Contemporary Challenges for the International Criminal Court

AF698359

Contemporary Challenges for the International Criminal Court

Edited by

Andraž Zidar and Olympia Bekou

BIICL

British Institute of International and Comparative Law

Published and Distributed by
The British Institute of International and Comparative Law
Charles Clore House, 17 Russell Square, London WC1B 5JP

© BIICL 2014

British Library Cataloguing in Publication Data
A Catalogue record of this book is available from the British Library

ISBN 978-1-905221-51-6

All rights reserved. No part of this publication may be reproduced or transmitted in any form or by any means, electronic, mechanical, photocopying, recording or otherwise, or stored in any restricted system of any nature without the written permission of the copyright holder, application for which should be addressed to the distributor. Such written permission must also be obtained before any part of this publication is stored in a retrieval system of any nature.

Typeset by Cambrian Typesetters
Camberley, Surrey
Printed in Great Britain by Polestar Wheatons
Cover Design: Nick Clarke
Cover Image Design: Dušan Zidar
Photo of the International Criminal Court: Wim Van Capellen
International Criminal Court architect drawing: Schmidt/Hammer/Lassen Architects

Contents

Preface

As with every judicial institution in history, the International Criminal Court is going through its growing pains. This is both natural and to be expected. The drafters of the Rome Statute could not have anticipated all of the exigencies of a functioning institution, particularly one operating in a highly political context. Experience is the only guide. But more importantly, it is the good judgment of the leaders of the institution which will prevent problems from arising, and resolve them when they do.

It is precisely for these reasons that a book such as this one is necessary and useful, and others like it in time will make a contribution to the doctrinal and practical evolution of this important institution.

One has barely to look at the history of such institutions as the International Court of Justice, the European Court of Human Rights, and the Inter-American Court of Human Rights to see how these institutions have evolved and how experience and doctrine have contributed to their progressive development. This book brings together the writings of 15 experts who have dealt with different subjects that are so important to enhanced understanding of the Court's norms, functions and better achievement of its goals.

The editors are to be congratulated for their initiative, as are the contributing authors whose work will surely prove to be of use not only to those who are interested in the Court's success and progress, but also to those working within it and desirous of achieving the same goals.

M. Cherif Bassiouni
Emeritus Professor of Law
DePaul University
President, ISISC
Honorary President, AIDP
Chair, Drafting Committee, Diplomatic Conference, Rome 1998

Foreword

When I attended some of the preparatory sessions of the Rome Statute debates in New York in 2000 as an independent barrister, my main objective was to assist in the lobbying for the defence to be a fully integrated part of the organic structure of the proposed International Criminal Court. Experience, sometimes hard, difficult and downright risky experience, gleaned from defending at the ICTY and ICTR had shown the necessity for such supportive integration from the outset.

My impression from listening to the debates and discussing issues with NGO representatives in the early stages was that the USA was going to be a committed partner but that it was going to be a hard sell to get a majority of African and South American states on board. How misleading first impressions can be.

Then came the euphoria in 2002 that the ICC was going to be a reality tinged with the disappointment that the USA, Russia, China, India, Israel and some other influential nations were not only on the sidelines but in some instances actively hostile. Raw nationalism and fears over sovereign dilution were rampant in some significant forums and a fear of a rogue prosecutor ran through debates that sometimes lacked logic and ignored the complementarity principles, or at least failed to comprehend them.

That the ICC was going to face huge challenges and criticism should never have come as a surprise. A court, without any police force and dependent upon State and Security Council assistance, that is to deal with the most prominent of accused and allegations of the most egregious offences whilst dispensing firmly with notions of immunity and impunity is a heady brew. I suspect that many politicians did not quite realise what they were signing up for. It may be relatively easy to accept that a foreign official is to be accountable, rather less easy when it gets closer to home. The strength of the ICC lies in its jurisdiction and jurisprudence, its daily health depends upon mature state responsibility.

The eleven years since its inception have seen many problems and some notable achievements. I am not engaging in any of the current 'political' debates as judicial restraint prevents that. What seems to me to be the case, however, is that the international criminal and humanitarian law world, as embodied in evolving domestic and supra-domestic political circles, is one that is moving away from the dominance of individual human rights. I perceive a shift back into the more protective cloak of sovereign and national interests with the good of the individual being subsumed, and perhaps diminished, in the cauldron of domestic or national community interests. The individual, and especially the 'international individual', is going to have to find a louder voice in order to be heard. Again this should not be a great surprise. As nations deal with austerity, the threat or reality of terrorist attacks and diminishing natural resources coupled with population growth the political will to give prominence to individual rights as opposed to general security is very likely to recede. The argument that community security is in fact enhanced by protecting individual rights can be a tough one to mount at election time.

The good news is that the ICC and its many and varied supporters exists. The bad news is that our human problems are going to get worse. We have had territorial, ideological, theological and pure greed wars, conflicts and genocidal events ever since we became societal. The bigger and more powerful nations became, the more potent were the conflicts. We now have to face terrorism on a variety of scales and bases; we will have more oil, gas and other mineral resource wars which I suspect will include food and water wars and living space conflicts on wider and more bitter scale than hitherto. The Geneva Conventions will be tested by more sophisticated weaponry, as the debate on drones signals, and electronic warfare will become increasing potent. The speed at which information now races to every corner of the globe by television, computer, tablets and smartphones will sharpen the responses and, dangerously, may give less time for reasoned debate and reaction to perceived threats. It is very easy to form a wrong first impression from an instant but partisan electronic source. We will have to face more, and more damaging, environmental crimes and consider the implications of unlawful activities by transnational corporations that may cross the threshold into crimes against humanity.

We underestimate at our collective and possibly global peril the spread of the Sunni-Shia divide and the conflicts that division will generate and sustain in coming years. It does little good simply to look at the situation in Iraq or Syria or elsewhere in relative isolation. The problem is at least as wide as the Middle East region and is in my view likely to spread. That there will be more grave breaches of international criminal and humanitarian law I have no doubt. These are issues the ICC and the wider international legal and diplomatic community are going to have to recognise and constrain as best possible. It is plain that, for instance, interventions in Iraq and Afghanistan which have not given sustainable priority to the rule of law and good governance will neither meet the aspirations of war-weary civil society nor prevent radical and bloody unrest.

To counter these challenges it is even more crucial that the rule of law and the rule of international law prevail. We have domestic courts and we have the ICC. Together they are the most powerful aid to the non-military maintenance of civilised values. The ICC and the Assembly of States Parties need to ensure that the principles of complementarity are understood and applied and, in my personal view, that more is done by the ICC and the international legal community, not least through the good offices of the Coalition for the International Criminal Court, to encourage, enable and develop national courts dealing with crimes against humanity and war crimes. More outreach and training will require more funding. You get what you pay for or, perhaps more starkly, what you do not pay for. International criminal and humanitarian justice is never cheap, but compared to the costs of war and conflicts in monetary terms it is a tiny fraction of the costs of weapons spending alone. Add the more important considerations of human suffering and the equation in favour of spending more on international justice is self-explanatory.

This incisive and important collection of contributions from well established experts takes the debates to newer and higher levels. The contemporary challenges are set out and underscored and explained. This is a collection of views and opinions that needs to be read by practitioners, academics and judges alike. It will be an essential tool in the debates that these challenges will generate and provides vital material for consensus and understanding.

Having been involved in international criminal law as a practitioner, teacher and judge since 1997, with some years ahead of me at the ICC, I see the value of this work in fine and appreciative focus. I thank the authors and editors for their hard erudite work.

Judge Howard Morrison
The Hague
January 2014

The International Criminal Court at Ten: Contemporary Challenges

Olympia Bekou and Andraž Zidar

The book 'Contemporary Challenges for the International Criminal Court' is the culmination of a celebration of the tenth anniversary of the functioning of the International Criminal Court (ICC). To mark this solemn occasion the British Institute of International and Comparative Law (BIICL) and the University of Nottingham Human Rights Law Centre joined forces to organise an international conference on the ICC. The conference, which took place on 21 June 2012, and was sponsored by the Foreign and Commonwealth Office (FCO) and Temple Garden Chambers, brought together 25 speakers and 110 participants from all over the world. In addition to chapters written by some conference speakers, the book contains contributions from experts affiliated with BIICL or the University of Nottingham.

Contributors to this book come from a variety of professional backgrounds and include academics and researchers; defence counsel before the ICC; members of non-governmental organisations and professional associations; a politician and former high-level diplomat; officials working at the ICC; and both a sitting and a former judge of the Court. In this sense, the contributors constitute a representative 'international college of experts', engaged in the functioning and monitoring of the ICC. The aim of the book is to present thoughts on the ICC at the intersection of practical experience and academic knowledge. The book seeks to highlight some of the key challenges faced by the Court in the first decade of its operation and to identify those areas which have been a success and those in which improvement can be made. Although the contributions vary in their emphasis on practical realities or scholarly assessment, they all provide analysis and evaluation of the functioning of the ICC and proffer concrete recommendations on how to overcome the current challenges. The book does not purport to cover all areas of the vast international criminal law practice nor all issues relevant to the Rome Statute. It does, however, offer an in-depth approach to a number of key issues which have occupied the Court's early practice. Premised on Kant's statement that '[t]houghts without content are empty, intuitions without concepts are blind', the book combines positive with constructively critical approaches to provide insights on the past, present and prospective functioning of the ICC.

The lengthy process leading to the adoption of the Rome Statute started in earnest following the Second World War and the completion of the work of the International Military Tribunals for Nuremberg and Tokyo. However, the Cold War impeded the fruition of those early efforts. The tragic events in the former Yugoslavia and Rwanda and the creation of two ad hoc International Criminal Tribunals in the 1990s provided fresh impetus for the creation of a permanent international criminal court. Discussions at the UN General Assembly resulted in the preparation by the International Law Commission of the first draft of the Statute in 1994, which, in the liberal atmosphere that ensued after the fall of the Berlin Wall and following skilful negotiations, provided fertile ground for a revolutionary leap in support of an emerging international criminal justice system. Determination to end impunity for serious international crimes united the international community at the Diplomatic Conference in Rome in 1998. The conference concluded with the adoption of the Rome Statute of the International Criminal Court, which was lauded as one of the greatest developments in modern international law.

The Court is a permanent judicial institution with jurisdiction over individuals accused of genocide, crimes against humanity and war crimes. Following its first Review Conference which took place in Kampala, Uganda in 2010, the ICC will eventually also have jurisdiction over the crime of aggression. The Rome Statute came into force on 1 July 2002, and States Parties currently number 122. The year 2012 marked 10 years since the entry into force of the Rome Statute establishing the ICC. In that decade, the international community has made remarkable strides in building a functioning court, able to investigate and prosecute individuals suspected of committing crimes within its jurisdiction. However, the Court has also faced a complex set of challenges which may affect its daily operation. Some of the concerns include: the universality of the Rome Statute and its relationship with State sovereignty; tension between the UN political organs (eg the Security Council) and the Court; the relationship between peace and justice; the role of municipal legal traditions in the interpretation of the Rome Statute and the use of jurisprudence of other international courts and tribunals.

With the institution-building process now complete, the ICC is at a crossroads: there are a number of challenges before the Court, the outcomes of which will be critical to determining its legitimacy and long-term success.

The structure of the book has been crafted to reflect issues pertinent to the maturation of the ICC. Following some introductory thoughts, the book comprises four substantive parts which address the following themes: the ICC and domestic legal systems; trigger mechanisms of the jurisdiction of the ICC; the ICC and victims; and the ICC at ten and prospects for the future.

The book finishes with some concluding remarks and a set of annexes which provide useful facts and figures related to the activities and functioning of the Court.

The introduction to the book is the opening address of the 2012 conference, delivered by Henry Bellingham MP, then an FCO Minister. In his speech he points to the fast development of international criminal law, especially after the fall of the Berlin Wall, and hails the creation of the ICC as an exceptional achievement in international justice. Bellingham emphasises that apart from being a permanent criminal court of universal aspiration, the ICC is also an independent judicial body. This independence is important because it represents the source of the Court's international legitimacy and the fashion in which it dispenses justice. Bellingham reaffirms the United Kingdom's strong support for the Court and its judicial independence, and underlines that there should be no impunity for perpetrators of the most serious international crimes.

The first part of the volume deals with the interplay between the ICC and domestic legal systems, which is of crucial importance to both the ICC and States. Olympia Bekou focuses on the effects produced by the ICC at the domestic level in her contribution on the domestic implementation of Rome Statute crimes. She offers a detailed overview of the transposition of genocide, crimes against humanity and war crimes from the Rome Statute into national legal systems and discusses the instances of legislation that exceed or fall short of the Rome Statute. Her analysis reveals that approximately half of the States Parties have enacted implementing legislation, which is an extraordinary fact in itself, but indicates that there remains a long way to go. Implementing legislation denotes a State's willingness to investigate and prosecute core international crimes at the domestic level and functions as a catalyst, facilitating cooperation with the ICC. Equally important is the realisation that the transposition of the norms enshrined in the Rome Statute into domestic legal systems empowers national systems to trigger proceedings against perpetrators of core international crimes domestically and to keep the ICC at bay. In that sense, the system established by the Rome Statute comprises not only the Court, but also a wider network of national judicial institutions.

Mark Ellis and Federica Gioia both examine the domestic level through the lens of the complementarity principle. Ellis considers the principle of complementarity in contemporary criminal justice. He notes that the principle of complementarity allocates primary authority to prosecute perpetrators of gross violations of international criminal law to States Parties. Only when States are unwilling or genuinely unable to carry out an investigation or prosecution is a case admissible before the ICC. Ellis analyses the prospects of judicial rivalry between the ICC and domestic courts on the basis of the criteria of 'willingness' and 'ability' of a State to carry out judicial proceedings.

The case law of the ICC on complementarity, he argues, demonstrates that the Court's approach is inconsistent and sometimes even contradictory. Ellis's proposal is that the Court nominate an independent expert body in the form of an International Advisory Group, tasked with making an objective assessment of the criteria of complementarity. This would increase the legitimacy of the ICC and contribute to greater coherence in its case law.

Gioia, on the other hand, elaborates on the topic of complementarity *in bonam partem*. She considers the principle of complementarity in the context of domestic judicial proceedings that manifest serious violations of due process rules to the detriment of the accused. Gioia emphasises that although some experts claim that the ICC was not conceived as a human rights court, it must resolutely uphold principles of due process to safeguard its legitimacy as the most prominent international criminal tribunal. Therefore, the Court should exercise its complementarity also in cases of violations of procedural rights of a defendant. For this purpose the Court should develop criteria that would secure the protection of the human rights of the accused, including the right to a fair trial. In addition, she suggests that the ICC should provide assistance to States Parties to enhance the functioning of national judicial institutions on the basis of international due process standards.

In the second part of the book, attention is shifted from the national to the international level. The mechanisms by which the Court's jurisdiction is triggered are discussed in considerable detail, in light of the practice that has ensued in the first ten years of the Court's operation. Annika Jones addresses the issue of State referrals, arguing that this trigger mechanism has attracted considerable debate, given the prevalence of self-referrals in the early practice of the ICC. Jones reviews both the State referral mechanism enshrined in the Statute and its relationship with admissibility before discussing the challenges raised by self-referrals. She argues that although self-referrals were not originally anticipated, the practice has been accommodated by the ICC. Her contribution sheds some light on the merits and disadvantages of such referrals and cautions of the dangers this practice may pose for the Court.

Fabricio Guariglia considers the powers of the Prosecutor to initiate investigations through a review of the drafting history of Article 15 and examination of its goals and how this trigger mechanism has been used in practice. He focuses on preliminary examinations and the procedural steps taken therein and argues that it is up to the ICC to define the modalities and scope of this provision before concluding that there is still some uncertainty and ambiguity which will need to be resolved by the Court in its upcoming practice.

The final contribution in this part is by Amal Alamuddin, who addresses the role reserved in the Rome Statute for the Security Council and the law relating to referrals and deferrals. She discusses how the system encourages conflict with the principles of independence and freedom from what she calls, 'politicised selectivity.' She then reviews the practice of Security Council referrals, or absence thereof, with respect to Darfur (Sudan) and Syria as well as attempts to defer the ICC's jurisdiction, which she considers has not undermined the work of the ICC in practice. She concludes by putting forward a number of recommendations on preservation of the Court's independence and limitation of the discretion of the Security Council.

The third part of the book focuses on victims. The Rome Statute is progressive in its stance on the status of victims. Gaëlle Carayon addresses the operation of the provisions that recognise victims as active participants before the Court. The participation of victims in judicial proceedings has important implications: it gives them recognition and helps restore their dignity; it contributes to societal healing and rehabilitation; it can contribute useful information to proceedings; and it can bring the ICC closer to its constituents. However, as Carayon notes, victim participation has become a victim of its own success. From the very beginning, the ICC has been flooded with applications for victim participation, which have inevitably slowed down proceedings. Victim participation has been improved through the role of the Legal Representative for Victims, who acts as a representative of numerous victims, and through simplification of bureaucratic application procedures. Garayon concludes that a further review of the Court's procedures is needed to facilitate meaningful and active victim participation in judicial proceedings.

Another progressive aspect of the Rome Statute is the introduction of a reparations mechanism and implementing organ – the Trust Fund for Victims (TFV). This mechanism represents a paradigm shift from retributive to transformative justice and is aimed at social reconciliation in war-torn societies. Pieter de Baan focuses on the mandate of the Trust Fund for Victims (TFV) to assist victims in conflict-affected societies and presents its functioning in more detail. Not only can the TFV provide reparations to victims as ordered by the Court, but it can also undertake projects for the greater benefit of the victims within the Court's jurisdiction. He outlines the forms of general assistance that the TFV can provide, including physical rehabilitation, psychological rehabilitation and material support initiatives. De Baan explains that the TFV can engage with victims outside the scope of a particular trial, which proved particularly useful in the eastern Democratic Republic of Congo where the TFV offered support to victims of sexual and gender-based violence.

Nevertheless, a reparations regime, a novelty in international criminal justice, has inevitably given rise to some tensions in the functioning of the Court. Mia Swart addresses these tensions in the context of reparations. Swart identifies a first tension in the different nature of the mandates of the Court and the TFV respectively. She argues that this tension could be overcome if the Court were to frame general principles of reparations and entrust their practical implementation to the TFV, as in the *Lubanga* case. The second tension lies in that Civil Law systems accord a greater role to the victims in contrast to the absence of victims as participants in Common Law criminal proceedings. Since the Rome Statute regime is a mixture of criminal law systems, it is argued that this tension can be resolved by the integration of some elements of the *partie civile* mechanism into the operation of the ICC. The third tension lies in a different approach to reparations in criminal proceedings and in civil (tortious) proceedings. Although reparations may resemble the payment of damages in a civil trial, it is also possible to perceive them as an extension of a criminal trial and to nonetheless conduct proceedings in a fair and expeditious way.

The final part of the book revisits the major achievements of the ICC in the first ten years of its operation and discusses its prospects for the future. The first contribution in this part, by William Schabas, discusses the ICC 'at ten.' Schabas offers a critical review of a number of issues. He examines some missed opportunities that the Assembly of States Parties and Review Conference could have used to improve procedural aspects of the functioning of the Court in particular with regard to confirmation of charges hearings and appellate proceedings. Schabas questions the utility of both the confirmation of charges hearing and interlocutory appeals. He then focuses on the issue of victims and the operation of the TFV and discusses the associated challenges posed by voluntary contributions. Schabas moves on to discuss the thorny issue of selectivity through an examination of the distinction between 'situations' and 'cases' as well as the exercise of the *proprio motu* powers of the Prosecutor. In the final part of his contribution, some of the failings of the Court's operation are discussed alongside some encouraging signs that the ICC has exhibited regarding evolving crises, as well as the successful adoption of the Kampala amendments.

The contribution by Andraž Zidar focuses on the first case before the ICC, that of Thomas Lubanga Dyilo. Zidar examines the use of intermediaries by the Prosecution and the problems encountered during the trial regarding their trustworthiness and impact on the evidence gathered before discussing the proposed amendments to the current system. In addition, Zidar reviews the principle of legality in light of the Court's interpretation of 'active participation in hostilities' and the 'harm caused to the victims'. In particular, he discusses the non-pursuance of the allegations of sexual violence and the interpretation of the meaning of active participation by the Chamber and the approach taken by Judge Odio Benito in that respect. To complete the review of the legality principle in this instance, Zidar focuses on sentencing procedures. The final part of his contribution addresses co-perpetration and *dolus eventualis* before putting forward a view based on the approach of the Model Penal Code informed by insights from comparative law. He concludes that although the *Lubanga* judgment is a remarkable achievement, it is but a first step in the right direction.

Marek Marczynski gives a perspective from civil society, discussing some of the ICC's successes before focusing on the challenges that lie ahead, which he identifies as the budget, the role of Security Council and the Court's relationship with African States. Besides these, Marczynski argues that the ICC needs to look beyond Africa and better respond to the needs of the situation on the ground regarding the use of intermediaries, understanding local dynamics and tackling gender-based violence. He concludes that the ICC needs strategic, political and financial support from the international community in order to live up to expectations.

The 2012 conference was concluded with a speech by Sir Adrian Fulford, the first ICC judge from the United Kingdom. Sir Adrian considers the challenges and opportunities faced by the judges of a new institution, the effect of the ICC on political figures, and the position of non-States parties. He then shifts his attention to the rhetoric surrounding the expectation that the ICC put an end to impunity before turning to practical steps that would enhance the efficacy of the ICC, such as increased use of a single judge, innovations regarding the giving of testimony and evidence and ensuring the latter is secure at the outset for use at later stages in proceedings. Also discussed are the role of intermediaries and ensuring that assistance is given to the prosecution with a view to enhancing investigations through consistent and reliable evidence. Overall, however, Sir Adrian celebrates the 'surprising and impressive triumphs' that the ICC has recorded in its operation to date.

In order to provide a comprehensive representation of the breadth of the activities and functioning of the ICC, we have included a number of annexes that illustrate some key aspects of the Court's operation. We are grateful to the ICC Public Affairs Unit for providing us with this information, which we hope the readers of this book will find useful. The first annexe shows the spread of the situations under investigation, those under preliminary examination as well as the jurisdictional trigger mechanisms used for each of the situations currently before the ICC, the accused and the stages at which their proceedings currently stand. The second annexe gives an overview of the cost of the administration of international criminal justice at the ICC, as well as the individual State and voluntary contributions. The final annexe gives a breakdown of the human infrastructure of the Court.

In closing, we would like to thank all those who participated in the process of making this book a reality. Our sincere gratitude goes, first and foremost, to all the contributing authors. In addition, we are indebted to the director of BIICL Professor Robert McCorquodale and Professor M Cherif Bassiouni for many valuable suggestions on the format and contents of the book. We would also like to thank the research assistants at the Institute for their invaluable contribution to the editing process. Our warm thanks go, in particular, to Sotirios Lekkas and Shehara de Soysa who spent considerable time editing the book and who also provided many useful suggestions along the way. We would also like to thank Aletta van der Merwe, Ruth Kennedy, Hadrian Tulk and Natalia Spyridaki who participated in various stages of the editing process. Finally, we are thankful also to Anna Riddell for putting the final, but nevertheless important touches to the book.

PART 1

Introduction

The International Criminal Court: Ten Years On

*Henry Bellingham**

Today is an historic day as we have a Nobel Prize winner here in the Foreign Office (Aung San Suu Kyi). It is also an historic day as we have you here to mark the tenth anniversary of the coming into force of the Rome Statute. I am honoured to address such a distinguished audience, and on a subject of such great importance. You represent some of the world's leading experts in international justice. And while I usually feel comfortable talking about this subject given my own background in law, I am conscious that I am sharing the platform today with Sir Adrian Fulford – who will deliver his remarks a little later on.

As a concept, international justice dates back generations, and while the institutions underpinning it are still in their infancy, they have already established themselves in the international system.

Nowhere has this been more evident than in the landmark judgment made two months ago by the Special Court for Sierra Leone, against former Liberian President Charles Taylor. His fifty-year prison sentence has demonstrated to his many victims that even the most powerful cannot escape justice, no matter how long it takes to be administered. It is when you think about the victims of these crimes that you begin to understand the importance of these institutions in combatting impunity. The International Criminal Court, now ten years old, is at the forefront of this.

I will argue today that the decision to establish the world's first permanent international criminal court marked a watershed in international justice. But it should be recognised that both the ICC and the State Parties can and must do better. So I will also share with you the United Kingdom's vision for the Court in its next ten years and how I think we can overcome the challenges it faces.

---

* MP, Minister for Africa, the Caribbean, the Overseas Territories, the UN and conflict issues at the Foreign and Commonwealth Office from May 2010 to September 2012. In that capacity Mr Bellingham gave the opening address on 21 June 2012 at the International Conference on 10th Anniversary of the International Criminal Court, which took place at the Foreign and Commonwealth Office, the proceedings of which form the background to this book.

It is important that it does. Over the past year, we have seen countless examples – not least the absolutely terrible atrocities happening in Syria – that demonstrate why individuals must be held to account for their actions, and why we need to invest in the institutions to do that.

While today we are marking ten years since the establishment of the International Criminal Court, we all know that its origins can be traced back much earlier. To the calls in the nineteenth century for a global criminal court – not least from Gustave Moynier, a co-founder of what became the Red Cross. Or, more recently, to 1948 – when the UN General Assembly adopted the Convention on the Prevention and Punishment of the Crime of Genocide. The push to create a Court was renewed after the Cold War ended, and accelerated following the conflicts in the Balkans and Rwanda in the early 1990s. The tribunals established in their wake continue to dispense justice to this day.

So the International Criminal Court came into being at a time when the importance of international justice was becoming increasingly recognised. At its heart, the Court is an independent judicial body; and it is this judicial independence that is both the source of its legitimacy and the means by which it dispenses justice.

But what made the Court different was its ambition for universality. Unlike those that had gone before it, or indeed the more recent Courts for Cambodia and Lebanon, the International Criminal Court aspired to create a framework for the proper dispensation of justice, both at the domestic and the international level. Its inception, therefore, was a recognition that justice can reach beyond the confines of national boundaries, that impunity could and must be challenged and that all are accountable for their actions regardless of where they come from.

Ten years in, the Court has established itself as the cornerstone of international criminal justice. After six years of hard work, it delivered its first verdict just a few months ago – convicting the Congolese militia leader, Thomas Lubanga, of war crimes. The investigations set in motion last year into the events in Libya and Côte d'Ivoire have been handled with speed and efficiency. There has been progress in other cases, including the investigation into the post-election violence in Kenya in 2007 to 2008. Collectively, these developments are engendering an increasing confidence in the Court, and in international justice more generally.

And the Court has been able to do this because of the way it was set up; because of its mandate. It does not seek to bypass or undermine the judicial processes of individual countries. It is not a political tool, nor is it something 'imposed' on the rest of the world by the West. The ICC is a 'court of last resort', providing for the primacy of national jurisdictions: it only steps in when a country cannot or will not investigate and, where necessary, prosecute fairly the most heinous of crimes. And, most importantly, it puts victims at the centre of its work.

Nor is it, as some have argued, a Court focused solely on Africa. Accusations to that effect are understandable: all 15 cases formally under investigation at present are, after all, from the African continent.

But I do not think we should get hung up on this. Other courts have dealt with similar issues in other places, as I have already highlighted. And the ICC itself is conducting preliminary examinations outside Africa, including in Afghanistan and Colombia. Civil society in Africa is strongly supportive of the work of the Court and the justice that it can and will deliver for many Africans. Nor should we forget that in every African situation where the Court has been involved, either the country in question, or where relevant, all African states on the UN Security Council, have supported the involvement of the ICC. Fatou Bensouda's appointment as Prosecutor by the consensus of all States Parties is a clear indication of Africa's important role in the Court. I hope it will go some way to addressing the concern expressed by some African countries that their voices were not being heard.

For our part, the United Kingdom has been a staunch supporter of the Court and its judicial independence. We are committed to the principle that there should be no impunity for the most serious international crimes. Indeed, we are actively engaged in all six existing international criminal tribunals – as a State Party to the Rome Statute of the ICC; as a member of the Security Council which oversees the tribunals for the former Yugoslavia and Rwanda; and as a major donor and member of the management bodies of the tribunals for Sierra Leone, Cambodia and Lebanon.

We have worked tirelessly to support and develop management and oversight of the Court, helping to ensure that it continues to mature as an efficient and effective institution.

The UK contributes almost ten percent of the Court's budget – which this year will amount to over €10m of a budget of €111m. We also donated £500,000 to the Court's Trust Fund for Victims, to help assist victims as they rebuild their lives and communities. And I am pleased that following his election in December 2011, Howard Morrison QC is set to become a UK judge at the ICC later in 2012, following in the footsteps of Sir Adrian Fulford.

It is clear, then, that we in the UK have much invested in the International Criminal Court's success. We want to see the Court fulfil its true potential.

The President of the ICC, Judge Sang-Hyun Song, said himself on 4 June 2012 that whilst we can be truly proud of what the ICC community has achieved it is far more important that we recognise the shortcomings and the obstacles that remain.

And so we should: the Court is by no means perfect, not perhaps surprising given that it is still in its youth. Its critics understandably point to the completion of just one case in ten years, arguing that it is a poor return on the investment of dozens of governments – an investment totalling close to $1bn since 2003.

So the task before us is how we make the Court work better; how we ensure that its next ten, twenty, thirty years builds on what it has achieved over the past decade. The answer is by no means obvious, but I think there are three fundamentals we need to address.

The first is further establishing the ICC as a truly universal court. One strand of this is for us to continue to encourage all countries to become State Parties to the Rome Statute, particularly those that have signed but not ratified it. Alongside this, we should recognise that there is a need to demonstrate clearly that the Court's reach extends beyond the African continent. This will only happen if the reach of the Court is universal and countries around the world take the step that those in Africa and Europe have done to shine the light of accountability on themselves.

Second, we need to address the issue of non-cooperation. I do not deny that this is a difficult issue, given that the International Criminal Court relies entirely on state cooperation to ensure that its arrest warrants are enforced. But as long as those indicted by the Court are allowed to evade justice – President Bashir is the most visible example, though he is not the only one – the credibility of the Court will continue to be questioned. This is why the UK will continue to urge all countries to cooperate. We hope others will do the same, and commend those State Parties who have made clear that they would arrest ICC indictees should they visit, Malawi being the most recent example.

Last – but certainly not least; indeed, perhaps most importantly – the Court needs to become more efficient. Prudent budget management with a sharp eye for efficiency is crucial to this, particularly given the global economic backdrop.

I want to be clear now that I am not condoning the slashing of budgets. Indeed, the British Government supported an increase in the Court's budget for this year, taking into account the additional cases it has taken on. But this agreement was on the basis that the Court would improve its budgetary processes; that it would work to reform its system of legal aid; and that it would undertake a review of personnel conditions. It is also crucial, after ten years, for the Court to embark upon a review of its criminal procedures to ensure that the rules in place are effective.

We all recognise the additional complications of international justice, given the sheer scale of the crimes committed. But the Court is all too often criticised for simply being too slow. This is understandable: I remember one of the first lessons I learnt at the Bar was that, ultimately, justice delayed is justice denied. So it is heartening to see the Court taking this message on board as it undertakes a 'lessons learnt' exercise to review its criminal procedures. The UK, as the facilitator of this process, will work with the Court to ensure it produces tangible results leading to the conduct of fairer, more expeditious trials.

It is vital that the Court makes progress in all of these areas if it is to fulfil its potential.

That said, I do not want these challenges to overshadow what the Court has achieved over the past ten years. It is right that we look for ways to make it work better. Indeed, failing to do so is ultimately failing the victims, who look to the Court and the wider international community to bring to justice the perpetrators of crimes against humanity, war crimes and genocide – irrespective of their status or position in public office. But we should take this opportunity today to take stock. Would we have realistically believed even just twenty or thirty years ago that there would in 2012 be an established permanent, global court, a near universal means to challenge impunity? Because that is what the International Criminal Court has achieved.

I believe that the effects of the Arab Spring and the events of the last eighteen months show that we are living through an accountability revolution, where impunity will be challenged and victims will have a voice. Bodies like the ICC, the courts in Sierra Leone and elsewhere are helping to shine the light of accountability on those who commit serious international crimes. And the modern media is granting them fewer places to hide.

The UK is proud to have been at the forefront of this revolution, and we will work relentlessly to strengthen it further.

PART 2

The International Criminal Court and Domestic Legal Systems

National Approaches to the ICC Statute Crimes

*Olympia Bekou**

The creation of the International Criminal Court is an important milestone in the fight against impunity for core international crimes.[1] In the words of the ICC's Prosecutor on the occasion of her solemn undertaking: 'From a groundbreaking idea on paper in 1998 to an incredible international criminal justice experiment in 2003, [the ICC has] now, reaching [its] 10th anniversary, become an undisputed reality in the international arena.'[2]

The institution-building process has dominated the debate surrounding the first ten years of the Court's operation. With this process now complete and the Court fully operational, it is important to examine the impact the Court has had on domestic legal orders. Whilst the Court will continue its work and increase its case-load in The Hague, the readiness and ability of national jurisdictions to tackle such core international crimes both effectively as well as efficiently is becoming a new frontline issue. The institutional preparedness of national legal orders is of critical importance in that respect.

After ten years of ICC operation, a quick survey of the 122 State Parties to the Rome Statute to date reveals that less than half have implementing legislation enabling them to investigate and prosecute core international crimes before their national courts.[3] Still, this is an extraordinary achievement given the nature of the Rome Statute which needs to be celebrated.[4] The presence of implementing legislation denotes a State's willingness, in principle, to deal with the case within its domestic criminal realm. Implementing legislation

* Professor of Public International Law and Head, International Criminal Justice Unit, Human Rights Law Centre, University of Nottingham.

[1] In this contribution, the term 'core crimes' denotes genocide, crimes against humanity and war crimes.

[2] Ceremony for the solemn undertaking of the Prosecutor of the International Criminal Court, 15 June 2012 <http://www.icc-pi.int/NR/rdonlyres/561C232F-3C4F-47AC-91CB-8F78DCC6C3FD/0/15062012FBSolemn Undertaking.pdf>.

[3] Information on national implementing legislation referred to in this contribution is accessible through the National Implementing Legislation Database, which is part of the ICC's Legal Tools Project. See <http://www.legal-tools.org/en/go-to-database/national-implementing-legislation-database/>.

[4] Rome Statute of the International Criminal Court, (2002) 2187 UNTS 90.

also facilitates cooperation with the ICC, in accordance with Part 9 of the Rome Statute. The availability of procedures at the national level regarding cooperation is explicitly envisaged in the Statute.[5] There is no positive legal obligation in the Statute to incorporate the core crimes.[6] However, if a State proceeds with such incorporation, this constitutes the first step in being able to keep the case at the national level to the exclusion of the ICC. The chapter will therefore review the status of implementation with regard to the three core international crimes – genocide, crimes against humanity and war crimes – and will focus on some key examples of State practice. The choice of examples cannot be representative but is indicative of these provisions. However, the implementation of crimes of aggression will not be examined, given that the definition agreed upon at the Kampala review conference has yet to come into force, which means that the ICC cannot yet exercise its jurisdiction.[7]

I. GENOCIDE

Of the three core international crimes, genocide provokes the most emotive response. Described as the 'crime of crimes', the criminalisation of genocide at the international level first occurred with the adoption of the Genocide Convention in 1948.[8] The definition of the crime of genocide has not changed since and identical wording to that in the Convention can also be found in Article 6 of the Rome Statute. Valuable lessons can be learnt by States who have incorporated it at the national level, regardless of whether the incorporation is a result of ratifying the Genocide Convention,[9] in response to the creation of the ad hoc International Criminal Tribunals for the former Yugoslavia and Rwanda,[10] or owing to ratification of the Rome Statute.[11]

---

[5] Art 88 Rome Statute; O Bekou, 'A Case for Review of Article 88 ICC Statute: Strengthening a Forgotten Provision' (2009) 12 New Criminal Law Review 468–84.

[6] Cf JK Kleffner, 'The Impact of Complementarity on National Implementation of Substantive International Criminal Law' (2003) 1 Journal of International Criminal Justice 86, 90.

[7] For an overview of existing legislation see A Reisinger-Coracini, 'National Legislation on Individual Responsibility for Conduct Amounting to Aggression', in R Bellelli (ed), *International Criminal Justice. Law and Practice from the Rome Statute to Its Review* (Ashgate 2010) 547–78. The earliest the aggression amendment can come into force is 2017.

[8] Convention on the Prevention and Punishment of the Crime of Genocide (adopted 9 December 1948, entered into force 12 January 1951) 78 UNTS 277.

[9] Numerous States incorporated the crime of genocide domestically upon becoming parties to the Genocide Convention. See for example, Bahrain (1990), Brazil (1956), Ethiopia (1957), Fiji (1973), Germany (1955), Israel (1950), Jamaica (1986), Luxembourg (1985), the Netherlands (1966), the United States (1987).

[10] Burkina Faso (1996), France (1994), Ghana (1993), Rwanda (1996).

[11] Belgium (1999), Congo Brazzaville (1998), Costa Rica (1998), Estonia (2004), Kenya

Whilst most States tend to follow *verbatim* the wording of the Genocide Convention definition[12] and others incorporate it directly by means of direct reference to Article 6 of the Rome Statute,[13] there are notable aberrations, focusing either on extending or limiting the protection of groups covered by the crime of genocide or on expanding or restricting the punishable acts. These will be taken in turn.

In the first category of States, namely those whose legislation derogates from the definition of genocide in international instruments, with respect to the four protected groups, are mainly States from Latin America. Racial groups have been omitted by Bolivia,[14] Paraguay[15] and Nicaragua[16] with the latter also excluding national groups. This is to be contrasted to El Salvador[17] where ethnical groups are left out instead. Whether certain aspects of the international definition are included or indeed consciously excluded in the domestication process certainly belongs to the discretion of the relevant national legislator. From an international criminal law perspective however, a national definition, which is under-inclusive may lead to engagement of the ICC, provided the relevant jurisdiction and admissibility criteria are met.[18]

(2008), Latvia (1998), Mali (2001), Malta (2003), New Zealand (2000), Peru (1998), Poland (1997), Portugal (2004), Senegal (2007), South Africa (2002), Spain (2003), Uganda (2010), the United Kingdom (2000).

12 Austria, Art 321, Criminal Code 1958; Belgium, Loi relative à la repression des violations graves de droit international humanitaire, 10 février 1999; Canada, Amendment of Criminal Code, 1985; Cuba, Art 116, Ley No 62: Código Penal de Cuba & Ley No 87, modificative del Código Penal (note however that the genocidal acts are listed in the reverse order); Germany Art 220a, Criminal Code 1955; Ghana, Section 1, Criminal Code Amendment Act 1993; Ireland, Genocide Act, 1973, Liechtenstein, Art 321, Criminal Code 1987; Mali, Art 30, Criminal Code; Malta, ICC Act 2003; Netherlands, Law Implementing the Genocide Convention, 1966; New Zealand, ICC Act 2000; Portugal, Art 239, Criminal Code; Rwanda, Organic Law No 08/96 of August 30, 1996 on the Organization of Prosecutions for Offences constituting the Crime of Genocide or Crimes against Humanity committed since October 1, 1990; Tajikistan, Art 398, Criminal Code (note the rather unusual wording); Trinidad and Tobago, Genocide Act 1977; United Kingdom, ICC Act 2000. See also Schedule 1, South African Implementation of the Rome Statute of the International Criminal Court Act 27 of 2002. Similarly, Mauritius, Schedule 2, International Criminal Court Act 2011, of 25 January 2012. It is noteworthy that the definitions are found in the Schedules and not in the main body of the Act. See also Ghana re genocide in section 49A of the Criminal Code 1960 and for Zimbabwe, s. 4, Genocide Act, 9/2000.

13 For example, see s 6(4), Kenyan International Crimes Act 2008; and, s 7(2), 8(2) and 9(2), Ugandan International Criminal Court Act 2010 of 25 June 2010. In addition, Burundi refers directly to both the Genocide Convention as well as the Rome Statute, in the chapeau of Art 2 of its legislation which incorporates the crimes of genocide. See Loi No 1/004 du 08 Mai 2003 portant répression du crime de génocide, des crimes contre l'humanité et des crimes de guerre.

14 Art 138 Ley no 1768 de Modificaciones al Código Penal.

15 Art 319 Criminal Code.

16 Art 549 Criminal Code.

17 Art 361 Criminal Code.

18 Art 12 and 17 Rome Statute.

In the same category, one can also find States that actually are over-inclusive in their definitions. Coverage of additional groups, most commonly political groups, can be found in Colombia,[19] Costa Rica,[20] Ethiopia,[21] Ivory Coast,[22] Lithuania,[23] Panama,[24] Poland,[25] Switzerland,[26] to name a few. In addition, social groups have also been included in the definitions adopted by Lithuania,[27] Latvia[28] and Estonia,[29] with the latter also including 'groups resisting occupation'. Perhaps the most striking of those, is Poland's protection of 'groups of persons with a definite philosophical conviction.' This provision, besides being rather unique, may be hard to apply in practice, as it is difficult to determine its precise elements. Whilst recognising that States are at liberty to decide which groups they wish to extend their protection to, over-inclusiveness ought to be approached with caution. It may be that extending the protection of international criminal law is generally a welcome development. However, it is equally important to try not to dilute the essence of the genocide provision and its exceptional nature.

Yet some other States opt for determining which groups ought to be protected in an ad hoc manner, in addition to the four protected groups enshrined in the definition. Notably France, in its genocide provision, covers 'a group determined by any other arbitrary criterion'.[30] The same position has been adopted also by Burkina Faso[31], the Central African Republic[32] and the Republic of Congo[33] whose legal systems follow the francophone civil law tradition. Cape Verde, another State on the African continent, also adopts this position in its Penal Code.[34] The flexibility inherent in the ad hoc determination is its greatest advantage. This formulation offers protection to

---

[19] Art 101 Ley 599 de 2000 (24 de Julio) por la cual se expide el Código Penal.

[20] Art 375 Criminal Code 1998.

[21] Art 281 Criminal Code 1957.

[22] Art 137 Criminal Code.

[23] Art 99 Criminal Code.

[24] Art 311 Criminal Code.

[25] Art 118(1) Criminal Code 1997.

[26] Art 264 of the Loi fédérale portant modification de lois fédérales en vue de la mise en oeuvre du Statut de Rome de la Cour pénale international of 18 June 2010, covers both social and political groups.

[27] Art 99 Criminal Code.

[28] Section 71 Penal Code 1998.

[29] Art 90 Criminal Code 2004.

[30] Art 211-1 Criminal Code.

[31] See Art 16 Loi No 052-2009/AN Portant détermination des compétences et de la procédure de mise en œuvre du Statut de Rome relatif à la Cour Pénale Internationale par les juridictions Burkinabe.

[32] Art 152 Loi No 10.001 portant code pénal centrafricain of 06/01/2010.

[33] Art Premier Loi No 8-98 du 31 octobre 1998.

[34] Art 268 Legislative Decree 4/2003 of 18 November 2003, Penal Code.

additional groups, beyond the four included in the genocide definition (where a person is targeted simply on the basis of his or her membership of such a group). It is true to say that it echoes the findings of the ICTR *Akayesu* judgment, where '"stable" groups, constituted in a permanent fashion and membership of which is determined by birth', were also found to be covered by the genocide definition.[35] However, this approach has not been followed either by subsequent case law at the international level,[36] or by those States who subsequently incorporated the crime of genocide in their national laws.

As mentioned already, States also depart from the genocide provision with regard to punishable acts. Lithuania,[37] for instance, a State Party to the Rome Statute, refers to torturing, mutilating and disturbing mental health in its implementation of subsection (b) namely, 'causing serious bodily or mental harm to members of the group'. Similarly, Mexico[38] makes explicit reference to mass sterilization as the sole method of hindering the group's reproduction. Ethiopia, on the other hand, conflates two genocidal acts, ie (a) killing members of the group and (b) causing serious bodily or mental harm to members of the group[39] but reformulates the wording of the provision to widen it to 'any way whatsoever'.[40] Where punishable acts do not cover those found in the definition of genocide in international treaty law, it means that the national implementation of the provision falls short of the international one.

Additional punishable acts have also been included by a number of States in their national versions of the genocide provision. Of those additional acts, displacement or deportation are the most common.[41] Forced pregnancy,[42] illness,[43] imposition of distinctive signs,[44] sexual attack, transfer of adults from one group to another, causing loss or 'uselessness' of parts and bodily-

---

35 *Prosecutor v Akayesu* (Judgement) Case No ICTR096-4-T Trial Chamber (2 September 1998) para 511.

36 WA Schabas, 'Article 6' in O Triffterer (ed), *Commentary on the Rome Statute of the International Criminal Court – Observers' Notes, Article by Article* (2nd edn, CH Beck et al 2008) 149.

37 Art 99 Criminal Code. See generally, J Zilinskas, 'Broadening the Concept of Genocide in Lithuania's Criminal Law and the Principle of *Nullum Crimen sine Lege*' (2009) 4 (118) Jurisprudencija 333–348.

38 Art 149bis Federal Criminal Code.

39 Art 269(a) Criminal Code No 414/2004.

40 Idem.

41 Armenia, Bolivia, Ethiopia, Italy, Ivory Coast, Lithuania, Paraguay, Russia, Spain and South Africa.

42 See Colombia, Art 101 Ley 599 de 2000 (24 de Julio) par la cual se expide el Código Penal.

43 See Finland, Chapter 11, Section 6 Penal Code. Conditions of life have also been substituted by 'in any other way impairs the survival of the group' in the Finnish legislation.

44 See Italy, Law on Prevention and Punishment of Crime of Genocide 1967.

functions are also included in some States' legislation.[45] Moreover, a wider definition can be construed when certain elements of the punishable acts included in the Rome Statute are omitted. In the Republic of the Congo, 'forcible transfer of children'[46] has been used instead of '[f]orcibly transferring children of the group to another group', as in Article 6(e) of the Rome Statute. The desirability of expanding the punishable acts needs to be balanced against ensuring the effectiveness of the provisions. Whilst not violating the rationale behind the criminalisation of genocide, it is questionable whether all of the above punishable acts have in fact reached the level required to be considered suitable for inclusion in the domestic definitions of genocide.

A final observation is warranted with regard to the 'intent to destroy' element of the genocide definition. Both France[47] and Burkina Faso[48] have omitted the so-called specific intent which is the main characteristic of the crime of genocide and which sets it apart from crimes against humanity for instance. It is true that this omission significantly expands the possible incidents that would qualify as genocide. On the other hand, it would eliminate the very nature of the crime itself, ie the fact that, normally, the crime of genocide is reserved for very exceptional situations.

The above exposition demonstrates how States have treated the crime of genocide at the national level. Whilst most States follow the international definition to the letter, there are considerable variations which offer a useful insight into how States understand the crime for domestic purposes. With that in mind, it is important to also observe the reaction of States with regard to the rather less established crimes, such as crimes against humanity.

II. CRIMES AGAINST HUMANITY

Although provisions incorporating genocide or war crimes were commonly found in national laws, the adoption of the Rome Statute revealed States as largely unprepared regarding the implementation of crimes against humanity. Since then, a number of States have incorporated provisions on this crime with considerable success. This section will focus on two issues, namely the incorporation of Article 7(1)(k) of the Rome Statute which covers 'other

---

[45] See Spain, Art 607 Criminal Code, 2003. See E Carnero Rojo, 'National Legislation providing for the Prosecution and Punishment of International Crimes in Spain' (2001) 9 Journal of International Criminal Justice 699–728.

[46] Art Premier Loi No 8–98 du 31 octobre 1998.

[47] See Livre II, Titre 1er, Sous-titre 1er, Chapitre 1er, Art 211–1, Code Pénal (1994 consolidé).

[48] See Loi No 052-2009/AN (n 31) Art 16.

inhumane acts of similar character intentionally causing great suffering, or serious injury to body or to mental or physical harm' and on whether the policy element of Article 7(2)(a) has been implemented.

With regard to the implementation of the residual clause found in Article 7(1)(k), a surprising number of States implement the provision as it is, without voicing any concerns as to the whether the provision (especially given its open-ended nature) does in fact comply with the principle of legality. Belgium,[49] Georgia,[50] Malta,[51] the Netherlands,[52] New Zealand,[53] Norway,[54] Portugal,[55] South Africa,[56] Trinidad and Tobago,[57] and the UK[58] belong to that category.

Canada is amongst the countries that adopt a different approach to the issue. Under the Crimes against Humanity and War Crimes Act (CAHWCA) 2000, Canadian courts have jurisdiction over crimes against humanity, also when these are found in customary international law.[59] The provision is wider than the Rome Statute, allowing for additional flexibility, given that customary international law may evolve.

---

49 Art 7 Act of 5 August 2003 on Serious Violations of International Humanitarian Law inserting a new provision 136ter to the Criminal Code. Notably, The Serious Violations of IHL Act incorporates the crimes listed in Art 7(1) into domestic law, but does not make reference to the definitions of crimes against humanity outlined in Art 7(2) of the Rome Statute. However, the Serious Violations of IHL Act provides that the crimes must be interpreted 'in accordance with the Statute of the International Criminal Court', indicating that the crimes will be interpreted so as to be consistent with the definitions contained in Art 7(2) of the Rome Statute.

50 Art 408 Criminal Code of Georgia of July 22, 1999, which came into force on 1 June 2000.

51 First Schedule, Art 2 International Criminal Court Act of 13 December 2003.

52 Section 4, 270 Act of 19 June 2003 containing rules concerning serious violations of international humanitarian law (International Crimes Act).

53 Section 10 International Crimes and International Criminal Court Act of 1 October 2000.

54 Section 102 Penal Code Chapter 16 Sections 101–110, 7 March 2008.

55 Art 9 Law No 31/2004 Adaptation of Criminal Legislation to ICC Statute, 22 July 2004.

56 Schedule 1 Part 2, Act No 27 Implementation of the Rome Statute of the International Criminal Court, of 12 July 2002.

57 Section 10(2)(k) International Criminal Court Act 2006.

58 Schedule 8 International Criminal Court Act of 11 May 2001. Sections 50 and 51 of the ICC Act 2001 incorporate crimes against humanity into national law by reference to the Rome Statute. See M Brubacher, S Olleson, 'Report of the United Kingdom' (European Law Students Association, London 2004) 2; R Cryer and O Bekou, 'International Crimes and ICC Cooperation in England and Wales' (2007) 5 Journal of International Criminal Justice 441, 444. Further, the ICC Act 2001 provides that the crime should be interpreted in accordance with the Elements of Crimes, propagated under Art 9 of the Rome Statute, along with decisions of the ICC and other international tribunals.

59 Sections 4(3) and 6(3).

Another approach is taken by Germany, which restricts the provision to those acts that that involve severe physical or mental harm. By contrast, the Elements of Crimes refer to 'great suffering, or serious injury to body or to mental or physical health.' The qualification of 'severe' found in the German provision, makes the provision narrower than the Rome Statute.[60] The Republic of the Congo also specifies that the provision enshrines: forcing into prostitution, pillage, massive and systematic summary executions, and abductions of persons followed by their disappearance,[61] which differs from the wording in the Rome Statute and the Elements of Crimes.

When examining whether a policy requirement is essential to establishing the commission of crimes against humanity[62] and whether this, in turn, needs to be incorporated in domestic legislation, the response of States has been variable. This perhaps reflects the inconsistency enshrined in the Rome Statute. Malta,[63] the Netherlands,[64] the Republic of Korea,[65] South Africa[66] and the UK[67] have incorporated the policy requirement of Article 7(2)(a) ICC Statute, whereas Belgium, Benin, Burkina Faso, Burundi, Canada, Central African Republic, Georgia and Germany have chosen not to include it in their legislation. Of particular interest is Article 9 of the legislation of the Republic of the Congo.[68] Whilst it does not mention the policy requirement *per se*, it seems to merge crimes against humanity with war crimes committed in the execution of a concerted plan by referring to such crimes committed in a time of armed conflict against those who fight 'an ideological system' in the name of which crimes against humanity are committed. This is a very unusual provision, breach of which is punishable subject to the death penalty.[69]

---

[60] Section 7(1)(8) Act to Introduce the Code of Crimes against International Law of 26 June 2002, which implements this with reference to Art 226 German Criminal Code. See G Werle and F Jessberger, 'International Criminal Justice is Coming Home: the New German Code of Crimes Against International Law' (2002) 13 Criminal Law Forum 191, 206; H Satzger, 'German Criminal Law and the Rome Statute – A Critical Analysis of the New German Code of Crimes against International Law' (2002) 2 International Criminal Law Review 261, 275.

[61] Loi No 8-98 (n 33) Art 6(k).

[62] M de Guzman, 'The Road from Rome: The Developing Law of Crimes against Humanity' (2000) 22 Human Rights Quarterly 335; P Hwang, 'Defining Crimes against Humanity in the Rome Statute of the International Criminal Court' (1998) 22 Fordham International Law Journal 457; WA Schabas, 'State Policy as an Element of International Crimes' (2008) 98 Journal of Criminal Law and Criminology 953.

[63] International Criminal Court Act (n 51) First Schedule, Art 2.

[64] International Crimes Act (n 52) Section 4.

[65] Art 9 2007 Act on the Punishment of Crimes within the Jurisdiction of the International Criminal Court.

[66] Act No 27 Implementation of the Rome Statute of the International Criminal Court (n 56) Schedule 1, Part 2, Section 1.1.

[67] International Criminal Court Act (n 58) Schedule 8, Art 7.2.

[68] Loi No 8-98 (n 33).

[69] Ibid Art 9.

The above examples demonstrate that there is not a single approach with regard to the most controversial issues that arise in the implementation of crimes against humanity. Whilst many States follow the Statute, other States choose a path of their own. The implementation of this provision shows that States are confident enough to reinterpret the Statute and to make those choices that suit their interests when incorporating the provision for national application.

III. WAR CRIMES

When it comes to the incorporation of war crimes into domestic law, States are more familiar with this category of crimes than with the previous two. It can safely be assumed that most States will have incorporated some war crimes provisions into their national laws already. However, as the ICC war crimes provision enshrined in Article 8 of the Rome Statute is narrower than the war crimes stipulated by international humanitarian law instruments,[70] it is important to examine whether States have adopted particular implementation approaches.

In that respect, the Ugandan approach is noteworthy. Section (9)(4) of the Ugandan International Criminal Court Act 2010 provides that: 'Nothing in this section affects or limits the operation of section (2) of the Geneva Conventions Act (which makes a grave breach of the Geneva Conventions an offence under Uganda[n] law)'. This formulation essentially denotes that where the Rome Statute and Geneva Conventions Act are divergent as to grave breaches, the latter is applicable. This approach however is not common.

A couple of States make reference to other international treaties besides the Geneva Conventions. For instance, the Georgian Criminal Code[71] prohibits 'other war crimes, envisaged by the international treaties of Georgia and which are not punishable under articles 411 and 412 of the Criminal Code of Georgia'. If war crimes are included in other international treaties and they are wider than Article 8 of the Rome Statute, then the Georgian implementation would indeed be wider. The same approach is taken also by Costa Rica.[72]

---

[70] Despite the fact that most of the provisions of the grave breaches of the 1949 Geneva Conventions (75 UNTS 31) are covered, as are most grave breaches of the 1977 Additional Protocol I (1125 UNTS 3), common Art 3 and Art 23 of the Hague Regulations annexed to Convention (IV) respecting the Laws and Customs of War on Land, the Hague 1907, some of the 1977 Additional Protocol II (1125 UNTS 609) provisions are not included in Art 8 Rome Statute.

[71] Criminal Code (n 50) Art 413(d).

[72] Art 378 Criminal Prosecution to Punish War Crimes and Crimes against Humanity, No 8272 of 2 May 2002.

Taking account of other developments in international law regarding war crimes after the coming into force of the Rome Statute is another issue that States may wish to consider when implementing the war crimes provisions. In particular, given the role customary international law plays in this area as well as the body of jurisprudence emanating from the ad hoc tribunals, it is worth considering how, if at all, such developments need to be incorporated. One State that embraces taking account of developments in international law is Canada which in its CAHWCA 2000 criminalises any act or omission that is a war crime under conventional or customary international law.[73] This provision is wider than the war crimes provision in the Rome Statute and takes into account future developments in the law of war crimes, thereby enabling the Canadian courts to exercise criminal jurisdiction and prosecute war crimes beyond the constraints of the ambit of Article 8 of the Rome Statute.

The Samoan implementation of the war crimes provision takes a similar approach. The reference to the existence of genocide and crimes against humanity 'according to the general principles of law recognized by the community of nations' is omitted with regard to war crimes. The Samoan ICC Act 2007 includes in its prohibition 'any other act committed during an armed conflict which, at the time and in the place of its commission, constitutes a war crime according to customary international law or conventional international law applicable to armed conflicts, whether or not it constitutes a contravention of the law in force at the time and in the place of its commission'.[74] In that respect, this approach is wider than the wording of Article 8(2) of the Rome Statute.

The war crimes provision of the Rome Statute is characterised by the presence of a 'non-threshold threshold' in its chapeau which stipulates that the ICC has jurisdiction over war crimes 'in particular when committed as part of a plan or policy or as part of large-scale commission of such crimes'.[75] When a State implements this provision, a decision is necessary as to whether the above threshold should be implemented as well. This jurisdictional threshold has been included for the purposes of allocating the Court's limited resources better. This does not however mean that States ought to adopt this threshold in their legislation as well. Indeed, including it would perhaps unacceptably restrict the number of prosecutions that States would be able to oversee at the national level.

---

[73] See Section 4(1)(c), 4(3), 6(1)(c) and 6(3) Crimes Against Humanity and War Crimes Act 2000.

[74] Section 7(2) International Criminal Court Act No 26 of 9 November 2007.

[75] Art 8(1) Rome Statute.

Looking at the practice, States that have replicated the Rome Statute word for word, have also incorporated the threshold above. Ireland,[76] Malta[77] and South Africa,[78] fall in that category for instance. Some African States, namely, Burkina Faso,[79] the Republic of the Congo,[80] and Burundi,[81] have all chosen not to include any reference to a threshold. A variation of this approach can be detected in Norway and Spain which employ the above threshold to distinguish between serious and less serious war crimes in terms of applicable penalties. If a war crime is committed as part of large-scale commission, or as part of a plan or policy, harsher penalties would be applicable.[82] Whilst the breadth of the national criminal jurisdiction is certainly a matter of choice and an unfettered right of any sovereign State, it is important to recall that (owing to the complementarity principle enshrined in the Statute) States are expected to tackle the vast majority of the cases themselves, leaving for the Court only those situations where the State is genuinely unwilling or unable to investigate or prosecute. With that in mind, it would be important for the State to enable its own legal order to dispose of as many cases as possible, as the ICC even with respect to the few situations it addresses can only prosecute a handful of cases. States should therefore consider whether removing the threshold for war crimes prosecutions is feasible.

The implementation process offers an ideal opportunity for States to review the Rome Statute in light of their existing legislation and also to consider reinterpreting those provisions of the Statute that would perhaps benefit from a fresh approach. A key trend has developed with regard to disposing of the distinction between international and non-international armed conflicts. The Statute, in the war crimes provision, has maintained it as have the majority of States in their national implementing legislation. Notably, however, a number of States choose to extend the Statute coverage regarding crimes committed in an international armed conflict to those committed in non-international armed conflicts. Given the absence of such a provision in the Statute, this can only be effected by legislation enacted to implement it.

---

[76] International Criminal Court Act of 31 October 2006.

[77] International Court Act (n 51) First Schedule, Art 8.1.

[78] Act No 27 Implementation of the Rome Statute of the International Criminal Court (n 56), Schedule 1, Part 3.

[79] Loi No 10.001 (n 31) Art 19.

[80] Loi No 8-98 (n 33) Art 4.

[81] See Loi No 1/004 du 08 Mai 2003 portant répression du crime de génocide, des crimes contre l'humanité et des crimes de guerre.

[82] Section 130, Chapter 16 Norwegian Penal Code, 2008 and Provisions of the Spanish Criminal Code Concerning International Crimes and Art 614bis of the Integrated Text Containing the Amendments Introduced by the Ley Organica 15/2003 Implementing the Statute of the International Criminal Court, respectively.

The 1993 Belgian Act[83] which first incorporated war crimes into national law did not distinguish between crimes committed in international and non-international armed conflicts. The Belgian Act of 5 August 2003 on Serious Violations of International Humanitarian Law equally maintains this approach. In Article 136 *quater*, of the Belgian Criminal Code, the crimes that engage when committed in international armed conflicts (as defined in Common Article 2 of the Geneva Conventions and Article 1 of Additional Protocol I) and non-international armed conflicts (as defined in Article 1 of Additional Protocol II and Article 8(2)(f) of the Rome Statute) are listed. The reference to non-international armed conflicts defined in Article 8(2)(f) as an alternative to Additional Protocol II is significant insofar as Article 8(2)(f) only requires the existence of a protracted armed conflict. Additional Protocol II contains a narrower definition of non-international armed conflict.[84] Hence, the lack of distinction between the two types of conflict renders the coverage envisaged in the Serious Violations of IHL Act broader than that conferred by Article 8 of the Rome Statute.

Another State that has removed the distinction between the two types of conflict is Germany. Its 2002 Code of Crimes against International Law (CCAIL)[85] criminalises acts which amount to grave breaches of Additional Protocol I to the Geneva Conventions, thereby making the list of crimes that can be committed in non-international armed conflicts longer than that included in the Rome Statute.[86] German courts therefore do not need to determine whether a conflict was of an international or non-international character.[87] Instead, the CCAIL lists the crimes in accordance with the protected interest: namely crimes against persons, property and other rights, humanitarian operations and emblems. War crimes that can only be committed in an international armed conflict are listed separately.[88] The

---

[83] D Vandermeersch, 'The ICC Statute and Belgian Law' (2004) 24 Journal of International Criminal Justice 134.

[84] According to Art 1 of Additional Protocol II such conflicts are: 'conflicts which take place in the territory of a High Contracting Party between its armed forces and dissident armed forces or other armed groups which, under responsible command, exercise such control over a part of its territory as to enable them to carry out sustained and concerted military operations and to implement the Protocol.'

[85] The incorporation therefore of the conduct prohibited by Arts 8(2)(b)(ii), (iv), (vi), (vii), (xxiii), (xxv) of the Rome Statute coupled with the absent distinction of international and non-international armed conflict renders the CCAIL wider than the Rome Statute. On the issue of merging the international armed conflicts with the international non-armed conflicts provisions in Germany see A Eser, 'Das Rom-Statut des Internationalen Strafgerichtshofs als Herausforderung für die nationale Strafrechtspflege' in C Grafl (ed), *Festschrift für Martin Burgstaller zum 65. Geburtstag* (Neuer Wissenschaftlicher Verlag 2004) 371.

[86] Idem.

[87] Idem.

[88] Werle and Jessberger (n 60) 207.

CCAIL however continues to distinguish between Geneva Law, ie protected persons, and Hague Law, ie prohibited means and methods of warfare.[89]

The approach of grouping crimes in accordance with the object of protection is also followed by Ethiopia. Consequently, the following categories can be identified: 'War crimes against the civilian population', 'War crimes against wounded, sick and shipwrecked persons or medical services' and 'war crimes against prisoners and interned persons'.[90] Ethiopia does not distinguish between the two types of armed conflict either, nor does it refer to the Geneva Conventions in its legislation. However, all of the punishable acts have been thoroughly reviewed and redefined for the purposes of domestic implementation. For example, prohibition of 'unlawful or arbitrary taxes or levies disproportionate to the requirements of military necessity' has been included.[91] Also notably, the age for recruiting child soldiers is 18[92] as opposed to 15 as per the Rome Statute.[93] Ethiopia has not yet joined the ICC regime, so some adaptation may be required if and when it decides to become a State Party (to the Rome Statute). The same applies to Cape Verde whose Penal Code substantially codifies war crimes provisions,[94] which, however, having been adopted prior to Cape Verde's ratification of the Rome Statute in 2011, requires re-examination with the latter. Perhaps, however, it is worth mentioning Article 278 in that respect.[95] Although this article was not included with the Rome Statute in mind, its reference to 'other act that constitutes a breach or violation of the provisions contained in international agreements by which Cape Verde is bound' might be used to provide a legal basis for compliance with the Statute, should a determination of Cape Verde's readiness to investigate and prosecute ever be in question.

Another country that moves away from the distinction between international and non-international conflicts is the Republic of Korea.[96] In addition,

---

[89] Eser (n 85).

[90] See Arts 270, 271 and 272 respectively Criminal Code No 414/2004.

[91] Ibid Art 270(h).

[92] Ibid Art 270(m).

[93] See Art 8(2)(b)(xxvi) and (e)(vii) ICC Statute.

[94] See Legislative Decree 4/2003 (n 34) Arts 272–278.

[95] Art 278 (Other crimes against the international community): 'A penalty of one year's to three years' imprisonment shall be imposed as punishment upon anyone who, in time of war, armed conflict or occupation, carries out or orders the carrying out of any other act that constitutes a breach or violation of the provisions contained in international agreements by which Cape Verde is bound, relating to the conduct of hostilities, the protection of the injured, ailing and shipwrecked, the treatment of prisoners of war, and the protection of civilians in the event of war, armed conflict or occupation'. (Ibid.)

[96] See 2007 Act on the Punishment of Crimes within the Jurisdiction of the International Criminal Court (n 65) Arts 10–14. See T H Choi, S Kim, 'Nationalized International Criminal Law: Genocidal Intent, Command Responsibility, and an Overview of the South Korean

Switzerland, in its 2010 amendment of the Swiss Criminal and Military Criminal Code[97] follows the same approach.[98] Notably, the lists of war crimes introduced in the civil and military criminal codes are identical and are broader than in the previous Military Criminal Code;[99] as a result, this legislation is also more expansive than Article 8 of the Rome Statute.

Moving away from implementation efforts aimed at extending coverage of the Rome Statute, the approach taken by France deserves some further explanation. France was the first State to make use of Article 124 of the Rome Statute upon ratification. The said provision, when invoked, precludes the ICC from exercising jurisdiction over war crimes for a seven-year period.[100] Originally, the French Penal code in its Article 212–2 only referred to a very specific category of crimes against humanity committed in the context of armed conflict.[101] France had also deposited seven interpretative declarations pertaining to Article 8 of the Rome Statute. These declarations mirror the French reservations regarding Additional Protocol I and cover, amongst others, the right of self-defence and the use of nuclear weapons.[102] France amended its Penal Code in 2010 and brought it into line with the Rome Statute.[103] War crimes have been thoroughly incorporated in a manner which is generally consistent with the Rome Statute.[104] The omission however of rape, sexual slavery and some grave breaches of the Geneva Conventions, including torture and inhuman treatment is noteworthy. Consistent 'with its own practice (reservations to API) … the use of nuclear weapons in self-defence does not constitute a prohibited act (*une infraction*) and thus prosecution thereof is precluded.'[105] A further distinction is introduced between

---

Implementing Legislation of the ICC Statute' (2010) 19 Michigan State Journal of International Law 609.

[97] Loi n° 2010-930 du 9 août 2010 portant adaptation du droit pénal à l'institution de la Cour pénale internationale.

[98] Ibid Art 264b.

[99] Militärstrafgesetz (MStG) of 13 June 1927 (as amended on 23 January 2007). For a discussion of the various issues that had arisen with the application of the MStG provisions, see R Roth, I Jeanneret, 'Droit suisse' 275–297, in A Cassese and M Delmas-Marty (eds), *Jurisdictions nationales et crimes internationaux* (Presses Universitaires de France 2002) 278–281.

[100] France revoked the declaration in 2008.

[101] In its 1994 version, Art 212–2 of the Criminal Code provided: 'Where they are committed during war time in execution of a concerted plan against persons fighting the ideological system in the name of which are perpetrated crimes against humanity, the actions referred to under Art 212–1 are punished by criminal imprisonment for life'.

[102] For the text see: <http://www.icrc.org/ihl.nsf/NORM/6D97C3E21CCF24E2412566BB002F5C1A?OpenDocument>.

[103] Loi n° 2010–930 du 9 août 2010 portant adaptation du droit pénal à l'institution de la Cour pénale internationale.

[104] Book IV bis- Criminal Code, Arts 461–1 *et seq*.

[105] Ibid Art 462–11.

war crimes and war offences (*délits de guerre*), a lesser form of war crimes,[106] which incur lower penalties and are subject to a briefer period of limitation.[107] This distinction does not exist in the Rome Statute which also does not allow for the applicability of statutes of limitations for any of the core crimes.[108]

Despite being the oldest category of crimes incorporated at the national level, the implementation of the Rome Statute provision on war crimes offers a fresh opportunity for States to put their own stamp on the domestic implementation of international crimes. Considerable variation can therefore be observed, which at times, extends significantly beyond the provision of the Rome Statute. The fact that a notable trend is beginning to develop, particularly regarding the abolition of the distinction between international and non-international armed conflicts, might lead to progressive development of the law on war crimes at the international level. This would indeed be an interesting development, which would be further demonstrate the importance national approaches can play in the development of international law from a bottom-up perspective.

IV. CONCLUSIONS

The first ten years of the ICC are characterized by a number of significant achievements which have been examined elsewhere in this book. On the occasion of the tenth anniversary of the entry into force of the Rome Statute, it is fitting to explore how national legal orders have contributed to the success of the institution created by the Statute. Empowering national courts to become able first and – where possible – also willing to investigate and prosecute the core international crimes is key to all accountability efforts. This contribution has sought to offer an insight into how States have taken up this challenge. By and large, it has focused on those approaches that either go beyond the Rome Statute or do not fully encapsulate its provisions. An overview of available implementing legislation reveals that in most instances, the definitions of genocide, crimes against humanity and war crimes have largely been transposed unchanged. Aberrations denote a newly found sense of ownership on the part of the States. Where this is coupled with an

[106] See E Verges, 'La Loi n° 2010–930 du 9 août 2010 portant adaptation du droit pénal à l'institution de la Cour pénale internationale : une avancée marquante de la répression en France des crimes de guerre et des crime contre l'humanité' (2010) 4 Revue de science criminelles et de droit pénal comparé 896.

[107] Art 462–10 of the Criminal Code envisages a 30-year prescription for war crimes and 20 years for war offences.

[108] See Art 29 Rome Statute.

increased likelihood of national prosecutions, it is a welcome development. Where, however, it conceals an attempt to limit the reach of the accountability efforts at the national level, then the so-called 'impunity gap' is likely to be widened.

The varied approaches of domestic legislation examined here should be treated as a healthy reaction to a novel international institution, which in the not so distant past, looked like nothing more than a 'court of dreams'.[109] Setting up regimes at the national level which are able to rise to the challenge of undertaking effective national prosecutions is a step in the right direction. The outlook appears to be positive overall. When the ICC first became operational, the domestic implementation of the Rome Statute was not treated as a pressing matter. As the ICC has become a fully functioning body, attention at the national level has rightly increased. It may take some time before the extent of the ICC's effect can be fully appreciated. In the meantime, as Justice Robert Jackson commented on the performance of the Nuremberg International Military Tribunal: 'Many mistakes have been made and many inadequacies must be confessed' but one might take consolation in the fact that, 'in proceedings of this novelty, errors and missteps may also be instructive to the future'.[110] Given that the path to individual criminal accountability, as set out in the Rome Statute system, also passes through national jurisdictions, it is to be hoped that when it comes to the assessment of the ICC regime in the future, the errors and missteps will not be such that they tarnish its overall significance. If anything, national laws implementing the Statute may prove to be useful signposts along this path.

---

[109] D Rieff, 'Court of Dreams' (*New Republic* 7 September 1998) 16–17.

[110] R Jackson, 'Final Report to the President Concerning the Nuremberg War Crimes Trial' (1946) 20 Temple Quarterly 338.

Principle of Complementarity in Contemporary International Criminal Justice

*Mark Ellis**

Since 1945, there have been approximately 313 armed conflicts[1] in which an estimated 92 to 101 million people died – twice the number of victims in World War I and II combined.[2] While a staggering number of these deaths are directly attributable to war crimes and other atrocities, international and mixed model tribunals have indicted only 823 persons.[3] Most crimes have gone unpunished. Responding to the need for justice and accountability, the international community took a leap forward on 1 July 2002, when it established a permanent international criminal court to prosecute the most egregious international crimes: aggression, genocide, war crimes, and crimes against humanity. This vanguard court is a remarkable development in international law.

Debate continues, however, over whether and when gross violations of international criminal law should be tried by international courts or by national courts. It is reasonable and appropriate to question the role of domestic actors in handling the most heinous international crimes. There is incontrovertible evidence that national accountability for such crimes can be

* Dr Mark Ellis is Executive Director of the International Bar Association, London. This publication is based on Dr Ellis's address on 30 August 2011 at the 5th International Humanitarian Law Dialogs held in Chautauqua, New York, and the 10th Anniversary of the International Criminal Court: Its Achievements and Prospects for the Future organised by the British Institute of International and Comparative Law and the University of Nottingham Human Rights Law Centre, 21 June 2012. The previous version of this contribution was published as an article in the 2012 Humanitarian Dialogs Proceedings. Dr Ellis would like to thank Aleisha McLean and Shehara de Soysa for their research assistance in the course of preparation of the contribution.

[1] See C Mullins, 'Conflict Victimization and Post-conflict Justice: 1945–2008', in MC Bassiouni (ed), *The Pursuit of International Criminal Justice: A World Study on Conflicts, Victimization, and Post-conflict Justice* (Intersentia 2010) 79.

[2] See MC Bassiouni, 'Assessing Conflict Outcomes: Accountability and Impunity' in Bassiouni (n 1) 6.

[3] MC Bassiouni, *Crimes Against Humanity* (Cambridge University Press 2011) 650.

slow.[4] Yet this is gradually changing, and the Rome Statute of the International Criminal Court offers an important new mechanism to promote uniformity in the exercise of jurisdiction by domestic war crimes courts. As the International Criminal Court (ICC) evolves and continues to be tested, national jurisdictions will be challenged to build and showcase their capacity, and will increasingly become 'accountability centers' for international criminal trials.

The core mechanism for the devolution of judicial authority is the principle of complementarity. The Preamble and Article 1 of the Rome Statute establish that the ICC 'shall be complementary to national criminal jurisdictions.'[5] Complementarity gives national courts primary authority to prosecute individuals who have committed gross violations of international criminal law. The Rome Statute specifies that it is 'the duty of every state to exercise its criminal jurisdiction over those responsible for international crimes.'[6] As Judge Fausto Pocar, former President of the International Criminal Tribunal for the former Yugoslavia (ICTY), and former Chairman of the UN Human Rights Committee, stated:

> Developing domestic capacity for the prosecution of international crimes and the application [by domestic judiciaries] of international law as clarified by international courts [by domestic judiciaries] is ... a primary objective to be achieved.[7]

Complementarity addresses the presumed conflict between state sovereignty and the pursuit of supranational justice for the most pernicious international crimes – between a nation's right to control and enforce its own laws and the victims' right to objective justice. It is no surprise that most people believe it is better to prosecute crimes in local rather than international courts.[8] In concurrence, the former ICC Prosecutor, Luis Moreno-Ocampo, stated:

---

[4] See MS Ellis, 'Combating Impunity and Enforcing Accountability as a Way to Promote Peace and Stability – The Role of International War Crimes Tribunals' (2006) 2 Journal of National Security Law & Policy 112.

[5] Rome Statute of the International Criminal Court (adopted 17 July 1998, entered into force 1 July 2002) 2187 UNTS 90, Art 1.

[6] Ibid Preamble.

[7] F Pocar, 'UN Approach to Transitional Justice – Dialogue with Member States on Rule of Law at the International Level' (Rule of Law Unit 2 December 2009) <http://www.unrol.org/files/TJ%20panel%20discssion%20-%20FP%20statement.pdf>.

[8] See a discussion on Serbia's views on the International Criminal Tribunal for the former Yugoslavia (ICTY) in DF Orentlicher, *Shrinking the Space for Denial* (Open Society Justice Initiative 2008).

> National investigations and prosecutions, where they can properly be undertaken, will normally be the most effective and efficient means of bringing offenders to justice; States themselves will normally have the best access to evidence and witnesses.[9]

The ICC *will not* undermine national sovereignty, nor interfere with judicial matters that naturally fall within the jurisdiction of States. Through the principle of complementarity, the ICC dramatically expands the role of national courts in trials involving international crimes. This is because the ICC has jurisdiction only if there is a breakdown in the national system of justice or if a State Party simply fails to prosecute. The ICC *must* defer its jurisdiction to national courts except in situations where national jurisdictions have been 'genuinely unable' or 'unwilling' to investigate and/or prosecute the accused.[10] This is an irrevocable principle.

The ICC's impact on domestic law and national capacity building will be significant and far-reaching. Most dramatic will be the increase in the number of domestic war crimes courts, even in non-State Party jurisdictions. Complementarity will likely push States to retain control over investigating and prosecuting nationals charged with gross violations of international criminal law. Both State Parties and non-State Parties will stress the pre-eminence of domestic over international jurisdiction where they have the capacity to undertake domestic trials.

The risks are high if a State fails to maintain control over the proceedings – it will lose jurisdictional control. Because States will naturally be reluctant to admit inadequacies that might result in the transfer of a case to the ICC, they will do everything possible to retain jurisdiction unless it is in the State's clear interest to delegate matters to the Court. For instance, in a politically charged post-conflict environment, it might be less contentious to transfer a former head of state to the ICC. For most situations, however, it is inconceivable that a State with a functioning legal system would not at least investigate alleged crimes.

I. THE COMPLEMENTARITY PRINCIPLE

There nevertheless remains confusion as to when the ICC should intervene. Article 17(1)(a) of the Rome Statute states that a case is inadmissible to the ICC if it 'is being investigated or prosecuted by a State which has jurisdiction

---

[9] OTP, 'Paper on Some Policy Issues Before the Office of the Prosecutor' (September 2003) <http://www.icc-cpi.int/NR/rdonlyres/1FA7C4C6-DE5F-42B7-8B25-60AA962ED8B6/143594/030905_Policy_Paper.pdf>.

[10] Art 17(1)(a) Rome Statute.

over it, unless the State is unwilling or unable genuinely to carry out the investigation or prosecution.'[11] In consideration of the terms 'genuinely unwilling' and 'unable', the Rome Statute offers a limited definition. Article 17(2) states:

> In order to determine unwillingness in a particular case, the Court shall consider, having regard to the principles of due process recognized by international law, whether one or more of the following exist, as applicable:
> (a) The proceedings were or are being undertaken or the national decision was made for the purpose of shielding the person concerned from criminal responsibility for crimes within the jurisdiction of the Court ... ;
> (b) There has been an unjustified delay in the proceedings which in the circumstances is inconsistent with an intent to bring the person concerned to justice;
> (c) The proceedings were not or are not being conducted independently or impartially, and they were or are being conducted in a manner which, in the circumstances, is inconsistent with an intent to bring the person concerned to justice...

There are a number of issues that may demonstrate a State's *unwillingness* to prosecute. For example, certain extra-judicial proceedings, such as truth and reconciliation commissions, have been used to shield suspects from ICC jurisdiction. Blanket amnesties, which allow for a defendant's acquittal, short sentencing, and general disregard of material evidence, may also demonstrate a State's unwillingness to prosecute.[12] The use of these tools for the sole purpose of avoiding prosecution contravenes Article 17, and the ICC would be fully within its right to declare jurisdiction. However, an investigation would be required to determine if a State is acting in pursuit of reconciliation or to protect those criminally responsible. Such a determination should be made by an impartial, objective party independent from the ICC. This contribution will provide arguments in favour of such an approach.

In consideration of whether a State is shielding a suspect from criminal responsibility, the ICC must conduct an assessment of the subjective nature of the State's action.[13] The Rome Conference determined that a simple delay

---

[11] Idem.

[12] See D Robinson, 'Serving the Interests of Justice: Amnesties, Truth Commissions and the International Criminal Court' (2003) 14 European Journal of International Law 481–505, A Seibert-Fohr, 'The Relevance of the Rome Statute of the International Criminal Court for Amnesties and Truth Commissions' (2003) 7 Max Planck Yearbook of United Nations Law 553–590 and HA Moy, 'The International Criminal Court's Arrest Warrants and Uganda's Lord's Resistance Army: Renewing the Debate over Amnesty and Complementarity' (2006) 19 Harvard Human Rights Journal 267–273.

[13] See R Cryer et al, *An Introduction to International Criminal Law and Procedure* (Cambridge University Press 2010) 156.

resulting from State action is too low a threshold for deciding whether there was an unjustified delay in proceedings.[14] Instead, the Court would need to look toward the 'usual procedures and time-frames in that individual state' to determine whether there may be an indication that the State is unwilling to conduct proceedings.[15] Intent is an important factor which must not be overlooked. If the Prosecutor can prove that a State's inaction or delay, relative to usual timeframes, is for the purpose of evading prosecution, then the Court is within its right to claim jurisdiction.

Regarding lack of ability, the Rome Statute defines a State as *unable* if there is a:

> substantial collapse or unavailability of its national judicial system ... [in such a way that] the State is unable to obtain the accused or the necessary evidence and testimony or otherwise unable to carry out proceedings.[16]

There are a number of circumstances that may lead the ICC to question a State's ability: States engaged in domestic or international conflict; States experiencing political or economic crisis that threatens judicial independence; States lacking the rule of law and a judicial system capable of meeting international standards of fairness; States in transition that invariably lack a properly functioning judiciary; States that fail to incorporate necessary legislation into the judicial system; and States that fail to ensure fair trial proceedings.

States experiencing or emerging from armed conflict or civil unrest are unlikely to have the judicial capacity to properly investigate and prosecute those responsible for crimes under ICC jurisdiction. Yet, if all States currently engaged in conflict were deemed unable to conduct trials, it would fall upon the ICC to investigate and prosecute all cases. Given limited resources, however, it would be impossible for the ICC to investigate or obtain jurisdiction over all of these cases.

It is true that the criteria described in the Rome Statute are vague, and the burden of proof rests squarely with States. Perhaps as a result, there are a number of inconsistencies in the reasoning behind ICC jurisdictional claims. One could argue that the ICC has too much freedom to impose on state sovereignty and organize its own domestic courts. At the very least, however, there is an unresolved tension between the legitimate concerns of the ICC and States regarding the prosecution of heinous international crimes.

---

[14] See M Benzing, 'The Complementarity Regime of the International Criminal Court: International Criminal Justice between State Sovereignty and the Fight against Impunity' (2003) 7 Max Planck Yearbook of United Nations Law 608.

[15] Ibid 609.

[16] Art 17(3) Rome Statute.

II. EARLY TEST CASES

In 2007, targeted ethnic killings in Kenya left over 1,200 people dead, 3,500 injured and 600,000 displaced.[17] The ICC reported that;

> [d]uring the 60 days of violence there were hundreds of rapes, possibly more, and over 100,000 properties were destroyed ... They were crimes against humanity as a whole.[18]

It was initially believed that Kenya had the ability to conduct proceedings. The ICC Prosecutor announced:

> Kenya has strong capacity in many parts of its justice sector ... all agreed that there are no insurmountable technical challenges to the conduct of credible investigations, prosecutions and trials for international crimes in Kenya.[19]

However, numerous reports implicated 'serving police officers, security officials and powerful legislators for ordering attacks that were widespread, well-orchestrated and which unfolded in notable patterns.'[20] While Kenya may have had the judicial capacity to conduct proceedings, the government – marred by corruption, judicial interference, and lack of public confidence – was reluctant to prosecute members of its own ranks.[21]

Kenya's reluctance was clear from its relaxed approach to criminal investigation and prosecution. Although the government was adamant that it would conduct a thorough investigation, the ICC ruled that merely taking steps to launch an investigation does not demonstrate willingness.[22] Instead, the government would have to

---

[17] ICC Press Release, 'Kenya's Post-election Violence: ICC Prosecutor Presents Cases against Six Individuals for Crimes against Humanity' (15 December 2010) <http://www.icc-cpi.int/NR/exeres/BA2041D8-3F30-4531-8850-431B5B2F4416.htm>.

[18] Ibid.

[19] *Putting Complementarity into Practice: Domestic Justice for International Crimes in DRC, Uganda and Kenya* (Open Society Justice Initiative 2011) 86.

[20] P Siels, 'ICC's Kenya Decision Is No Cause for Celebration' (*Al Jazeera* 31 January 2012) <http://www.aljazeera.com/indepth/opinion/2012/02/201212812593161 7297.html>.

[21] See *Restoring Integrity: An Assessment of the Needs of the Justice System in the Republic of Kenya*, Report of the International Bar Association Human Rights Institute (IBA Human Rights Institute February 2010) 54 <http://www.ibanet.org/Document/Default.aspx?DocumentUid=DCD20276-7C7C-4321-92A1-DD43531F93A1>.

[22] See *Prosecutor v Francis Kirimi Muthaura et al* (Judgment on the appeal of the Republic of Kenya against the decision of Pre-Trial Chamber II of 30 May 2011 entitled "Decision on the Application by the Government of Kenya Challenging the Admissibility of the Case Pursuant to Article 19(2)(b) of the Statute") ICC-01/09-02/11-274 Appeals Chamber (30 August 2011).

> [take] steps to ascertain whether *those suspects* are responsible for the conduct ... such as interviewing witnesses and suspects, analyzing forensic information and collecting documentary evidence.[23]

Moreover, the government ignored the recommendations in the Kenya National Commission on Human Rights report,[24] Parliament failed to form an investigative tribunal comprised of local and international judges,[25] and the Waki Commission findings, recommending a Truth and Reconciliation Commission and Special Tribunal for Kenya, were also disregarded.[26]

As a result of Kenya's general unwillingness to do as required under international law, the Prosecutor claimed jurisdiction on behalf of the ICC. On 23 January 2012, the ICC confirmed it was formally charging four high-ranking Kenyan officials with crimes for their alleged roles in the post-election violence.[27] Charges included murder, persecution, and ethnic cleansing.[28]

As a result of the Court's decision, the Kenyan government has launched a wider campaign to have the ICC proceedings discontinued. This followed a failed attempt to seek a change of venue for trials from The Hague to either Kenya or Tanzania.[29] Its ambassador to the UN, Macharia Kamau, lodged a petition to the UN Security Council asking for the 'immediate termination' of the trials.[30]

At a recent African Union (AU) summit in Addis Ababa, AU Chariman Hailemariam Desalgn said that the AU was opposed to the ICC trying Kenyan President Uhuru Kenyatta, and that the cases against Kenyatta and his Deputy President William Ruto should be referred to domestic courts in

---

23 Ibid para 40 (emphasis in the original).

24 Siels (n 20).

25 Ibid.

26 Ibid.

27 The leader of the Opposition, William Ruto, and Jushua Arap Sang were formally charged 'with planning attacks on supporters of the ruling party', while Uhuru Kenyatta and Francis Muthaura were charged with 'financing and organising retaliatory attacks'. The charges against Francis Muthaura have since been withdrawn by the Prosecutor. See FN Nesbitt, 'Principled Intervention in Africa' (*The Epoch Times* 5 February 2012) <http://www.theepochtimes.com/n2/opinion/principled-intervention-in-africa-186875.html> and ICC, 'Statement by ICC Prosecutor on the Notice to Withdraw Charges against Mr Muthaura' (11 March 2013) <http://icc-cpi.int/en_menus/icc/press%20and%20media/press%20releases/Pages/OTP-statement-11-03-2013.aspx>.

28 Nesbitt (n 27).

29 ICC Press Release, 'Ruto and Sang Case: Trial to Open in The Hague' ICC-CPI-20130715-PR931 (15 July 2013) <http://www.icc-cpi.int/en_menus/icc/press%20and%20media/press%20releases/Pages/pr931.aspx>.

30 BBC News, 'Kenya Asks UN to Halt ICC Charges against Kenyatta' (9 May 2013) <www.bbc.co.uk/news/world-africa-22472242>.

Kenya.[31] All of this hostility has led to the Kenyan Parliament recently approving a motion to withdraw from the ICC.[32] Kenya is the first State Party to take such action.[33]

In another example, the UN Security Council referred the situation in Libya to the ICC Prosecutor in February 2011. The Prosecutor subsequently issued arrest warrants for Muammar Gaddafi, Saif Al-Islam Gaddafi, and Abdullah Al-Senussi for a 'systematic policy of suppressing any challenge to authority'[34] through 'abductions, mass arrests, torture and killing civilians.'[35] The National Transitional Council has always declared its intention to hold trials in Libya's domestic courts, but with the backing of prominent governments such as the United States, the ICC Prosecutor considered whether the trial should be held in The Hague.[36] On 31 May 2013, Pre-Trial Chamber I determined 'that the case against Saif Al-Islam Gaddafi is admissible'[37] before the ICC, noting, *inter alia*, that Libya has not indicated whether and how it will 'overcome the existing difficulties in securing a lawyer for the suspect' as well as the apparent inability of Libya to secure his transfer from the custody of the Zintan militia.[38] In response, the Libyan government filed an appeal, also requesting suspension of the order for the surrender of Saif Al-Islam Gaddafi pending handing down of the appeal decision.[39] The Court rejected the request and reminded Libya of its obligation to surrender Saif Al-Islam Gaddafi to the Court.[40]

There are compelling arguments for holding proceedings in The Hague. Despite the Libyan government's insistence that suspects would receive a fair

---

[31] BBC News, 'African Union Accuses ICC of "Hunting" Africans' (27 May 2013) <http://www.bbc.co.uk/news/world-africa-22681894>.

[32] BBC News, 'Kenya MPs Vote to Withdraw from ICC' (5 September 2013) <http://www.bbc.co.uk/news/world-africa-23969316>.

[33] Ibid.

[34] *Situation in the Libyan Arab Jamahiriya* (Prosecutor 's Application to Pre-Trial Chamber 1 Pursuant to Article 58 as to Muammar Mohammed Abu Minyar Gaddafi, Saif Al-Islam Gaddafi and Abdullah Al-Senussi) ICC-01/11-4Red (16 May 2011) 7.

[35] Idem.

[36] See I Sekularac, 'ICC Rejects Gaddafi Daughter's Appeal on Jailed Brother' (*Yahoo! News UK* 2 February 2012) <http://uk.news.yahoo.com/icc-rejects-gaddafi-daughters-appeal-jailed-brother-150620971.html>.

[37] *Prosecutor v Saif Al-Islam Gaddafi and Abdullah Al-Senussi* (Decision on the admissibility of the case against Saif Al-Islam Gaddafi) ICC-01/11-01/11 Pre-Trial Chamber I (31 May 2013) 91.

[38] Ibid para 215.

[39] See *Prosecutor v Saif Al-Islam Gaddafi and Abdullah Al-Senussi* (The Government of Libya's Appeal against Pre-Trial Chamber I's 'Decision on the admissibility of the case against Saif Al-Islam Gaddafi') ICC-01/11-01/11 Appeals Chamber (7 June 2013).

[40] *Prosecutor v Saif Al-Islam Gaddafi and Abdullah Al-Senussi* (Decision on the request for suspensive effect and related issues) ICC-01/11-01/11 OA 4 Appeals Chamber (18 July 2013) 1 and para 27.

trial in Libya, many believe that unlikely. Evidence from international human rights organizations suggests there is:

> rampant torture of inmates in makeshift prisons operated by militias accused of seeking to exact revenge against the slain leader's former supporters .... [V]arious former rebel groups are holding as many as 8,000 prisoners in 60 detention centers around the country.[41]

Furthermore, Amnesty International has claimed that 'torture is being carried out by officially recognized military and security entities as well as by a multitude of armed militias operating outside of any legal framework,'[42] leading to a general belief that the government lacks the capability and willingness to control the armed groups.[43]

Also at issue is the treatment of Saif Al-Islam Gaddafi, who has been held by militia in isolation at a secret location in the remote mountain village of Zintan since his capture on 19 November 2011. It is unclear to what extent he has been granted access to a lawyer,[44] though it was reported that two local lawyers had been appointed to represent him in domestic proceedings ensuing from a visit in 2012 by ICC staff,[45] including a defence lawyer.[46] His co-accused, Abdullah Al-Senussi, has not had access to a lawyer in connection with domestic proceedings since being taken into the custody of Libyan central authorities[47] after his extradition from Mauritania in September 2012.[48]

Notwithstanding, the ICC ruled on 11 October 2013 that the case against Al-Senussi is inadmissible before the Court on the basis that it is already

---

41 See R Al-Shaheibi, 'Libya to Niger: Al-Saadi Gaddafi Must Be Handed Over' (*The Huffington Post* 11 February 2012) <http://www.huffingtonpost.com/2012/02/11/libya-niger-al-saadi-gaddafi_n_1270293.html>.

42 See BBC News, 'Libyan Detainees Die after Torture, Says Amnesty International' (26 January 2012) <http://www.bbc.co.uk/news/world-africa-16741937>.

43 See V Walt, 'Why Libya is Becoming more Dangerous after Gaddafi's Fall' (*Time* 17 February 2012) <http://www.time.com/time/world/article/0,8599,2107024,00.html>.

44 See N Durkin, 'Saif Gaddafi's Trial in Libya is Victor's Justice' (*Huffington Post* 21 September 2013) <http://www.huffingtonpost.co.uk/neil-durkin/saif-gaddafi-trial_b_3956043.html>.

45 BBC News, 'ICC Holds Four ICC Staff after They Met Saif Gaddafi' (9 June 2012) <http://www.bbc.co.uk/news/world-africa-18380214>.

46 BBC News, 'Lawyers Appointed for Saif al-Islam Gaddafi' (2 May 2013) <http://www.bbc.co.uk/news/world-africa-22378116>.

47 *Prosecutor v Saif Al-Islam Gaddafi and Abdullah Al-Senussi* (Decision on the admissibility of the case against Abdullah Al-Senussi) ICC-01/11-01/11 Pre-Trial Chamber I (11 October 2013) paras 304–307.

48 Amnesty International, 'Libya Must Surrender Saif al-Islam al-Gaddafi to International Criminal Court' (18 September 2013) <http://www.amnesty.org/en/news/libya-must-surrender-saif-al-islam-al-gaddafi-international-criminal-court-2013-09-18>.

subject to domestic proceedings that the Libyan State is not unwilling or unable genuinely to carry out.[49] The decision marks the first time that the Court has found in favour of a challenging State in an admissibility decision.[50] The two decisions of the ICC on complementarity in cases against Saif Al-Islam Gaddafi and Abdullah Al-Senussi, respectively, are thus different, although they pertain to the same country and to a similar set of factual and legal circumstances.

Despite the rather dubious reasoning behind the Court's decision to find the case of Abdullah Al-Senussi inadmissible, there are factual differences between the Gaddafi and Al-Senussi cases that could merit different outcomes. However, I think the Court was unclear as to how the evidence provided by the Libyan government in the Al-Senussi case was any stronger than its admissions in the Gaddafi case. This discrepancy led to criticism about the consistency of the Court's reasoning in relation to complementarity.[51]

In the Gaddafi case, the Court concluded that Libya failed to demonstrate 'whether and how it will overcome the existing difficulties in securing a lawyer for the suspect',[52] owing to 'the security situation in Libya and the risk faced by lawyers who act for associates of the former regime.'[53] Yet, surely these same concerns still exist for any domestic trial against Al-Senussi.

On 19 September 2013 Saif Al-Islam Gaddafi was prevented from appearing in court in Tripoli for a pre-trial hearing in respect of domestic proceedings arising out of the 2011 civil war. The militia detaining him in Zintan had refused to permit his transfer on the basis of the security situation.[54] If Saif Al-Islam Gaddafi is found guilty, Libya could impose the death penalty whereas the ICC could only impose a life sentence.[55] The Libyan government has stood its ground and maintained that Saif Al-Islam Gaddafi will receive a fair trial.[56]

---

[49] *Prosecutor v Saif Al-Islam Gaddafi and Abdullah Al-Senussi* (Decision on the admissibility of the case against Abdullah Al-Senussi) (n 47) 151 and para 311.

[50] BBC News, 'Gaddafi-era Spy Chief al-Senussi to Be Tried in Libya' (11 October 2013) <www.bbc.co.uk/news/world-africa-24493885>.

[51] See, for example, JK Heller, 'PTC I's Inconsistent Approach to Complementarity and the Right to Counsel' (*Opinio Juris* 12 October 2013) <http://opiniojuris.org/2013/10/12/ptc-inconsistent-approach-right-counsel/>.

[52] *Prosecutor v Saif Al-Islam Gaddafi and Abdullah Al-Senussi* (Decision on the admissibility of the case against Saif Al-Islam Gaddafi) (n 37) para 215.

[53] Ibid para 212.

[54] BBC News, 'Saif al-Islam Gaddafi Tansfer for Tripoli Hearing Blocked' (19 September 2013) <http://www.bbc.co.uk/news/world-africa-24161544>.

[55] See Sekularac (n 36).

[56] See A Hileman, 'Libya Prime Minister Assures Fair Trial Success for Gaddafi's Son' (*Jurist* 22 November 2011).

Were Saif Al-Islam Gadaffi to be tried in The Hague, there is little doubt that he would receive a fair trial, but the ICC risks being accused of interfering in state sovereignty. That the United States – not even a party to the Rome Statute – is involved in the UN Security Council's referral is a good indication of the Libyan situation's politically-charged nature.

To maintain a sense of legitimacy and objectivity, it is imperative that an independent and impartial third party analyze the situation and provide input on which party is more capable of conducting fair proceedings; otherwise, it is likely the ICC will attract much criticism from those who believe it to be a tool used by the West to exert authority over other nations.

Recently, the conflict in Syria has led to international pressure to remove President Bashar Assad from power and try him for crimes against humanity. Inspired by the democratic protests of the Arab Spring, Syrians began calling for an end to Assad's authoritarian rule in March 2011.[57] The regime's response was a brutal crackdown, in which over 115,000 people, including 10,000 women and children, have been killed.[58] There are reports of 'continuing widespread, systematic and gross violations by security forces against civilians.'[59] In August 2011, the UN named fifty people suspected of committing crimes against humanity; including murder, torture and rape.[60] More recently, the employment of conventional weapons has been augmented by recourse to chemical weapons.[61] The most high profile incident, for which responsibility has not been attributed, took place on 21 August 2013, when the Ghouta agricultural belt on the outskirt of Damascus suffered aerial bombardment in which the nerve agent sarin was released.[62] In the aftermath of the attack, diplomatic pressure resulted in Syrian agreement to accede to the Chemical Weapons Convention.[63] Syria has since

---

57 See KY Oweis and S al-Khalidi, 'Syria Sends Tanks into Deraa where Uprising Began' (*Reuters* 25 April 2011) <http://www.reuters.com/article/2011/04/25/us-syria-idUSLDE73N02P20110425>.

58 See D Evans, 'More than 115,000 Killed in Syrian Conflict – Monitoring Group' (*Reuters* 1 October 2013) <http://uk.reuters.com/article/2013/10/01/uk-syria-crisis-toll-idUKBRE9900KD20131001>.

59 See UN News Centre, 'Political Solution Only Way to End Syria Crisis, UN Chief Stresses' (24 February 2012) <http://www.un.org/apps/news/story.asp?NewsID=41359&Cr=syria&Cr1=>.

60 See C Hartmann, 'UN: Syrian Officials Should Be Sent to ICC' (*Reuters* 10 February 2012) <http://www.jpost.com/MiddleEast/Article.aspx?id=257315>.

61 See UN Mission to Investigate Allegations of the Use of Chemical Weapons in the Syrian Arab Republic, 'Report on the Alleged Use of Chemical Weapons in the Ghouta Area of Damascus on 21 August 2013' (13 September 2013) <http://www.un.org/disarmament/content/slideshow/ Secretary_General_Report_of_CW_Investigation.pdf>.

62 Ibid.

63 BBC News, 'Syria Crisis: UN Receives Syria Chemical Treaty Papers' (12 September 2013) <http://www.bbc.co.uk/news/world-middle-east-24068867>.

transmitted an 'initial declaration' of its chemical weapons programme to the Organisation for the Prohibition of Chemical Weapons, which will draw up a plan for the destruction of Syria's chemical weapons arsenal.[64] As the conflict in Syria continues to escalate, calls for accountability against those responsible for atrocities will also increase. The Security Council may ultimately refer the situation to the ICC for investigation. However, the paragraph of a recent draft Security Council resolution[65] referring the Syrian situation to the ICC was deleted from the unanimously approved final text calling for Syria to renounce its chemical weapons.[66]

Accountability, however, may still be possible. I serve on a blue ribbon panel of former international tribunal chief prosecutors, international judges, and leading experts which has prepared a Draft Statute for a Syrian Extraordinary Tribunal to Prosecute Atrocity Crimes.[67] The purpose of a Syrian Extraordinary Tribunal would be to prosecute those on both sides of the conflict most responsible for atrocity crimes committed in Syria. It would exist along-side the ordinary criminal and military courts of Syria, which would prosecute lower level perpetrators, and to the ICC if it gains jurisdiction to prosecute the highest level perpetrators.

The ICC faces a difficult decision as to whether and how to take jurisdiction in cases like those of Libya and Syria, where conflict is ongoing and there is a desire to prosecute domestically. This in turn raises important issues of credibility. While the complementarity principle is a valuable mechanism, the Rome Statute simply fails to articulate how it should be interpreted and exercised.

At the time of the Rome Conference, many States expressed concern that the Court would have too much discretion in determining whether and when a State was willing and able to prosecute.[68] States were concerned that they would not be able to prevent the Court from exercising jurisdiction over national or international crimes committed on their territory.[69] They were

---

64 CBS, 'Syria Hands "Initial Declaration" on Chemical Weapons to Global Watchdog' (20 September 2013) <http://www.cbsnews.com/8301-202_162-57603851/syria-hands-initial-declaration-on-chemical-weapons-to-global-watchdog/>.

65 See <https://docs.google.com/file/d/0ByLPNZ-eSjJdX29vd2Y3WlNxQWc/view?sle=true>.

66 AFP, 'UN Resolution orders Syria chemical arms destroyed' (28 September 2013) <http://news.yahoo.com/un-council-passes-landmark-syria-chemical-resolution-004535372.html>.

67 See <http://publicinternationallawandpolicygroup.org/wp-content/uploads/2013/09/Chautauqua-Blueprint1.pdf>.

68 On the drafting history see, for example, B Perrin, 'Making Sense of Complementarity: The Relationship between the International Criminal Court and National Jurisdictions' (2006) 18 Sri Lanka Journal of International Law 307–308.

69 See JT Holmes, 'Complementarity: National Courts versus the ICC' in A Cassese, P Gaeta and JRWD Jones (eds), *The Rome Statute for an International Criminal Court* vol I (Oxford University Press 2002) 667–668, 673–674.

uncomfortable with the idea of the ICC passing judgment on their own courts.

Given the high stakes, and sometimes politically charged judgments that must be made, it would be advantageous for an objective, non-vested third party to evaluate domestic legal capacity. Not only could this help mediate claims of state sovereignty and ICC jurisdiction, it would bolster the legitimacy of the courts and the process.

III. THE ARGUMENT FOR AN INTERNATIONAL ADVISORY GROUP

The ICC was established as an independent and unbiased organization to preside over the 'most serious crimes of concern to the international community.'[70] As an international court, it is important that the ICC has the power to conduct proceedings when necessary, but the international community must also protect state sovereignty. Currently, the ICC relies on its own investigations to determine whether a State is willing and able to conduct fair and proper investigations and proceedings into alleged crimes. However, an International Advisory Group (IAG) could conduct independent investigations, acting as a buffer between States and the ICC. While not binding, an independent body such as an IAG could provide expert opinion upon which both the State and the ICC could rely.

The legal basis for such a group can be found in the Rome Statute. Article 54(3)(c) allows the ICC Prosecutor to '[s]eek the cooperation of any state or intergovernmental organization or arrangement in accordance with its respective competence and/or mandate' during the investigation. Similarly, Article 15(2) allows the ICC Prosecutor, when initiating investigations *proprio motu*, to 'seek additional information from States, organs of the United Nations, intergovernmental or nongovernmental organizations, or other reliable sources that he or she deems appropriate.' [71]Finally, Article 42(1) of the Rome Statute stipulates that the Prosecutor is 'responsible for receiving referrals and any substantiated information on crimes within the jurisdiction of the Court, for examining them and for conducting investigations and prosecutions before the Court.'[72] The authority granted under Articles 54, 42, and 15 is extraordinarily broad and would certainly allow the ICC to cooperate with an IAG.[73]

---

70 See ICC, 'About the Court' <http://www.icc-cpi.int/Menus/ICC/About+the+Court/>.

71 Art 15(2) Rome Statute.

72 Art 42(1) Rome Statute.

73 See WW Burke-White, 'Proactive Complementarity: The International Criminal Court and National Courts in the Rome System of International Justice' (2008) 49 Harvard International Law Journal.

The purpose of an IAG would be to ensure that an objective, impartial and non-political evaluation is made regarding a State's willingness and ability to carry out judicial proceedings in a manner consistent with international standards. The focus of the evaluation would be on a State's national judicial system and on areas germane to the investigation and prosecution of war crimes. An IAG would consult with a wide range of people, including legal experts and academics who might interview ministers, government officials, prosecutors, judges, lawyers and local civil society groups familiar with a State's domestic legal system. The IAG would ask questions such as: Can the proceedings be conducted impartially and independently? Does the domestic court have extensive backlogs resulting in long pre-trial detention? Is there adequate security for court personnel? Does the State have a sufficient number of trained defence lawyers and an effective legal aid program for indigent defendants? What is the level of court management? Are there undue delays in conducting trials? Are there sufficient guarantees against outside pressure on the judiciary? Is there unwarranted prosecutorial discretion in conducting investigations and trials? Does the State impose the death penalty? Can the court provide witnesses and victims with medical, psychological, and material support during and after trial through a victim and witness support office? Has the country concluded conventions on mutual assistance in criminal matters? Is there on-going political strife and repression in the country? Does the State have detention facilities that meet international standards?

As an unbiased and objective party, an IAG could also monitor domestic trials to ensure that the proceedings are consistent with international norms. Such monitoring would assist the ICC Prosecutor in carrying out his or her duties under Article 53(2) of the Rome Statute. Finally, a body such as the International Bar Association might oversee the group, or draft a standard of ethics and protocols for the investigative and monitoring process.

IV. CONCLUSION

The ICC was created as a permanent international criminal court to ensure that those most responsible for egregious atrocities are brought to justice. Yet the Court does not stand alone; the Rome Statute facilitates a new and symbiotic relationship with domestic jurisdictions. Under the principle of complementarity, the Court has jurisdiction only over situations that a State is unable or unwilling to prosecute. Still, there is a natural tension between international and domestic courts, and in times of conflict or state breakdown, there can be conflicts between claims of sovereignty and the need to protect vulnerable people from the State. At the same time an objective and comprehensive assessment of domestic capacity and ability to conduct judicial proceedings for international crimes would prevent the Court from reaching diverging decisions in similar cases, as happened in two Libyan cases against Saif Al-Islam Gaddafi and Abdullah Al-Senussi. The creation of an independent IAG would help to resolve these tensions while bringing perpetrators to trial.

As the number of violent conflicts grows, the ICC will continue to evolve and be tested. Also, as justice and accountability are increasingly focused within national jurisdictions, the need for careful, unbiased assessment of State judicial capacity will increase. Currently, when States are found to lack the willingness or ability to prosecute, ambiguity surrounding the principle of complementarity makes it difficult for the ICC to justify jurisdictional claims. The creation of an independent, unbiased group tasked with assessing whether a State is able and willing to fairly conduct trials for the most serious crimes would give greater legitimacy to these decisions. In addition, an IAG would be a useful tool to ensure proceedings conducted at both the State and international levels meet international standards. An expert, independent and objective assessment of the State's willingness and ability to prosecute would also contribute to greater coherency in case law of the ICC. As the ICC continues to play an increasingly important role in the pursuit of international justice, the need to establish an IAG has never been greater.

Ten Years of International Criminal Court and Complementarity 'In Bonam Partem'

*Federica Gioia**

I. INTRODUCTION

On 31 July 2012, Saif Al-Islam Gaddafi, son of the former Libyan Head of State Muammar Gaddafi, conveyed to Pre-Trial Chamber I of the International Criminal Court (ICC), through his lawyers,[1] his preference for a trial before the ICC over one taking place before the judicial authorities of his own country.[2] On 31 May 2013, Pre-Trial Chamber I rejected the Libyan Government's challenge to the admissibility of the case against Saif Al-Islam Gaddafi and determined that the case was admissible.[3] Saif Al-Islam's 'unsworn statement' goes straight to the heart of one critical issue concerning the complementary role of the ICC, which in the same year (2012) celebrated ten years from the entry into force of the Rome Statute. As was to be expected, the milestone anniversary prompted numerous opportunities for discussion and debate, many of which focussed on complementarity. While many facets of the principle have undergone critical and careful scrutiny, one issue went relatively undetected: would the complementary nature of the Court allow that a violation of due process occurring not to the benefit, but *to the detriment* of the person subjected to criminal proceedings in a State,

---

* Legal Officer, International Criminal Court, The Hague, The Netherlands; Associate Professor, Università Cattolica, Piacenza, Italy (on leave). The views expressed in this article are solely of the author.

[1] Saif Al-Islam Gaddafi has been initially represented by the ICC 'Office of Public Counsel for the Defence (OPCD)' in the proceedings pending before the ICC.

[2] For more details see *Prosecutor v Gaddafi and Al-Senussi* (Public Redacted Version of the Corrigendum to the 'Defence Response to the "Application on behalf of the Government of Libya pursuant to Article 19 of the ICC Statute"') ICC-01/11-01/11-190-Corr-Red Pre-Trial Chamber I (31 July 2012).

[3] *Prosecutor v Gaddafi and Al-Senussi* (Decision on the admissibility of the case against Saif Al-Islam Gaddafi) ICC-01/11-01/11-344-Red Pre-Trial Chamber I (31 May 2013). This Decision was appealed by the Government of Libya (ICC-01/11-01/11-370-Red2, 24 June 2013).

result in that State being held as unwilling and/or unable, and the case being therefore admissible before the Court? This question would for instance arise in the event of a conviction issued following summary proceedings, without giving the accused a chance to submit crucial pieces of exculpatory evidence; or of a court obviously biased against the indicted or, more broadly, operating under procedural rules aimed at making a defendant 'easier to convict'.[4] I will refer to this particular reading of the principle as complementarity '*in bonam partem*'; other scholars prefer the term 'due process thesis'.[5] The purpose of this essay is to determine whether, in light of the history, the practice, the statutory texts of the Court, including the broader framework of international criminal law, Saif Al-Islam Gaddafi's wishes can be considered as consistent with the complementary role of the Court *vis-à-vis* national jurisdictions.

II. THE HISTORY AND THE PRACTICE

A. The early days

In the early days,[6] and for many years,[7] the chapter on complementarity was

[4] For this language see KJ Heller, 'The Shadow Side of Complementarity: The Effect of Article 17 of the Rome Statute on National Due Process' (2006) 17 Criminal Law Forum 257.

[5] Among many, see: Heller (n 4) 257, M Benzing, 'The Complementarity Regime of the International Criminal Court: International Criminal Justice between State Sovereignty and the Fight Against Impunity' (2003) 7 Max Planck Yearbook of United Nations Law 598, E Carnero Rojo, 'The Role of Fair Trial Considerations in the Complementarity Regime of the International Criminal Court: From "No Peace without Justice" to "No Peace with Victor's Justice"?' (2005) 18 Leiden Journal of International Law 852–3.

[6] MA Newton, 'Comparative Complementarity: Domestic Jurisdiction Consistent with the Rome Statute of the International Criminal Court' (2001) 167 Military Law Review 26 ('the complementarity principle is intended to preserve the power of the ICC over irresponsible states that refuse to prosecute nationals who commit heinous international crimes'); Heller (n 4); WA Schabas, '"Complementarity in Practice": Some Uncomplimentary Thoughts' (2008) 19 Criminal Law Forum 24.

[7] As recently as 2008 Jakob Pichon wrote that 'the ICC Statute's drafting history contradicts the applicability of the complementarity regime to fair trial rights other than the right to an independent judiciary'. More specifically, the author recalls that the Rome Conference rejected the proposal of including a reference to fair trial rights and argues that 'the delegations … showed no interest in establishing procedural fairness (other than the independence of the judiciary) as a ground for the purpose of defining complementarity and consequently rejected both proposals'. Having regard to the scenario and notion of inability, he observes that the requirement that 'the State also has to be unable to obtain the accused or the necessary evidence and testimony or otherwise unable to carry out its proceedings … suggests that the drafters of the ICC Statute only wanted to avoid ineffective national proceedings' and that 'unfair national proceedings had not been part of these considerations.' Accordingly, the author concludes that 'the complementarity principle does not apply to violations of the right to independent and impartial proceedings which are disadvantageous to the accused'. (See J Pichon, 'The Principle of

almost unanimously read as relying on the assumption that the Court was only meant to remedy failures of States resulting in a 'cover-up' to the benefit of the accused. Little (if any) attention was given to the role the ICC would be able and likely to play with regard to the observance of human rights standards. The debate over the fight against impunity, and rejoicing about the existence of an institution capable of addressing and curing the shameful shielding of heinous criminals from the rule of law, were at the forefront. Compliance with human rights standards of the accused was sometimes referred to and used as a criterion to determine whether alternative forms of justice to the criminal trials could be considered for the purpose of ascertaining a state's compliance with the principle of complementarity.[8] Usually, however, such reference would occur within a context far more concerned with scenarios of undue impunity rather than with unjust persecution of innocent individuals.[9] Those few voices[10] advocating for an impartial role of the Court in addressing any shortcoming or weakness of national jurisdictions, irrespective of their ultimate impact on the position of the individual, remained virtually isolated. The largely prevailing view was that the ICC was not a human rights court[11] or a 'human rights monitoring body',[12] that its role was 'not to ensure perfect procedures and compliance with all international standards'.[13] Further, it was highlighted that it did not possess the necessary resources to recast itself as one and that more suitable remedies

---

Complementarity in the Cases of the Sudanese Nationals *Ahmad Harun* and *Ali Kushayb* before the International Criminal Court' (2008) 8 International Criminal Law Review 192–3, 194.)

[8] See J Dugard, Possible Conflicts of Jurisdiction with Truth Commissions, in A Cassese, P Gaeta and JRDW Jones (eds), *The Rome Statute of the International Criminal Court – A Commentary* (Oxford University Press 2002) 693; C Van den Wyngaert and T Ongena, '*Ne bis in idem* principle, Including the Issue of Amnesty', in ibid 705; D Robinson, Serving the Interests of Justice: Amnesties, Truth Commissions and the International Criminal Court' (2003) 14 European Journal of International Law 481; EW Schabacker, 'Reconciliation or Justice and Ashes: Amnesty Commissions and the Duty to Punish Human Rights Offenses' (1999) 12 New York International Law Review 1; MP Scharf, 'The Amnesty Exception to the Jurisdiction of the International Criminal Court' (1999) 32 Cornell International Law Journal 507. More recently, L Mallinder, 'Amnesties' Challenge to the Global Accountability Norm? Interpreting Regional and International Trends in Amnesty Enactment', in F Lessa and LA Payne (eds), *Amnesty in the Age of Human Rights Accountability: Comparative and International Perspectives* (Cambridge University Press 2012) 69–96.

[9] C Stahn, 'Complementarity, Amnesties and Alternative Forms of Justice' (2005) 3 Journal of International Criminal Justice 713.

[10] F Gioia, 'State Sovereignty, Jurisdiction and "Modern" International Law: The Principle of Complementarity in the International Criminal Court' (2006) 19 Leiden Journal of International Law 1110–1113.

[11] OTP Informal Expert Paper, 'The principle of complementarity in practice' para 23 (annexed as Annex A to ICC-01/04-01/07-1008-AnxA) <http://www.icc-cpi.int/iccdocs/doc/doc654724.pdf> (OTP Expert Paper on Complementarity).

[12] Ibid para 49.

[13] Idem, see also para 52.

for these kinds of breaches were available under international law. At the most, it was acknowledged that human rights standards might 'be of relevance and utility in assessing whether the proceedings are carried out genuinely', without clarifying the content of such relevance.[14] Concerns were raised to the effect that allowing the Court to step in *in lieu* of a State 'to correct a perceived miscarriage of justice for any reason' would be tantamount to transforming its role into one of 'a "super" international appellate court' rather than a complementary one.[15] Sometimes, the role of the ICC in remedying national shortcomings in matters of fair trial rights was viewed as a matter for review and amendment of the Statute, and hence in a *de iure condendo* perspective.[16]

Curiously, as years elapsed and the first situations were referred to or taken up by the Court, the debate seemed to ignore the fact that none of the scenarios coming before the Court were affected by issues consisting of undue shielding of suspected criminals from fair judgement. Both the Democratic Republic of the Congo (DRC) and Uganda (the first two self-referrals) offered rather examples of failures of national legal systems and judicial apparatus to tackle grave crimes, be it as a matter of technical inadequacy (the DRC) or as a matter of political expediency (Uganda). The fact that both the DRC and Uganda had themselves referred their own countries to the Court made it unlikely that issues of undue 'shielding' would take centre stage in either of those situations; by the same token, the very inaction of both countries prevented them from becoming scenarios in which the possible intervention by the Court with a view to preventing fair trial violations to the detriment of the accused would be tested.

B. *Darfur, Kenya and Libya*

The terms of the debate started to shift in 2005, with the ground-breaking referral of the situation in Darfur, Sudan by the United Nations Security Council.[17] This referral paved the way for an intervention where the Court's role would not only be aimed at remedying a State's failure to act, but also possibly at preventing domestic judicial proceedings from becoming a tool whereby the governing powers would summarily dispose of their legitimate opponents. The Report issued on 25 January 2005 by the International Commission of Inquiry established in October 2004 by the UN

---

[14] Ibid para 23.

[15] J Gurulé, 'United States Opposition to the 1998 Rome Statute Establishing an International Criminal Court: Is the Court's Jurisdiction Truly Complementary to National Criminal Jurisdictions?' (2001–2) 35 Cornell International Law Journal 8–9, 45.

[16] Heller (n 4) 260, 279–80.

[17] UNSC Res 1593 (31 March 2005) UN Doc S/RES/1593.

(Commission),[18] headed by Antonio Cassese,[19] was damning in exposing the shortcomings manifest in the Sudanese legal system in terms of compliance with human rights standards and, more specifically, fair trial rights. The country's justice system was found 'unable and unwilling to address the situation in Darfur',[20] due to factors including the following: (i) breadth of powers vested in the executive and ensuing undermining impact on the effectiveness of the judiciary; (ii) enactment of laws contravening basic human rights standards; (iii) failure to adequately proscribe war crimes and crimes against humanity; (iv) presence, in the Sudan Criminal Procedure Code, of provisions preventing effective prosecution of these acts.[21] Victims reported having little confidence in the impartiality of the justice system, and fearing reprisals in the event they had recourse to it. Most of those (few) cases where complaints had been made had not been properly pursued; procedural hurdles limited victims' access to justice; very few individuals had been prosecuted.[22]

In surveying the initiatives taken by the Government of Sudan with the purported goal to stop and remedy violations, the Commission pointed out loud and clear that most of those had resulted in a 'window-dressing operation' which had done little, if anything, to prevent or remedy impunity.[23] As to the Sudanese 'National Commission of Inquiry', the Commission found that its findings and recommendations were 'insufficient and inappropriate to address the gravity of the situation', in particular since it attempted 'to justify the violations rather than seeking effective measures to address them'.[24] In respect of the 'Committees against rape', the Commission noted that they had been given no guidance regarding the proper methods of investigation, were allotted grossly inadequate time for the completion of their task and relied far too heavily on the affected population to produce evidence.[25]

These observations show that, in recommending the Security Council to refer the situation in Darfur to the ICC, the Commission certainly embraced the view that 'sham trials', whereby a case is investigated and/or prosecuted with a view to shielding one or more persons from any meaningful judicial determination, possibly because of political implications or complicity of the judiciary, may trigger a finding of the unwillingness of a State to proceed genuinely. By the same token, however, it seemed to take a significantly

---

18 Pursuant to UNSC Res 1564 (18 September 2004) UN Doc S/RES/1564.
19 See <http://www.un.org/news/dh/sudan/com_inq_darfur.pdf>.
20 Ibid 5.
21 Idem.
22 Ibid 6.
23 Idem.
24 Ibid para 462.
25 Ibid paras 469–471.

broader view when, assessing (and denying) Sudan's ability to genuinely investigate and prosecute the relevant crimes, it also referred to several factors which would only be problematic in a perspective of violations likely to have a detrimental impact on the position of the person on trial. The victims' lack of confidence in the ability of the judiciary to act independently and impartially; the weakened credibility of the judiciary; the fact that the judiciary had been 'manipulated and politicised'[26] in spite of the constitutional guarantees and that judges disagreeing with the Government had suffered harassment and dismissals;[27] and the creation of 'special' and 'specialised' courts failing to meet basic standards of fair trial[28] were listed as shortcomings of the Sudanese legal and judicial framework making it unsuitable to tackle the serious crimes being committed in the country. In evoking scenarios such as the use of 'confessions' extracted under torture, or other forms of duress,[29] as evidence; the failure to ensure that the accused was represented by counsel of choice;[30] the enactment of unfeasible deadlines for the lodging of appeals, including against death sentences and[31] the failure to draw distinctions between adult and minor offenders,[32] the Commission openly drew on instances of failures and shortcomings which had resulted in the accused's deprivation of fundamental tenets of the right to a fair trial.

It seems reasonable to hold that, in so doing, the Commission was acting on the assumption that those violations occurring to the detriment of the accused would be suitable to trigger the intervention of the Court. This assumption also surfaces when considering the Commission's assessment of Sudanese laws. The Commission noted, *inter alia*, that fundamental constitutional guarantees had been suspended for a long time, due to the protracted state of emergency;[33] that the parliamentary process was 'a charade'[34] and the country was mainly ruled by decrees; that detainees were held in custody for long periods (longer than 12 months) without charges, visitors or access to a lawyer. The advisability of ensuring a neutral atmosphere for the trials was also explicitly listed as one reason warranting the Commission's recommendation to the Security Council that the situation in Darfur be referred to the ICC.[35]

---

[26] Ibid para 432.

[27] Idem.

[28] Ibid para 439.

[29] Ibid para 96.

[30] Ibid para 446.

[31] Ibid para 447.

[32] Ibid para 448.

[33] Ibid para 450.

[34] Idem.

[35] Other reasons included the Court being the best suited organ for ensuring a veritably fair trial, due to its 'entirely international composition and well-defined rules of procedure and evidence'; the fact that the Court could be activated immediately, without any delay (unlike the

When first Bahar Idriss Abu Garda,[36] then Abdallah Banda and Saleh Jerbo[37] (leaders of 'rebel' groups opposing the Sudanese government) appeared on a voluntary basis before Pre-trial Chamber I of the Court on the basis of summonses to appear issued for the attack on the African Union Mission in Haskanita in 2007, they provided the first example of individuals favouring ICC proceedings over proceedings in their own country.

Most commentaries on the ICC's action in Sudan did not explicitly comment on the fact that many of the shortcomings detected by the Commission in the Sudanese legal system would be detrimental to the accused, or whether this fact might have an impact on the scope of complementarity.[38] Nevertheless, the years that followed showed that Sudan was only the first step down a road which witnessed an ever-increasing commitment and involvement of the Court in situations where erosion of the rule of law manifests itself also (if not exclusively) to the detriment of the accused.

In 2011, the Government of Kenya challenged the admissibility of the two cases brought by the Prosecutor[39] (following an investigation of request by the Prosecutor to initiate investigation *proprio motu* authorised by the Pre-Trial Chamber)[40] to a large extent based on the country's recent enactment of far-reaching constitutional reforms. These reforms, the Government submitted, 'significantly strengthen[ed] fair trial rights and procedural guarantees within the Kenyan criminal justice system', aimed as they were at 'guarantee[ing] the independent and impartial dispensation of justice', as well as 'the independence of the State's investigative services'.[41] Pre-Trial Chamber II would eventually reject the challenge, observing that it 'relied mainly on judicial reform actions and promises for future investigative activities', as such inapt to ground an affirmative outcome of the assessment of the state's willingness

---

establishment of ad hoc tribunals or so called mixed or internationalized courts); and the fact that criminal proceedings before the ICC, at the request of the Security Council, would not necessarily involve a significant financial burden for the international community.

[36] On 18 May 2009 (ICC-02/05-02/09-T-4-ENG ET WT 18-05-2009 1-11 NB PT).

[37] Both made their first appearance before the Court on 17 June 2010 (ICC-02/05-03/09-T-4-ENG ET WT 17-06-2010 1-27 SZ PT).

[38] DY Hewett, 'Sudan's Courts and Complementarity in the Face of Darfur' (2006) 31 Yale Journal of International Law 276, 280 ('[T]he Prosecutor would need to inspect procedural and institutional features of the national trials to ascertain whether they were conducted independently, impartially, in accordance with due process, and without undue delay, political interference, or the express purpose of shielding culpable individuals').

[39] *Prosecutor v Ruto, Kosgey and Sang* (ICC-01/09-01/11) and *Prosecutor v Muthaura, Kenyatta and Ali* (ICC-01/09-02/11).

[40] *Situation in Kenya* (Decision Pursuant to Art 15 of the Rome Statute on the Authorization of an Investigation into the Situation in the Republic of Kenya) ICC-01/09-19-Corr Pre-Trial Chamber II (31 March 2010).

[41] *Prosecutor v Ruto, Kosgey and Sang* and *Prosecutor v Muthaura, Kenyatta and Ali* (Application on behalf of the Republic of Kenya pursuant to Art 19 of the ICC Statute) ICC-01/09-01/11-19 Pre-Trial Chamber II (31 March 2011) para 2.

and ability to genuinely proceed.[42] It appears however significant that the Government of Kenya chose to support its challenge with neutral reference to reforms which would ensure full compliance of the Kenyan legal system and judiciary with fair trial rights, irrespective of the direction that a departure from such rights might or would take.

In 2011, following another referral by the Security Council,[43] the situation in Libya and the cases of Saif Al-Islam Gaddafi (son of the former leader Muammar Gaddafi and leader *in pectore* of the country) and Abdullah Al-Senussi (head of the intelligence services of the deposed regime) would provide the first scenario where an admissibility challenge[44] would be openly brought and fought on the question of which forum would be best suited to provide the accused with a genuinely fair trial. It was universally known that Libya's human rights compliance record was far from immaculate, with many departures from the rule of law. These violations were operating first to the detriment of opponents of Gaddafi's regime[45] and then, following the latter's disgrace, to that of supporters of the *ancien regime*.[46] These two elements resulted in some studies openly questioning the role, if any, to be given by the Court to 'due process and sentencing considerations' in the context of making an assessment of domestic proceedings.[47] While some of the old arguments continued to be repeated, some doubts started to surface. The existence of an 'inherent tension' in the Rome Statute was, at last, openly acknowledged: whilst reiterating that the ICC admissibility system was not 'a forum or an appeal instance to remedy general human rights violations in domestic criminal proceedings', by the same token it was conceded that 'the Court is mandated to uphold fair trial principles and human rights guarantees under Article 21(3)'.[48] It should therefore come as no surprise that some authors pointed to the existence of 'compelling arguments for holding proceedings in The Hague', since 'despite the Libyan

[42] *Prosecutor v Ruto, Kosgey and Sang* (Decision on the Application by the Government of Kenya Challenging the Admissibility of the Case Pursuant to Article 19(2)(b) of the Statute) ICC-01/09-01/11-101 Pre-Trial Chamber II (30 May 2011) para 64 (Kenya Admissibility Decision).

[43] UNSC Res 1970 (26 February 2011) UN Doc S/RES/1970.

[44] The admissibility challenge relating to the case of Saif Al-Islam Gaddafi was brought on 1 May 2012 (ICC-01/11-01/11-130-Red); the one relating to Al-Senussi on 2 April 2013 (ICC-01/11-01/11-307-Red2).

[45] B Leanos, 'Cooperative Justice: Understanding the Future of the International Criminal Court through its Involvement in Libya' (2012) 80 Fordham Law Review 2295–6.

[46] M Mancini, 'The Day After: Prosecuting International Crimes in Libya' (2011) 21 Italian Yearbook of International Law 90-93; Leanos (n 45) 2299.

[47] C Stahn, 'Libya, the International Criminal Court and Complementarity' (2012) 10 Journal of International Criminal Justice 343.

[48] Ibid 344.

government's insistence that suspects would receive a fair trial in Libya, many believe that unlikely'.[49] On 31 May 2013, Pre-Trial Chamber I rejected the challenge brought by the Libyan Government and found that the case against Saif Al-Islam Gaddafi was admissible.[50] The Government of Libya filed an appeal of the Pre-Trial Chamber I decision on 7 June 2013, on which the Appeals Chamber is yet to rule. The decision of Pre-Trial Chamber I was on the basis that it was not satisfied that Libya was 'investigating the same case as that before the Court'[51] and that it found Libya 'unable genuinely to carry out the investigation or prosecution against Mr Gaddafi'.[52] Accordingly, it decided it did not need to address the alternative requirement of 'willingness'[53] and, more specifically, 'the implications of the alleged impossibility of a fair trial for Mr Gaddafi on Libya's willingness genuinely to carry out the investigation or prosecution',[54] which had been extensively argued by Mr Gaddafi's defence.[55]

III. THE LEGAL FRAMEWORK

The ICC practice shows that the views propounding the limitation of the Court's role is those shortcomings of national proceedings working to the benefit of the accused had little, if any, impact. While it may be true that throughout the negotiation process of the Rome Statute the ICC was never conceived of as a fully-fledged 'human rights court',[56] its judges obviously did not think that this would or should be an obstacle. They apparently took to heart the idea that the Court, as an international body complementing national jurisdictions in meting out fair punishment for the most serious crimes by abiding by the highest international human rights standards,[57] could and should have a word to say also in cases of trials unfairly twisted to the detriment of the accused. Pre-Trial Chamber I refused to address the issue in deciding the admissibility challenge in the case against Saif Al-Islam

49 M Ellis, 'Principle of Complementarity in Contemporary International Criminal Justice' (2012) 10 Journal of International Criminal Justice 9. See also Mancini (n 46) 103.

50 See *Prosecutor v Saif Al-Islam Gaddafi and Abdullah Al-Senussi* (Decision on the admissibility of the case against Saif Al-Islam Gaddafi) (n 3).

51 *Prosecutor v Saif Al-Islam Gaddafi and Abdullah Al-Senussi* (Decision on the admissibility of the case against Saif Al-Islam Gaddafi) (n 3) para 134.

52 Ibid para 138.

53 Idem.

54 Ibid para 218.

55 Ibid paras 154–171.

56 OTP Expert Paper on Complementarity (n 11) para 23.

57 See, inter alia, Art 55 (Rights of persons during an investigation) and Art 67 (Rights of the accused) of the Rome Statute.

Gaddafi.[58] However, it took a different approach in its recent decision on the challenge by the Libyan Government to the admissibility of the case against Al-Senussi. The finding, of inadmissibility, was predicated on a full consideration of both of 'the two limbs of the admissibility test':[59] on one hand, whether domestic proceedings cover the same case as that before the Court;[60] and on the other, unwillingness and inability to carry out the proceedings.[61] With respect to the latter criterion, the Pre-Trial Chamber considered the failure to secure legal representation of Al-Senussi in respect of domestic proceedings but seemingly found that this was no impediment to the ability of Libya to carry out proceedings and accordingly of no effect on the inadmissibility of ICC proceedings, as a remedy to 'the problem of legal representation'[62] was envisaged in the short-term.

In its earlier decision regarding Saif Gaddafi, Pre-Trial Chamber I inverted the second limb of the admissibility test and based its conclusion exclusively on the inability to genuinely carry out the investigation of prosecution,[63] the analysis of which led to the Court's omission of analysing of the other branch of the second limb – unwillingness to carry out the investigation or prosecution.[64] It is worthy of note that similar deficiencies regarding the appointment of defence counsel were identified and were a contributing factor in the finding of admissibility, in contrast to the finding of inadmissibility with respect to the case against Al-Senussi. In light of these decisions of contrasting scope and outcome, the time seems ripe to try and make an assessment of the appropriateness of the Court's decision to embrace a more comprehensive (as such potentially much more influential) role as a powerful 'catalyst' for the enactment of human rights standards at the national level.

The broad approach first taken by the International Commission of Inquiry in Sudan (ie, that complementarity allows the ICC jurisdiction to also be triggered when human rights guarantees are violated to the detriment of suspects), now vigorously defended also by counsel for Saif Al-Islam Gaddafi in opposing the country's challenge to admissibility, seems indeed to be supported by solid arguments. They are rooted both in the statutory framework and in the broader perspective on the role of the ICC as a perma-

---

58 *Prosecutor v Saif Al-Islam Gaddafi and Abdullah Al-Senussi* (Decision on the admissibility of the case against Saif Al-Islam Gaddafi) (n 3) para 218.

59 *Prosecutor v Saif Al-Islam Gaddafi and Abdullah Al-Senussi* (Decision on the admissibility of the case against Abdullah Al-Senussi) ICC-01/11-01/11-466-Red Pre-Trial Chamber I (11 October 2013) para 210.

60 Ibid para 167.

61 Ibid para 289 *et seq*.

62 Ibid para 307.

63 See *Prosecutor v Saif Al-Islam Gaddafi and Abdullah Al-Senussi* (Decision on the admissibility of the case against Saif Al-Islam Gaddafi) (n 3) para 215.

64 Ibid para 216.

nent court complementing national systems in meting out fair justice for the most serious crimes.

A. Textual arguments

The Preamble to the Statute states *inter alia* that 'the most serious crimes of concern to the international community as a whole must not go unpunished'; that 'their effective prosecution must be ensured by taking measures at the national level and by enhancing international cooperation'; and that, in so doing, the Court 'shall be complementary to national criminal jurisdictions'. More specific guidance as to how this complementary role is to be concretely carried out is enshrined in Article 21(3) of the Statute, which provides that the application and interpretation of the applicable law by the Court (be it its statutory instruments, applicable treaties and principles and rules of international law, or general principles of law derived by the Court from national laws of legal systems of the world)

> must be consistent with internationally recognised human rights, and be without any adverse distinction founded on grounds such as gender ... age, race, colour, language, religion or belief, political or other opinion, national, ethnic or social origin, wealth, birth or other status.

The Court having to abide by the highest international human rights standards, allowing it to remedy all sorts of failures of national courts to comply with due process rules, irrespective of their outcome on the position of the accused, seems entirely consistent with this role.

More direct hints can be found in the statutory provisions governing the complementarity regime. The central provision is Article 17 of the Statute, setting forth the relevant criteria for the purpose of assessing the admissibility of a case:

> Having regard to paragraph 10 of the Preamble and article 1, the Court shall determine that a case is inadmissible where:
> (a) The case is being investigated or prosecuted by a State which has jurisdiction over it, unless the State is unwilling or unable genuinely to carry out the investigation or prosecution;
> (b) The case has been investigated by a State which has jurisdiction over it and the State has decided not to prosecute the person concerned, unless the decision resulted from the unwillingness or inability of the State genuinely to prosecute;
> (c) The person concerned has already been tried for conduct which is the subject of the complaint, and a trial by the Court is not permitted under article 20, paragraph 3;

> (d) The case is not of sufficient gravity to justify further action by the Court.

As regards unwillingness, Article 17(2) provides as follows:

> In order to determine unwillingness in a particular case, the Court shall consider, having regard to the principles of due process recognized by international law, whether one or more of the following exist, as applicable:
> (a) The proceedings were or are being undertaken or the national decision was made for the purpose of shielding the person concerned from criminal responsibility for crimes within the jurisdiction of the Court referred to in article 5;
> (b) There has been an unjustified delay in the proceedings which in the circumstances is inconsistent with an intent to bring the person concerned to justice;
> (c) The proceedings were not or are not being conducted independently or impartially, and they were or are being conducted in a manner which, in the circumstances, is inconsistent with an intent to bring the person concerned to justice.

Article 17(2)(b) seems to be particularly relevant: the existence of 'an unjustified delay in the proceedings which in the circumstances is inconsistent with an intent to bring the person concerned to justice' allows the Court to determine the unwillingness of a State. It is submitted that an unjustified delay in the proceedings can either be the result of the will to shield the accused from conviction, or of the will to persecute an individual who has been unjustly accused and brought to trial. Both shielding and persecution seem indeed to conflict with the idea of 'bringing a person to justice', at least where 'justice' is read as requiring an impartial assessment of the position and role of the accused. As conceded even by those reading the reference to the bringing to justice as exclusively addressing 'national proceedings that aim at making the defendant more difficult to convict',[65] helpful criteria in order to interpret the terms used in Article 17 should be inferred from the chapeau of Article 17(2). Article 17(2) mandates the Court to consider the existence of any of the scenarios it lists 'having regard to the principles of due process recognized by international law'. Consideration of this chapeau has in recent years led some scholars to advocate extending the scope of application of the notion of admissibility beyond the boundaries of sham trials: it has, for instance, been stated that the formula suggests 'an assessment of the quality of justice from

[65] Pichon (n 7) 193.

the standpoint of procedural and perhaps even substantive fairness'.[66] It seems therefore reasonable to argue that those principles, at the very minimum, require that the term 'justice' be given a broad meaning, so as to also encompass situations whereby the denial of justice takes the form of violations of the rule of law to the detriment of the accused. As noted by the Office of Public Counsel for the Defense in its submissions in the case of Saif Al-Islam Gaddafi, '[t]o equate "justice" with "convictions" would be fundamentally contrary to the presumption of innocence'.[67]

Indeed, the reference to 'bringing the person to justice' – as a benchmark against which departure from principles of due process is to be assessed for the purposes of unwillingness – appears neutral enough for it to be read as encompassing not solely ascertainment of guilt and subsequent punishment, but rather as mandating an impartial assessment of the actual position and role of the accused. Furthermore, if the Court were, given a departure from due process standards, to determine whether such departure actually worked to the benefit as opposed to the detriment of the accused (with a view to intervening only in the case of the former), it seems reasonable to fear that a conspicuous amount of uncertainty would be introduced. This would appear paradoxical, in particular since the reference to 'principles of due process recognized by international law' appearing in the chapeau of Article 17 seems aimed at limiting the Court's margin of discretion in assessing a State's unwillingness.

The need for national proceedings to meet 'genuineness', a qualifier that Article 17 applies to issues of both unwillingness and inability, seems to lend further support to the thesis of complementarity *in bonam partem*. Indeed, most of the sparse references to the relevance of human rights standards when assessing national proceedings for the purposes of complementarity are to be found in commentaries on the requirement of genuineness. Since the early days, it has been conceded that the term, by evoking 'a certain basic level of objective quality', would likely result in vesting the Court with some leeway in assessing the level of compliance of the relevant national system with established and recognised human rights standards.[68] By the same token, however, those same views did not extend to the far-reaching implications of such admissions, emphasising that the very insertion of that term had been the result of painstaking negotiations aimed at excluding that any shortcoming in terms of a State compliance with human rights standards, no matter how trivial, might lead to an assessment of national proceedings as not genuine.[69]

---

66 WA Schabas, 'Article 17' in O Triffterer (ed), *Commentary on the Rome Statute of the International Criminal Court – Observer's notes, Article by article* (2nd edn, CH Beck et al 2008) 623.

67 *Prosecutor v Gaddafi and Al-Senussi Defence Response* (n 2) para 40.

68 OTP Expert Paper on Complementarity (n 11) para 23.

69 Idem.

It is submitted that the theory of complementarity *in bonam partem* may well offer a solution to this conundrum: only an assessment carried out on an entirely objective basis, irrespective of the ultimate effect on the position of the accused, is suitable to pre-empt possible grievances by a state. 'Scripted trials', to borrow one expression used to describe a scenario warranting a finding of lack of genuineness of national proceedings,[70] can certainly go either way. More broadly, it should be noted that the Statute as a whole seems to foster the objective and fair assessment of the truth, as opposed to a one-sided approach necessarily leading to the conviction of the accused. Article 54(1), setting forth the duties and powers of the Prosecutor with respect to investigations, mandates the Prosecutor to 'investigate incriminating and exonerating circumstances equally' with a view to 'establish[ing] the truth'.[71] The principle of impartiality seems therefore to be meant as an overarching principle which is to guide the Court in the exercise of all of its functions, starting with the investigative phase.

Arguments in support of the theory of complementarity *in bonam partem* can also be found in the provisions governing the scenario of inability of a State to carry out the investigation or prosecution. Article 17(3) of the Statute mandates the Court to determine the inability of a State by considering *inter alia*

> whether, due to a total or substantial collapse or unavailability of its national judicial system, the State is unable to obtain the accused or the necessary evidence and testimony or otherwise unable to carry out its proceedings.

The reference to the State being 'otherwise unable to carry out the proceedings',[72] especially when read through the lens of the overarching need to read all of the statutory provisions so as to make them compatible with human rights standards, appears broad enough to support the argument that a State failing to comply with basic fair trial guarantees is *per se* 'unable' to carry out (genuine) criminal proceedings.

This broad reading of Article 17(3) and of the notion of inability enshrined therein reverberates on the scope of application of the principle of the *ne bis in idem* mirrored in Article 20 of the Statute. The Court can only proceed to try a person who has been tried by another court for acts proscribed by Articles 6, 7 or 8 with respect to the same conduct when the proceedings in the other court:

---

70 Ibid para 35.

71 This seems to contradict those arguing that 'nothing in the Rome Statute suggests that Article 17 requires States to guarantee defendants due process'. (Heller (n 4) 266.)

72 Art 17(1)(a) Rome Statute.

> (a) Were for the purpose of shielding the person concerned from criminal responsibility for crimes within the jurisdiction of the Court; or
> (b) Otherwise were not conducted independently or impartially in accordance with the norms of due process recognized by international law and were conducted in a manner which, in the circumstances, was inconsistent with an intent to bring the person concerned to justice.

Article 20 operates as an *ex-post pendant* of Article 17, whereby the Court's assessment of the requirements of admissibility is made *after* proceedings have taken place at the national level. In spite of the neutral formulation of Article 20(3)(b), most scholars read it as providing additional support to the view that the Court cannot step in where violations of due process are occurring to the detriment of the accused. On the one hand, they argue, it would not make any sense to retry someone who was acquitted by a national court, albeit in an unfair way; on the other hand, the appropriate remedy in case of an unfair conviction would be the annulment of the conviction, rather than a new trial before the Court.[73] Some of the arguments developed above on the interpretation of Article 17 seem suitable for reiteration here. First, as stated above, limiting the intervention of the Court to instances of violations of due process guarantees favouring the person tried at the national level makes such intervention conditional upon a determination which might not always be straightforward and as such is apt to introduce an unpalatable degree of uncertainty in proceedings before the Court. Second, it appears beyond controversy that Article 20(3)(b) is drafted in neutral terms, triggering the application of the provision upon the conclusion of any trial at the national level and rendering the outcome of such proceedings irrelevant for the purposes of determining the Court's right and duty to step in. A person who was convicted following violations of due process of which the object was to make his or her conviction easier cannot be said to have been a person 'brought to justice', at least not in the sense conveyed earlier in this article.

Finally, some further light seems to be shed by Rule 51 of the Rules of Procedure and Evidence.[74] Under the neutral heading 'Information provided under Article 17', the provision states that

> in considering the matters referred to in article 17, paragraph 2, and in the context of the circumstances of the case, the Court may consider, inter alia, information that the State referred to in article 17, paragraph 1, may

---

[73] Ibid 268.

[74] Rules of Procedure and Evidence, adopted by the Assembly of States Parties (3–10 September 2002) OR ICC-ASP/1/3.

choose to bring to the attention of the Court showing that its courts meet internationally recognized norms and standards for the independent and impartial prosecution of similar conduct.

It is uncontested, and openly stated in the official records, that the Rules 'are an instrument for the application' of the Statute, 'to which they are subordinate in all cases'.[75] Nevertheless, it appears significant that in matters of complementarity the drafters of the Statute chose to decline the instrumental and ancillary function of the Rules by drawing the attention of a State involved in an admissibility challenge to the advisability of submitting information related to its fair trial record and that such information is deemed useful to the Court in the exercise of its adjudicative role.

B. Systematic arguments

If the textual arguments attempting to reject the theory of complementarity *in bonam partem* do not seem persuasive, nor do other views more broadly relying on the framework of the Rome Statute. A further argument against complementarity *in bonam partem* is sometimes based on the absence of a procedural mechanism allowing the individual purportedly suffering violations of fair trial rights at the domestic level to challenge the admissibility of the case before the Court.[76] This argument places undue weight on the idea that the relevant provision (Article 19 of the Rome Statute) makes literal reference to admissibility only, instead of 'inadmissibility': indeed, a challenge to admissibility can, and should, be read as encompassing any motion soliciting the Court to review its determination of the matter, whatever the substance of that determination.

Even less persuasive are the arguments highlighting the absence, in the Rome Statute, of a referral mechanism at the disposal of the individual,[77] or the fact that only a State can have recourse to a referral in respect of a situation in which one or more crimes within the jurisdiction of the Court appear to have been committed.[78] Such arguments appear irremediably flawed, as they unduly overlap issues of jurisdiction with issues of admissibility. The fact that the jurisdiction of the Court can only be triggered by referrals initiated by either a State, the Security Council or the Prosecutor (upon the authorisation of the Pre-trial Chamber) is a procedural matter exclusively pertaining to the triggering mechanism, and cannot therefore be used to give content to the issue of admissibility, which – by its very nature – is a substantive matter.

---

[75] Explanatory note to the Rules of Procedure and Evidence.
[76] Heller (n 4) 266.
[77] Ibid 266–7.
[78] Ibid 267.

Finally, an additional element in favour of complementarity *in bonam partem* seems to flow from the broader architecture of 'modern' international criminal justice. Pursuant to Article 21(3) of the Statute, the Court is mandated to apply 'where appropriate, applicable treaties and the principles and rules of international law, including the established principles of the international law of armed conflict'. This makes it possible for the ICC to go beyond its own statutory instruments, whenever an interpretive uncertainty arises. Rule 11 *bis* of the Rules of Procedure and Evidence of the UN International Tribunal for the Former Yugoslavia (ICTY) makes the Chamber's satisfaction as to the fact that the accused 'will receive a fair trial' a condition for the case being referred back to the judicial authorities of a state, in furtherance of the ICTY's 'closing strategy'. It seems beyond controversy that the 'fair trial' referred to in this rule is meant to encompass full compliance with the relevant rules and that failure to comply with any of such rules results in an obstacle to the case being referred to the national jurisdiction, irrespective of whether such failure may benefit or disadvantage the accused. Precisely because of its neutral formulation, the provision does not set any limit or boundary as to the grounds on which such a challenge may be based; as a provision of a procedural nature, it is *per se* not aimed at providing any insight as to the substantive arguments suitable to appropriately trigger its functioning.

It is worth highlighting that Rule 11 *bis* was written at a time when the Rome Statute, and its Article 17, were well known to the judges authoring it: it has indeed been noted that the provision 'bears a striking similarity to the ICC's Article 17 complementarity regime'.[79] It seems unlikely that the issue of complementarity *in bonam partem* did not cross the minds of the drafters.

On balance, it seems therefore reasonable and in line with the overall objectives underlying the Statute to submit that *any* violation of internationally recognised principles of due process inconsistent with meting out fair judgment of the accused might create a *prima facie* case in favour of admissibility, based upon either the unwillingness or the inability of the State to carry out the investigation or prosecution, irrespective of whether such violation resulted in unduly improving or worsening the position of the accused.

IV. COMPLEMENTARITY *IN BONAM PARTEM* AND COOPERATION

Cooperation has long been regarded as a one-sided process. Recent studies have however drawn attention to Article 93(10) of the Statute and to what

[79] J Shih, 'Restoring the balance between the International Criminal Court and national jurisdictions' (2012) <http://ssrn.com/abstract=2198140> (working paper).

has been labelled as 'reverse cooperation',[80] a term which has since come to be regularly used in the academic debate.[81] The view taken on the scope of the principle of complementarity – namely, whether one favours or rejects the theory of complementarity *in bonam partem* – may have an impact on the suitable scope of the assistance to be provided by the Court to a State under this heading. With respect to the situation in Kenya, Pre-Trial Chamber II recently ruled that a request for assistance under Article 93 'has no linkage with the issue of admissibility', on the basis that a determination of the admissibility of a case pursuant to Article 17 of the Statute 'does not depend on granting or denying a request for assistance under Article 93(10) of the Statute'.[82] However, when one considers that the very notion of complementarity ultimately relies on an assessment of the adequacy of initiatives taken at the national level, and that a request for assistance might or should precisely be aimed at addressing alleged inadequacies or shortcomings of the requesting State, whether in matters of an investigative nature or otherwise linked to the judicial process, the link between the two areas appears less tenuous or inappropriate.[83] Indeed, as early as 2003, in the context of a policy paper broadly addressing the challenges likely to be posed by the complementarity regime, the Office of the Prosecutor saw the fact of 'exchang[ing] information and evidence to facilitate a national investigation or prosecution' not only as consistent with the Prosecutor's mandate, but even as 'an incentive to encourage co-operation on the part of the State concerned', provided this would not be turned into an instrument at the disposal of a State acting in bad faith to abuse the Court.[84] Accepting that the ICC stepping in is also warranted in scenarios of violations of due process guarantees occurring to the detriment of the accused, whether actual or threatened, would result in *ipso facto* broadening of the appropriate ambit of the assistance to be lent by the Court.

---

[80] F Gioia, 'Complementarity and "Reverse Cooperation"', in C Stahn and MM El Zeidy (eds), *The International Criminal Court and Complementarity – From Theory to Practice* (Cambridge University Press 2011) 807–829.

[81] Stahn (n 47) 347.

[82] *Prosecutor v Ruto et al*, Kenya Admissibility Decision (n 42) para 34.

[83] See Mancini (n 46) 108, explicitly suggesting that the Libyan Government could make use of Art 93(10) with respect to the investigation and prosecution of crimes perpetrated on its territory.

[84] OTP Expert Paper on Complementarity (n 11) para 10.

V. COMPLEMENTARITY *IN BONAM PARTEM* AS A TOOL FOR (IMPROVING) SHARING RESPONSIBILITIES BETWEEN THE COURT AND NATIONAL JURISDICTIONS

In 2003, the Office of the Prosecutor issued a policy paper outlining the fundamental principles that would govern its action in the forthcoming years, as well as some criteria against which it was to measure its effectiveness and success.[85] The central view was that the Court, on the one side, and the national jurisdictions, on the other, would have to operate on the basis of a 'division of labour', whereby they would coexist and pursue one and the same goal, albeit through different, complementary methods. Interestingly, the scenario of 'a territorial State incapacitated by mass crimes' where '[g]roups bitterly divided by conflict may oppose prosecutions at each other's hands and yet agree to a prosecution by a Court perceived as neutral and impartial' was identified as deserving attention and legitimately triggering the intervention of the court.[86] Partiality in prosecution may well amount to shielding a perpetrator from fair assessment and subsequent punishment. However, fear of prosecution by the 'other side' rather evokes a scenario of undue persecution of innocent individuals based on opposite political allegiances. The idea that the Court would better serve the cause of fair investigations and prosecutions in a scenario of deeply entrenched political hostilities is one which seems entirely consistent with the approach favouring the idea of complementarity *in bonam partem*. This seems to be the basis for the statement in the policy paper that: 'the principle underlying the concept of complementarity is that States remain responsible and accountable for investigating and prosecuting crimes committed under their jurisdiction and that national systems are expected to maintain and enforce adherence to international standards'.[87]

VI. FINAL ASSESSMENT: THE COMING OF AGE OF AN IDEA

One may argue that the very idea of crediting the ICC with the power to address, through the operation of the complementarity principle, human

---

[85] Paper on some policy issues before the Office of the Prosecutor (September 2003) <http://www.icc-cpi.int/NR/rdonlyres/1FA7C4C6-DE5F-42B7-8B25-60AA962ED8B6/143594/030905_Policy_Paper.pdf> (OTP 2003 Policy Paper).

[86] Ibid 5. See also OTP Expert Paper on Complementarity (n 11) para 61. More recently, see Leanos (n 45) 2272, arguing that 'when conflicts are severe and atrocities are committed, public resentment may be so strong in the conflict state that a fair trial and certain due process rights would be unavailable to the defendant'.

[87] OTP 2003 Policy Paper (n 85) 5.

rights violations in the area of due process, irrespective of their ultimate outcome on the position of the accused, would only result in unduly raising expectations. Violations of human rights standards and guarantees tend to be systemic and systematic, while the ICC, as a judicial institution with strictly limited funds and resources can only remedy shortcomings and lacunae arising in respect of a specific trial, lacking tools to otherwise sanction the relevant State or to impact its general practices with respect to due process. Yet, the considerations developed in this article support the view that complementarity *in bonam partem* is not only entirely consistent and compliant with the statutory texts and the overall mission of the Court, but also likely to enhance the predictability and ultimate legitimacy of its role. Significantly, even those authors rejecting the idea of complementarity *in bonam partem* cannot help noting the unpalatable nature of the outcome of their own theoretical approach, and its fundamental contrariness to the very idea of the rule of law.[88]

The very fact that the issue has now come before the Court in the context of the admissibility challenges in the Libyan cases of Saif Al-Islam Gaddafi and Abdullah Al-Senussi might lead one to conclude that time may be ripe for a new venture, both irrespective of the fact that it did not turn out to be the deciding factor in the decision of Pre-Trial Chamber I on the admissibility of the case against Saif Al-Islam Gaddafi and because it indeed was a factor in the finding of inadmissibility of the case against Al-Senussi. The situation of Syria, whose legal framework has been long since exposed by the Office of the High Commissioner for Human Rights for its failure to comply with basic human rights guarantees,[89] may well prove a more suitable candidate for complementarity *in bonam partem*, and prove to be the next step.

---

[88] Heller (n 4) 280: 'if the ICC simply turns a blind eye to unfair national trials – the inevitable effect of Article 17 as written – it will simply permit States to replace one kind of impunity with another.'

[89] 'Report of the United Nations High Commissioner for Human Rights on the situation of human rights in the Syrian Arab Republic' (15 September 2011) A/HRC/18/53, paras 16-19. The High Commissioner stated that Syrian domestic law cannot 'be adequately relied on because it violates constitutional guarantees and encourages impunity' and that crimes such as 'spreading false or exaggerated information with the aim of harming the State', 'publishing mendacious information liable to weaken the nation's moral[e]', or 'belonging to a secret society that aims to change the State's political and social structure', broadly defined as they are, may result in the violation of freedom of expression and association. Provisions allowing for suspects to be held for up to seven days pending investigation and the interrogation of suspects for certain crimes, renewable for up to a maximum of 60 days, as well as 'emergency laws' providing inter alia for the detention for crimes not defined in the law and for unlimited unsupervised preventive detention by security forces, were also stigmatised.

PART 3

Trigger Mechanisms of the International Criminal Court

State Referrals at the International Criminal Court: From Vision to Practice

*Annika Jones**

Article 13 of the Rome Statute lists the referral of a situation by a State Party to the Rome Statute as one of the three mechanisms that can trigger the jurisdiction of the International Criminal Court (ICC), along with the referral of a situation by the Security Council and the initiation of an investigation by the Prosecutor *proprio motu*.[1] The ICC's State referral mechanism has attracted considerable attention in the early years of the Court's operation, largely because it has not been used as the drafters of the Rome Statute had anticipated. The drafters did not foresee that State referrals would be used as frequently as they have been since the Court began to function in 2002; nor did they expect States to be as eager as they have been to refer situations occurring on their own territory. So far, the ICC has received five State referrals, all of which concern conduct alleged to have taken place on the territory on the referring State. The early practice of 'self-referrals'[2] has raised a number of interesting issues of law and policy, which will be addressed in the course of this chapter. Before turning to these issues, the chapter will briefly outline the legal framework for State referrals at the ICC and look at how the trigger mechanism has been used to date. The chapter will conclude by reflecting on whether the practice of self-referrals should be seen as positive development or as a cause for concern.

* Lecturer in Law, University of Exeter.

[1] Rome Statute of the International Criminal Court, Adopted by the United Nations Diplomatic Conference of Plenipotentiaries on the Establishment of an International Criminal Court (signed 17 July 1998, entered into force 1 July 2002) 2187 UNTS 3.

[2] The term 'self-referral' has been used to describe referrals by State Parties to the Rome Statute concerning crimes committed on their own territory. See D Robinson, 'The Controversy over Territorial State Referrals and Reflections on ICL Discourse' (2011) 9 Journal of International Criminal Justice 357. Such referrals have also been termed 'voluntary referrals' and 'auto-referrals'. See AT Müller and I Stegmiller, 'Self-Referrals on Trial: From Panacea to Patient' (2010) 8 Journal of International Criminal Justice 1271.

I. THE ICC'S STATE REFERRAL MECHANISM AND EARLY PRACTICE

Articles 13 and 14 of the Rome Statute, which provide the legal framework for State referrals to the ICC, allow any State Party to the Rome Statute to refer a situation to the Court. Following the referral of a situation by a State Party to the Rome Statute, the responsibility lies with the Prosecutor to determine whether or not one or more individuals should be charged with crimes within the Court's jurisdiction.[3] A State referral will not necessarily result in the initiation of an investigation by the Prosecutor of the ICC. On receipt of a State referral, the Prosecutor must determine whether or not there is a 'reasonable basis to proceed', taking into consideration whether or not there is a reasonable basis to believe that a crime within the jurisdiction of the Court has been or is being committed, whether or not the Court's admissibility criteria have been satisfied and whether or not an investigation is in the 'interests of justice'.[4]

The drafters of the Rome Statute did not expect State referrals to play a significant role in triggering the jurisdiction of the ICC.[5] The State referral mechanism was envisaged to operate primarily as an inter-State complaints mechanism, whereby States would refer situations concerning the territory or nationals of another State.[6] The infrequent use of inter-State complaint mechanisms in human rights treaties had demonstrated the reluctance of States to make complaints in relation to the conduct of other States unless their 'geopolitical or other interests [were] at stake'.[7] It was thought, therefore, that the ICC would be dependent on the Court's other trigger mechanisms, particularly the use of the Prosecutor's *proprio motu* powers of investigation, to establish a caseload.[8]

In practice, State referrals have had a strong role to play in triggering the Court's jurisdiction. In fact, the State referral mechanism has been the most frequently used trigger mechanism to date. Five State referrals have been submitted to the Court so far.[9] The first came from Uganda in December

---

[3] Art 14(1) Rome Statute.

[4] Art 53(1) Rome Statute.

[5] C Kress, '"Self-Referrals" and "Waivers of Complementarity"' (2004) 2 Journal of International Criminal Justice 944; WA Schabas, *An Introduction to the International Criminal Court* (4th edn, Cambridge University Press 2011) 159.

[6] Schabas (n 5) 161-63; P Akhavan, 'Self-Referrals before the International Criminal Court: Are States the Villains or the Victims of Atrocities' (2010) 21 Criminal Law Forum 104–105.

[7] Akhavan (n 6) 105; See also Kress (n 5) 944; A Marchesi, 'Article 14' in O Triffterer (ed), *Commentary on the Rome Statute of the International Criminal Court: Observers' Notes, Article by Article* (2nd edn, CH Beck and others 2008) 577; Schabas (n 5) 159.

[8] Marchesi (n 7) 578; Akhavan (n 6) 105.

[9] See <http://www.icc-cpi.int/en_menus/icc/structure%20of%20the%20court/office%20of%20the%20prosecutor/comm%20and%20ref/Pages/communications%20and%20referrals.aspx>.

2003.[10] The Ugandan referral was followed by referrals from the Democratic Republic of the Congo (DRC),[11] the Central African Republic (CAR),[12] Mali,[13] and, most recently, the Union of the Comoros.[14] Whilst the investigation in the Côte d'Ivoire was based on the use of the Prosecutor's *proprio motu* powers, the preceding declaration under Article 12(3) of the Rome Statute (accepting the jurisdiction of the Court) indicates that the initiation of the investigation was strongly supported by the territorial State.[15] The first four State referrals triggered four of the eight investigations initiated by the Prosecutor of the ICC. The Prosecutor has not yet refused to initiate an investigation in respect of a situation referred by a State Party to the Rome Statute.[16]

All five of the State referrals that have been received by the Court to date have been 'self-referrals', in other words, referrals of situations occurring on the territory of the referring State.[17] The majority of situations that have been referred have concerned nationals of the referring State. The referral from the Union of the Comoros is an exception in that it concerns allegations of crimes committed by Israeli nationals during a raid on the Humanitarian

---

10 ICC Press Release, 'President of Uganda refers situation concerning the Lord's Resistance Army (LRA) to the ICC' (29 January 2004) <http://www.icc-cpi.int/en_menus/icc/press%20and%20media/press%20releases/2004/Pages/president%20of%20uganda%20refers%20situation%20concerning%20the%20lord_s%20resistance%20army%20_lra_%20to%20the%20icc.aspx>.

11 ICC Press Release, 'Prosecutor receives referral of the situation in the Democratic Republic of Congo' (19 April 2004) <http://www.icc-cpi.int/en_menus/icc/press%20and%20media/press%20releases/2004/Pages/prosecutor%20receives%20referral%20of%20the%20situation%20in%20the%20democratic%20republic%20of%20congo.aspx>.

12 ICC Press Release, 'Prosecutor receives referral concerning Central African Republic' (7 January 2005) <http://www.icc-cpi.int/en_menus/icc/press%20and%20media/press%20releases/2005/Pages/otp%20prosecutor%20receives%20referral%20concerning%20central%20african%20republic.aspx>.

13 Letter of Referral from the Government of Mali (13 July 2012) <http://www.icc-cpi.int/NR/rdonlyres/A245A47F-BFD1-45B6-891C-3BCB5B173F57/0/ReferralLetterMali130712.pdf> (Mali Letter of Referral).

14 Letter of Referral from the Government of the Union of the Comoros (14 May 2013) <http://www.icc-cpi.int/iccdocs/otp/Referral-from-Comoros.pdf> (Union of the Comoros Letter of Referral).

15 See further *Situation in the Republic of Côte d'Ivoire* (Decision Pursuant to Article 15 of the Rome Statute on the Authorisation of an Investigation into the Situation in the Republic of Côte d'Ivoire) ICC-02/11-14 PTC III (3 October 2011) 10–15.

16 The Prosecutor has not yet announced whether or not an investigation will be initiated in relation to the referral from the Union of the Comoros.

17 The referral from the Union of the Comoros differs slightly from the other State referrals in that it relates to conduct alleged to have taken place on a vessel registered in the territory of the referring State, as opposed to conduct taking place within the borders of the referring State. See Union of the Comoros Letter of Referral (n 14).

Aid Flotilla bound for the Gaza Strip.[18] It was not anticipated during the drafting of the Rome Statute that States would be keen to refer situations occurring on their own territory or involving their own nationals to the Court. On the contrary, it was assumed that States would prefer to investigate and prosecute such crimes at the domestic level, rather than relinquish jurisdiction to the ICC.[19]

The early wave of self-referrals can be explained, in part, by the policy of the Office of the Prosecutor of the ICC (OTP). A policy paper produced by the OTP in 2003 had hinted at the prospect of self-referrals by envisaging the possibility of a 'consensual division of labour' between the Court and a territorial State incapacitated by mass crimes.[20] An annexe to the OTP's policy paper goes further, stating that 'given that under the Statute, the Prosecutor relies on cooperation to carry out his investigations, the Prosecutor will in general seek where possible to make this support explicit through a referral'.[21] The OTP's policy of 'soliciting' self-referrals is also apparent from a report on the activities of the OTP performed during the first three years.[22] The report acknowledges that 'the Prosecutor adopted the policy of inviting and welcoming voluntary referrals by territorial states as a first step in triggering the jurisdiction of the Court' and that this policy 'resulted in referrals for what would become the Court's first two situations'.[23] These documents show that the ICC's first Prosecutor openly followed a policy of pursuing self-referrals, despite the lack of a clear legal basis for doing so under the Rome Statute or the Court's Rules of Procedure and Evidence (RPE).[24]

---

[18] Idem.

[19] MH Arsanjani and WM Reisman, 'The Law-In-Action of the International Criminal Court' (2005) 99 American Journal of International Law 386–87; See also P Kirsch, 'The International Criminal Court: From Rome to Kampala' (2010) 43 John Marshall Law Review 520.

[20] ICC Office of the Prosecutor, 'Paper on some policy issues before the Office of the Prosecutor' (September 2003) 5 <http://www.icc-cpi.int/NR/rdonlyres/1FA7C4C6-DE5F-42B7-8B25-60AA962ED8B6/143594/030905_Policy_Paper.pdf> (OTP 2003 Policy Paper). See further Kress (n 5) 945.

[21] Annex to the 'Paper on some policy issues before the Office of the Prosecutor': Referrals and Communications, 5 <http://www.icc-cpi.int/NR/rdonlyres/278614ED-A8CA-4835-B91D-DB7FA7639E02/143706/policy_annex_final_210404.pdf> (Annex to OTP 2003 Policy Paper).

[22] Office of the Prosecutor, Report on the Activities Performed during the First Three Years (June 2003 – June 2006) (12 September 2006) 7 <http://www.icc-cpi.int/NR/ rdonlyres/D76A5D89-FB64-47A9-9821-725747378AB2/143680/OTP_3yearreport20060914_English.pdf> (OTP 2006 Report). See further WA Schabas (n 5) 160.

[23] OTP 2006 Report (n 22) 7.

[24] Rules of Procedure and Evidence, Adopted by the Assembly of States Parties (3–10 September 2002) OR ICC-ASP/1/3. It has been highlighted that the relevant provisions of the Rome Statute (Articles 14 and 42(1)) and the ICC's RPE (Rule 45) envisage a 'passive' role for the Prosecutor, who acts as the 'recipient of a referral'. See Kress (n 5) 947.

Non-States Parties to the Rome Statute have also shown a willingness to support the activities of the Court in relation to conduct occurring on their own territory by accepting the exercise of the Court's jurisdiction under Article 12(3) of the Rome Statute. Article 12(3) allows States that are not party to the Rome Statute to accept the exercise of the Court's jurisdiction by lodging a declaration with the Registrar. In April 2003, the Republic of Côte d'Ivoire made a declaration pursuant to Article 12(3) accepting the jurisdiction of the Court in relation to acts committed on Ivorian territory since 19 September 2002.[25] Subsequently, in January 2009, the Palestinian National Authority lodged a declaration accepting the jurisdiction of the Court in relation to acts committed on the territory of Palestine since 1 July 2002.[26] It has been argued that declarations pursuant to Article 12(3) of the Rome Statute can be viewed as 'analogous to a referral by a State Party under Articles 13(a) and 14 of the Rome Statute'.[27] However, Article 12(3) declarations and State referrals are clearly distinguished in the Rome Statute. Declarations under Article 12(3) are referred to under the heading 'preconditions to the exercise of jurisdiction' and are not mentioned in Article 13, which outlines the mechanisms that can trigger the jurisdiction of the Court.[28] The ability to refer a situation to the ICC, and thus trigger the Court's jurisdiction, is expressly limited to State Parties to the Rome Statute under Articles 13(a) and 14.[29] Consequently, where a declaration under Article 12(3) is made by a non-State Party to the Rome Statute, the jurisdiction of the Court must be triggered by one of the three mechanisms outlined in Article 13. Following the declaration by the Côte d'Ivoire, the Prosecutor initiated an investigation on the basis of his *proprio motu* powers.[30] No investigation has been initiated in respect of the situation in Palestine. In April 2012, the OTP issued a statement asserting that the OTP did not have the competence to determine whether or not Palestine qualified as a State for the purposes of Article 12(3)

---

[25] See Declaration Accepting the Jurisdiction of the International Criminal Court (18 April 2003) <http://www.icc-cpi.int/NR/rdonlyres/74EEE201-0FED-4481-95D4-C8071087102C/279844/ICDEENG.pdf>.

[26] See Declaration Recognizing the Jurisdiction of the International Criminal Court (21 January 2009) <http://www.icc-cpi.int/NR/rdonlyres/74EEE201-0FED-4481-95D4-C8071087102C/279777/20090122PalestinianDeclaration2.pdf>.

[27] See, for example, S Freeland, 'How Open Should the Door Be? – Declarations by non-States Parties under Article 12(3) of the Rome Statute of the International Criminal Court' (2006) 75 Nordic Journal of International Law 224. This approach has been rejected by Stahn and others. See C Stahn, MM El Zeidy & H Olásolo, 'The International Criminal Court's Ad Hoc Jurisdiction Revisited' (2005) 99 American Journal of International Law 424.

[28] Stahn and others (n 27) 423–24.

[29] Ibid 424–25.

[30] *Situation in the Côte d'Ivore,* (Decision Pursuant to Article 15 of the Rome Statute on the Authorisation of an Investigation into the Situation in the Republic of Côte d'Ivore) ICC-02/11-14 PTC III (3 October 2011) para 2.

of the Rome Statute.[31] Article 12(3) declarations have raised a number of interesting legal issues, which fall beyond the scope of the present chapter. The focus of the remaining sections will be on the issues raised by the practice of State referrals since the Court came into operation.

II. ARE SELF-REFERRALS PERMITTED UNDER THE ROME STATUTE?

The early practice of State referrals has raised a number of legal issues. Perhaps the most fundamental of these issues is whether or not the Rome Statute permits the referral of situations from the territorial State.

It is clear from the text of Article 14 that self-referrals are indeed permitted under the Rome Statute.[32] Article 14(1) allows any State Party to refer a situation to the Prosecutor, without exception. There is no restriction in the text of Article 14 that would prevent a State from referring a situation arising from its own territory. This interpretation of Article 14 is consistent with the intentions of the drafters of the Rome Statute. Throughout the drafting process, some delegates were in favour of restricting the authority to refer situations to the ICC to 'interested States', namely the 'territorial State, the custodial State or the State of nationality of the victim or suspect'.[33] It is clear from the drafting history of Article 14 that the drafters of the Rome Statute contemplated the prospect of self-referrals, and even considered them to be desirable.[34] Questions have been raised as to whether or not the drafters of the Rome Statute foresaw self-referrals of a purely internal nature, in other words, the referral of situations concerning the nationals as well as the territory of the referring State. It has been highlighted that the change in termi-

---

[31] See Statement of the OTP on the Situation in Palestine (3 April 2012) 5 <http://www.icc-cpi.int/NR/rdonlyres/C6162BBF-FEB9-4FAF-AFA9-836106D2694A/284387/SituationinPalestine030412ENG.pdf>. The approach of the Prosecutor has prompted a considerable amount of academic discussion. See J Dugard, 'Palestine and the International Criminal Court: Institutional Failure or Bias?' (2013) 11 Journal of International Criminal Justice 563. For a recent submission to the OTP in favour of considering Palestine as a State see Al-Haq and the Palestinian Centre for Human Rights, 'Position Paper on the Scope of the International Criminal Court's Jurisdiction over the Situation in Palestine' (August 2013) <http://www.alhaq.org/images/stories/PDF/2012/Al-Haq_and_PCHR_Position_Paper-International_Criminal_Court_.pdf>.

[32] Kress (n 5) 945; R Cryer and others, *An Introduction to International Criminal Law and Procedure* (2nd edn, Cambridge University Press 2010) 165; Robinson (n 2) 359–61.

[33] 'Report of the Preparatory Committee on the Establishment of an International Criminal Court Vol I' *United Nations General Assembly Official Records Fifty-First Session, Supplement No. 22* UN Doc A/51/22 (1996) para 112. See also 'Summary of the Proceedings of the Preparatory Committee during the Period of 25 March–12 April 1996' (7 May 1996) UN Doc A/AC.249/1 para 163.

[34] Cryer and others (n 32) 165; Robinson (n 2) 363.

nology from 'complaint' to 'referral' during the drafting of Article 14 suggests that the drafters of the Rome Statute contemplated a complaint by a State Party 'against *another* State'.[35] It does, however, seem unlikely that the drafters would have intended self-referrals to be restricted to situations involving the nationals of a third State without mentioning such a restriction during the drafting process.[36]

An interpretation of Article 14 that permits States to refer situations arising from their own territory could be understood to conflict with the preamble of the Rome Statute.[37] Article 14 affirms that the effective prosecution of the most serious crimes of concern to the international community 'must be ensured by taking measures at the national level',[38] and recalls 'the duty of every State to exercise its criminal jurisdiction over those responsible for international crimes'.[39] The preamble of the Rome Statute is not legally binding, but provides context for the interpretation of the Statute's operative provisions.[40] The duty referred to in the preamble could be understood to require States to investigate and prosecute crimes occurring on their own territory at the domestic level. Such an interpretation could, however, be seen to conflict with the principle of *aut dedere aut judicare*, which allows a State in whose territory a suspect is present to relieve itself of its obligation to prosecute by acceding to a request for extradition.[41] It would also be undesirable as a matter of policy. Situations are likely to arise where the ICC would provide a more appropriate forum for the pursuit of justice than the territorial State. This might be the case, for example, where domestic proceedings could trigger violence or instability in the affected region, or where the territorial State lacks the capacity to oversee criminal proceedings, or to do so impartially.[42] In these situations, referrals to the ICC could be considered preferable to proceedings at the domestic level. The duty referred to in the preamble should, therefore, be interpreted broadly as a duty to 'ensure that a genuine investigation [is] undertaken', regardless of whether this is through domestic proceedings, extradition to another State or surrender to

---

35 Schabas (n 5) 163. See also WA Schabas, 'First Prosecutions at the International Criminal Court' (2006) 27 Human Rights Law Journal 27–32.

36 Robinson (n 2) 365–66.

37 Kress (n 5) 945.

38 Preamble to the Rome Statute para 4.

39 Ibid para 6.

40 Vienna Convention on the Law of Treaties (adopted 23 May 1969, entered into force 27 January 1980) 1155 UNTS 331, Art 31(2).

41 MM El Zeidy, 'The Ugandan Government Triggers the First Test of the Complementarity Principle: An Assessment of the First State's Party Referral to the ICC' (2005) 5 International Criminal Law Review 103. See further *Questions relating to the Obligation to Prosecute or Extradite (Belgium v. Senegal)* (Judgment), 20 July 2012, para 95.

42 This issue is discussed in greater depth in section V below.

an international criminal jurisdiction.[43] Following this approach, self-referrals would be consistent with the preamble to the Rome Statute, as well as the intentions of the drafters and the text of Article 14.

III. SELF-REFERRALS AND THE ICC'S ADMISSIBILITY CRITERIA

Another legal issue that has been raised by the practice of self-referrals is whether or not cases are admissible under Article 17 of the Rome Statute in the event that a State fails to initiate domestic proceedings, regardless of its 'willingness' or 'ability' to do so (the 'inaction' scenario).[44] The question of whether or not the Court can proceed in such a situation was raised by the first referral to the ICC, from Uganda. Ever since the referral, the Ugandan authorities have appeared both willing and able to investigate and prosecute under the terms of Article 17.[45] The failure of the Ugandan authorities to initiate proceedings has not been due to 'unwillingness' or 'inability', as defined in the Rome Statute, but difficulties faced in securing custody of the alleged perpetrators.[46]

Article 17 of the Rome Statute has been understood by some to require a determination of unwillingness or inability in order for the Court to proceed.[47] This reading of Article 17 is, however, inconsistent with the plain text of the provision, which requires a determination of unwillingness or inability only if a case 'is being' or 'has been' investigated by a State with jurisdiction over it.[48] The text of Article 17 makes it clear that a case will automatically be admissible before the ICC if no proceedings have been initiated at the domestic level, provided that it is of sufficient gravity to justify further

---

[43] Kress (n 5) 946.

[44] OTP 2003 Policy Paper (n 20) 5. See also Müller and Stegmiller (n 2) 1282. D Robinson, 'The Mysterious Mysteriousness of Complementarity' (2010) 21 Criminal Law Forum 72; Akhavan (n 6) 109.

[45] Art 17(2) and (3) Rome Statute. See Arsanjani and Reisman (n 19) 395; P Akhavan, 'The Lord's Resistance Army Case: Uganda's Submission of the First State Referral to the International Criminal Court' (2005) 99 American Journal of International Law 415; M Happold, 'The International Criminal Court and the Lord's Resistance Army' (2007) 8 Melbourne Journal of International Law 166; DE Goldstone, 'Embracing Impasse: Admissibility, Prosecutorial Discretion, and the Lessons of Uganda for the International Criminal Court' (2008) 22 Emory International Law Review 784.

[46] Arsanjani and Reisman (n 19) 395; Akhavan (n 45) 415; Happold (n 45) 166; Goldstone (n 45) 784; Schabas (n 5) 167.

[47] Akhavan (n 45) 413; WA Schabas, 'Prosecutorial Discretion v. Judicial Activism at the International Criminal Court' (2008) 6 Journal of International Criminal Justice 757; Robinson (n 44) 72.

[48] Art 17(1)(a) and (b) Rome Statute. See Akhavan (n 45) 414; Robinson (n 44) 70–71, 81–85; Robinson (n 2) 373.

action by the Court.[49] An interpretation of Article 17 that requires a determination of unwillingness or inability also conflicts with the object and purpose of the Rome Statute because it could lead to impunity for those responsible for the commission of international crimes.[50] The concepts of unwillingness and inability have been defined narrowly under the Rome Statute because they were envisaged to operate in situations where domestic proceedings had been initiated.[51] Article 17(3), for example, requires 'a total or substantial collapse or unavailability' of the State's national judicial system for a finding of inability. Situations are likely to arise where States are not 'unwilling' or 'unable' to investigate and prosecute under the terms of the Rome Statute, but nonetheless face difficulties in overseeing the investigation and prosecution of international crimes. In such situations, it may be appropriate for States to seek assistance from the ICC by making a referral. The effect of reading a requirement of a determination of unwillingness or inability into Article 17 would be to prevent the ICC from stepping in to ensure that individuals are held accountable for their actions, contrary to the Statute's goal of fighting impunity for the commission of international crimes.

A more convincing approach to the interpretation of Article 17 sees the tests of inability or unwillingness as relevant only in the event that a State has initiated proceedings at the domestic level.[52] Not only is this approach consistent with the text of Article 17, it also promotes the object and purpose of the Rome Statute by ensuring that perpetrators are held to account in the event of inaction at the domestic level.[53] The Office of the Prosecutor of the ICC has adopted this approach. Whilst emphasising the duty of States to exercise criminal jurisdiction over those responsible for the commission of international crimes, the 2003 policy paper released by the OTP states that '[t]here is no impediment to the admissibility of a case before the Court where no State has initiated any investigation' and that in cases of inaction 'there will be no question of "unwillingness" or "inability" under article 17'.[54] The same approach was adopted in the informal expert paper produced for the OTP in 2003, which stated that in the scenario where no State has initiated any investigation 'there is no need to examine the factors of unwill-

---

49 Art 17(1)(d) Rome Statute.

50 El Zeidy (n 41) 104–105, Robinson (n 44) 90; Robinson (n 2) 376.

51 Robinson (n 44) 90. See further JT Holmes, 'Complementarity: National Courts *versus* the ICC' in A Cassese, P Gaeta and JRWD Jones (eds), *The Rome Statute of the International Criminal Court: A Commentary* vol I (Oxford University Press 2002) 673, 675.

52 El Zeidy (n 41) 104; Akhavan (n 45) 414; Happold (n 45) 169; Cryer and others (n 32) 157; Robinson (n 44) 68; Robinson (n 2) 373.

53 El Zeidy (n 41) 103.

54 OTP 2003 Policy Paper (n 20) 5.

ingness or inability; the case is simply admissible under the clear terms of Article 17'.[55]

The Chambers of the ICC have interpreted Article 17 in the same way when dealing with self-referrals.[56] In the case of *Prosecutor v Thomas Lubanga Dyilo*, Pre-Trial Chamber I considered that since 'no State with jurisdiction over the case against Mr. Thomas Lubanga Dyilo is acting, or has acted in relation to [the] case ... the Chamber need not make any analysis of unwillingness or inability'.[57] The same approach has been taken in other decisions of the Pre-Trial Chamber.[58] It has also been affirmed by the Appeals Chamber of the ICC in the case of *Prosecutor v Germain Katanga and Mathieu Ngudjolo Chui*, where the judges agreed with the submission of the Prosecutor that 'the question of unwillingness or inability of a State having jurisdiction over the case becomes relevant only where, due to ongoing or past investigations or prosecutions in that State, the case appears to be inadmissible.[59] It explained that:

> in considering whether a case is inadmissible under article 17(1)(a) and (b) of the Statute, the initial questions to ask are (1) whether there are ongoing investigations or prosecutions, or (2) whether there have been investigations in the past, and the State having jurisdiction has decided not to prosecute the person concerned. It is only when the answers to these questions are in the affirmative that one has to look to the second halves of sub-paragraphs (a) and (b) and to examine the question of unwillingness and inability ... It follows that in case of inaction, the question of unwillingness or inability does not arise.[60]

The Appeals Chamber went on to say that the alternative approach, according to which unwillingness and inability must be considered in the case of

---

[55] Informal Expert Paper: The Principle of Complementarity in Practice, ICC-01/04-01/07-1008-AnxA, (30 March 2009) 7 <http://www.icc-cpi.int/iccdocs/doc/doc654724.PDF> (Informal Expert Paper).

[56] Cryer and others (n 32) 157.

[57] *Prosecutor v Thomas Lubanga Dyilo* (Decision on the Prosecutor's Application for a Warrant of Arrest, Art 58) ICC-01/04-01/06-8-US-Corr PTC I (10 February 2006) para 40.

[58] See, for example, *Prosecutor v Omar Hassan Ahmad Al Bashir* (Decision on the Prosecution's Application for a Warrant of Arrest against Omar Hassan Ahmad Al Bashir) ICC-02/05-01/09-3 PTC I (4 March 2009) para 48; *Prosecutor v Joseph Kony, Vincent Otti, Okot Odhiambo, Dominic Ongwen* (Decision on the Admissibility of the Case under Art 19(1) of the Statute) ICC-02/04-01/05-377 PTC II (10 March 2009) paras 36, 52.

[59] *Prosecutor v Germain Katanga and Mathieu Ngudjolo Chui* (Judgment on the Appeal of Mr. Germain Katanga against the Oral Decision of Trial Chamber II of 12 June 2009 on the Admissibility of the Case) ICC-01/04-01/07-1497 Appeals Chamber (25 September 2009) para 75.

[60] Ibid para 78.

inaction, is 'not only irreconcilable with the wording of the provision, but is also in conflict with a purposive interpretation of the Statute'. Such a purposive interpretation seeks to 'put an end to impunity' and ensure that 'the most serious crimes of concern to the international community as a whole must not go unpunished'.[61] The Appeals Chamber has taken a similar approach to the interpretation of Article 17 in the context of the Kenyan situation, in which the jurisdiction of the Court was triggered by the use of the Prosecutor's *proprio motu* powers of investigation.[62]

It is now settled in the jurisprudence of the ICC that cases are admissible before the Court if a State has failed to undertake proceedings at the domestic level. If a State decides to refer a situation occurring on its own territory to the ICC, the fact that the State is both 'willing' and 'able' to investigate and prosecute under the terms of Article 17 will not prevent the ICC from intervening.

IV. WITHDRAWAL OF SELF-REFERRALS AND SUBSEQUENT ADMISSIBILITY CHALLENGES

A further legal issue associated with the practice of self-referrals is whether or not a State can withdraw a referral once it has been submitted to the Prosecutor of the ICC. This issue was raised by reports of an announcement from the President of Uganda in 2004 that Uganda might seek to 'withdraw' its self-referral.[63] There may be legitimate reasons for a State to attempt to withdraw a self-referral, such as concern for peace and security or a decision

[61] Ibid para 79.

[62] *Prosecutor v Francis Kirimi Mutharura and others* (Judgment on the appeal of the Republic of Kenya against the decision of Pre-Trial Chamber II of 30 May 2011 entitled "Decision on the Application by the Government of Kenya Challenging the Admissibility of the Case Pursuant to Art 19(2)(b) of the Statute) ICC-01/09-02/11-274 Appeals Chamber (30 August 2011) para 40; *Prosecutor v Ruto* (Judgment on the Appeal of the Republic of Kenya against the Decision of Pre-Trial Chamber II of 30 May 2011 entitled 'Decision on the Application by the Government of Kenya Challenging the Admissibility of the Case pursuant to Art 19(2)(b) of the Statute') ICC-01/09-02/11-307 Appeals Chamber (30 August 2011) para 41. See further TO Hansen, 'A Critical Review of the ICC's Recent Practice Concerning Admissibility Challenges and Complementarity' (2012) 13 Melbourne Journal of International Law 218.

[63] Amnesty International Press Release, 'Uganda: Government cannot prevent the International Criminal Court from investigating crimes' (16 November 2004) <http://www.amnesty.org/en/library/asset/AFR59/008/2004/en/db815a8b-fa9d-11dd-999c-47605d4edc46/afr590082004en.pdf>. See further MP Scharf and P Dowd, 'No Way Out? The Question of Unilateral Withdrawals of Referrals to the ICC and Other Human Rights Courts' (2009) 9 Chicago Journal of International Law 574; AKA Greenawalt, 'Complementarity in Crisis: Uganda, Alternative Justice, and the International Criminal Court' (2009) 50 Virginia Journal of International Law 108.

to pursue justice locally. However, an attempt to withdraw a self-referral could also be underpinned by a desire to obstruct criminal proceedings and shield individuals from accountability, perhaps following a change of government where newly elected officials are implicated in crimes within the jurisdiction of the Court.

There is no express provision for the withdrawal of a State referral in the text of the Rome Statute.[64] Once a situation has been referred to the Court, the decision as to whether or not to proceed with an investigation lies with the Prosecutor and Pre-Trial Chamber under Article 53 of the Rome Statute, and with the Security Council, in accordance with Article 16.[65] In this respect, the Rome Statute is consistent with the founding documents and case law of other human rights treaty bodies.[66] The absence of a right of withdrawal prevents States from obstructing the Court's activities and wasting the Court's time and resources in situations where justice is not being pursued at the domestic level. Even if a referring State decides to withdraw from the Rome Statute altogether, it would still be bound by its obligations under the treaty.[67] Article 127(2) provides that the withdrawal of a State from the treaty shall not 'prejudice in any way the continued consideration of any matter which was already under consideration by the Court prior to the date on which the withdrawal became effective.'[68]

A State can, however, bring an admissibility challenge under Articles 18 or 19 of the Statute on the basis that proceedings have been, or are being, undertaken by a State with jurisdiction.[69] There is nothing in the text of either Article to prevent a State that has referred a situation to the ICC from making a subsequent admissibility challenge. It could be argued that a State that has referred a situation to the ICC has automatically 'waived' its right to challenge admissibility under Article 18 or 19 of the Rome Statute.[70] There is, however, nothing in the text of the Rome Statute to suggest that this is the case. Furthermore, it has been highlighted that a State wishing to bind itself under international law must express a clear intention to do so.[71] It is conceivable, albeit unlikely, that a State might make a statement expressly

[64] Scharf and Dowd (n 63) 586; Schabas (n 5) 167.

[65] Schabas (n 5) 167.

[66] Scharf and Dowd (n 63) 593-608. Scharf and Dowd highlight a 'narrow exception' in the practice of the Inter-American Court of Human Rights that could be transferred to the ICC, which would allow a referral to be withdrawn in the 'very narrow temporal window between when a referral is made to the Court and when the Court actually exercises its jurisdiction over that case or referral'. See Scharf and Dowd (n 63) 610.

[67] Art 127(2) Rome Statute. See further Scharf and Dowd (n 63) 586–87.

[68] Art 127(2) Rome Statute.

[69] Arts 18(2) and 19(2)(b) Rome Statute.

[70] See discussion in El Zeidy (n 41) 107–110.

[71] Müller and Stegmiller (n 2) 1288.

waiving its right to make an admissibility challenge following the referral of a situation to the ICC, or where the jurisdiction of the Court has been triggered by another trigger mechanism.[72] It may be considered preferable for the Court to treat such a statement of waiver as binding since this would prevent waste of the Court's resources and allow the ICC to continue with its proceedings, unhindered by an admissibility challenge. However, this approach would conflict with the rationale underpinning the Court's complementarity regime, which gives States priority in the investigation and prosecution of international crimes.[73] If States are willing and able to undertake proceedings at the domestic level, and to do so genuinely, they should be given the opportunity to do so, regardless of the existence of a statement expressly relinquishing this right.

It is worth noting that the Court has set a high bar for a challenge to the admissibility of a case under Article 19 of the Statute. To succeed in such a challenge, it has been held that a State must show that it is investigating the same individuals for the same conduct being addressed by the Court.[74] Consequently, a State will not be able to regain control over proceedings following a referral without being able to show that it has taken concrete steps to pursue justice at the domestic level.

V. IS THE REFERRAL OF SITUATIONS BY THE TERRITORIAL STATE A DESIRABLE PRACTICE?

The early practice of self-referrals has not only raised issues of law, it has also raised the question of whether or not the tendency of States to refer situations occurring on their own territory to the ICC is a desirable practice.

Self-referrals do have potential benefits for the ICC. The active pursuit of self-referrals by the OTP has been driven, in part, by the belief that a self-referral enhances the prospect of a good level of cooperation between the Court and the territorial State. The annexe to the OTP's policy paper recognises that where a self-referral has been received 'the Prosecutor has the advantage of knowing that that State has the political will to provide his Office with all the cooperation within the country that it is required to give

[72] Ibid 1289.

[73] Holmes (n 51) 667.

[74] See, for example, *Prosecutor v Thomas Lubanga Dyilo* (Decision Concerning Pre-Trial Chamber I's Decision of 10 February 2006 and the Incorporation of Documents into the Record of the Case against Mr Thomas Lubanga Dyilo) ICC-01/04-01/06-8-US-Corr PTC I (24 February 2006) para 31; *Prosecutor v Francis Kirimi Mutharura and others* (n 56) para 39; *Prosecutor v Saif Al-Islam Gaddafi and Abudllah Al-Senussi* (Decision on the Admissibility of the Case Against Saif Al-Islam Gaddafi) ICC-01/11-01/11-344-Red PTC I (31 May 2013) paras 73–77.

under the Statute'.[75] The cooperation of the territorial State is crucial for the effective operation of the ICC. The Court relies on States for various forms of cooperation, including access to witnesses and evidence and the transfer of accused persons to the Court.[76] A good level of State cooperation is particularly important in the early years of the Court's operation. Without it, there is a danger that the fledgling Court will be viewed as weak and ineffective. When the Court first began to function, it was logical for the Prosecutor of the ICC to seek out self-referrals rather than initiate investigations *proprio motu*, which were more likely to be resisted by the territorial State.[77] Whilst strong cooperation from the territorial State may be more likely where the jurisdiction of the Court is triggered by a self-referral, it is certainly not guaranteed.[78] The cooperation of a referring State could be lost following a change in government, or its priorities. It could also be lost following a decision of the Prosecutor to investigate the conduct of State officials.[79] In such situations, however, the self-referral would not put the Court at a disadvantage: the OTP would simply face the same situation that it would have faced if a different mechanism had been used to trigger the Court's jurisdiction.

Self-referrals have also been considered beneficial for the ICC insofar as they help to generate an image of the Court as a supportive and non-threatening institution.[80] Such an image could lead to greater acceptance of the Court amongst States, and even encourage wider ratification of the Rome Statute. It has been observed that by soliciting self-referrals, the first Prosecutor of the ICC managed to build a caseload for the Court without relying on the use of his controversial *proprio motu* powers of investigation.[81] Consequently, the ICC managed to

> make its first steps in the guise of an institution that can assist states to obtain justice in the face of mass atrocities committed within their boundaries, rather than as an interfering international watchdog against which states have to defend themselves.[82]

---

[75] Annex to OTP 2003 Policy Paper (n 21) 5.

[76] A Ciampi, 'The Obligation to Cooperate' in Cassese and others, vol II (n 51) 1607–08.

[77] P Gaeta, 'Is the Practice of 'Self-Referrals' a Sound Start for the ICC?' (2004) 2 Journal of International Criminal Justice 950.

[78] See, for example, A Wartanian, 'The ICC Prosecutor's Battlefield: Combating Atrocities While Fighting for States' Cooperation Lessons from the U.N. Tribunals Applied to the Case of Uganda' (2005) 36 Georgetown Journal of International Law 1311–1312.

[79] Gaeta (n 77) 952.

[80] Ibid 950; Happold (n 45) 166.

[81] Happold (n 45) 166.

[82] Gaeta (n 77) 950.

Whilst there is no empirical evidence to confirm that the early practice of self-referrals has led to greater acceptance of the Court amongst States, it is certainly possible that they could have this effect.

The early spate of self-referrals to the ICC has, however, raised some concerns. One concern is that States could use self-referrals as a 'political weapon' against their opponents by seeking to '[expose] internationally the crimes allegedly being perpetrated by the other side'.[83] It is important to note at the outset that concerns about the use of the Court as a political tool are not confined to self-referrals and could be raised in relation to the use of the Court's other trigger mechanisms,[84] or referrals from non-territorial States.[85] The concern that self-referrals could be used by States to achieve political goals is reinforced, to some extent, by the fact that many of the self-referrals received by the Court to date have been made by governments against rebel groups or non-governmental parties to a conflict occurring on their territory.[86] The self-referral from Uganda focused explicitly on the conduct of the Lord's Resistance Army (LRA).[87] The referral from Mali also focused on the conduct of rebel groups on the territory.[88] The risk of the Court being used as a political tool in the hands of States has been reduced by the OTP's practice of interpreting self-referrals to ensure that they embrace the conduct of both sides of a conflict.[89] For example, following the Ugandan self-referral in December 2003, the OTP 'informed the Government of Uganda that, in compliance with its obligations of impartiality, the Office would interpret the referral to include all crimes committed in Northern Uganda'.[90]

Despite the OTP's interpretation of the Ugandan referral to encompass 'all crimes committed in Northern Uganda', the ICC's investigations have focused on the conduct of the LRA, and not the Ugandan army.[91] The OTP

---

83 Ibid 951–52. This concern is addressed in the context of Art 12(3) declarations by Rule 44(2) of the ICC RPE, which provides that the Registrar shall inform the State concerned that the declaration under Art 12, paragraph 3, has as a consequence the acceptance of jurisdiction with respect to the crimes referred to in Art 5 of relevance to the situation'.

84 Robinson (n 2) 368. Robinson highlights that 'Security Council members may have geostrategic, domestic and reputational considerations in mind when referring situations'.

85 Akhavan (n 6) 119.

86 Müller and Stegmiller (n 2) 1270.

87 ICC Press Release, 'President of Uganda refers situation concerning the Lord's Resistance Army (LRA) to the ICC' (29 January 2004) <http://www.icc-cpi.int/en_menus/icc/press%20and%20media/press%20releases/2004/Pages/president%20of%20uganda%20refers%20situation%20concerning%20the%20lord_s%20resistance%20army%20_lra_%20to%20the%20icc.aspx>.

88 Mali Letter of Referral (n 13).

89 Kress (n 5) 946.

90 OTP 2006 Report (n 22) 25.

91 Ibid. This approach has received criticism from human rights groups. See Akhavan (n 45) 411; Schabas (n 5) 165.

has justified its focus on the conduct of the LRA on the basis that the crimes allegedly committed by members of the LRA are of a 'higher gravity' than those allegedly committed by any other group.[92] However, suspicions have been raised that the first Prosecutor of the ICC may have had 'a tacit, if not an explicit, understanding with the Ugandan authorities that he [would] prosecute the rebel leaders only'.[93] Some commentators have even gone so far as to claim that self-referrals 'will often be accompanied and burdened by "understandings" between The Hague and the referring state'.[94] There is, however, no tangible evidence to suggest that understandings have been concluded between the OTP and a referring State.[95] Furthermore, even if such understandings had been concluded, they are not an inevitable consequence of a self-referral.[96] There is no reason to believe that the independence and impartiality of the OTP will be undermined in situations where the jurisdiction of the Court is triggered by the referral of a situation by the territorial State.

Another concern associated with the practice of self-referrals is that it may take the pressure off States to play a leading role in the investigation and prosecution of international crimes.[97] Not only could this inhibit the strengthening of domestic criminal justice systems and domestic rule of law, it could also risk overburdening the Court, which has limited resources at its disposal. The Court's investigation in Uganda has been described as 'a clear example of this free-rider problem' due to the fact that 'in all likelihood, the Ugandan government is itself capable of bringing key members of the LRA to justice'.[98] Whilst there is a risk that States could use the State referral mechanism to avoid investing time and resources in the investigation and prosecution of crimes when they are capable of doing so, there may, in some situations, be good reason for States to hand over situations to the ICC for investigation. The OTP's 2003 policy paper recognises a number of different situations where State inaction could be considered the most appropriate way to proceed.[99] These include situations where the territorial state is 'incapaci-

---

[92] OTP 2006 Report (n 22) 25.

[93] Schabas (n 5) 165. See also P Clark, 'Chasing Cases: The ICC and the Politics of State Referral in the Democratic Republic of the Congo and Uganda' in C Stahn and MM El Zeidy (eds), *The International Criminal Court and Complementarity: From Theory to Practice* vol II (Cambridge University Press 2011) 1201.

[94] Müller and Stegmiller (n 2) 1285.

[95] Robinson (n 2) 369.

[96] Idem.

[97] W Burke-White, 'Proactive Complementarity: The International Criminal Court and National Courts in the Rome System of International Justice' (2008) 49 Harvard International Law Journal 62; Schabas (n 5) 166.

[98] W Burke-White (n 97) 62.

[99] OTP 2003 Policy Paper (n 20) 5.

tated by mass crimes', situations where groups divided by conflict 'oppose prosecutions at each other's hands and yet agree to a prosecution by a Court perceived as neutral and impartial' and situations where 'a third State has extra-territorial jurisdiction, but all interested parties agree that the Court has developed superior evidence relating to that situation'.[100] Where such circumstances arise, the referral of a situation to the ICC by the territorial State could be seen as 'a step taken to *enhance* the delivery of effective justice', in accordance with the object and purpose of the Rome Statute and the State's obligations under international law.[101] Proceedings before the ICC could also be more appropriate where domestic prosecutions risk triggering further violence in an unstable region.[102] The trial of Charles Taylor in The Hague, rather than at the seat of the Special Court of Sierra Leone in Freetown, was, for example, justified on the basis of such concerns.[103]

The risk that a high frequency of self-referrals could lead to an overburdening of the Court is a serious one. There are, however, measures that the Court can take to ensure that its limited resources are not stretched too far. The first is to pursue a policy of actively encouraging States to undertake domestic proceedings wherever it is possible for them to do so.[104] An emphasis on domestic proceedings would not only reduce pressure on the Court's limited resources, it could also result in the strengthening of domestic criminal justice systems and domestic rule of law. The OTP has expressed its commitment to a policy of positive complementarity, which seeks to promote national proceedings in a number of different ways.[105] The risk of overburdening the Court with State referrals can also be minimised through careful use of the Prosecutor's discretion under Article 53 of the Rome Statute.[106] It was highlighted at the beginning of this chapter that following the referral of a situation by a State Party to the Rome Statute, the Prosecutor must decide whether or not to initiate an investigation. In doing so, the Prosecutor must consider whether '[t]aking into account the gravity of the crime and the interests of victims, there are nonetheless substantial reasons to believe that

---

100 Idem.

101 Informal Expert Paper (n 55) 19 (emphasis in the original).

102 Akhavan (n 45) 414–15; Akhavan (n 6) 111.

103 Akhavan (n 6) 111.

104 Müller and Stegmiller (n 2) 1284; Robinson (n 44) 93.

105 Office of the Prosecutor, Prosecutorial Strategy 2009-2012 (February 2010) paras 16, 17 <http://www.icc-cpi.int/NR/rdonlyres/66A8DCDC-3650-4514-AA62-D229D1128F65/281506/OTPProsecutorialStrategy20092013.pdf>. See also Office of the Prosecutor, Report on Prosecutorial Strategy (14 September 2006) 5 <http://www.icc-cpi.int/NR/rdonlyres/D673DD8C-D427-4547-BC69-2D363E07274B/143708/ProsecutorialStrategy20060914_English.pdf>.

106 Art 53(1) Rome Statute. See further Robinson (n 44) 93.

an investigation would not serve the interests of justice'.[107] In making this determination, the Prosecutor can control the division of labour between the Court and domestic authorities and reduce the risk that the Court will be overwhelmed by situations referred by States Parties to the Rome Statute.[108]

Overall, the early trend towards self-referrals should not be viewed as a cause for concern. Whilst self-referrals do carry some risks, these risks are not unique to the practice of self-referrals and can be mitigated by measures that can be taken within the Court itself. Furthermore, in light of the benefits associated with self-referrals, both for the ICC and for States that would otherwise struggle to hold individuals accountable for crimes committed on their territory, the practice of self-referrals can be considered a positive practice, with potential benefits both within and beyond the Court.

VI. CONCLUSION

When the ICC came into operation, it was not anticipated that the State referral mechanism would be used so readily by States to resolve situations occurring on their own territory. Since the Court began to function, States Parties to the Rome Statute have shown that they are prepared to use the ICC as a source of assistance in holding individuals accountable for crimes committed on their territory. In its early jurisprudence, the ICC has confirmed that not only is this practice accommodated by the text of the Rome Statute, it is also consistent with its object and purpose, which seeks to end impunity for international crimes and ensure that the most serious crimes of concern to the international community do not go unpunished.

The willingness of States to refer situations occurring on their own territory should be viewed in a positive light. In situations where States refer their own situations to the Court, there is a possibility that the referral will be accompanied by a good level of cooperation, allowing the Court to operate efficiently and effectively. Self-referrals could also help to foster an image of the Court that is palatable for States and encourage greater cooperation and support for its activities. Most importantly, self-referrals may result in the investigation and prosecution of international crimes in situations where individuals would otherwise have gone unpunished. There is a risk that States Parties to the Rome Statute may seek to use the self-referral mechanism as a political tool against opposition groups on their territory. However, it has been argued that the risk of politicisation of the Court is not confined to self-referrals and can be reduced by a firm commitment to independent and

---

107 Art 53(1)(c) Rome Statute.

108 Müller and Stegmiller (n 2) 1285.

impartial proceedings within the ICC. There is also a danger that the practice of self-referrals may overburden the Court with situations that could be addressed at the domestic level. In light of this risk, it is crucial that States are actively encouraged by the Court and other actors to pursue justice at the domestic level whenever it is possible and appropriate for them to do so. If the trend towards self-referrals continues, the Prosecutor may also come to play a pivotal role in preventing the Court from being overwhelmed by refusing to initiate investigations under Article 53 where it 'would not serve the interests of justice' to do so.

Propio motu *Powers of the Prosecutor to Commence Investigations*

*Fabricio Guariglia**

I. INTRODUCTION

Article 15 is a central provision of the procedural system enshrined in the Rome Statute. It is also a critical component of the model of international justice; by providing for the commencement of *proprio motu* investigations, (ie investigations triggered at the sole initiative of the Prosecutor without any other external stimulus, such as a State or Security Council referral) it reduces the risk of impunity prevailing due to a lack of political will to refer a situation to the International Criminal Court (ICC).

Yet Article 15 remained a controversial provision until the very end of the Rome Conference, with some States robustly resisting its inclusion in the Rome Statute. Those States feared an exorbitant and politicized use of the provision, leading to frivolous prosecutions. Such fears proved to be unsubstantiated. In practice, the Article 15 mechanism has been used sparingly to date by the ICC Office of the Prosecutor (OTP), with only two out of the eight situations being dealt with in this way. Nothing in the manner it has been used suggests that the safeguards contained in the provision are insufficient or that this procedural device is otherwise prone to abuse.

However, the existing practice does point at some ambiguities and inconsistencies, which will have to be clarified in subsequent rulings by the Court. The following pages will describe those problematic areas after briefly explaining the background to the current text of Article 15.

* Prosecutions Coordinator, Office of the Prosecutor, International Criminal Court. Senior Appeals Counsel, Office of the Prosecutor, International Criminal Court (2004–2013). Appeals Counsel, Office of the Prosecutor, International Criminal Tribunal for the Former Yugoslavia (1998–2003). Member of the Argentine Delegation to the ICC Preparatory Committee and the Rome Conference (1996–1998). The views expressed herein are solely the author's and should not be attributed to the Office of the Prosecutor or the International Criminal Court.

II. THE CREATION OF ARTICLE 15

A. Pre-draft Article 15 discussions

Discussions about whether the triggering mechanisms for activating the ICC's jurisdiction should include the possibility of the Prosecutor of the ICC commencing investigations on his or her own motion (*proprio motu*) only appear to have started once the International Law Commission (ILC) presented its draft Statute to States.[1] The ILC draft did not include any provision similar to Article 15 and Article 26 only allowed for investigation upon receipt of a 'complaint' by a State Party or a 'decision' by the Security Council.[2] This was viewed as inadequate by various delegations and observers, considering, *inter alia*, the poor record of States reporting other States in existing human rights mechanisms, as well as the Security Council's highly selective use of its Chapter VII powers.[3] This perception led to initiatives allowing the Prosecutor to initiate investigations

> on his or her own motion on the basis of information provided not only by Governments or the Security Council but also by other sources, including individuals (especially victims) and non-governmental organizations.[4]

Other States feared the risk of frivolous and/or politically motivated investigations and prosecutions as a result of vesting the Prosecutor with *ex officio* powers.[5] The imaginary character of a 'frivolous and politically motivated' Prosecutor was repeatedly used throughout the negotiations by those opposing the inclusion of *proprio motu* powers in the Statute.[6] The tension between these two opposing positions remained unresolved until the very end of the Rome Conference.

---

[1] 'Draft Statute for an International Criminal Court' in *Report of the International Law Commission on its forty-sixth session*, UN Doc A/49/10 (1994) *Yearbook of the International Law Commission* vol II, 20.

[2] Ibid Art 26. On previous drafts see J Crawford, 'The ILC's Draft Statute for an International Criminal Tribunal' (1994) 88 American Journal of International Law 140, 148.

[3] W Schabas, *An Introduction to the International Criminal Court* (4th edn, Oxford University Press 2011) 177.

[4] S Fernández, 'The Role of the Prosecutor' in R Lee (ed), *The International Criminal Court: The Making of the Rome Statute* (Martinus Nijhoff Publishers 1999) 177.

[5] P Kirsch & D Robinson, 'Initiation of Proceedings by the Prosecutor' in A Cassese, P Gaeta & JRWD Jones (eds), *The Rome Statute for the International Criminal Court: A Commentary* vol I (Oxford University Press 2002) 659.

[6] One of the examples provided was the alleged excesses of the investigation carried out by 'independent counsel' Ken Starr into the alleged misconduct of then US president Clinton.

B. The first drafts

The current text of Article 15 is the result of the combination of two different proposals. One of them goes back to 1996 and was the first initiative to afford *propio motu* powers to the Prosecutor.[7] The second was tabled by Argentina in August 1997, and subsequently presented as a joint Argentinean-German proposal in the last Preparatory Committee (PrepCom) session in April 1998.[8]

The first proposal established the authority of the Prosecutor to conduct *proprio motu* investigations. It was adjusted in the so-called Zutphen Draft and in the 1997 PrepCom Draft Statute.[9] Its language, with some modifications, is that contained in the first two paragraphs of current Article 15.[10] The second proposal established a procedure for the exercise of those powers, involving the Pre-Trial Chamber. The process was structured around the following principles: (1) victims, associations, regional or international organizations, etc, could submit information to the Prosecutor; (2) the Prosecutor could not start an investigation on this basis, but only a preliminary examination, which could include seeking additional information and receiving written and oral testimony at the seat of the Court; (3) if the Prosecutor considered that there was a 'reasonable basis' to proceed, then a request for authorization would have to be submitted to the Pre-Trial Chamber, together with any supporting materials. Until such time as an investigation was authorized, the prosecutor was 'frozen' in The Hague, so to speak. This proposal is what now constitutes paragraphs (2)(*in fine*) to (6) of Article 15.[11]

How was the procedure conceived? There had been one previous attempt to establish an internal control mechanism in the form of an 'Indictment Chamber'. The proposal involved an *ex parte,* in camera review of indictments issued by the Prosecutor.[12] Although the idea of judicial control was

---

[7] See 'Proceedings of the Preparatory Committee During the Period 25 March–12 April 1996, Draft Summary' UN Doc A/AC.249/CRP.9/Add.2, 4; 'Report of the Preparatory Committee on the Establishment of an International Criminal Court vol II' UN Doc. A/51/22 (1996) *United Nations General Assembly Official Records Fifty-First Session, Supplement No. 22A*, 109, para 2 *quat*.

[8] 'Proposal submitted by Argentina and Germany, Article 46, Information submitted to the Prosecutor' UN Doc A/AC.249/1998/WG.4/DP.35.

[9] Text reproduced in MC Bassiouni, *The Legislative History of the International Criminal Court: An Article-by-Article Evolution of the Statute* vol 2 (Transnational Publishers 2005) 136.

[10] W Schabas, *The International Criminal Court – A Commentary on the Rome Statute* (Oxford University Press 2010) 316.

[11] Ibid 317.

[12] 'Report of the Preparatory Committee on the Establishment of an International Criminal Court vol I' *United Nations General Assembly Official Records Fifty-First Session, Supplement No. 22* UN Doc. A/51/22, 35.

welcomed, the mechanism was viewed as insufficient.[13] First, it occurred too late in the process, when an investigation had already been carried out and indictments had been issued. Elements of this proposal, however, are present in the current text of Article 58 of the Rome Statute, which requires judicial review of any application for a warrant of arrest or summons to appear prior to any such warrant or summons being issued.

The concept behind the original Argentine draft was actually an old one: in those civil law jurisdictions which still have investigative magistrates, the latter may not start an investigation without a specific request from the public prosecutor, who will only make such a request if he or she is satisfied that the information available provides sufficient indicia of the commission of a crime under the jurisdiction of the magistrate. No judicial investigation may thus commence if the public prosecutor decides not to activate the investigative magistrate's exercise of jurisdiction (*ne procedat iudex ex officio*).[14] This mechanism, which is the product of the Enlightenment's reaction to the inquisitorial criminal procedure and the concentration of unlimited power in the inquisitor, tempers the otherwise very broad authority of the investigative magistrate and operates as a limit to the exercise of his or her authority. The drafters of the Rome Statute inverted these elements and created a system whereby it is the prosecutorial initiative to investigate *ex officio* what is subject to an internal (judicial) review. By way of anecdote, the very important words 'victims may make representations to the Pre-Trial Chamber' in Article 15(3) were written on a paper napkin in the context of informal discussions between delegates of the first rough version of the draft in the UN's Vienna Cafe, and then added to the proposal that was finally tabled.

(c) *The adoption of Article 15*

The basic parameters for the proposal for the current Article 15 were first presented orally by Argentina in the August 1997 Preparatory Committee session. As already advanced, in the last session of the Preparatory Committee (April 1998) a detailed proposal was tabled by Argentina and Germany. The proposal, which, as stated by the delegation presenting it (Argentina) sought not only to allow for *proprio motu* powers for the prosecutor, but also to provide victims with a voice in relation to the exercise of those powers, received favourable responses by some delegations, which considered that the inclusion of internal safeguards could avert the dangers of frivolous and/or politically motivated prosecutions.[15]

---

13 Fernández (n 4) 183.

14 See J Maier, *Derecho Procesal Penal I* (1996) 351–360 and 418–420.

15 Fernández (n 4) 184.

At the Rome Conference, a significant number of delegations supported the draft provision, all of the view that the safeguards included in the draft were sufficient and adequate. Initiatives to include a requirement of State consent were ultimately rejected as they would have duplicated the safeguards already included in Article 18 (preliminary rulings regarding admissibility).[16] The draft provision was finally included in the 'final package', despite continued resistance from the few delegations that remained opposed to the very notion of *proprio motu* powers.[17]

III. THE GOALS OF ARTICLE 15

The provision seeks to establish an independent avenue to trigger the jurisdiction of the Court, in order to avoid a situation of paralysis stemming from the lack of political will of any of the external actors vested with the authority to refer situations to the Court. It also provides for a system of internal review which substitutes internal judicial endorsement for external political support while simultaneously removing the possibility of unfounded or frivolous investigations. Although the use of referrals by States has certainly been more frequent than anticipated, the examples of Kenya, where the State failed to make a referral despite the commission of crimes within the jurisdiction of the Court in its territory, and Côte d'Ivoire, where arguably no State referral could have taken place due to the limitations of Articles 12(3) and 13(a) combined, show that the mechanism is indeed necessary.

Simultaneously, Article 15 provides the Prosecution with some basic tools to perform the critical analysis of the relevant situation and determine whether there is a proper basis to proceed. As will be explained below, while the Prosecutor may not move to the field and/or actively undertake investigative steps, the Prosecutor may receive information from multiple sources and even take testimony at the seat of the Court. This aims at ensuring that the Prosecution has at its disposal sufficient material enabling it to make a proper determination as to whether there is a sufficient basis to commence an investigation.

IV. ARTICLE 15 IN PRACTICE

A. *Preliminary examinations*

Once seized of a communication informing the alleged commission of crimes allegedly falling within the jurisdiction of the Court, the Prosecution

16 Kirsch & Robinson (n 5) 661.

17 Fernández (n 4) 187.

commences its preliminary inquiry. Under the existing practice, such inquiry is composed of three elements: (a) examination of jurisdiction (existence of crimes falling within the jurisdictional parameters of the Court); (b) admissibility (complementarity and gravity); and (c) the interests of justice (countervailing consideration).[18] This reflects the prescriptive language of Rule 48 of the Rules of Procedure and Evidence,[19] which mandates that the Prosecution consider the factors set out in Article 53(1)(a)-(c) for the purposes of its determination under Article 15(3) (reasonable basis to proceed with an investigation).

'Jurisdiction' has been defined by the Appeals Chamber as encompassing four different facets:

> subject-matter jurisdiction also identified by the Latin maxim jurisdiction *ratione materiae*, jurisdiction over persons, symbolized by the Latin maxim jurisdiction *ratione personae*, territorial jurisdiction – jurisdiction *ratione loci* – and lastly jurisdiction *ratione temporis*.[20]

'Admissibility', in turn, involves, at this early stage, an analysis of one or more *potential* cases within the broader context of the 'situation'. Finally, the Prosecution must assess whether, taking into account the gravity of the crime and the interests of victims, there are nonetheless substantial reasons to believe that an investigation would not serve the interests of justice.[21]

The analysis process entails four phases: Phase 1 is devoted to eliminating communications pertaining to crimes or events manifestly outside the jurisdiction of the Court. Phase 2 represents the formal commencement of preliminary examination, and entails closer scrutiny of the crimes and the jurisdictional requirements. Phase 3 focuses on admissibility and Phase 4 on interests of justice. The situation in Afghanistan is in an 'advanced' Phase 2 (focused on the crimes allegedly committed), while the situation in Colombia is in Phase 3.[22]

---

[18] See eg K Ambos and S Bock, 'Procedural Regimes' in L Reydams, J Wouters and C Ryngaert (eds), *International Prosecutors* (Oxford University Press 2012) 535–537.

[19] Rules of Procedure and Evidence, Adopted by the Assembly of States Parties (3-10 September 2002) OR ICC-ASP/1/3.

[20] *Prosecutor v Lubanga* (Judgment on the Appeal of Mr. Thomas Laubanga Dyilo against the Decision on the Defence Challenge to the Jurisdiction of the Court pursuant to article 19(2) of the Statute of 3 October 2006) ICC–01/04–01/06-772 (14 December 2006) para 22.

[21] For a description of the manner in which the Prosecution approaches this particular element, see OTP, 'The Interests of Justice' (September 2007) <http://www.icc-cpi.int/NR/rdonlyres/772C95C9-F54D-4321-BF09-73422BB23528/143640/ICCOTPInterestsOfJustice.pdf>.

[22] See OTP, 'Report on Preliminary Examination Activities 2012' (November 2012) <http://www.icc-cpi.int/NR/rdonlyres/C433C462-7C4E-4358-8A72-8D99FD00E8CD/285209/OTP2012ReportonPreliminaryExaminations22Nov2012.pdf>.

1. Permissible activities at the examination stage:

As already advanced, Article 15(2) vests the Prosecution with a limited authority to gather and analyse information with a view to making a proper determination as to whether there is a reasonable basis to proceed. In particular, the Prosecution may:

- Perform analysis: the Prosecution can map the situation, detect the groups engaged in criminal activity, analyse their structure, identify the worst episodes of victimization, etc;
- Receive information and material and proactively request that information be shared with the OTP;
- Receive testimony at the seat of the Court under Rule 47 (rules for statement-taking apply); if the Prosecution considers that there is a serious risk of the evidence becoming subsequently unavailable, measures similar to those envisioned by Article 56 of the Rome Statute may be used to secure the testimony (Rule 47(2));
- Other activities? The Rome Statute and the Rules of Procedure and Evidence are silent on other types of preparatory activities that the Prosecution may need to engage in before launching an investigation. These include, *inter alia*, performing security assessments, entering into cooperation agreements, identifying possible sources of cooperation, issuing preventative statements, etc. As long as they fall short of constituting investigative steps performed outside the framework of Articles 15 and 53, these activities are compatible with the Rome Statute and the role and authority of the Prosecutor.

2. Presentation of an Article 15 request:

Rule 50 and Regulation 49 of the Regulations of the Court[23] establish the legal requirements for the submission of a request by the Prosecution under Article 15. The request must be made in writing. The Prosecution has a duty to inform victims known to it, unless it considers that so doing 'would pose a danger to the integrity of the investigation or the life or well-being of victims and witnesses' (Rule 50(1)). The Prosecution may also decide to issue a public notice.

The Pre-Trial Chamber may request additional information (Rule 50(4)). In practice, Chambers have availed themselves of this possibility and have requested supplementary submissions and information. Under Regulation 49, the request for authorization must include a reference to the crimes

---

[23] Regulations of the Court, Adopted by the Judges of the Court (26 May 2004) ICC-BD/01-01-04.

allegedly committed and a 'statement of facts' indicating places of alleged commission, time, persons and/or groups involved, as well as a declaration by the Prosecutor that the relevant crimes fall within the jurisdiction of the Court (Regulation 49(1)).

3. *The Pre-Trial Chamber's authorization:*

The process leading to a Pre-Trial Chamber's authorization under Article 15 involves different issues. First, the *scope* of the review: under Rule 48, the Prosecutor must consider for the purposes of any Article 15 determination the same factors as in Article 53(1)(a)-(c), namely: whether there is a reasonable basis to believe a crime within the jurisdiction of the Court has occurred (which involves the lowest evidentiary standard in the Rome Statute and requires an initial assessment of jurisdiction); whether the case appears to be admissible (as already explained, a determination to be made in relation to *potential* cases); and whether it is in the interests of justice to commence an investigation. The Pre-Trial Chamber's analysis will include scrutiny of the manner in which these factors have been assessed by the Prosecution.

As to the Chamber's analysis of supporting information, it must be noted that this is undoubtedly an important tool for the Chamber to verify whether the Prosecution's determination under Article 15 is sound and sufficiently substantiated. However, the Pre-Trial Chamber's role at this embryonic stage of the Court's activities in the relevant situation should not be construed as a fact-finding one. On the contrary, the Chamber's scrutiny is limited to verifying that there is a proper foundation for the Prosecution's request and not to make authoritative findings on the situation and the alleged crimes committed therein.[24]

An interesting question that has arisen out of the practice of the Court is whether the Pre-Trial Chamber is limited by the facts described in the application. The issue arose in the context of the Cote d'Ivoire situation, where a discussion took place about the appropriateness of a Pre-Trial Chamber making autonomous findings pertaining to incidents and crimes not included in the Prosecution's request. In the decision, a majority of the judges effectively departed from the Prosecution's request and made findings in relation to what it called 'underlying acts not presented by the Prosecutor'.[25] Judge Fernández, dissenting, stressed that the Pre-Trial Chamber is not an investigative chamber, and should not make independent inquiries on the facts based on the material presented by the Prosecution; rather, the Chamber's

---

[24] See eg Schabas (n 3) 180.

[25] *Situation in Côte d'Ivoire* (Decision pursuant to article 15 of the Rome Statute on the Authorisation of an Investigation into the Situation in the Republic of Côte d'Ivoire) ICC-02/11-14-Corr (15 November 2011) paras 86, 116, 148, 165, inter alia.

role is limited to verifying the accuracy of the factual and legal underpinnings of the request made.[26] In relation to this, it is important to note that the Prosecution is expected to include in its request those incidents and crimes which, in its professional assessment, are duly supported by the information and evidence available to him or her. One would expect that, absent exceptional circumstances, the Chamber would defer to that professional assessment as far as the selection of incidents and crimes is concerned. In addition, as long as it stays within the parameters of the situation, the Prosecution is free to depart from the incidents that were offered as illustrative examples of the overall victimization, which means that it can both add incidents that were not included in the original request and discard for the purposes of an in-depth investigation and/or prosecution incidents that were originally included.

Finally, the *temporal scope* of the authorization also requires some discussion. In the Kenya situation, the Pre-Trial Chamber imposed a cut-off date (26 November 2009), which was the date of the Prosecution's Article 15 request.[27] The Chamber considered that it could not leave the situation open-ended, and accordingly an outer temporal limit was needed. This practice, if adopted as a general rule, would create a complicated problem in the case of on-going crimes clearly connected to the situation. It has accordingly been argued that the focus should not be on establishing an end-date, but on requiring that any subsequent investigations be ***materially related*** to the focus of the authorized situation.[28] In contrast, in the Côte d'Ivoire situation, Pre-Trial Chamber III did not impose a cut-off date but required that any subsequent investigation be limited to 'continuing crimes'. This would mean that, at a minimum, subsequent investigations would be possible only insofar as the contextual elements remained the same.[29] For instance, if the underlying new crimes constituted crimes against humanity, a fresh investigation would only be authorized if the new crimes formed part of the same 'widespread or systematic attack against the civilian population'.[30]

Judge Fernández, dissenting, objected to the adoption of the 'continuing crimes' criterion, noting that this is a term of art, related to a narrow category

---

[26] Separate and partially dissenting opinion of Judge Fernández de Gurmendi, *Situation in Côte d'Ivoire* (Decision pursuant to article 15 of the Rome Statute on the Authorisation of an Investigation into the Situation in the Republic of Côte d'Ivoire) ICC-02/11-15-Corr (3 October 2011) paras 34–42.

[27] *Situation in the Republic of Kenya* (Decision Pursuant to Article 15 of the Rome Statute on the Authorization of an Investigation into the Situation in the Republic of Kenya) ICC-01/09-19-Corr (31 March 2010) para 207.

[28] See R Rastan, 'The Jurisdictional Scope of Situations before the International Criminal Court' (2012) 23 Criminal Law Forum 20–23.

[29] *Situation in Côte d'Ivoire* (n 25) paras 178–179.

[30] Rome Statute of the International Criminal Court (adopted 17 July 1998, entered into force 1 July 2002) 2187 UNTS 90, Art 7(1).

of crimes which continue to be committed over a period of time, such as enforced disappearance of persons or enslavement, among others. Therefore, the majority's approach could exclude the investigation of war crimes and crimes against humanity which are linked to the same attack or same armed conflict but do not fall within the legal category of 'continuing crimes'. In her view, the relevant criterion was not the nature of the crime(s) in question, but whether they are linked to the same situation.[31] This reasoning is persuasive, but only to the extent that the intention of the majority was to effectively restrict the scope of investigations authorized by the Pre-Trial Chamber pursuant to Article 15 to a small circle of crimes. It is possible however to interpret the majority's reference to 'continuing crimes' in a non-technical way, and include in its scope those crimes which fit into the same contextual elements underpinning the original authorization (be it an attack against the civilian population or an armed conflict, or both), regardless of the specific nature of the underlying acts and whether they would qualify as 'continuing crimes' in a technical sense.

V. CONCLUSIONS

Article 15 was born as an effort to bridge the gap between positions that looked irreconcilable, but also as an attempt to provide the Prosecution, and the Court as a whole, with a practical device capable of activating the Court's jurisdiction in situations of State or Security Council inaction. As in the case of many procedural devices included in the Rome Statute, it was left to the Court to define the modalities and scope of the mechanism articulated in the provision. The Court's initial jurisprudence is doing that, by supplementing the requirements set forth in the Rules of Procedure and Evidence and the Regulations of the Court and providing some clarity to the grey areas of the provision. However, some uncertainty and ambiguity remain and it will be the task of the Court to deal with them in the coming situations and cases.

---

[31] *Situation in Côte d'Ivoire* (n 25) paras 68–73.

The Role of the Security Council in Starting and Stopping Cases at the International Criminal Court: Problems of Principle and Practice

*Amal Alamuddin**

I. INTRODUCTION

The Security Council (the Council) is the body that kick-started international criminal justice in the 1990s by creating courts to try those suspected of international crimes in the former Yugoslavia and Rwanda. After an almost-50-year hiatus that followed the Nuremberg trials of World War II, the resolution that created the Yugoslavia court (ICTY) in 1993[1] was a new and innovative use of the Council's powers to restore international peace and security under the UN Charter. Since then, the Security Council has established another international criminal tribunal for the conflict in Rwanda (ICTR),[2] a hybrid Court for Lebanon and internationally-assisted Courts in Kosovo and East Timor.[3]

The International Criminal Court (ICC) is different. When it opened its doors in 2002, it became the world's first *permanent* international criminal court, covering crimes worldwide, not just in a particular country. It was created as the result of a treaty – the Rome Statute – not a Council resolution, meaning the Court would only have jurisdiction over States that had ratified the Rome Statute. It is not part of the United Nations, but there is still an intrinsic link to the Council. Under Article 13 of the ICC's Statute, the Council can refer a 'situation' in a State to the Court, even if that State

* Barrister at Doughty Street Chambers specializing in international law and human rights. Ms Alamuddin appears in English and international courts (including the International Criminal Court and the International Court of Justice) and advises individuals and governments.

1 UNSC Res 827 (25 May 1993) UN Doc S/RES/827.

2 UNSC Res 955 (8 November 1994) UN Doc S/RES/955.

3 UNSC Res 1757 (30 May 2007) UN Doc S/RES/1757; UNSC Res 1244 (10 June 1999) UN Doc S/RES/1244; UNSC Res 1272 (25 October 1999) UN Doc S/RES/1272 . Courts for Cambodia and Sierra Leone were established by treaty between the State involved and the UN.

has not ratified the Rome Statute. This power to trigger the Court's jurisdiction is controversial; it was hotly debated in Rome when the Statute was drafted, and now – as the Court reaches its ten-year anniversary – it remains divisive.[4]

The Council has used its referral power to send the Darfur and Libya situations to the Court, allowing the ICC judges to issue arrest warrants against Presidents Bashir and Gaddafi when the judges would otherwise have been unable to act.[5] The Council also has the power under Article 16 of the Court's Statute to 'defer' a case, which means that it can pause an ongoing investigation or prosecution by the ICC for a renewable one-year period, when, in its view, the interests of peace and security so require. Article 16 has so far not been used to pause an imminent or ongoing case, but it has been *misused* in certain resolutions to shield peacekeepers from non-States Parties from prosecution.[6]

The ability of the Security Council to trigger or stunt the Court's work is the basis for two of the most serious criticisms leveled against the ICC: first, that justice is dispensed in a *political* rather than independent manner; and second that, as a result, the judicial process is carried out *selectively*, and therefore unfairly. When the Security Council unanimously referred the situation in Libya to the Court, approximately 300 people had been killed. But with over 80,000[7] already killed in Syria, and no referral, can the system be credible?

This chapter will examine the Security Council's power to start (refer) and stop (defer) proceedings at the ICC, and its practice over the Court's ten-year lifespan. It argues that while there are checks and balances in the Rome Statute to ensure the Court's independence and neutrality, these must be respected by the Council, and strongly defended by the ICC's Prosecutor and judges in practice, if the Court's integrity is to be maintained. It concludes by putting forward recommendations to strengthen the Court's independence and ensure greater consistency of Council action.

II. THE LAW

The legal framework governing the relationship between the Security

---

[4] Cf E Wilmshurst, 'Jurisdiction of the Court' in RS Lee (ed), *The International Criminal Court – The Making of the Rome Statute: Issues, Negotiations, Results* (Kluwer Law International 1999) 127.

[5] UNSC Res 1593 (31 March 2005) UN Doc S/RES/1593; UNSC Res 1970 (26 February 2011) UN Doc S/RES/1970.

[6] See section IV. B.

[7] UN estimate released in May 2013. UN News Centre, 'UN announces largest ever humanitarian appeal for conflict-torn Syria' (7 June 2013) <http://www.un.org/apps/news/story.asp?NewsID=45112&Cr=syria&Cr1=#.UbXv3-u6XyE>.

Council and the Court is set out in Articles 13, 16 and 53 of the Rome Statute.[8]

Under Article 13, the ICC's power to investigate crimes within its jurisdiction can be triggered in three ways. First, Article 13(a) (read together with Article 12(2)) suggests that a State Party can itself refer a situation to the Court when genocide, crimes against humanity or war crimes[9] have allegedly been committed on its territory or by its nationals. This has happened in four of the eight situations currently before the Court: Uganda, the Democratic Republic of Congo, the Central African Republic and Mali. In two other situations, Kenya and Ivory Coast, a second trigger method was used; the Prosecutor acted on his own initiative – '*proprio motu*' – to investigate crimes within the Court's mandate. The third route envisaged under Article 13 is referral by the Security Council, and this is how the investigations in Darfur and more recently Libya were triggered. Regardless of how an investigation was triggered,[10] the Security Council has the power under Article 16 to require that 'no investigation or prosecution may be commenced or proceeded with' for a renewable one-year period.

The drafting of the language that ultimately became Articles 13 and 16 was one of the most controversial issues at the Rome Conference at which State representatives drafted the Rome Statute. The debate around Article 13 centered on the issue of *what* would be referred: a specific prosecution or a broader 'situation' for the Court to work on? Some States argued that to reduce Council interference with the Court's independent functioning, the power of referral had to be broadly defined to ensure that the Council was not dictating to the Court who should be prosecuted or for what crimes. It had been proposed that the Council could refer a 'case' or a 'crime' to the Court, but the final language on referral allows the Council to send a 'situation' to the Court – rather than the prosecution of a specific individual or persons associated with one political group or side of a conflict.[11] As the summary of the negotiations made clear:

---

8 Two other provisions mention the Security Council but these relate to funding (Art 115) and State cooperation (Art 87).

9 Art 5 Rome Statute. The Court's jurisdiction over the crime of aggression is not yet effective.

10 Some commentators argue that deferral is not appropriate when the case relates to a situation that was referred to the Court by the Security Council. However, the text of Art 16 contains no such limitation. Cf, eg, D Scheffer, 'The Security Council's Struggle over Darfur and International Justice' (*JURIST* 20 August 2008) <http://jurist.law.pitt.edu/forumy/2008/08/security-councils-struggle-over-darfur.php> and R Cryer, 'The Security Council, Article 16 and Darfur' (Oxford Transitional Justice Working Paper Series 29 October 2008) <http://www.csls.ox.ac.uk/documents/CryerFi.pdf>.

11 SA Williams & WA Schabas, 'Article 13' in O Triffterer (ed), *Commentary on the Rome Statute of the International Criminal Court: Observer's Notes, Article by Article* (2nd edn Hart and Nomos Publishing 2008) 568.

> The Council, it was observed, would merely refer a general matter or situation to the court, as opposed to bringing a case against a specific individual – which would preserve the independence and autonomy of the court in the exercise of its investigative, prosecutorial and judicial functions.[12]

Delegates ultimately even rejected the possibility that the Council could refer a 'matter' on the basis that this was more specific than a 'situation' and could therefore risk limiting the Court's independence.[13] As a result, the final text of Article 13 ultimately provided that the Court may exercise its jurisdiction if a

> *situation* in which one or more ... crimes [within its jurisdiction] appears to have been committed is referred to the Prosecutor by the Security Council acting under Chapter VII of the Charter of the United Nations.[14]

Article 13 must be read with Article 53, which provides a basis for the Prosecutor to refuse to initiate a prosecution, even where a situation has been referred by the Security Council. Article 53(1) sets out grounds upon which the Prosecutor may decline to conduct an *investigation*. Relevant factors that the Prosecutor 'shall consider' include; (a) whether there is a 'reasonable basis' to believe that a crime within the jurisdiction of the Rome Statute has been committed; (b) whether the case is 'admissible' based on the criteria set out in Article 17;[15] and (c) whether a prosecution is 'in the interests of justice'. This would appear to include scenarios where a situation has been referred by the Security Council. The next subparagraph – Article 53(2) – sets out similar grounds on which the Prosecutor can refuse to initiate a *pros-*

---

[12] UNGA, 'Report of the Ad Hoc Committee on the Establishment of an International Criminal Court' UNGAOR 51th Session Supp No UN Doc. A/50/22 (1995), para 120.

[13] Williams & Schabas, 'Article 13' (n 11) 568.

[14] Art 13(b) Rome Statute (emphasis added).

[15] The criteria in Art 17 are whether there are adequate judicial proceedings at the national level and whether the alleged crimes are sufficiently grave. Note however that the requirement in Art 18 to notify States which may have jurisdiction over the offences in question – presumably for purposes of a complementarity analysis – is conspicuously not applicable to Security Council referrals. See Rome Statute Art 18(1): 'When a situation has been referred to the Court pursuant to *article 13 (a)* and the Prosecutor has determined that there would be a reasonable basis to commence an investigation, or the Prosecutor initiates an investigation pursuant to *articles 13 (c)* and 15, the Prosecutor shall notify all States Parties and those States which, taking into account the information available, would normally exercise jurisdiction over the crimes concerned.' (Emphases added.) In practice, complementarity still applies for UN Security Council referrals, as is clear in the Prosecutor's reports and the Chambers' decisions on Darfur and Libya. See, eg, *Situation in Darfur, Sudan* (Decision on Application under Rule 103) ICC-02/05-185 Pre-Trial Chamber I (4 February 2009) para 31.

ecution, and here *explicitly* includes the scenario where there has been an investigation following a Security Council referral. Under Article 53(2), if the Prosecutor decides not to prosecute following a Council referral, she 'shall inform ... the Security Council ... of ... her conclusion and the reasons for the conclusion'. The next sub-paragraph allows the Council to request a review of this decision by the Pre-Trial Chamber. So the Court – either through the Prosecutor or the Pre-Trial Chamber[16] – has the final word.

The debate at the Rome Conference on the Council's *deferral* power also focused on the issue of judicial independence. At one end of the spectrum, delegates argued that the Court should be totally independent of the Council and that the Council should therefore not have any power to interfere with an ongoing process. This would have meant no Article 16 deferral power. Others argued that, given the role of the Security Council as the principal guardian of international peace and security,[17] all the Court's work should be subject to Security Council approval if the Council were taking action in relation to a 'situation' in the same State.[18] This was also the view put forward by the International Law Commission (ILC) in their draft Statute of 1994, which provided that

> [n]o prosecution may be commenced under this Statute arising from a situation which is being dealt with by the Security Council as a threat to or breach of the peace or an act of aggression under Chapter VII of the Charter, unless the Security Council otherwise decides.[19]

Given the breadth of the Council's activities, the effect of this could easily have been to require Security Council authorization – blockable by a single veto – for an investigation to proceed in almost every situation likely to be covered by the Court.[20]

The deadlock was eventually broken by the 'Singapore Compromise', a text put forward by Singapore which proposed that '[n]o investigation or prosecution may be commenced or proceeded with under this Statute where the Security Council has[,] acting under Chapter VII of the Charter of the United Nations, given a direction to that effect'.[21] This language was ultimately

---

16 See also Art 53(3)(b) Rome Statute.

17 See United Nations Charter (adopted 26 June 1945, entered into force 24 October 1945) 1 UNTS XVI, Art 24.

18 For an overview of discussions see L Yee, 'The International Criminal Court and the Security Council: Articles 13(b) and 16' in Lee (n 4) 146–152.

19 ILC, 'Draft Statute for an International Criminal Court' in *Report of the International Law Commission on its fourty-sixth session*, UN Doc A/49/10 (1994) Yearbook of the International Law Commission vol II, Art 23(3).

20 See ILA, 'International Criminal Court' (Report: Berlin Conference 2004) 1–2.

21 M Bergsmo & J Pejić, 'Article 16: Deferral of Investigation or Prosecution' in Triffterer

tweaked to clarify that the Council could stop an investigation or prosecution for a one-year renewable period.

The trend in the negotiations was therefore to limit Council interference in the Court's work. Under Articles 13 and 53, the Council can expand the Court's jurisdiction but not dictate what it does with it. And the final text of Article 16 turns the ILC Draft on its head, so that instead of needing the Council's blessing to proceed with a case, ICC proceedings continue unless the Council formally acts to stop them. Nine votes would be required to have a deferral resolution passed, and a single veto prevents the Council's *blocking power* rather than preventing a green light to Court action.[22] As a result, the Council's ability to stop the Court remains, but is substantially reduced from what was initially proposed.

In addition to these provisions in the Rome Statute, the Court entered into a Treaty with the UN in 2004, which further clarifies the respective roles of the two bodies. This 'Relationship Agreement' recognizes in Article 2(1) that the ICC is a 'permanent judicial institution which … has international legal personality'.[23] Article 2(3) declares the principle that the 'United Nations and the Court respect each other's status and mandate';[24] one dealing with peace and security and the other with justice.

III. THE PROBLEM OF PRINCIPLE

All prosecutors – whether domestic or international – have to make choices about who to charge and what crimes to pursue. They may prioritize the most serious crimes, or case files that contain the most promising evidence.[25] When it comes to crimes committed in States that are parties to the Rome Statute, the Prosecutor exercises his or her prosecutorial discretion to investigate cases in line with objective criteria, as laid down in the Rome Statute: the gravity of the crimes, the prospects for justice at the national level and

(n 11) 375. Some delegations stated during the negotiations that the General Assembly should have referral power so that no veto would be possible. However this was ultimately rejected as *ultra vires* on the basis that the General Assembly is not the body that is responsible for dealing with situations under Chapter VII of the UN Charter.

22 See Art 27(3) UN Charter.

23 ICC, 'Negotiated Relationship Agreement between the International Criminal Court and the United Nations' (adopted on 4 October 2004, entered into force 22 July 2004) <http://www.icc-cpi.int/NR/rdonlyres/916FC6A2-7846-4177-A5EA-5AA9B6D1E96C/0/ICCASP3Res1_English.pdf>.

24 Idem.

25 For example; in the US some district attorneys' offices assign seasoned prosecutors to a specialized screening unit, which reviews and investigates incoming cases and decides whether the case is serious enough and whether the evidence is strong enough to justify the charges.

more broadly the 'interests of justice'.[26] But in cases where the Court would not otherwise have jurisdiction, it is the Security Council that initially decides[27] whether or not the Court can investigate, by choosing whether to refer the situation in that country. And it can decide to stop an investigation or prosecution that is planned or underway.[28]

The problem that arises from this legal framework is one of principle; judicial legitimacy depends on independence from government (or executive) interference.[29] But at the international level the judicial and executive organs are connected and have defined roles that may conflict; hence the age-old debate about peace versus justice.

The problem with allowing the Council to have a role in triggering proceedings is the risk of politicized selectivity. Decisions on whether to refer and defer – in other words start or stop – cases may depend on the vagaries of politics and States' interests, particularly those that have a veto power. Support for a particular regime based on political or trade ties could become the defining factor in whether an investigation can be triggered or is allowed to proceed, instead of the gravity or types of crimes committed.[30] This can explain why the Council has referred Libya and Sudan to the Court, but ignored calls to refer the situations in Sri Lanka and Gaza, despite UN findings that international crimes have been committed there.[31] And while the United States, Russia and China can comfortably refer Libya to the Court, they have a veto-power that guarantees that they themselves – as non-States Parties to the Rome Statute – will not face a similar fate. This problem of selectivity has also been raised in relation to the system of international criminal justice as a whole; why did the Council set up a court to try crimes in Rwanda, but not Zimbabwe? Why Yugoslavia, but not Iraq? Why did the Council vote to establish a court for a terror attack that killed former Prime Minister Hariri in Lebanon in 2005, but not the crimes committed in the same country during the Israeli bombing of 2006, or next door in Syria?

---

[26] See Art 17 and Art 53 Rome Statute. See OTP, 'Policy Paper on the Interests of Justice' (2007) ICC-OTP-2007, 1, 9; OTP, 'Draft Policy Paper on Preliminary Examinations' (4 October 2010) paras 50, 74.

[27] Art 13 Rome Statute. But see also Art 53 (see discussion in section II).

[28] Art 16 Rome Statute (see discussion in section II).

[29] See T Bingham, *The Rule of Law* (Penguin Books 2011) 25, 91–93.

[30] The debates about the Council's role in triggering the court's jurisdiction over the crime of aggression, potentially beginning in 2017, raise similar concerns.

[31] UNSG, 'Report by the secretary-general's panel of experts on accountability in Sri Lanka' (31 March 2011) <http://www.un.org/News/dh/infocus/Sri_Lanka/POE_Report_Full.pdf>; 'Report by the Report of the United Nations Fact-Finding Mission on the Gaza Conflict (25 September 2009) <http://www2.ohchr.org/english/bodies/hrcouncil/docs/12session/A-HRC-12-48.pdf>.

Critics of the referral system point out that all States should be equal before the law and the Court should not be limited to prosecuting persons in weak States that have no friends on the Council. Indeed, one of the fundamental ingredients of the rule of law is that the law should apply equally to all, except to the extent that objective differences justify differentiation.[32] But the jurisdiction of the ICC is complementary to that of national systems and is not universal so long as some States refuse to ratify the Rome Statute. Referral action by the Council therefore adds to the limited jurisdiction of the Court and allows it to act where it would otherwise be impotent.[33] The true test of the Court's independence or fairness should therefore be applied *once* the Court has the power to act: to the prosecutorial discretion exercised between and within situations that the Prosecutor has the power to investigate; to the investigation process; to the decision taken on whether to charge a particular suspect; and to the conduct of any ensuing trial. As long as the Court exercises its discretion – within and between all situations within its reach – responsibly, and conducts any proceedings that are initiated fairly, this should be sufficient to ensure its legitimacy.[34]

However this defence to alleged selectivity within the ICC system only holds so long as the Council and the Court stick to the respective roles they are given in the Rome Statute: Article 13 limits the Council's role to referring 'situations', *not* to deciding which particular individuals are to be charged or what specific incidents or crimes are pursued. Article 53 even allows the Court to say 'no' to the Council and refuse to conduct a prosecution even after a referral has been made on the objective grounds set out in that provision.

The Court's power to reject a referral was highlighted by the Office of the Prosecutor in the first debate on the relationship between the Council and the Court at the UN Security Council in October 2012. The representative of the Office stated that:

> the Council may unilaterally trigger, but cannot impose acceptance of jurisdiction by the ICC ... Once the Security Council decides to refer a

---

[32] Bingham (n 29) 55 *et seq*.

[33] Cf *Prosecutor v Ayyash et al* (Decision on the defence challenges to the jurisdiction and legality of the tribunal) STL-11-01/PT/TC Trial Chamber (27 July 2012) paras 86–87 ('these tribunals ... are intended to replace or supplement national systems but only in tightly defined circumstances. The ICTY, the ICTR and the SCSL, for example, have jurisdiction confined to specified circumstance-geographic, temporal or related to the triable crimes and classes of perpetrators ... "selectivity" is part of the history of international criminal jurisdictions, and an inevitable consequence of establishing an international criminal court or tribunal. ... [but the] Tribunal's restrictive jurisdiction does not violate any fundamental human right to a fair trial').

[34] For the meaning of discretion in judicial decision-making and constrains upon it see, in general, Bingham (n 29) 48–54.

situation to the Prosecutor, the judicial process has been triggered and the matter is fully in the hands of the Prosecutor and the Judges.[35]

It is more difficult to counter concerns about politicization and selectivity when it comes to deferral. Article 16 is a straightforward interference with the judicial process, allowing the Council to prevent a specific investigation or prosecution – as opposed to a broader 'situation'. It is supposed to allow the requirements of peace to prevail over justice – when justice would not contribute to peace and only for a limited time. This is not the approach that would be taken by the Prosecutor, whose stated policy is that the interests of peace do not justify delaying or abandoning a prosecution.[36] Article 16 therefore allows the Council, as the guardian of international peace, to stop the judicial process in its tracks when and while it is in the Council's view necessary to do so.

This power to interfere and stop proceedings affects any case before the Court – not just one that was initially referred by the Council.[37] It is a sweeping power that could potentially bring the entire machinery of the Court to a standstill. Still, pragmatists would say, Article 16 can serve an important purpose: to delay justice where its immediate imposition threatens peace. It is not difficult to imagine circumstances where insistence on immediate accountability in a situation where a leader is fighting to the death could mean trading redress for those who have been killed against the protection of those who are still alive. As several States highlighted at the UN Security Council in October 2012, the timing of the ICC's involvement in a situation 'needs to be very carefully judged' especially where a conflict is ongoing.[38]

---

[35] P Mochochoko, 'Open Debate of the United Nations Security Council on "Peace and Justice, with a special focus on the role of the International Criminal Court"' (Address on behalf of the Prosecutor, 17 October 2012) 3 <http://www.iccnow.org/documents/Phakiso_Mochochoko_at_UNSC_17102012__2_.pdf>.

[36] In an OTP policy paper the Prosecutor has made clear that 'the interests of justice do not cover the interests of peace', the reasoning being that there is a difference between the concepts of the interests of justice and the interests of peace and that the latter falls within the mandate of institutions other than the Office of the Prosecutor. See OTP Policy Paper on Preliminary Examinations (n 26), para 6. Of course, the new Prosecutor Fatou Bensouda may take a different view.

[37] Cf above n 10.

[38] J Mclay, 'United Nations Security Council- Peace and justice, with a special focus on the role of the International Criminal Court' (New Zealand statement to SC, 17 October 2012) <http://www.mfat.govt.nz/Media-and-publications/Media/MFAT-speeches/2012/0-17b-Oct-2012.php>. See also Statement by Russia that '[w]hile it is important that the Court independently conduct its functions in the criminal-legal sphere, its activities must be carried out in the light of common efforts to settle crisis situations'. See UNSC, 'The promotion and strengthening of the rule of law in the maintenance of international peace and security' (Transcript of morning session of 6849th meeting, 17 October 2012) UN Doc S/PV.6849, 19–20.

The Council, it is argued, should consider whether a role for the Court would be an 'incentive or a disincentive' for prolonging violence in a particular situation, and the Council can also consider the likelihood of actually bringing indictees to trial.[39] Some States, such as China, have gone further and argued that 'justice *cannot be pursued* at the expense of peaceful processes, nor should it impede the process of national reconciliation'.[40] And, the argument goes, it is the Council that is best-placed and uniquely authorized to make these determinations in the international system.

This reasoning also needs to take account of the fact that according to UN principles,[41] and the views of many States and organizations, both peace and justice are UN values. Justice can, at most, be delayed but not forgotten in the name of peace – indeed a sustainable peace is not possible without it.[42] This is also recognized in the Rome Statute's Preamble, which notes that the crimes within the jurisdiction of the Court are 'grave crimes [that] threaten the peace, security and well-being of the world.' The premise of Article 13 is also that the referral of a situation to the Court is a measure to restore international peace.[43] Article 16 should therefore be seen as an exceptional and temporary measure.

The best defence of Article 16 from the perspective of the independence of the Court is therefore a pragmatic one: that it is narrow, and should be exercised only when – and only for as long as – the circumstances require the Council to act to save lives. The Council's deferral power is after all only legally justified when the stopping of a particular case is a measure that restores international peace and security under Chapter VII of the UN Charter – not to achieve any other aim.[44] The drafting of Article 16 also ensures that it would be invoked only where there is a majority vote in the Council, and no veto. Finally, the Council's power is limited to 'pausing' an investigation for one year at a time, though there is no provision for maximum number of renewals in Article 16. Ultimately, the more exceptional the use of Article 16 is in practice, and the more temporary its application, the easier it is to defend in principle.

---

[39] Mclay (n 38).

[40] Transcript of Morning Session (n 38) 12.

[41] UN, 'United Nations Approach to Transitional Justice' (Guidance Note of the Secretary-General, March 2010).

[42] UNGA, 'Nuremberg Declaration on Peace and Justice' (19 June 2008) UN Doc A/62/885, 2: 'Peace and justice, if properly pursued, promote and sustain one another. The question can never be whether to pursue justice, but rather when and how'.

[43] Arts 39-41 UN Charter.

[44] This is the prerequisite to the use of Chapter VII powers by the Council – at least in theory – under Art 39 of the UN Charter. But see section IV.

IV. THE PRACTICE

A. The practice on starting an investigation: the Security Council's power to refer a situation to the Court

In the ten years since the Court opened its doors, it has dealt with eight situations, two of which have been referred to it by the Council: Darfur and Libya. The Darfur situation was referred to the Court in Resolution 1593 passed in 2005, with the US abstaining. Then in 2011, the Council unanimously passed Resolution 1970 referring the situation in Libya to the ICC.[45]

Despite the role of the Council – a political organ – in triggering the Court's jurisdiction, the Statute provided a guarantee that the Court's independence would be preserved through two mechanisms. First, it could only refer a 'situation', not a specific case against an individual suspect or group. Second, under Article 53, the Prosecutor (or Pre-Trial Chamber) could decide *not* to pursue a prosecution in a referred situation.[46]

Unfortunately these guarantees have not been fully respected in practice. On a plain reading of Article 13, one would expect that a situation would blandly refer to a State that is not Party to the Rome Statute, and nothing more. This would bring the State within the jurisdiction of the Court as if it had ratified the Rome Statute. A referral resolution would then read: 'The Council refers the situation in [country X] to the ICC'. It might then add the time and place 'in which one or more [international] crimes appears to have been committed' as per the wording of Article 13:[47] for instance, 'the situation in [country X] since 1 July 2002' or 'the situation in Eastern [country X] since 2004'. In practice, however, the Council has sought, through referrals, to limit the Court's power to investigate not only on the basis of *geography* and *time* but – more worryingly – on the basis of *potential suspects' nationality*.

1. Narrowing a 'situation' based on time and place

A geographical limitation was used in Resolution 1593. Instead of referring 'Sudan', the Council referred 'Darfur', the territory in the west of the country. Then in Resolution 1970, the Council referred a situation that was limited in time; although it covered all of Libya and was open-ended as to its end-date, the Council '[d]ecide[d] to refer the situation in the Libyan Arab Jamahiriya *since 15 February 2011* to the Prosecutor of the International Criminal Court'.[48] (The resolution on Darfur allowed the Prosecutor to investigate as far back as the Rome Statute allows – the date of its entry into

---

[45] See above n 5.

[46] See section II.

[47] Art 13 Rome Statute.

[48] UNSC Res 1970 (26 February 2011) UN Doc S/RES/1970, 2 (emphasis added).

force on 1 July 2002.) The Libya time-restriction might be explained as an attempt to shield western countries from investigation into acts of the Gaddafi regime that they may have been considered criminally complicit in.[49] The less cynical view is that the chosen start-date corresponds to the beginning of protest-related violence during Libya's 'Arab Spring'.[50]

In principle, a referral that defines the temporal or geographic parameters of a situation – if neutrally limited to correspond to where and when international crimes appear to have been committed – would comply with the wording of Article 13 and not be problematic. After all, the Rome Statute already restricts the Court's jurisdiction in any case to post-2002; to the territory of States that have ratified[51] the Statute or territories where State Party nationals commit crimes, and to only the most serious international crimes. Similarly, other international tribunals created by the Council have also held – albeit in different contexts – that it was legitimate for the Council to focus on a particular time and place in defining a court's jurisdiction. [52]

2. *Narrowing a situation based on the nationality of the suspect*

Unlike objectively-defined time and date restrictions, dictating to a prosecutor which individuals or parties should be investigated – or excluding certain individuals or parties from her reach – directly interferes with her ability to act as an independent judicial organ and follow the evidence wherever it leads. It would also amount to referring a specific *case* to the Court – a possibility the drafters specifically sought to exclude.[53]

---

[49] Cf: '[I]t is important to remember just how cozy Western leaders have been with Gaddafi in recent years. With this jurisdictional limitation, relations between the regime in Libya and the international community cannot be investigated.' (M Kersten, 'Libya Referred to the ICC – Initial Thoughts' in *Justice in Conflict*, 27 February 2011 <http://justiceinconflict.org/2011/02/27/libya-referred-to-the-icc-initial-thoughts/>.)

[50] *Situation in the Libyan Arab Jamahiriya* (Warrant of Arrest for Saif Al-Islam Gaddafi) ICC-01/11 Pre-Trial Chamber I (27 June 2011). See also *Prosecutor v Muammar Mohammed Abu Minyar Gaddafi, Saif Al-Islam Gaddafi and Abdullah Al-Senussi* (Decision on the 'Prosecutor's Application Pursuant to Article 58 as to Muammar Mohammed Abu Minyar GADDAFI, Saif Al-Islam GADDAFI and Abdullah ALSENUSSI') ICC-01/11-01/11-1 Pre-Trial Chamber I (27 June 2011) para 7 ('In relation to the jurisdiction *ratione temporis*, the Chamber notes that ... the Prosecutor refers in his application to acts which were allegedly committed from 15 February 2011 to 28 February 2011 at the latest').

[51] Or filed a declaration under Art 12(3).

[52] See *Prosecutor v Tadić* (Decision on the Defence Motion for Interlocutory Appeal on Jurisdiction) IT-94-1 Appeals Chamber (2 October 1995) para 45 and *Prosecutor v Ayyash et al* (Decision on the defence challenges to the jurisdiction and legality of the tribunal) STL-11-01/PT/TC Trial Chamber (27 July 2012) and *Prosecutor v Ayyash et al* (Decision on the defence appeals against trial chamber's 'decision on the defence challenges to the jurisdiction and legality of the tribunal') STL-11-01/PT/AC/AR90.1 Appeals Chamber (24 October 2012).

[53] See section II.

Circumscribing an investigation based on nationality also violates basic principles of the rule of law and international human rights.[54] Under the International Covenant on Civil and Political Rights, the law should prohibit any discrimination and guarantee to all persons equal and effective protection against discrimination on any grounds, such as *race*, *colour*, sex, *language, religion, political or other opinion, national or social origin*, *property, birth or other status*.[55] In line with this standard, other international courts have held that selective jurisdiction or prosecutions would not be appropriate if a defendant could establish that there was, '(i) an unlawful or improper purpose (including discriminatory) motive for the prosecution and (ii) … that other similarly situated persons were not prosecuted'.[56] This is also the position in many national systems.[57] In the US, for instance, a 'selective prosecution' would be unconstitutional if a defendant can establish that he has been unfairly singled out and charged while 'similarly situated individuals of a different race [gender, ethnic or protected class] were not prosecuted'.[58]

Of course, it is possible that limiting a jurisdiction geographically or temporally – especially in an absurdly narrow manner – can simply mask a limitation regarding persons. In the Kenya case, which involved an investigation triggered by exercise of the Prosecutor's *proprio motu* powers, the Court noted the potential for temporal restrictions to undermine

> the purpose behind investigating an entire situation as opposed to subjectively selected crimes and … the Prosecutor's duty to establish the truth by extending the investigation to cover all facts and evidence pursuant to article 54(1) of the Statute.[59]

Similarly in the context of a Council referral, a resolution on Syria that excluded the Golan Heights could be said to be a way to exclude Israeli

[54] See Art 21(3) Rome Statute.

[55] Optional Protocol to the International Covenant on Civil and Political Rights (adopted 16 December 1966, entered into force 23 March 1976) 999 UNTS 302 (Optional Protocol) Arts 2(1) and 26 (emphasis added).

[56] *Prosecutor v Delalić and others* ('Ćelebići') (Judgment) IT-96-21-A Appeals Chamber (20 February 2001) paras 569-619.

[57] *Prosecutor v Milošević* (Decision on Preliminary Motions) IT-02-54 Trial Chamber III (8 November 2001) paras 8-11. See also P Krug, 'Prosecutorial Discretion and its Limits' (2002) 50 American Journal of Comparative Law 643.

[58] *United States v Armstrong*, 517 US 456 (1996) 465. See also *United States v Berrios*, 501 F 2d 1207 (2nd Cir 1974) 1211. Cf *Prosecutor v Delalić et al* (n 56) para 189: 'It is preposterous to suggest that unless all potential indictees who are similarly situated or brought to justice, there should be no justice done in relation to a person who has been indicted and brought to trial'.

[59] *Situation in the Republic of Kenya* (Decision Pursuant to Art 15 of the Rome Statute on the Authorization of an Investigation into the Situation in the Republic of Kenya) ICC-01/09-19-Corr Pre-trial Chamber II (31 March 2010) para 205.

nationals from the Court's reach, though the referral-restriction would ostensibly be framed geographically. Or if, for instance, it was suspected that a certain group was responsible for a massacre that took place on a single day – and the referral was limited to that day – this would in effect be a personal limitation masquerading as a temporal one.

As it turns out, the Council has felt no need for the masquerade and has limited the Court's *personal* jurisdiction *explicitly*. In the resolutions on both Darfur and Libya, there has been a paragraph inserted (originally at the insistence of the US) to exclude ICC jurisdiction over individuals who might otherwise be suspects but who are not nationals of States Parties or the country to which the situation primarily referred (ie Sudan and Libya).[60] The almost-identical clauses inserted into the Resolutions to achieve this read as follows:

> [The Security Council] [d]ecides that nationals, current or former officials or personnel from a ... State outside [Sudan/Libya] which is not a party to the Rome Statute of the International Criminal Court shall be subject to the exclusive jurisdiction of that ... State for all alleged acts or omissions arising out of or related to operations in [Sudan/Libya] established or authorized by the Council ... unless such exclusive jurisdiction has been expressly waived by [the] State...[61]

So each referral resolution explicitly provides that only some persons can be prosecuted by the Court, namely those who are citizens of States that have ratified the Rome Statute or are from the situation-country. Individuals from other States who serve as part of UN missions in Libya and Darfur are excluded. When this language featured for the first time in Article 6 of the Resolution referring the situation in Darfur to the Court, various States voiced strong objections. Brazil stated that Article 6 was against international law.[62] The Philippines remarked that Article 6 'kill[ed] [the resolution's] credibility' and added:

> [w]e may ask whether the Security Council has the prerogative to mandate the limitation of the jurisdiction of the ICC under the Rome Statute once

[60] For the resolution on Darfur see R Cryer, 'Sudan, Resolution 1593, and International Criminal Justice' (2006) 19 Leiden Journal of International Law 204–205, 208–214.

[61] UNSC Res 1593 (31 March 2005) UN Doc S/RES/1593, para 6 (Sudan). This was repeated almost verbatim in the UNSC Res 1970 (2011) concerning Libya at para 6. Also of interest is the United States' comment at the time of Resolution 1593 that 'the language providing protection for the United States and other contributing States was precedent-setting': UNSC, 'Reports of the Secretary-General on the Sudan' (31 March 2005) UN Doc S/PV.5158, 3 (Reports of the Secretary-General on the Sudan, March).

[62] Reports of the Secretary-General on the Sudan, March (n 61) 11.

> the exercise of its jurisdiction has advanced. Operative paragraph 6 subtly subsumed the independence of the ICC into the political and diplomatic vagaries of the Security Council.[63]

At the other end of the spectrum, some commentators have suggested that in the future the Council could place specific *named individuals* beyond the Court's reach. For instance, in relation to a possible referral of Syria, David Scheffer (who led the US delegation at the Rome Conference) has suggested that:

> If, for example, the Security Council gave Assad and his colleagues one week to quit power and leave the country for asylum in, say, Tunisia (or perhaps Russia), the Council *would explicitly omit their names* from its referral of the Syrian situation to the Court. Such officials would have to demonstrate indefinitely their complete withdrawal from political and military power in Syria in order to qualify for continued omission from the Court's jurisdiction.[64]

If a resolution could refer 'the situation in Syria except for any crimes committed by Bashar Al Assad and his family', it could also presumably refer 'the situation in Syria except for any crime committed by a member of the Free Syrian Army' or 'the situation in Syria except for any crimes committed by a Christian'. But this goes squarely against the intention of the drafters, who chose to limit the Council's power to referring a 'situation' as opposed to a 'case',[65] and it would make a mockery of the judicial process. Article 13 was not intended to allow such referrals, and there could be nothing more threatening to the Court's legitimacy and independence than a mandate that instructs the Court to go after specific individuals – or leave others alone – regardless of what the evidence uncovers about crimes that have been committed.

A more convincing reading of what Professor Scheffer and others propose might be that the Council can effectively make partial or limited referrals by

---

[63] Ibid 6.

[64] D Scheffer, 'Fanning the Flames of Justice in Syria' (*Project Syndicate* 1 March 2012) <http://www.project-syndicate.org/commentary/fanning-the-flames-of-justice-in-syria> (emphasis added).

[65] See 'Statement by Hans-Peter Kaul Head of the German delegation on United Nations negotiations on the establishment of an International Criminal Court (ICC) Complementarity, Trigger Mechanism', delivered to the Preparatory Committee on the Establishment of an International; Criminal Court (04 August 1997): 'We support the ILC proposal that the statute should give to the Security Council the explicit competence to submit to the court situations involving threats to or breaches of international peace and security and acts of aggression. But it would be in our view quite inappropriate if the Security Council could submit individual cases.'

exercising its powers under Articles 13 and 16 simultaneously – since Article 16 allows the postponement of a specific investigation. It might be argued that a combined referral-and-deferral would allow for instance referring 'Syria' under Chapter VII in the interest of maintaining international peace and security while simultaneously deferring any investigation involving top regime figures for a limited time in order to advance those same interests. But the resolutions on Darfur and Libya do not explicitly invoke Article 16, nor do they comply with that Article's stipulation that the Council can only postpone an investigation or prosecution for one year at a time. More fundamentally, such use of Article 16 would have to be based on the need to take an urgent and exceptional measure to preserve international peace and security, in line with Articles 39 to 41 of the Charter. This is clearly not the case in the resolutions on Darfur and Libya given that the exemption refers to the nationals of over 70 countries (non-States Parties) against whom there was no planned charge.

Article 16 should therefore not be used to legitimize referrals that narrow the scope of a situation based on the perpetrators' nationalities, and arguably the Prosecutor would be free to simply refuse to apply such purported restrictions. The Prosecutor must of course act within jurisdictional boundaries, but she is also required, under Article 42(1) of the Rome Statute, to 'act independently' and 'not seek or act on instructions from any external source'. In addition, Article 21(3) of the Rome Statute requires the Court to act in compliance with 'internationally recognized human rights ... without any adverse distinction founded on grounds such as ... race, colour, language, religion ... political or other opinion, [or] national, ethnic or social origin...'. Once a referral is made, the prosecution should therefore follow the evidence wherever it leads, as it would in any other active case.

Early statements on this issue by the Court's first Prosecutor, Luis Moreno Ocampo, have been encouraging. When faced with a state referral that sought to exclude certain potential perpetrators from his reach, he pushed back. Uganda had sought to define the scope of its referral as related only to the acts of the Lord's Resistance Army. The Prosecutor ignored this and stated in a letter to the President that he would be investigating any crimes committed by the Ugandan army as well.[66] This was explained on the basis that 'no such exception *ratione personae* could be effective'.[67]

---

[66] See *Situation in Uganda* (Decision Assigning the Situation in Uganda to Pre-Trial Chamber II) ICC-02/04-1 Presidency (5 July 2004) (annexing a letter from the Prosecutor to the President of the Court on the scope of the referral). The same independence would apply with respect to the lists of suspects submitted to the Office of the Prosecutor by the United Nations International Commission of Inquiry for Darfur and by the Commission of Inquiry into the Post-Election Violence in Kenya.

[67] *Situation in Uganda* (Decision to Convene a Status Conference on the Investigation in the

There are also indications that the Prosecutor has ignored the purported restriction in Security Council Resolution 1970 on investigating non-State Party actors (other than Libya) in Libya. The Prosecutor's report on Libya in May 2012 suggests that his Office did analyse the actions of all parties, including NATO, which is largely comprised of US (a non-State Party) troops.[68] As the Prosecution report to the Security Council explained:

> [t]he Office does not have jurisdiction to assess the legality of the use of force and evaluate the proper scope of NATO's mandate in relation to UNSC Resolution 1973. ... The Office *does have a mandate*, however, to investigate allegations of *crimes by all actors*. This includes allegations of crimes against humanity ... and of war crimes, in particular when committed as part of a plan or policy or as part of large scale commission of such crimes ....[69]

More generally, the Prosecutor has made clear that, consistent with Article 53, he exercises his discretion as to whether to launch an investigation and prosecution against particular individuals following a Council referral. For instance, after Darfur was referred, the Prosecutor commented in his report to the Council that '[t]he admissibility assessment is ongoing';[70] he did not automatically start to build prosecution files. It was the same with Libya. As he explained to the Council:

> [f]ollowing the unanimous Security Council referral, the Office conducted a factual and legal analysis during its preliminary examination of the situation. As a result of this analysis, covering issues of jurisdiction, admissibility [complementarity and gravity] and the interests of justice, on 3 March 2011 the Office determined that the statutory criteria for opening an investigation into the situation in the Libyan Arab Jamahiriya had been met.[71]

Situation in Uganda in Relation to the Application of Article 53) ICC-02/04-01/05 Pre-Trial Chamber II (2 December 2005) paras 3-4. See also WA Schabas, *An Introduction to the International Criminal Court* (4th edn, Cambridge University Press 2011) 173–174.

[68] ICC, 'Third report of the prosecutor of the international criminal court to the UN security council pursuant to UNSCR 1970 (2011)' (16 May 2012) <http://www.icc-cpi.int/NR/rdonlyres/D313B617-6A86-4D64-88AD-A89375C18FB9/0/UNSCreportLibyaMay2012Eng.pdf>.

[69] Ibid paras 53-54 (emphasis added).

[70] UNSC, 'Report of the Secretary-General on the Sudan' (29 June 2005) UN Doc S/PV.5216, 3.

[71] 'Report of the International Criminal Court to the United Nations for 2010/11' (19 August 2011) UN Doc A/66/309, 14–15.

The Prosecutor has also commented that 'referral of a situation by the Security Council does not affect the right under Article 19(2)(b) of the Rome Statute of any State with jurisdiction to lodge an admissibility challenge before this Court' since 'the legal framework of the Statute applies in the situations referred by the Security Council' just like any other.[72] This has since been confirmed by the ICC Judges.[73] So although the former ICC Prosecutor did not in any case actually pursue those who the Council sought to exclude in its resolutions, and in Uganda he only issued indictments against the Lord's Resistance Army (LRA) and none against the Ugandan army (UPDF), he did say that he *could* do so, despite the attempts to limit the 'situation'.[74] His independence had therefore been declared but not fully tested.

The Court, on the other hand, has acknowledged that personal parameters can in some circumstances be part of the legitimate definition of a 'situation'.[75] And in the case against Jean-Pierre Bemba which followed a referral by the Central African Republic, the Court did not question the referral 'letter [which] specifically requested the ICC Prosecutor "to open an investigation into this situation with a view to determining whether Mr Ange Felix PATASSE, Mr Jean-Pierre BEMBA [and others] can be accused" of the crimes listed therein'.[76] These statements by the Court were not however

---

[72] The Prosecutor has however indicated that where there has been a Council referral he may give the Council advance notice of certain actions. See OTP Statement to the United Nations Security Council on the situation in the Libyan Arab Jamahiriya, pursuant to UNSC Res 1970 (4 May 2011) para 22 ('Further cases will be opened as necessary, taking into account the full scope of criminality – including war crimes – allegedly committed by different individuals in the context of the Libya situation. *Before proceeding, I will inform this Council in advance*.') (Emphasis added.)

[73] *Prosecutor v Gaddafi and Al-Senussi* (Decision on the "Urgent Application on behalf of Abdullah Al-Senussi for Pre-Trial Chamber to order the Libyan Authorities to comply with their obligations and the orders of the ICC) ICC-01/11-01/11 Pre-Trial Chamber I (6 February 2013) para 21 ('The entire legal framework of the Statute applies equally to situations referred by the Security Council, including its complementarity and cooperation regimes').

[74] This inaction on the part of the OTP has since been used by Ugandan President Museveni to argue that his regime was 'cleared' by the ICC.

[75] *Prosecutor v Thomas Lubanga Dyilo* (ICC Decision Concerning Pre-Trial Chamber I's decision of 10 February 2006 and the Incorporation of Documents into the Record of the Case against Mr Thomas Lubanga Dyilo) ICC-01/04-01/06-8 Pre-Trial Chamber I (24 February 2006) para 21. See also *Situation in the Democratic Republic of Congo* (Decision on the Applications for Participation in the Proceedings of VPRS 1, VPRS 2, VPRS 3, VPRS 4, VPRS 5 and VPRS 6) ICC-01/04-101 Pre-Trial Chamber I (17 January 2006) para 65. This may be inevitable, however, if jurisdiction is based on nationality rather than territory, for instance if the ICC were to investigate to acts of British troops in Iraq.

[76] *Prosecutor v Jean Pierre Bemba Gombo* (Decision on the Prosecutor's Application for a Warrant of Arrest against Jean Pierre Bemba Gombo) ICC-01/05-01/08 Pre-Trial Chamber III (10 June 2008) para 16; *Prosecutor v Jean Pierre Bemba Gombo* (Corrigendum to Judgment on the appeal of Mr Jean-Pierre Bemba Gombo against the decision of Trial Chamber 3 of 24 June 2010 entitled *'Decision on the Admissibility and Abuse of Process Challenges'*) ICC-01/05-01/08 OA3 Appeals Chamber (19 October 2010) para 44.

made in the case of a Security Council referral that might on its face strike the Court as *ultra vires*, such as a referral that excluded certain nationals or directed the Court to pursue specified individuals to the exclusion of others. So the Court's practice, if faced with such a referral, is not yet known.

B. The practice on stopping an investigation: the Security Council's power to defer an investigation or prosecution by the Court

In the Court's ten-year lifespan, no ongoing investigations or prosecutions have been deferred by the Security Council under Article 16 of the Rome Statute. However, in the two years following the adoption of the Rome Statute, there was reference to Article 16 in three Resolutions – 1422 (2002), 1487 (2003) and 1497 (2003).[77]

In each of these resolutions the US successfully pushed for language that excluded ICC jurisdiction over nationals of non-State Parties who were part of peacekeeping missions. Resolution 1422 was passed just weeks after the Rome Statute came into force and at a time when the Council was considering whether to renew peacekeeping operations in Bosnia. The Resolution provided very broadly that:

> consistent with the provisions of article 16 of the Rome Statute … if a case arises involving … personnel from a contributing State not a Party to the Rome Statute over acts or omissions relating to a United Nations established or authorized operation, [the Court] shall for a twelve-month period starting 1 July 2002 not commence or proceed with investigation or prosecution of any such case, unless the Security Council decides otherwise.[78]

The two subsequent resolutions contained similar language specifically in relation to troops that were part of UN peacekeeping missions in Bosnia and Liberia.[79] These resolutions exempted citizens of the US (and other non-State Parties) from the jurisdiction of the Court even though the chance that

---

77 UNSC Res 1422 (12 July 2002) UN Doc S/RES/1422; UNSC Res 1487 (12 June 2003) UN Doc S/RES/1487; and UNSC Res 1497 (1 August 2003) UN Doc S/RES/1497.

78 UNSC Res 1422 (12 July 2002) UN Doc S/RES/1422.

79 UNSC Res 1487 (12 June 2003) UN Doc S/RES/1487, para 1 and UNSC Res 1497 (1 August 2003) UN Doc S/RES/1497, para 7: '*[decides]* that current or former officials from a contributing State, which is not a party to the Rome Statute … shall be subject to the exclusive jurisdiction of that contributing State for all alleged acts or omissions arising out of or related to the Multinational Force … unless such exclusive jurisdiction has been expressly waived by that contributing State'.

they would ever be investigated for any Rome Statute crimes was hypothetical and remote.[80]

These early Resolutions do not appear to be compatible with Article 16 of the Rome Statute. First, they are not explicitly adopted under Chapter VII of the UN Charter, as the Article requires. The first (1422) does not even relate to a specific country so could hardly be based on a determination that the situation in that country constitutes a threat to international peace and security (the trigger for invoking Chapter VII according to the Charter).[81] They establish a permanent deferral by automatic renewal instead of the maximum one-year renewable deferral period provided for in Article 16. And, rather than deferring a specific 'case or investigation', as Article 16 allows, the resolutions provide a blanket exemption for all peacekeepers from a large number of countries.

At the time of these Resolutions, several members of the Security Council expressed serious reservations about them[82] and the UN Secretary-General Kofi Annan warned the Council that its actions appeared to violate international law. In his words, 'article [16] ... was not intended to cover such a sweeping request, but only a more specific request relating to particular situation'.[83] He also emphasized the problem of principle, highlighting that if such a practice were to become routine:

> the world would interpret it as meaning that this Council wished to claim absolute and permanent immunity for people serving in the operations it establishes or authorizes. And if that were to happen, it would undermine not only the authority of the ICC but also the authority of this Council, and the legitimacy of United Nations peacekeeping.[84]

This practice by the Security Council under Article 16 is disappointing, because the Article was invoked not to temporarily stop a case in the name of peace but rather to provide unlimited legal cover for the nationals of certain States. But this practice did not affect any live case, and has not been

---

[80] See K Annan, 'Secretary-General's statement to the Security Council on the renewal of a resolution regarding the International Criminal Court and peacekeeping' (United Nations 12 June 2003): 'in addition to my concern about its conformity with article 16 of the Rome Statute, I do not believe this request is necessary' since it deals 'only with a hypothetical case [and] a highly improbable one') <http://www.un.org/sg/statements/?nid=389>.

[81] Art 39 UN Charter.

[82] See Coalition for the International Criminal Court, 'Compilation of Documents on UN Security Council Resolutions 1422/1487' (2004) and C Stahn, 'The Ambiguities of Security Council Resolution 1422' (2003) 14 European Journal of International Law 85–104.

[83] See Annan (n 80). The word 'situation' is used here in a non-technical sense, since Article 16 in fact refers to an 'investigation' or 'prosecution'.

[84] Idem.

repeated since 2004. As Christian Wenawesser, speaking on behalf of the three former presidents of the ICC Assembly of States Parties (ASP), told the Security Council in October 2012:

> [S]ome of the most controversial and questionable resolutions to come out of this Council [are] resolutions 1422 and 1487 which we consider contrary to both the Charter of the United Nations and the Rome Statute. Today, thankfully this topic belongs to the past...[85]

Indeed, in more recent times the Council has been invited to use its powers under Article 16 and refused to do so, notably in the case against Sudanese President Omar Bashir,[86] and in the cases involving post-election violence in Kenya.[87] The practice on Article 16 cannot, therefore, be said to have actually undermined the work of the Court.

V. CONCLUSION

In general terms, a broad power to refer situations to the Court is to be encouraged. After all, the Council could just as well set up a new international court and determine its jurisdiction in a resolution. The referrals have filled a jurisdictional (though not yet accountability) gap in two serious crises – Darfur and Libya – but without fragmenting the international system and increasing costs through the creation of new criminal courts.

---

85 C Wenawesser, 'Peace and Justice, with a Special Focus on the Role of ICC' (Speech to the United Nations, 17 October 2012) 1 <http://www.regierung.li/uploads/media/2012-10-17_SC_Open_Debate_Peaceand_Justice-ICC-LIE_Statement_as_read.pdf>.

86 Sudan argued that the comprehensive peace agreement was precarious and that arrest warrants would undermine that process.

87 UNSC Res 1828 (31 July 2008) UN Doc S/RES/1828, 2: 'took note' of the African Union's Communique of the 142nd Peace and Security Council [which asked the Council to issue a deferral compliant with Article 16] and said it was considering the matter. The US abstained. Then in November 2013, a draft resolution submitted by Kenya deferring the prosecution of President Kenyatta and Deputy President Ruto before the ICC for a one-year period failed to achieve the required nine votes out of fifteen. Of the permanent members of the Council, only China and Russia voted in favour of the resolution; the US, UK and France abstained. Liu Jieyi, the Chinese permanent representative to the United Nations expressed his disappointment with the outcome of the vote and remarked that 'deferring ICC proceedings against Kenya ... is indeed an urgent need dictated by the interest of maintaining regional peace and stability.' Meanwhile, delegates from Latin America and Western states declined to vote in favour of the resolution because of concerns that it could lead to impunity. See M Nichols, 'African Bid for Kenya Trials Deferral Fails at UN Security Council' (*Reuters* 15 November 2013) <http://uk.reuters.com/article/2013/11/15/uk-kenya-icc-un-idUKBRE9AE0S020131115>; All Africa, 'Kenya: China Regrets Security Council Failure to Defer ICC Trials of Kenyan Leaders' (18 November 2013) <http://allafrica.com/stories/201311180202.html>.

It should also be recalled that Council referrals are not the only way in which the Court acquires the power to act – investigations can also be triggered by State referrals or the decision of the Prosecutor to investigate crimes committed on the territory of a State Party or by its nationals. This is an improvement on the previous system of establishing new tribunals on a case-by-case basis, which meant that the Council was the *only* mechanism for triggering a new investigation at the international level unless the State involved consented to it. The ICC system gives the Court more leeway, since, regardless of Council action, the Prosecutor already has jurisdiction over the 122[88] States Parties to the Rome Statute and their changing governments.

However, the role of the Security Council in referring and deferring cases raises questions of principle that are at the heart of the system of international justice: judicial independence versus political influence, selectivity versus equality and the interests of peace versus those of justice.

The bargain struck in Rome included important checks and balances to ensure that the Court's independence – and the interests of justice more generally – would be safeguarded. The Council's referrals are not problematic if they are as general as they should be under Article 13, and simply add an objectively-defined 'situation' – as opposed to a specific case – to the jurisdiction of the Court. As long as the Council does not interfere with the judicial process thereafter (except on incidental issues such as enforcing cooperation obligations and funding), and so long as the Court's investigation and prosecution process is fair, the system can work. Similarly Article 16, properly interpreted, is an exceptional measure that allows a political body, the Council, to make a political choice that it is uniquely placed to make: namely to pause a judicial process in order to maintain or restore international peace and only for so long as it is strictly necessary to do so. This is the position in law and in principle.

In practice though the Council has misused its powers under Articles 13 and 16 and in so doing has threatened the Court's independence and legitimacy. Although many commentators celebrate the role that the Council has played in the first decade of the Court's life – because they expected no referrals and some deferrals, and have witnessed the opposite – there have been worrying developments over the last decade. Two fundamental problems remain.

First, there has been a trend to exempt certain nationals from the Court's reach – this was initially done through misuse of Article 16 and later by unacceptably narrowing referrals on the basis of nationality. The Council must act properly within the bounds of the legal framework that is in place by referring 'situations' and not pre-cooked referrals that arbitrarily limit the pool of

---

[88] As of May 2013.

possible defendants. The Council must also use Article 16 for its intended narrow purpose, and not as it did in its early practice to effectively grant mass amnesties. So far, it does not seem that the Court has allowed such mangled referrals, or the initial dubious invocation of Article 16, to impede its work, but if such a practice were to continue, it would threaten the Court's independence and credibility. The proper scope of referrals and deferrals needs to be clarified so that the Council's actions are objectively reined in.

The second major problem with the referral/deferral system today is that there are situations which cry out for referral, but remain out of reach because of one or more vetoes. The most striking is of course Syria, where over 80,000 people have been killed and the UN has confirmed that international crimes have been committed on an alarming scale. The Council does not accept that it has a responsibility to respond to objectively similar situations in objectively similar ways – and so far its decisions on referral/deferral are entirely discretionary and political. As the UN Secretary-General has stated:

> [T]here remain serious challenges in pursuing accountability. Some situations which, by any objective analysis, would have warranted some form of action by the Security Council, have faced serious obstacles or languished entirely. This has eroded the Council's credibility. There is a need to address this problem, and to bring some consistency to the effort.[89]

This criticism about Council *in*action[90] is not the Court's fault *per se* and it should not lead to the conclusion that the entire ICC system is tainted and should be abandoned. The system is necessarily imperfect given that all international criminal jurisdiction is created through a political process, but as one commentator has put it, 'neither justice nor victim is served by making the perfect the enemy of the good. Denying justice to those who have suffered unspeakable crimes in Darfur would provide no comfort to victims in Gaza

---

[89] Secretary-General 'Honouring Geneva Conventions, Secretary-General Says Debate 'No Longer between Peace and Justice but between Peace and What Kind of Justice', (26 September 2009) UN Doc SG/SM/12494, L/T/4417, HR/5002.

[90] Council inaction *following* a referral is another variation of this problem. As the Court has stated in a report to the ASP, a 'referral of a situation to the Court is crucial to ensure accountability, but without the necessary follow-up in terms of ensuring cooperation, and in particular arrest and surrender of the individuals identified by the Prosecutor, justice will not be done. On the contrary, a perception of inactivity or reticence from the Council to take further measures to ensure the cases can be brought to the courtroom and the Court is not isolated, would only undermine the Court's credibility and legitimacy and could be seen by the international community as a lack on the Council's part of the necessary commitment to uphold the rule of law generally and accountability in particular'. Assembly of States Parties, 'Report of the Court on the Status of Ongoing Cooperation between the International Criminal Court and the United Nations, Including in the Field' (14 October 2013), Doc No ICC-ASP/12/42, para 55.

who are denied access to the ICC'.[91] The Court's performance should be judged once it has the power to act, according to the standards set out in the Rome Statute. We might need to be satisfied, for now, that some justice is better than none – but only as long as the judicial course, once initiated, is fair and meets international due process requirements.[92]

VI. RECOMMENDATIONS

So long as large swathes of territory remain beyond the Court's reach, the political and selective nature of referrals and deferrals, even if not the Court's fault, will continue to be one of the principal objections to its work. Improvements to the system should therefore focus on ways to limit the potential for abuse of the Council's discretion and to protect the Court's independence, both real and perceived. This is a critical time to take stock and work to improve the practices and principles underlying the relationship between Council and Court, particularly as the Court's jurisdiction over the crime of aggression will require even closer cooperation between the two bodies as of 2017. Six reforms would help this cause.[93]

1. *Universal ratification of the Rome Statute and credible domestic prosecutions should be encouraged.*

A referral by the Security Council, like the creation of a new international court, fills a jurisdictional gap by making prosecutions possible where national courts are not willing or able to put suspects on trial for international crimes. Of course, the Council would not be needed if the State concerned had ratified the Rome Statute or otherwise recognized the jurisdiction of the Court.[94] Currently almost two thirds of UN Member States are States Parties to the Rome Statute.[95] If the jurisdictional gap is reduced, the role of the Council becomes less relevant as there is less of a need for it to step in – States would have voluntarily submitted to the Rome Statute and the jurisdiction it gives the Court over international crimes. The other way to fill the jurisdictional gap without the need for Council intervention is if there are more

---

[91] R Dicker, 'A Flawed Court in Need of Credibility' (*The New York Times* 21 May 2012) <http://www.nytimes.com/2012/05/22/opinion/a-flawed-court-in-need-of-credibility.html>.

[92] Compare H Al Hamoudi, 'The Problem of Legitimacy in International Criminal Justice' (*Jurist* 7 July 2011) <http://jurist.org/forum/2011/07/haider-hamoudi-libya-legitimacy.php>: 'we judge the legitimacy of the tribunal before it begins, not by the process by which it proceeds'.

[93] These recommendations do not address matters of state-cooperation and funding, which have clearly been problematic but are beyond the scope of this chapter.

[94] See Art 12(3) Rome Statute.

[95] See n 88.

national prosecutions for international crimes, reducing the need for the Court to act at all.[96]

2. The Security Council should stop the practice of exempting categories of nationals from the Court's jurisdiction.

ICC referrals should be based on the severity of crimes – not the nationality of the alleged perpetrators. As the former Presidents of the Assembly of States Parties,[97] individual States[98] and experts have argued, in order to reduce the suspicion that the Court is a tool for selective justice, the Council should in future referrals not include language exempting certain nationals from the Court's jurisdiction.[99]

3. The ICC should not be bound by limitations in Security Council referrals that are not in line with the Court's Statute.

If the Court considers part of a referral resolution to be *ultra vires* in that it limits jurisdiction in a manner that is incompatible with the Rome Statute, the Court should not be bound by it. The Court is not a State, and it is therefore not subject to the obligation in Article 25 of the UN Charter to comply with the Council's decisions. It is subject instead to its own founding document, the Rome Statute.[100] The Court cannot *generally* review the legality of Security Council action under the UN Charter,[101] but it would likely find

---

96 States' laws vary on which crimes within the Court's Statute are considered 'universal jurisdiction crimes' and prosecutable as such. See, for example UNGA 'The scope and application of the principle of universal jurisdiction (agenda item 84)' (64th session of the General Assembly, Decision 63/568, 2009) <http://www.un.org/en/ga/sixth/64/UnivJur.shtml>.

97 Wenawesser (n 85).

98 See UNSC, 'The promotion and strengthening of the rule of law in the maintenance of international peace and security' (Transcript of afternoon session of 6849th meeting, 17 October 2012) UN Doc S/PV.6849, 4-5 where Brazil expressed opposition to the 'exemption of certain categories of individuals' and 'selective criminal accountability', commenting that this is not in the interests of justice. New Zealand also commented that the Council should not use its powers to shield certain categories of individuals and that justice should not be seen to be discriminatory. See also D Kaye et al, *The Court and the Council: Improving Security Council Support to the International Criminal Court* (University of California-Irvine 2013) 22 <http://councilandcourt.org/files/2013/05/The-Council-and-the-Court-FINAL.pdf> and D Akande, 'The Security Council and the ICC' (*EJIL: Talk!* 3 July 2013) <http://www.ejiltalk.org/the-security-council-and-the-icc/>.

99 Kaye at al (n 98) 22.

100 Art 1 Rome Statute: 'the jurisdiction and functioning of this Court shall be governed by the provisions of this Statute'.

101 *Questions of Interpretation and Application of the 1971 Montreal Convention Arising from the Aerial Incident at Lockerbie (Libya v UK)* (Preliminary Objections, Judgment) [1998] ICJ Rep p 9; *Legal Consequences for States of the Continued Presence of South Africa in Namibia (South-West Africa) Notwithstanding Security Council Resolution 276 (1970)*, (Advisory Opinion) [1971] ICJ Rep para 89.

that it could assess, in determining its own jurisdiction, whether the resolution referring a situation was *ultra vires*.[102] The Court could therefore hold either that an entire resolution is null and void or – more likely – that an offending provision is severable from the resolution and will not be applied.[103]

4. *Guidelines setting out objective criteria for the use and parameters of Security Council referrals and deferrals should be adopted.*

To encourage the Council to act objectively and with a greater degree of consistency, guidelines could be adopted governing (i) when the Council should consider referring a situation[104] and (ii) when the permanent five members will or will not use their veto to block a referral. Guidelines should also be adopted to guide the use of Council powers under Article 16.

The guidelines in relation to referrals could specify that there should be no exemptions of individuals or based on nationalities of the perpetrators and that geographical and temporal limitations (other than the 2002 start-date provided for in the Rome Statute) should relate objectively to the time and place in which international crimes appear to have been committed. The guidelines could also provide that where a UN-appointed commission has concluded that international crimes have been committed, this automatically triggers the tabling of a discussion at the Council on referral.

There can also be guidelines on the appropriate use of vetoes when it comes to possible referrals. States and regional organizations have been pushing for some time for guidelines limiting the use of vetoes in resolutions involving the Court.[105] Since 2006, Switzerland together with Costa Rica, Liechtenstein, Jordan and Singapore (labeled the 'Small Five') proposed that the permanent five members of the Council should agree not to use their veto power to block action 'in response to genocide and mass atrocities which would otherwise pass by a majority'.[106] Such a standard could be further elaborated upon.

---

[102] Cf *Prosecutor v Ayyash et al* (Decision on the defence appeals against trial chamber's "decision on the defence challenges to the jurisdiction and legality of the tribunal") STL-11-01/PT/AC/AR90.1 Appeals Chamber (24 October 2012); *Prosecutor v Duško Tadić* (Decision on the Defence Motion For Interlocutory Appeal on Jurisdiction) IT 94-I-AR72 Appeals Chamber (2 October 1995). See also Schabas, (n 67) 185: 'The [ICC] could assess whether or not the Council was validly acting pursuant to Chapter VII'.

[103] See Cryer (n 60) 195, 214.

[104] See also Kaye at al (n 98) 22 and Akande (n 98).

[105] In the debate on 17 October 2012 at the Security Council, New Zealand stated that Permanent Members should voluntarily agree not to use their veto in situations involving mass atrocities. See Transcript of afternoon session (n 98) 5.

[106] Citizens for Global Solutions, 'The Responsibility Not To Veto – A Way Forward' (2010) 2 <http://globalsolutions.org/files/public/documents/RN2V_White_Paper_CGS.pdf>.

The idea of a moratorium on the use of vetoes in certain situations has been called the 'responsibility not to veto' and presented as an element of the doctrine of Responsibility to Protect (R2P).[107] This doctrine provides that if a State fails to protect its populations from mass crimes,[108] the world's governments will 'take collective action, in a timely and decisive manner, through the Security Council, in accordance with the Charter'.[109] R2P was unanimously endorsed by UN member States in October 2005 and the UN Under-Secretary-General for Legal Affairs and Legal Counsel has called the resolution referring Libya to the Court 'the most explicit and robust application of R2P to date'.[110] However the contours and application of the doctrine are still unclear and it is therefore not yet a practical basis for guidelines on the use of vetoes to stop referrals or deferrals by the Council.[111]

Guidelines on Article 16 should seek to ensure that this provision does not get overused or manipulated by diplomats to allow for blanket exclusions from the Court's jurisdiction. The guidelines could make clear that it should only be in the narrowest of situations (akin to rare instances in a domestic system where an Attorney General or other political actor is required to approve a prosecution); only to be invoked where less restrictive measures (for example, the possibility of plea bargains once at the Court) could not be sufficient; and for the shortest possible time.

Ultimately the permanent five members of the Security Council are unlikely to agree to be bound by any guidelines that restrict their discretion in this area – they have no incentive to do so, and current debates over Syria reveal very different approaches to the issue of ICC referrals among the permanent five. Such guidelines could however be adopted by the Assembly of States Parties (ASP), as members of the ASP are the governing body of the Court and the Assembly includes two of the five permanent members of the

---

107 See A Blätter and PD Williams, 'The Responsibility Not To Veto' (2011) 3 Global Responsibility to Protect 301–322.

108 Which are comprised of: genocide, war crimes, ethnic cleansing and crimes against humanity as well as their incitement.

109 UNGA, 'Implementing the Responsibility to Protect' (12 January 2009) UN Doc A/63/677, 4.

110 P O'Brien, '55th Annual meeting of the Russian Association of International Law, "Current issues of modern international law"' (Roundtable discussion on the concept of "Responsibility to Protect", Moscow, 27 June 2012) 8. See also BK Moon, 'Statement by the Secretary-General on Libya' (United Nations, 17 March 2011): 'Resolution 1973 affirms, clearly and unequivocally, the international community's determination to fulfill its responsibility to protect civilians from violence perpetrated upon them by their own government' http://www.un.org/sg/statements/?nid=5145"http://www.un.org/sg/statements/?nid=5145>.

111 UNGA Res 60/1 (24 October 2005), 'World Summit Outcome', UN Doc A/RES/60/1. See also Implementing the Responsibility to Protect (n 109).

Council. The existence of such objective guidelines may at least require these States to explain themselves when they disagree or act contrary to the guidelines, and this may ultimately lead to greater reflection and consistency of action.

5. *Guidelines setting out the practical consequences of an Article 16 deferral should be adopted.*

Other guidelines – perhaps developed by legal and academic experts – could provide suggestions on the practical consequences of an Article 16 deferral for an ongoing case: should it lead to immediate release of the person from prison or could the Court continue to hold the suspect or accused in pre-trial detention? Would the ICC arrest warrant be cancelled? Can the person be re-tried somewhere else? How would a re-triggered prosecution affect the right to trial without undue delay? What measures can be taken to preserve evidence in the meantime? The guidelines should address these and other legal and practical questions that would arise in this context.

6. *The Office of the Prosecutor should issue guidelines on how it interprets referrals and should be transparent about its reasons when it does not proceed with investigations in situations that have been referred.*

In the past, the Office of the Prosecutor has published its policy on how it exercises its prosecutorial discretion in situations that come within the Court's jurisdiction.[112] It has also published explanations for why it did not proceed to investigate alleged crimes that were reported by citizens (in Iraq and Venezuela); why it did not investigate following an attempted State declaration (by Palestine); or why the situation remains under preliminary examination (for example, in Colombia).[113] A transparent and reasoned approach would also be warranted in any case where the Prosecutor refused to investigate a situation referred by the Security Council, or where the Prosecutor refused to follow instructions by the Council which were considered *ultra vires*.

[112] See above n 26.

[113] See 'Preliminary Examinations: Completed-Decision not to Proceed' <http://www.icc-cpi.int/en_menus/icc/structure%20of%20the%20court/office%20of%20the%20prosecutor/comm%20and%20ref/pe-cdnp/Pages/default.aspx#Iraq> and OTP, 'Report on Preliminary Examination Activities' (November 2012).

PART 4

The International Criminal Court and Victims

Victims as Participants in Proceedings before the ICC: A Success Story?

*Gaëlle Carayon**

For the first time in the history of international criminal justice, the Rome Statute recognised victims as distinct stakeholders in international criminal proceedings.[1] It acknowledged the right of victims to participate in proceedings in their own right, and not just as witnesses for the Prosecution.[2] After the experiences of the international ad hoc tribunals, which were criticized by many for their lack of provisions relating to victims, and the re-traumatisation victims suffered through the process,[3] the recognition of victims as active participants in proceedings before the International Criminal Court (ICC) is generally seen as a major achievement of the Rome Statute.[4]

* Legal Officer on the ICC program at the REDRESS Trust. In that capacity Ms Carayon has worked extensively with victims in ICC Situation countries such as the Democratic Republic of the Congo (DRC), Ivory Coast, Kenya and Uganda. The views expressed in this article are those of the author and do not necessarily reflects those of REDRESS.

1 The drafting of the present article was greatly facilitated by a report of REDRESS on the issue of victims' participation. See REDRESS, 'The Participation of Victims in International Criminal Court Proceedings, A Review of the Practice and Consideration of Options for the Future' (2012).

2 In this sense Pulchérie Makiandakama, a victim participating in the Bemba case, made the following statement to the International Criminal Court: 'I am a human being. Judges need to pay attention to my situation. Judges have to rule on this case and give me justice. This is all I want from the ICC.' ('Victim Testifies Publicly in the Bemba Trial: "I lost my Dignity"' (2012) 20 VRWG Bulletin 1.)

3 E Haslam, 'Victim Participation at the International Criminal Court: A Triumph of Hope Over Experience?' in D McGoldrick et al (eds), *The Permanent International Criminal Court: Legal and Policy Issues* (Hart Publishing 2004) 315; D Donat-Cattin, 'Article 68: Protection of Victims and Witnesses and their Participation in the Proceedings', in O Triffterer (ed), *Commentary on the Rome Statute of the International Criminal Court* (Nomos Verlag 1999) 869–871.

4 G Bitti and H Friman, 'Participation of Victims in the Proceedings', in Lee Roy et al (eds), *The International Criminal Court: Elements of Crimes and Rules of Procedure and Evidence* (Transnational Publishers 2001) 456–457.

The ability of victims to participate in criminal proceedings was recognized in a number of international standard setting documents[5] and also in some domestic – mostly civil law – jurisdictions. However, of all the international criminal justice processes, this was the first formal recognition by the international community that the victims' voice matters and that they have a role to play.[6] This formal act reflects the argument that participation, in itself, is a form of recognition for victims and that through participation victims can achieve a sense of 'healing and rehabilitation'.[7] It can also help bring the ICC closer to its constituents.[8] Some victims, and the activists working with them, have indeed reported that there has been a positive impact of direct legal participation in that it has allowed victims to feel valued through their involvement in the legal process. They have also pointed out that if the process is right, the mere fact of having gone through it will affect victims positively. [9] As one victim's counsel in the *Katanga* case stated:

> Victims want … their fate [to] be acknowledged … The sole purpose of victims participating in this trial is not to obtain compensation. That will

---

[5] See the UN *Declaration of Basic Principles of Justice for Victims of Crime and Abuse of Power*, which provides that:

> [t]he responsiveness of judicial and administrative processes to the needs of victims should be facilitated by: (b) allowing the views and concerns of victims to be presented and considered at appropriate stages of the proceedings where their personal interests are affected, without prejudice to the accused and consistent with the relevant national criminal justice system.

Declaration of Basic Principles of Justice for Victims of Crime and Abuse of Power (adopted 29 November 1985) UNGA Res 40/43, UN Doc A/RES/40/34 Annex; also *Basic Principles and Guidelines on the Right to a Remedy and Reparation for Victims of Gross Violations of International Human Rights Law and Serious Violations of International Humanitarian Law* (adopted on 16 December 2005) UNGA Res 60/147, UN Doc A/RES/60/147 (2006) para 12 (b)–(d), which provide that states should: '(*c*) Provide proper assistance to victims seeking access to justice; (*d*) Make available all appropriate legal, diplomatic and consular means to ensure that victims can exercise their rights to remedy for gross violations of international human rights law or serious violations of international humanitarian law.'

[6] C Ferstman, 'The Role of the Victims at the International Criminal Court: Key Prospects' in E Vetere and D Pedro (eds), *Victims of Crime and Abuse of Power: Festschrift in Honour of Irene Melup* (United Nations 2005) 156.

[7] F McKay, 'Universal Jurisdiction in Europe: Criminal Prosecutions in Europe since 1990 for War Crimes, Crimes Against Humanity, Torture & Genocide' (REDRESS 1999) 15 <http://www.redress.org/downloads/publications/UJEurope.pdf>.

[8] Bitti & Friman (n 4) 457.

[9] Victims Rights Working Group, 'The impact of the ICC on victims and affected Communities' (2010) 19 <http://www.redress.org/downloads/publications/Stocktakingreport 2010.pdf>.

> be oversimplifying matters, even amounting to an insult .... Victims seek to ... get recognition for the suffering that they have been through.[10]

A total of 11,042 applications for participation from victims have received by the Court as of 1 January 2012.[11] This should be seen as a success and an indication that victims want to engage with the ICC. But has the participation of victims itself been the success story envisaged by the drafters of the Rome Statute?

This contribution will look first at the framework set for victim participation before the ICC, and then consider some of the achievements of the system of victims' participation so far. It will then concentrate on some of the challenges victims have faced when seeking to participate actively and meaningfully in proceedings before the ICC, and conclude by looking at the efforts necessary to improve the existing system.

I. STATUTORY FRAMEWORK FOR VICTIM PARTICIPATION BEFORE THE ICC AND MODALITIES OF PARTICIPATION

A. Application and framework for participation

The Rome Statute sets out a general framework under which victims can participate in proceedings.[12] Participation is envisaged in respect of specific proceedings, such as a request from the Prosecutor for authorisation to open an investigation or to seek a ruling regarding a question of jurisdiction or admissibility.[13] However, under Article 68(3) of the Rome Statute, there is also a more general right for victims to present their views and concerns when their personal interests are affected.[14] Victims entitled to that right will be those fulfilling the definition of a victim provided for in Rule 85 of the

---

[10] *Prosecutor v Katanga & Ngudjolo* (Hearing transcript, Closing statement of Me Nsita Luvengika) ICC-01/04-01/07-T-337-Red-ENG Trial Chamber II (16 May 2012) 54, 57.

[11] 2,228 in the situation in the Democratic Republic of the Congo, 1,039 in the situation in Uganda, 209 in the situation in Darfur, 4,993 in the situation in the Central African Republic and 2,572 in the situation in Kenya, 1 in the situation in Libya. A further 1,287 applications were received in 2012.

[12] Rome Statute of the International Criminal Court, (2002) 2187 UNTS 90 (Rome Statute).

[13] Authorisation of an investigation initiated by the Prosecutor (Art 15(3)); Challenges to the jurisdiction of the court or admissibility of a case (Art 19(3)), and reparations (Art 75).

[14] Art 68(3) of the Rome Statute spells out that:

> Where the personal interests of victims are affected, the Court shall permit their views and concerns to be presented and considered at stages of the proceedings determined to be appropriate by the Court and in a manner which is not prejudicial to or inconsistent with the rights of the accused and a fair and impartial trial.

Rules of Procedure and Evidence.[15] Under the above framework, it is for the Judges to define the concepts of 'personal interests', 'appropriate stage of the proceedings' and 'views and concerns'.

While a detailed review of the requirements that victims must meet to qualify for participatory status would go beyond the scope of this contribution, the general approach followed by the ICC's Chambers has been as follows: (1) the victim applicant is a natural person or an organization or institution; (2) a crime within the jurisdiction of the Court appears to have been committed; (3) the victim applicant has suffered harm; and (4) such harm arose 'as a result' of the alleged crime within the jurisdiction of the Court.[16] Some Chambers have also reformulated it into a tripartite test, namely whether: (1) the identity appears duly established; (2) the events described in the application for participation constitute the crime(s) within the jurisdiction of the Court with which the suspects are charged; and (3) whether the applicant has suffered harm that appears to have arisen 'as a result' of the crime(s) charged.[17] If it is established that a victim meets these criteria to a *prima facie* standard, a Judge – or a panel of Judges – will then go on to evaluate: a) if it is appropriate for the victim to be allowed to participate in a given stage of the proceedings; b) if victims' interests are affected by that proceeding and, finally; c) if participation in the manner requested is appropriate and consistent with the rights of the defence to a fair and expeditious trial.[18]

---

[15] Rule 85 of the Rules of Procedure and Evidence provides that:

> For the purposes of the Statute and the Rules of Procedure and Evidence:
> (a) 'Victims' means natural persons who have suffered harm as a result of the commission of any crime within the jurisdiction of the Court;
> (b) Victims may include organizations or institutions that have sustained direct harm to any of their property which is dedicated to religion, education, art or science or charitable purposes, and to their historic monuments, hospitals and other places and objects for humanitarian purposes.

(Rules of Procedure and Evidence, adopted by the Assembly of States Parties (3–10 September 2002) OR ICC-ASP/1/3.)

[16] *Situation in the Democratic Republic of Congo* (Decision on the Applications for Participation in the Proceedings of VPRS 1, VPRS 2, VPRS 3, VPRS 4, VPRS 5 and VPRS 6) ICC-01/04-101-tEN-Corr Pre Trial Chamber I 1(7 January 2006) para 79; *Prosecutor v Kony, Otti, Odhiambo & Ongwen* (Decision on victims' applications for participation a/0014/07 to a/0020/07 and a/0076/07 to a/0125/07) ICC 02/04-01/05-356 Pre Trial Chamber II (21 November 2008) para 7; *Prosecutor v Bemba* (Fourth Decision on Victims' Participation) ICC-01/05-01/08-320 Pre Trial Chamber III (12 December 2008) para 30; *Situation in Kenya* (Decision on Victims' Participation in Proceedings) ICC-01/09-24 Pre Trial Chamber II (3 November 2010) para 19.

[17] *Prosecutor v Muthaura, Kenyatta and Ali* (Decision on Victims' Participation at the Confirmation of Charges Hearing and in the Related Proceedings) ICC-01/09-02/11-267 Pre Trial Chamber II (26 August 2011) para 40.

[18] Ibid.

In practice, the initial stage is already marred with challenges relating to access to information, assistance and resources. A prerequisite to a judge recognising a victim as a participant in ICC proceedings is that a victim first submits an application with relevant proof of identity, kinship and other personal information. The Court has adopted form, which the victims can fill in in order to apply for participation. This usually requires that victims have been informed about the court's mandate, what their rights are and what they can hope to achieve by exercising their rights before the ICC. It also requires that the victims – many of whom are illiterate – and those assisting them devote a significant amount of time to the process of filling in the forms. This is not a straightforward process, but it is a mandatory step if victims want a chance of exercising their rights before the ICC.[19]

B. Modalities of participation, participation through Legal Representative of Victims

Turning to the modalities of victim participation, it is important to emphasise that victims are not parties to, but *participants* in proceedings. The modalities of participation are strictly regulated by the Rome Statute and Rules of Procedure and Evidence.[20] It has been found by the Court that participation could, under some circumstances, take place as early as the 'situation' phase, when no case has yet been identified, if a proceeding arises which impacts the personal interest of a victim applicant.[21] In relation to a case, victims' participation has been recognized at the pre-trial phase, at trial and also during sentencing and reparations proceedings.[22]

The Statute and the Rules leave it to the Chamber to 'specify the proceedings and manner in which participation is considered appropriate'.[23] Judges are left with a wide margin of discretion as to the parameters of victims'

---

19 In the *Prosecutor v Kenyatta* and *Prosecutor v Ruto, Sang*, a new approach was implemented whereby only victims wanting to appear in person need to fill in a full application. Others can still register with the Registry but their registration will not be subject to a decision by the Chamber. See Participation of Victims in International Criminal Court Proceedings (n 1) 38.

20 *Prosecutor v Lubanga* (Judgment on the appeals of The Prosecutor and The Defence against Trial Chamber I's Decision on Victims' Participation of 18 Jan 2008) ICC-01/04-01/06-1432 Appeals Chamber (11 July 2008) para 93.

21 *Situation in the Democratic Republic of Congo* (Decision on victims' participation in proceedings relating to the situation in the Democratic Republic of the Congo) ICC-01/04-593 Pre Trial Chamber I (11 April 2011) para 2. See also, *Situation in Kenya* (Decision on Victims' Participation in Proceedings) (n 16) para 1; *Situation in Libya* (Decision on Victims' Participation in Proceedings Related to the Situation in Libya) ICC-01/11-18 Pre-Trial Chamber I (24 January 2012); *Situation in Uganda* (Decision on Victim's Participation in Proceedings) ICC-02/04-191 Pre Trial Chamber II (12 March 2012).

22 Participation of Victims in International Criminal Court Proceedings (n 1) 46–55.

23 Rule 89(1) of the Rules of Procedure and Evidence.

participation, the specific nature of their participation and the form this participation will take. In practice, victims' participation has mostly been exercised through a Legal Representative of Victims (LRV), tasked with representing victims' interests in the proceedings. The LRV attends all public, and sometimes closed, hearings on behalf of the victims. LRVs have been allowed to make opening and closing statements in confirmation of charges hearings and at trial, and to put questions to witnesses.[24] They have also been allowed to examine and challenge the admissibility of evidence on a case by case basis.[25] Trial Chamber II in the *Katanga & Ngudjolo* case underlined the constructive role that the participation of victims can play in this regard, preventing 'the Chamber from being misled by relying on inadmissible or irrelevant evidence – or dismissing evidence that is in fact admissible and relevant – in order to establish the facts.'[26]

Chambers have also found that under some circumstances, victims could apply to submit evidence themselves, including by appearing in person.[27] Trial Chamber I in the *Lubanga* case indeed stressed that:

> the participating victims have an undoubted interest in setting their personal experiences, and the harm it is said they individually experienced, in their true historical, economic, and social context, which is, *inter alia*, the underlying circumstances in which the alleged crimes of enlisting, recruiting, or using child soldiers were committed.[28]

---

[24] *Prosecutor v Lubanga* (Decision on the Defence observations regarding the right of the legal representatives of victims to question defence witnesses and on the notion of personal interest on the defence application to exclude certain representatives of victims from the Chamber during the non-public evidence of various defence witnesses) ICC-01/04-01/06-2340 Trial Chamber I (11 March 2010).

[25] *Prosecutor v Lubanga* (Judgment on the appeals of The Prosecutor and The Defence against Trial Chamber I's Decision on Victims' Participation of 18 Jan 2008) (n 20) para 101; *Prosecutor v Katanga & Ngudjolo* (Decision on the Modalities of Victim Participation at Trial) ICC-01/04-01/07-1788-tENG Trial Chamber II (22 January 2010) para 104.

[26] Ibid.

[27] Art 69(3) of the Rome Statute states that 'The Court shall have the authority to request the submission of all evidence that it considers necessary for the determination of the truth.' This has been interpreted as recognising the ability of victims, with the Chamber's authorisation to induce evidence and also to appear in person to testify. *Prosecutor v Katanga & Ngudjolo* (Decision on the Modalities of Victim Participation at Trial) (n 25) para 101; *Prosecutor v Lubanga* (Transcript of hearing on 17 June 2009) ICC-01/04-01/06-T-193-ENG Trial Chamber I (17 June 2009) p 8, lines 15-25; *Prosecutor v Lubanga* (Judgment on the appeals of The Prosecutor and The Defence against Trial Chamber I's Decision on Victims' Participation of 18 Jan 2008) (n 20)).

[28] *Prosecutor v Lubanga* (Transcript of hearing on 17 June 2009) (n 27) p 8, lines 15–25.

Victims have also been able to bring their views and concerns to the relevant chambers on issues such as challenges to the jurisdiction of the Court;[29] interim release;[30] challenges on the basis of admissibility;[31] and whether it was desirable that confirmation of charges hearings be conducted in the Republic of Kenya.[32] The possibility of victims to appear as witnesses before the Court, as well as presenting their views and concerns in person, has also been recognized and will be discussed below.

Whilst the Court is still in an early stage of its existence, the *Lubanga* and *Katanga & Ngudjolo* trials are now complete and the *Bemba* trial is soon to conclude. Victims have also been able to participate in nine confirmation of charges hearings. With growing calls for the current system of victim participation to be reviewed, we will now examine some of the achievements of the system of victim participation and some of the challenges this system faces.

II. AN IMPORTANT RIGHT FOR THE COURT AND FOR VICTIMS

Victim participation can allow victims to contribute to the overall establishment of the truth. Victims have an interest in the outcome of the proceedings and may not always have the same views on what might constitute the truth. However, apart from the accused, they will often be the only persons with knowledge of the facts and of the context in which they took place. Victims will also often be the only ones in the courtroom apart from the accused who have been to and lived in the regions where the crimes took place. Through their participation, victims may be able to assist the Chamber to 'better understand the contentious issues of the case in light of their local

---

29 *Prosecutor v Lubanga* (Observations of Victims a/0001/06, a/0002/06 and a/0003/06 Regarding the Challenge to Jurisdiction Raised by the Defence in the Application of 23 May 2006) ICC-01/04-01/06-349 Pre Trial Chamber I (24 August 2006); *Prosecutor v Mbarushimana* (Observations on behalf of victims on the Defence Challenge to the Jurisdiction of the Court) ICC-01/04-01/10-417 Pre-Trial Chamber I (12 September 2011).

30 *Prosecutor v Lubanga* (Observations of victims a/001/06, 1/002/06 and a/003/06, in respect of the application for release filed by the Defence) ICC-01/04-01/06-530 Pre-Trial Chamber I (9 October 2006).

31 In the *Ruto* case, victims were invited to participate through the Office of Public Council for Victims (OPCV) in the proceedings on the admissibility challenge by the Government of the Republic of Kenya. See *Prosecutor v Ruto, Kosgey & Sang* (Decision on the Application by the Government of Kenya Challenging the Admissibility of the Case Pursuant to Article 19(2)(b) of the Statute) ICC-01/09-01/11-101 Pre-Trial Chamber II (30 May 2011).

32 See *Prosecutor v Ruto, Kosgey & Sang* (Decision Requesting Observations on the Place of the Proceedings for the Purposes of the Confirmation of Charges Hearing) ICC-01/09-01/11-106 Pre-Trial Chamber II (3 June 2011).

knowledge and socio-cultural background.'[33] In the *Lubanga* case, after the identity of witnesses became the subject of repeated questioning by counsel of the defence, victims, through their counsel, suggested that an expert witness on names and other social conventions in the DRC should testify. Such an expert was called in by the Chamber and he clarified that it was not unusual for Congolese citizens to change names over their lifetime, or not know their exact date of birth.[34]

Participants can also play an important role in bringing to light crimes which could be different from the charges presented by the Prosecution. Victims' participation was crucial, for example, in bringing to light concerns about the limited nature of the charges against Lubanga. In May 2009, victims' representatives brought a motion asking the judges to re-characterize the facts of the case to include the charges of sexual slavery that, in their opinion, better reflected sexual violence against female child soldiers. Although the Chamber originally granted the request, the decision was overturned on appeal.[35] Despite the final outcome, the request by victims was useful in bringing to the forefront the plight of girl child soldiers, which had not been explicitly recognized in the Prosecution case. In the *Ruto* case, counsel for victims Surety Chana kept emphasising before the Pre-Trial Chamber, and then the Trial Chamber, that the crimes in the charges did not fully reflect the victimisation of her clients and that acts of destruction and/or burning of property should be recognised in the charges.[36]

While these requests, aiming at broadening the scope of a case, have not been successful, they still represent a positive way in which victims can contribute to the establishment of the truth. They also ensure that victims' concerns about the scope of the case will form part of the record. The judges of the Trial Chamber I, in sentencing Lubanga in July 2012, notably criticized the failure of the Prosecution to bring charges for crimes of sexual

---

[33] *Prosecutor v Katanga & Ngudjolo* (Directions for the conduct of the proceedings and testimony in accordance with Rule 140) ICC-01/04-01/07-1665-Corr Trial Chamber II (1 December 2009) para 82.

[34] *Prosecutor v Lubanga* (Redacted version of 'Submission of Mr Kambayi Bwatshia's Expert Report') ICC-01/04-01/06-2025-Anx1 Trial Chamber I (3 August 2009).

[35] *Prosecutor v Lubanga* (Decision giving notice to the parties and participants that the legal characterisation of the facts may be subject to change in accordance with Regulation 55(2) of the Regulations of the Court) ICC-01/04-01/06-2049 Trial Chamber I (14 July 2009); *Prosecutor v Lubanga* (Judgment on the appeals of Mr Lubanga Dyilo and the Prosecutor against the Decision of Trial Chamber I of 14 Jul 2009 entitled 'Decision giving notice to the parties and participants that the legal characterisation of the facts may be subject to change in accordance with Regulation 55(2) of the Regulations of the Court') ICC-01/04-01/06-2205 Appeals Chamber (8 December 2009).

[36] *Prosecutor v Ruto, Kosgey & Sang* (Decision on the 'Renewed Request by the Victims' Representative for authorisation by the Chamber to make submissions on specific issues of law and/or fact') ICC-01/09-01/11-338 Pre Trial Chamber II (22 September 2011).

violence. The Court's decision on the principles to be applied for setting reparations placed a strong emphasis on the need for reparations to be gender inclusive and for the Court to 'formulate and implement reparations awards that are appropriate for the victims of sexual and gender-based violence.'[37] The Prosecutor's request for charges of sexual slavery to be added against Bosco Ntaganda, who served as an aide to Lubanga, can arguably be seen as a response to the concerns expressed by victims in relation to the *Lubanga* case and a positive outcome of their original request. Victims have also successfully requested to be heard in person by the Chamber at trial. While in the *Lubanga* and the *Katanga & Ngudjolo* cases victims only appeared in person in order to present evidence on the case, in the *Bemba* case three victims were granted the right to present their views and concerns via video link.[38] Victims have appeared in all the trials so far to present additional evidence to the relevant chambers. In the *Lubanga* case, the Chamber authorized three participating victims to give evidence under oath, recognising that the region about which the victims provided evidence had been referred to in the evidence and the prosecutor's summary of evidence, but had not been addressed thus far at trial.[39] In the *Katanga* case, Trial Chamber II held that the testimonies could 'shed new light on the events which took place', provide the Chamber with 'a clearer picture of the existing family, ethnic and social networks there' and 'provide new and useful information about possible methods of selecting houses to attack based on ethnicity'.[40] In the *Bemba* case, two victims were granted the right to testify.[41] One of them, testifying without the cover of anonymity, candidly stressed that all she wanted was to 'say before the Judges and before the whole world what [she] had suffered' and for the judges of the ICC to give her justice.[42]

---

[37] *Prosecutor v Lubanga* (Decision establishing the principles and procedures to be applied to reparations) ICC-01/04-01/06 Trial Chamber I (7 August 2012) para 207.

[38] *Prosecutor v Bemba* (Decision on the supplemented applications by the legal representatives of victims to present evidence and the views and concerns of victims) ICC-01/05-01/08-2138 Trial Chamber III (22 February 2012).

[39] *Prosecutor v Lubanga* (Decision on the request by victims a/0225/06, a/0229/06 and a/0270/07 to express their views and concerns in person and to present evidence during the trial) ICC-01/04-01/06-2032 Trial Chamber I (9 July 2009). In that case the credibility of the three victims later came under scrutiny by the Defense and the Trial Chamber I disregarded their testimonies.

[40] *Prosecutor v Katanga & Ngudjolo* (Décision aux fins de comparution des victimes a/0381/09, a/0018/09, a/0191/08 et pan/0363/09 agissant au nom de a/0363/09) ICC-01/04-01/07-2517 Trial Chamber II (9 November 2010). In the end only two victims testified.

[41] *Prosecutor v Bemba* (Decision on the supplemented applications by the legal representatives of victims to present evidence and the views and concerns of victims) (n 38).

[42] *Prosecutor v Bemba* (Hearings Transcripts) ICC-01/05-01/08-T-220-ENG CT WT Trial Chamber III (1 May 2012) p 53.

Another way in which the Court has heard victims is through victims presenting their views and concerns in person. In the *Bemba* case, for the first time, participating victims requested to be heard as participants only (and not witnesses) in order to bring their views and concerns to the Judges. The issue had already arisen in the *Lubanga case*, as the three victims who had come to testify had originally asked to present their views and concerns as well. Trial Chamber I had explained that this was, in essence, 'the equivalent of presenting submissions, and although any views and concerns of the victims may assist the Chamber in its approach to the evidence in the case, these statements by victims ... will not form part of the trial evidence.'[43]

In the *Bemba* case, the Chamber authorized three victims to appear before it only for the purpose of presenting their views and concerns and stressed that the victims would not be questioned by the parties; rather they would be guided through their statement by their counsel. On 25th and 26th June 2012, the three victims appeared before the Chamber through video-link from the Central African Republic (CAR) and described to the Court their individual accounts of events, the harm they suffered, the physical, social, and financial consequences of the attacks, the harm they experienced and in particular the stigmatisation suffered as a result of violence. This process was perceived as a relief by the victims, with one explaining that she felt 'a sense of satisfaction, because [she] ha[d] been able to come before the International Criminal Court'.[44]

The decisions by Chambers to admit testimonies, views and concerns in person send a strong signal that victims' views, concerns and voices matter; and that the Court, while remote, is willing and open to hear from those who have suffered the most and to recognize that they have something to add to the legal process. While these are positive examples of how victims have been able to engage and participate in proceedings before the ICC, the challenges they face in exercising this right should not be overlooked.

III. CHALLENGES TO THE PARTICIPATION OF VICTIMS

Despite the achievements highlighted above, implementing victims' right to participate in proceedings has proved challenging. Often the procedures and bureaucracies relating to the management of victim participation have been at odds with the realities in the field. In many cases victims and other indi-

---

[43] *Prosecutor v Lubanga* (Decision on the request by victims a/0225/06, a/0229/06 and a/0270/07 to express their views and concerns in person and to present evidence during the trial) (n 39) para 25.

[44] *Prosecutor v Bemba* (Hearing transcripts) ICC-01/05-01/08-T-228-Red-ENG WT Trial Chamber III (26 June 2012) p 8.

viduals in affected communities still perceive the Court as a geographically distant institution.

Victims often live in precarious security conditions, with fighting ongoing or only recently ended. Despite the Court's best efforts to protect victims, for example by redacting their identities from public documents, participation remains a risky choice. Even an assumption of participation in proceedings may present a serious risk for an individual. Additional considerations also include possible pressure from communities. For example, in the *Lubanga* case, many of the children recruited by the UPC/FPLC came from the same tribe as Lubanga and victims wanting to engage with the Court often still lived in communities where his supporters were present and active. Consequently, those who came forward as victims were sometimes perceived as 'traitors' by their own communities. Recently, this came to the fore in the *Ruto and Sang* case where victims from a community allegedly requested to withdraw from the case. Their legal representative later informed the Chamber of several incidents which shed doubt on the process that led to the withdrawal and the genuine willingness of some of the victims in question to do so. The legal representative requested that the Chamber further investigate the root causes of the withdrawal including alleged intimidation by the local administration.[45]

In addition, for victims to participate in proceedings, they will first need to receive information about the Court and the possibility of participating in proceedings. In many countries where the Court is currently conducting investigations, many victims are illiterate and have little or no access to the media and other electronic communication facilities. When they do have access to the media, additional issues arise. For example, in countries such as Kenya, the media reportedly contributed[46] to misinformation. The Court has increased its outreach efforts and endeavors through its field presence to provide timely and neutral information to victims and affected communities. However, the Court remains unable to reach all victims potentially affected by the judicial proceedings.

The jurisprudence has established that only victims' applications that are complete (ie, which provide all the information required for a ruling) should be transmitted to a Chamber for the purpose of decision on participatory status.[47] In 2011, while 90 per cent of applications received from CAR were

---

[45] *Prosecutor v Ruto & Sang* (Common Legal Representative for Victims' comprehensive Report on the Withdrawal of Victims from the Turbo area by Letter dated 5 June 2013) ICC-01/09-01/11- 896-Corr-Red Trial Chamber V(A) (5 September 2013).

[46] Prosecutor's Statement in relation to Kenya (5 April 2013) <http://www.icc-cpi.int/en_menus/icc/structure%20of%20the%20court/office%20of%20the%20prosecutor/reports%20and%20statements/statement/Pages/otp-statement-05-04-2013.aspx>.

[47] *Situation in Democratic Republic of Congo* (Decision on the Requests of the Legal Representative of Applicants on application process for victims' participation and legal representation) ICC-01/04-374 Pre-Trial Chamber I (17 August 2007).

properly completed, this was the case for only 40 per cent of the DRC related applications and 50 per cent of the Kenya related ones.[48] Whilst the relevant application form to be used has been greatly simplified and shortened over the years, it is still unrealistic to expect victims to be able to fill out these forms without some assistance. The Court still receives a high number of incomplete applications from countries where it has been active for some time. This fact is a reminder of the persisting challenges that victims face in order to see their applications reach an ICC judge.

In addition, to enable victims to participate, they need to have their applications decided upon in a timely manner. Difficulties have come to light in recent years in relation to the Court's capacity to process applications. While originally a low number of victims sought to participate in proceedings (only 129 and 364 victims participated in the *Lubanga* and *Katanga & Ngudjolo* cases respectively), the Court should nevertheless have been prepared to handle much higher numbers. As Ferstman emphasised, 'high numbers [of victims] is a fact when dealing with crimes like genocide, war crimes or crimes against humanity, and not a problem or an inconvenience – large numbers are to be expected.'[49] However, in 2011, the ICC received an unprecedented number of applications for participation (6,771 applications were received), and the court's capacity to process these applications was pushed to its limits with many victims missing out on an opportunity to participate in key proceedings. In the *Ruto et al* case[50] and *Muthaura et al*[51] case, the Victims Participation and Reparations Section (VPRS) seized the Court and requested additional time to submit applications after it received over 2,000 applications for participation in the cases. In the end the Registry was able to assess, for the purpose of completion, most, if not all the applications received, and transmitted complete applications to the Chamber. However 1,700 applications were deemed incomplete by the Registry in the *Ruto et al* case and never transmitted to the Chamber. Similarly, in the *Mbarushimana* case, 470 victims who applied to participate ahead of the deadline set by the Chamber were denied the opportunity to have their applications adjudicated because the Registry could not process them in time. The reasons given were limited human resources and the demands from other

[48] 'Report on activities and programme performance of the International Criminal Court for the year 2011' ICC-ASP-11/8 (4 May 2012) 51.

[49] C Ferstman, 'Speech presented at the Celebration of the tenth anniversary of the Rome Statute of the International Criminal Court, organized by the Dutch Ministry of Foreign Affairs together with the French Embassy in The Hague and the Coalition for the International Criminal Court' (Celebration of the tenth anniversary of the Rome Statute of the International Criminal Court conference, The Hague, 3 July 2008) (document on file with author).

[50] *Prosecutor v Ruto, Kosgey & Sang* (Request for instructions on the processing of victims' applications) ICC-01/09-01/11-144 Pre Trial Chamber II (24 June 2011).

[51] Ibid.

proceedings.[52] In the *Bemba* case, the volume of received submissions led to applications being submitted and ruled upon on a rolling basis, well after the trial had started. Over 1,700 victims were granted participatory status after the Prosecution had already concluded the presentation of its evidence, which was too late to be considered for the purpose of appearing in person before the Court.[53] In the *Lubanga* case, seven victims were granted participatory status as late as July 2011, just before the closing statements of the trial[54] and 27 applications were not ruled upon as a consequence of the Registry's inability to process and file them ahead of the closing arguments in the trial.[55] Despite the Trial Chamber's indication that these applications would be considered in the event of a conviction for the purpose of sentencing and reparation proceedings, this was not the case. Only recently, and in the context of the appeals against the conviction and sentencing decisions were these applications finally ruled upon.[56]

Participation of victims, who are granted participatory status, is unlikely to be meaningful if they are not kept informed of all relevant proceedings and their outcome in accordance with Rule 92 of the Rules of Procedure and Evidence. However, accessing the internet and/or telecommunications is frequently problematic. It is costly and often not safe for victims, many of whom live on less than $3 a day, to communicate in that manner. In the most remote places internet may only be accessible in internet cafés, with little protection in terms of confidentiality of the information exchanged. This has led some victims to feel abandoned or forgotten by the ICC. The length of

52 *Prosecutor v Mbarushimana* (Proposal on victim participation in the confirmation hearing) ICC-01/04-01/10-213 Pre Trial Chamber I (6 June 2011).

53 The Prosecutor concluded its evidence in March 2012. 1,377 victims were granted participatory status in May 2012 while another 331 were granted participatory status in July 2012. See *Prosecutor v Bemba* (Decision on 1400 applications by victims to participate in the proceedings) ICC-01/05-01/08-2219 Trial Chamber III (21 May 2012) and *Prosecutor v Bemba* (Public redacted version of 'Decision on the tenth and seventeenth transmissions of applications by victims to participate in the proceedings') ICC-01/05-01/08-2247 Trial Chamber III (19 July 2012).

54 *Prosecutor v Lubanga* (Redacted version of the Decision on the applications by 7 victims to participate in the proceedings) ICC-01/04-01/06-2764-Red Trial Chamber I (25 July 2011).

55 *Prosecutor v Lubanga* (Request for instructions on victim's applications for participation and reparations received by the Registry) ICC-01/04-01/06-2817 Trial Chamber I (2 November 2011).

56 In doing so, the Appeals Chamber stressed that these applications ought to have been ruled upon earlier, by the Trial Chamber. In order not to deprive the newly accepted victims from the opportunity to present their views and concerns in the appeals – submissions from victims had already been filed – the Appeals Chamber directed their legal representatives to ascertain their views and, should they differ from those already submitted, file an additional submission. *Prosecutor v Lubanga* (Decision on 32 applications to participate in the proceedings) ICC-01/04-01/06- 3045-Red2 Appeals Chamber (27 August 2013).

proceedings and lack of information explaining delays can also lead to frustration and tensions on the ground. For example, in 2012, the postponement of the hearing on the confirmation of charges in the *Gbagbo* case was wrongly understood by some victims as the end of the case. In Eastern DRC, some victims believed they had missed out on the opportunity to claim reparations after the Trust Fund for Victims started implementing activities under its assistance mandate, not understanding the difference between the two mandates of the Fund. Without adequate, regular, neutral and prompt information, it is easy for victims who may not understand all complexities of legal proceedings, to lose faith in the ICC's ability to deliver meaningful justice to them.

The participation of victims in the proceedings is mostly achieved through their legal representative, who will be representing their interests throughout the proceedings. When victims are indigent, their legal representation will be funded through the Court's legal aid system, which is administered by the Registrar. The Chambers have highlighted the need 'to ensure that the participation of victims, through their legal representatives, is as meaningful as possible, as opposed to 'purely symbolic'.[57] It is generally recognized that counsel funded by the legal aid system of the Court should be provided with a support structure that allows them to: respond to a reasonable number of specific legal inquiries from individual victims; receive general guidelines or instructions from his or her clients as a group and particular requests from individual victims; maintain up to date files of all participating victims and their whereabouts; obtain qualified legal support on a need basis; store and process any confidential filings or other information, including the identity of his or her clients, in a safe and secure manner; and communicate with victims in a language they understand.[58]

Legal representatives and their teams are also reliant on the Court's aid system for travel expenses incurred to meet with their clients, which are often spread over long distances, in order to keep them informed and consult with them. With increasing pressure on the Registrar to reduce the cost of legal aid, victims' counsel have, in the past, questioned whether the resources made available to them truly allow them to fulfil their obligations. In the *Ruto* case, the former common legal representative of victims seized the Chamber on

[57] *Prosecutor v Katanga & Ngudjolo* (Order on the organisation of common legal representation of victims) ICC-01/04-01/07-1328 Trial Chamber II (22 July 2009) para 10; *Prosecutor v Bemba* (Decision on common legal representation of victims for the purpose of trial) ICC-01/05-01/08-1005 Trial Chamber III (10 November 2010) para 9.

[58] *Prosecutor v Katanga & Ngudjolo* (Order on the organisation of common legal representation of victims) (n 57) para 17; *Prosecutor v Bemba* (Decision on common legal representation of victims for the purpose of trial) (n 57) paras 20-21; *Prosecutor v Muthaura, Kenyatta and Ali* (Decision on Victims' Participation at the Confirmation of Charges Hearing and in the Related Proceedings) (n 17) para 32.

numerous occasions to stress that she was not in a position to adequately meet with her clients.[59] In the *Katanga* case, ahead of the closing arguments in the trial, one legal representative of victims requested additional resources in order to travel to DRC to: i) inform his clients of developments and collect their instructions regarding final arguments and ii) meet them individually to obtain additional information. The Registry rejected the request stating that a single Legal Assistant in the field would suffice and the Chamber confirmed that 'personal contact with victims was unnecessary for the purposes of the mission'.[60] While personal contact between victim and their counsel may not be mandated in relation to each issue coming before the Chamber, it is arguable whether participation can truly be meaningful without at least some level of personal contact between victims and their counsel.

IV. LOOKING AT THE WAY FORWARD

Further efforts are necessary to improve the process by which victims interact with their counsel and the Court in their role as a participant. Without a two-way communication channel between the Court and victims, and also between victims and their counsel, participation cannot be meaningful or active. While the presence of victims' counsel at court hearings acts as a reminder that victims are present throughout the proceedings, for participation to be meaningful and active there needs to be a field based aspect. In the *Muthaura et al* case, the Chamber emphasized that either the counsel or an assistant should be based in the field.[61] In the *Ggagbo* case the Single Judge also requested that the common legal representative should be assisted by a team member with wide knowledge of the context and based in Côte d'Ivoire.[62] In addition to ensuring the presence of part of the legal representation team close to the location of the victims, the ICC also has other tools at its disposal to bring the proceedings closer to victims. *In situ* hearings, for one, remain an untested possibility envisaged in the Rome Statute through which participation could be brought closer to victims.[63]

---

59 *Prosecutor v Ruto & Sang* (Urgent request by the Victims' Representative pursuant to Regulation 83(4) of the Regulations) ICC-01/09-01/11-420 Trial Chamber V (1 June 2012).

60 *Prosecutor v Katanga & Ngudjolo* (Decision on the Urgent Requests by the Legal Representative of Victims for Review of Registrar's Decision of 3 April 2012 regarding Legal Aid) ICC-01/04-01/07-3277 Trial Chamber II (23 April 2012).

61 *Prosecutor v Muthaura, Kenyatta and Ali* (Decision on Victims' Participation at the Confirmation of Charges Hearing and in the Related Proceedings) (n 17) para 92.

62 *Prosecutor v Bemba* (Decision on common legal representation of victims for the purpose of trial) (n 57).

63 Art 3(3) of the Rome Statute provides that 'The Court may sit elsewhere, whenever it considers it desirable, as provided in this Statute'. The possibility to hold part of the *Ruto and*

Discussions on how to improve the judicial processes of the Court are continuing, with alternative models under consideration. Judges have a wide margin of discretion as to the parameters of victims' participation, the specific nature of their participation and the form this participation would take. They thus have the ability to streamline the process by which victims' applications for participation are processed and ruled upon by the Court. Over the last year or so, this has translated into different approaches being tested in ongoing cases. In the *Gbagbo* case, the Single Judge used her discretion to impose a partly collective approach to victims' applications for participation in addition to the traditional individualized one.[64] It was hoped that by replacing the need for each individual victim to fill in a separate form, which is then individually processed and assessed, the collective approach would render the process more efficient and less resource intensive. Some have expressed strong reservations in relation to the collective application process[65] and the efficiency gains expected are yet to be confirmed by the Court. The Registry has since indicated that 'it will not always be feasible or advisable to bring together groups of victims physically for the purposes of an application process.'[66] In the Kenya cases, Trial Chamber V set out a new procedure and ruled that only victims wishing to appear in person before the Court should fill in a full application form while others could register with the Registry through a less detailed process, which does not involve a judicial decision on their participation.[67] In the *Ntaganda* case, a new approach was again adopted whereby a new, shorter, application form is to be used. While these attempts at finding solutions to address some of the challenges described in this paper are encouraging, the lack of common vision and consistency in

---

Sang trial in Kenya or Tanzania was recently considered by the plenary of Judges however the majority of judges ruled in favour of the proceedings remaining in The Hague. In that instance, the overwhelming majority of victims participating in the case had expressed concerns with holding the proceedings in Kenya. *Prosecutor v Ruto & Sang* (Decision of the Plenary of Judges on the Joint Defence Application for a Change of Place where the Court Shall Sit for Trial) ICC-01/09-01/11-875-Anx Plenary (26 August 2013).

[64] *Prosecutor v Gbagbo* (Second decision on issues related to the victims' application process) ICC-02/11-01/11-86 Pre Trial Chamber I (5 April 2012).

[65] See *Prosecutor v Gbagbo* (Request to appear before the Chamber pursuant to Regulation 81(4)(b) of the Regulations of the Court on the specific issue of victims' application process) ICC-02/11-01/11-40 Pre Trial Chamber II (14 February 2012); *Prosecutor v Gbagbo* (Second Request to appear before the Chamber pursuant to Regulation 81(4)(b) of the Regulations of the Court on issues related to the victims' application process) ICC-02/11-01/11-51 Pre Trial Chamber I (8 March 2012).

[66] *Prosecutor v Ntaganda* (Registry Observations in compliance with the Decision ICC-01/04-02/06-54-Conf) ICC-01/04-02/06-57 Pre Trial Chamber II (6 May 2013).

[67] *Prosecutor v Muthaura & Kenyatta* (Decision on victims' representation and participation) ICC-01/09-02/11-498 Trial Chamber V (3 October 2012); *Prosecutor v Ruto & Sang* (Decision on victims' representation and participation) ICC-01/09-01/11-460 Trial Chamber V (3 October 2012).

how Chambers approach the way victims apply to and participate in proceedings is also problematic.[68]

Constraints on human and financial resources have made it increasingly difficult for the Court to adapt to the increasing number of victims' applications. Calls for additional resources have come at a time when States Parties, responsible for financing the Court's activities, are facing difficult economic circumstances, and have been reluctant to increase the budget of the Court. However, although there is a need for the revision of the system of victims' participation, efforts to review the system run the risk of being overshadowed by financial considerations. Some have also expressed doubts as to whether the current system does in fact provide a form of participation that is sufficiently meaningful and effective to justify its costs.[69] While it is time for the Court to review the system of victims' participation, such a review should be driven with the interests of victims at heart.

V. CONCLUSION

In conclusion, can we determine that the participation of victims in ICC proceedings has been the success many had hoped for when the Rome Statute was drafted? Perhaps we can. Imperfect as the system may be, the ability of victims to participate in the proceedings before the Court bears tremendous potential to make the justice of the ICC truly restorative, and to place victims at the centre of the justice it delivers. A lot of work remains to be done so that the system can be articulated in a way that truly provides victims with meaningful and active participation in the proceedings. A warranted review of the system has begun and recommended steps, some of which have already been attempted, could lead to improvements. Reform is underway and as it progresses, relevant actors should take into account the high number of victims who may wish to engage with the Court, and seek to assert their right, not privilege, to participate in such proceedings, in as meaningful a manner as possible.

---

[68] See REDRESS, 'Independent Panel of Experts Report on Victim Participation at the International Criminal Court' (July 2013) <http://www.redress.org/downloads/publications/130711%20panel%20report%20FINALfor%20dissemination.pdf>.

[69] C Van den Wyngaert, 'Victims before International Criminal Courts: Some Views and Concerns of an ICC Trial Judge' (2011) 44 Case Western Reserve Journal of International Law 475–496.

The Mandate of the Trust Fund for Victims to Assist Victims in Conflict Affected Communities

*Pieter de Baan**

Ten years ago, the International Criminal Court (ICC) became the world's first permanent international tribunal, dedicated to investigating and prosecuting those responsible for the most serious war crimes, crimes against humanity and genocide.[1] Since then, 122 countries, or nearly two-thirds of the United Nations General Assembly, have ratified the Rome Statute to become States Parties to the Court.[2] During this decade, the Court has carried out investigations in eight countries, resulting in 15 cases. In March 2012 it issued its first judgment convicting Thomas Lubanga of war crimes related to child soldiers.[3]

But the Court has not only become a threat to the perpetrators of the most serious crimes, including high-level individuals accused of orchestrating brutal policies resulting in murder, widespread sexual violence, or use of child soldiers. It has also become the source of hope to hundreds of thousands of victims, not least because of another creation of the Rome Statute: the Trust Fund for Victims (the Trust Fund).[4]

The Trust Fund is an integral part of the Rome Statute. Its fate is intrinsically linked with that of the Court, and yet its mission is a particular one. The Trust Fund may not only be tasked with facilitating reparations to victims

* Executive Director of the Trust Fund for Victims. The author wishes to acknowledge the contribution to this article by Katharina Peschke, Legal Adviser at the Trust Fund (2010–2012).

[1] Rome Statute of the International Criminal Court, (2002) 2187 UNTS 90, Art 129 (Rome Statute).

[2] See <http://www.icc-cpi.int/en_menus/asp/states%20parties/Pages/states%20parties%20_%20 chronological%20list.aspx>.

[3] See *Prosecutor v Thomas Lubanga Dyilo* (Judgment pursuant to Article 74 of the Statute) ICC-01/04-01/06-2842 (14 March 2012).

[4] See <http://www.trustfundforvictims.org>. See also M Jennings, 'Article 79' in O Triffterer (ed), *Commentary on the Rome Statute of the International Criminal Court: Observers' Notes, Article by Article* (CH Beck, Hart, Nomos 2008) 1439–1442 and WA Schabas, *The International Criminal Court: A Commentary on the Rome Statute* (Oxford University Press 2010) 909–917.

ordered by the Court, but it also implements projects for the benefit of victims of crimes recognized as falling within the Court's jurisdiction under its general assistance mandate, without such victims having to be directly linked to proceedings of a particular case before the Court.[5] The creation of the 'Trust Fund' with these two distinct mandates is a remarkable step forward in terms of considering the rights and needs of victims – which cannot be met by the Court's judgments against those most responsible alone. In other words, the Trust Fund's reparative justice approach directly benefitting victims complements the mission of the ICC to bring the perpetrators of the worst crimes of humanity to justice by offering victims tangible assistance.

Envisaged in Article 79 of the Rome Statute, the Trust Fund was established as an entity by the Assembly of States Parties in September 2002.[6] In late 2007, it began carrying out its first activities for the benefit of victims in countries where the ICC is active and it has continued to widen its operations.

The Trust Fund benefits from the leadership and guidance of a five-member Board of Directors elected by the Assembly of States Parties, which represents the States Parties to the Rome Statue, for 3 year terms.[7] The Trust Fund Secretariat manages the day-to-day operations of the Fund. Half of the Secretariat staff is based in the field.

Under its general assistance mandate, the Trust Fund uses voluntary contributions from donors to provide victims and their families in situations before the Court with the following categories of assistance:

- *Physical Rehabilitation* which includes reconstructive surgery, bullet and bomb fragment removal, the fitting of prosthetic and orthopaedic devices, referrals to services like fistula repair and HIV screening, treatment and support;
- *Psychological Rehabilitation* which includes both individual and group-based trauma counselling; music, dance and drama groups to promote social cohesion and healing; community sensitization workshops and large-scale community meetings; and
- *Material Support* initiatives may include livelihood activities, vocational training, or access to referral programmes that offer income generation and training opportunities to focus on longer-term economic empower-

[5] Art 79 Rome Statute; Rules of Procedure and Evidence, adopted by the Assembly of States Parties (3-10 September 2002) OR ICC-ASP/1/3, Rule 98(5) (Rules of Procedure and Evidence).

[6] 'Establishment of a fund for the benefit of victims of crimes within the jurisdiction of the Court, and of the families of such victims' (9 September 2002) Res ICC-ASP/1/Res 6.

[7] Ibid, Annex para 2.

ment. Material support may also include education grants for victim survivors and their children. Furthermore, the Trust Fund encourages community saving schemes.[8]

In the past five years, the Trust Fund has operated in the eastern part of the Democratic Republic of the Congo (DRC) and in northern Uganda, reaching out to over 110,000 beneficiaries, ie victims of crimes under the jurisdiction of the ICC.[9] Operations in the Central African Republic were scheduled to start in early 2013, but were suspended in March 2013 until further notice in consideration of the security situation in the country. These activities of the Fund are financed by voluntary contributions, by donations of private and public donors, including States, and not by the Court's regular budget. In the currently depressed global economic situation, the mobilization of sufficient resources is particularly challenging, although the Fund's income in 2011 reached an unprecedented level of 3.2 million Euros. That being said, raising sufficient resources remains one of the most important challenges for the Trust Fund.

The Trust Fund provides its assistance through partnerships with national and international implementing partners.[10] These partners include international non-governmental organizations, local grassroots organizations, women's associations, faith-based organizations and the private sector. The Fund aims to ensure that they have the financial resources, technical expertise and oversight that they need to adequately rehabilitate victims.

It is important to understand that the Trust Fund's assistance mandate is related to the existence of the Court's jurisdiction in a certain situation and that its operation does not depend on the existence or the outcome of proceedings in a particular case. This allows the Trust Fund to engage also with victims and communities that fall outside of the scope of the charges brought by the Office of the Prosecutor. However, procedurally the Trust Fund must notify the respective Pre-Trial Chamber of its intention to undertake activities for the benefit of victims so as to ensure that its activities will 'not pre-determine any issue to be determined by the Court'.[11]

The combination of the two mandates, assistance and reparations, is unprecedented and provides the Trust Fund with key powers for meeting the needs of victims of the gravest crimes in international law. In particular, the Trust Fund can engage with victims outside of the scope of any particular trial and prior to, as well as after, the conclusion of ICC proceedings. This means

---

[8] See 'Regulations for the Trust Fund for Victims' Res ICC-ASP/4/Res.3 (3 December 2005) Reg 50(a)(i). (TFV Regulations).

[9] For an overview see <http://www.trustfundforvictims.org/projects>.

[10] Regs 47–48 TFV Regulations.

[11] Reg 50(a)(ii) TFV Regulations.

that its intervention can be timely – trials often take a long time to complete or, as the case of northern Uganda shows it, may take a long time for the perpetrators to be apprehended and brought to justice.

It also means that the Trust Fund can react in a more flexible way to the most vulnerable victims. In the eastern DRC the Trust Fund has been supporting girls forcibly conscripted into and sexually abused by armed groups. Such crimes were not part of the charges against Thomas Lubanga. Assistance to victims of sexual and gender based violence (SGBV) has been a key feature of the Trust Fund's activities and incorporates physical and psychosocial rehabilitation services, material support, and reconciliation efforts at family level and with the victims' communities.[12]

The Trust Fund is also a valuable source of information for the Court. Lessons learnt from its assistance mandate may inform the judges who have to decide on reparations about what victims need and how the Court may best engage with victims and give them a voice in the process. This was recognized in the Decision of Trial Chamber I, issued on 7 August 2012, establishing the principles and procedures to be applied to reparations, in which the Trial Chamber adopted a consultative, community-based approach for the development of a collective reparations award.[13]

So how does the Trust Fund concretely go about repairing harm to victims under its assistance mandate? The Trust Fund addresses harm at two levels: firstly, at the individual level the Trust Fund seeks to support the empowerment and restoration of dignity of victims through concrete activities which directly benefit them; and secondly, at the collective level, the Trust Fund supports efforts to promote reconciliation within affected communities and to restore the social fabric that has been torn by conflict.

One positive example of an intervention at an individual level can be found in the Trust Fund's summer 2011 Programme Progress Report, which tells the story of Santa, a 35 year old survivor of a Lord's Resistance Army (LRA) attack that left her severely disfigured because of burns to her neck and face. Excluded from her community because of the horrible scars that she sustained, she underwent plastic surgery and learnt how to earn her own living again. She stated: 'my eyes could not see, my lips were twisted and coupled with a stiff neck, I was unable to cook or dig.' After the medical intervention, her life has turned around; now she is more engaged in village

---

[12] See also the TFV Programme Progress Report, 'Moblising Resources and Supporting the Most Vulnerable Victims through Earmarked Funding' (Winter 2012) <http://www.trustfundforvictims.org/sites/default/files/media_library/documents/pdf/TFV%20Programme%20Progress%20Report%20Winter%202012Finalcompressed.pdf>.

[13] *Prosecutor v Thomas Lubanga Dyilo* (Decision establishing the principles and procedures to be applied to reparations) ICC-01/04-01/06-2904 Trial Chamber I (7 August 2012). This decision is currently at the stage of appeal proceedings.

life and can contribute to supporting her family by working on a small plot of land.[14]

To bring about positive change at the collective level, the Trust Fund supports community reconciliation projects, for example in the Eastern Democratic Republic of the Congo, where the situation is still unstable and local conflict persists. In this context, the Trust Fund's local partners work closely with communities to develop community-focused programs that help mobilize victims around their rights and to transform their lives and communities in the aftermath of the conflict. These programs support community-led initiatives, such as remembrance and historic memory activities with a view to promoting individual and community healing, peace and reconciliation, the promotion of human rights, and cultures of respect, tolerance, and gender equality. They use dance, music, drama and sports to raise awareness around rights and current issues that matter to victims, as well as assisting communities affected by war to discuss and agree on key actions that need to be taken at the community level to heal and move forward with peace and tolerance, and to ensure that the voices of vulnerable and marginalized community members are heard. Several thousand victims have attended such activities at a community level, learning about ways to address underlying causes as well as results of conflict.

Unfortunately, the Trust Fund also experiences serious challenges to its important mission.

The first challenge stems from the fact that victims live in conflict-affected communities where insecurity often persists. This fragile security situation has direct effects, such as security concerns for the victims themselves and also for the Trust Fund's implementing partners, as well as indirect effects.

In particular, whether the Trust Fund can play the important role of concretely manifesting the Rome Statute's promise to victims will depend largely on the manner in which the Trust Fund's support is publicly explained and acknowledged. As Martti Koskenniemi has noted, often victims 'do not so much expect the punishment (though of course that is not insignificant) but rather the recognition of the fact that what they were made to suffer was "wrong", and that their moral grandeur is symbolically reaffirmed.'[15] However, because of the difficult security situations in some of the regions where the Trust Fund operates (for example, the persistent instability in eastern Congo), as well as for more global concerns (international NGOs with

---

14 TFV, 'Reviewing Rehabilitation Assistance and Preparing for Delivering Reparations – Programme Progress Report Summer 2011' (TVF 2011) 23. <http://www.trustfundforvictims.org/node/28/documents/word%20files/TFV%20Programme%20Report%20Summer%202011.pdf>.

15 See M Koskenniemi, 'Between Impunity and Show Trials' (2002) 6 Max Planck Yearbook of United Nations Law 10–11.

operations in Darfur/Sudan, for instance, may have an interest not to be seen as being close with the Court), some of the Trust Fund's implementing partners have in the past been reluctant to be 'too publicly' associated with the ICC – and with the Trust Fund. Accordingly, they have asked to keep their link to the Trust Fund confidential. And yet, it is important to underline that the Trust Fund does not provide any humanitarian assistance in the narrow sense of the term. Instead, because of its link to the ICC, any assistance it provides has a very important symbolic dimension: it implies the recognition of the fact that the harm suffered was 'wrong', to use Koskennieni's words. Its aim must be the moral rehabilitation of victim-survivors from any stigma that might be associated with the harm that they so unfairly suffered.

A second fundamental limitation stems from the ambitious scope of the Trust Fund's mandate to be a tool of reparative justice in the face of crimes over which the Court has jurisdiction. War crimes, genocide and crimes against humanity inherently affect a large number of victims, and affect them severely.

The Trust Fund depends on voluntary donations by States and private donors.[16] Without those resources it will not be able to carry out its work. The Trust Fund is grateful for the commitment and the donations it has received since it started functioning. In total, 28 countries as well as private donors have contributed since 2004. Some of these donations have been earmarked for victim survivors of sexual violence, a particularly vulnerable group of victims. However, the Trust Fund will need continued and additional support in the future. To respond to the challenge of limited resources, the Trust Fund acts strategically. For example, it undertakes specific actions targeting the most vulnerable victim groups, such as victims of sexual violence or former child soldiers.

Finally, while the main focus of this chapter is the Trust Fund's assistance mandate, a few observations related to the reparations mandate need to be made. Under this mandate, the Trust Fund may be tasked with implementing Court-ordered reparations awards against a convicted person when directed by the Court to do so.[17] The reparations mandate is not completely defined yet: several cases are pending before the ICC and only in the *Lubanga* case has the Court issued a decision on reparations.[18]

The Trust Fund's reparations mandate is directly linked to a criminal case against an accused before the ICC. Resources are collected through fines or forfeiture and awards for reparations, and complemented with 'other

---

[16] An overview of contributions received so far is available at <http://www.trustfundforvictims.org/financial-info>.

[17] Arts 75(2), 78(2) Rome Statute.

[18] *Prosecutor v Thomas Lubanga Dyilo* (Decision establishing the principles and procedures for reparations) ICC-01/04-01/06-2904 (7 August 2012).

resources of the Trust Fund' if the Board of Directors so determines.[19] It is important to note that reparations to, or in respect of victims, can take many different forms, including restitution, compensation and rehabilitation, and can be individual or collective, or both.[20] This broad mandate leaves room to identify the most appropriate forms of reparation in light of the context of the situation and the wishes of the victims and their communities. Much will depend on how the Court – and the Trust Fund – moves forward with regards to reparations. A lot is at stake. If the ICC's reparations system fails to deliver meaningful reparations to victims, this will have a serious effect on the rights of victims even outside the cases before it. If all goes well, however, the ICC's reparation system may even serve as an inspiration and catalyst for reparations in a wider context at national level in countries in need of transitional justice.

Principles related to reparations, foreseen in Article 75 of the Rome Statute, will be developed through a case law approach. The Trust Fund has, in its submission to Trial Chamber I, which dealt with the *Lubanga* case, explained why it considers that such principles should also address the need for transformative measures where appropriate.[21] Transformative reparations may serve not only as a form of reparative justice, but also as an opportunity to overcome structural conditions of inequality and exclusion.[22] In particular, in the aftermath of war crimes, crimes against humanity and genocide, it will often not be appropriate to restore the *status quo ante* that gave rise to such crimes, in particular because the majority of victims of such crimes were likely to have been the powerless and dispossessed at the time when the conflict erupted.[23] The need for transformation may seem particularly true in the context of addressing harm suffered by women and girls whose reality is often negatively shaped by structural inequalities.

In conclusion, a first decade has passed since the Assembly of States Parties created the ICC and the Trust Fund. This gives reason for celebration as well as for stocktaking and reflection. However, one should not forget that a decade is only a short period of time in the life of permanent institutions.

Time will show whether the Trust Fund will make the most of its important mission to transform victims of the worst crimes of humanity into empowered survivors and whether it can even contribute to reconciliation

---

19 Reg 56 TFV Regulations.

20 Art 75(2) Rome Statute; Rule 98(2)(3) Rules of Procedure and Evidence.

21 *Prosecutor v Thomas Lubanga Dyilo* (Observations on Reparations in Response to the Scheduling Order of 14 March 2012) ICC- 01/04-01/06-2872 (25 April 2012).

22 Ibid para 72.

23 Ibid para 73.

and the prevention of international crimes. To succeed, the Trust Fund depends on continued commitment and support from States as well as from individuals. With the benefit of such support, the Trust Fund will strive to develop into a beacon of reparative justice, making a real difference to victims.

Legal Space for Reparations: The Tensions Inherent in the ICC's Reparation Regime

*Mia Swart**

I. INTRODUCTION

Much has been said of the innovative approach to victim recognition, participation and reparation by the International Criminal Court (ICC). By placing victims at the centre of its concerns, the ICC challenges the old notion that victims should suffer in silence. In line with the Basic Principles and Guidelines on the Right to Reparation for Victims, the ICC affirms its solidarity with victims of violations of international law as well as with 'humanity at large.'[1] By including victims in its mandate, the ICC recognises that international criminal law is too complex to be contained within the traditional paradigm of prosecution and punishment. If one accepts that the ICC also has the function of reparation and restoration, it is vital to go beyond the prosecution paradigm.

Whereas there can be little doubt that the ICC's initiative to protect and include victims in its work is a salutary development which deserves to be celebrated, a preliminary question that should be addressed is: should the ICC have a reparations mandate at all? Is there legal space for this? Is an international criminal court the correct forum for reparations?

The concern that the ICC should not have a reparations role is often raised both by domestic and international lawyers. It is felt that the conflation of the

* Professor of International Law, University of Johannesburg. The research for this article was conducted in part during a fellowship at the Stellenbosch Institute for Advanced Studies (STIAS).

[1] 'Basic Principles and Guidelines on the Right to a Remedy and Reparation for Victims of Gross Violations of International Human Rights Law and Serious Violations of International Humanitarian Law', adopted and proclaimed by General Assembly on 16 December 2005 and annexed to UN Doc A/RES/60/147 (21 March 2006), state in their preamble: '*Convinced* that, in adopting a victim-oriented perspective, the international community affirms its human solidarity with victims of violations of international law, including violations of international human rights law and international humanitarian law, as well as with humanity.'

prosecutorial and reparatory roles of the Court is problematic and that this conflation creates tensions within the ICC regime that are difficult to resolve.

Common law lawyers very often raise the argument that it is inappropriate for a criminal court to decide on reparations[2] and so it seems appropriate that this paper will begin by commenting on the distinguishing factors of the civil and common law systems. I will highlight the fact that it is not at all uncommon for a court – particularly at the domestic level – to have a dual role of both deciding criminal cases and awarding reparations. There is an emerging trend in common law jurisdictions, such as the United States and United Kingdom, of increasingly providing 'space' for victims in criminal matters.[3] If one accepts the hybrid nature of the ICC it is easier to accept the Court's reparation role.

The reparations mandate of the ICC also raises the following questions: will the reparations mandate affect the objectivity of the judges in deciding on the guilt of the accused? Will judges feel a moral obligation to compensate victims? And if so, will this moral obligation make them more inclined to convict the accused than would otherwise be the case? Another important question is: What is the relationship between the guilt of the accused and the suffering of many thousands of victims?

Critics such as Liesbeth Zegveld have argued that it is inappropriate for the ICC to have a reparations mandate at all.[4] This proposition calls for more academic attention. I will proceed to consider some of the tensions brought to the fore by the ICC's reparations mandate: first, the tension between the reparations mandate of the Court and the general assistance mandate of the Trust Fund for Victims (TFV); secondly, the factors distinguishing the civil and common law systems, particularly as regards the awarding of reparations; and, thirdly, the tension between civil (tort) law and criminal law proceedings.

---

[2] See E Posner, 'A Minimalist Reparations Regime for the International Criminal Court' ICC Forum <http://iccforum.com/reparations>.

[3] With regard to the United Kingdom see P Rock, *Constructing Victims' Rights* (Oxford University Press 2005) 263-330. With regard developments in the United States see CS Goddu, 'Victim's "Rights" or Fair Trial Wronged' (1993) 41 Buffalo Law Review 245. See also JH Stark & HW Goldstein, *The Rights of Crime Victims* (Bantam Books 1985) 3-4 and N Marques, 'Victims' Reparation: What Lessons Can We Take from the International Criminal Court?' Stanford University Program on Human Rights (12 February 2013) <http://humanrights.stanford.edu/news/victims_reparation_what_lessons_can_we_take_from_the_international_criminal_court_20130212>.

[4] See L Zegveld, 'Victims Reparations and International Criminal Courts Incompatible Values?' (2010) 8 Journal of International Criminal Justice 94.

II. BACKGROUND TO THE ICC REPARATIONS REGIME

Awarding reparations for serious human rights violations is increasingly a subject of great interest and importance in international law and transitional justice. The movement to highlight the making of reparations to victims of serious human rights violations is a manifestation of the international movement to accord victims greater recognition in international law. Barkan writes of a new sense of civil rights informed by a new morality.[5]

With regard to reparations, the ICC chose to follow a more progressive approach than the ad hoc international criminal tribunals. The statutory frameworks of the International Criminal Tribunals for the former Yugoslavia (ICTY) and Rwanda (ICTR) did not stipulate a victims' reparation regime. Both tribunals, however, had the power to order the restitution of property.[6] Nevertheless, neither institution has hitherto exercised this power.[7]

The work of the ICC with regard to reparations can have a substantial impact on the lives of tens of thousands of victims. In spite of this, little is known about how the ICC reparations regime will operate in practice. This is due partly to the fact that the documents governing the ICC establish the scheme in very general terms, and partly to the fact that the scheme is *sui generis*.

The issue of reparations at the ICC is governed by Article 75 of the Rome Statute.[8] The Statute caters for victims in two principal ways. First, Article

---

[5] E Barkan, *The Guilt of Nations* (John Hopkins University Press 2001) xx.

[6] Art 24(3) of the ICTY Statute provides that 'in addition to imprisonment, the Trial Chambers may order the return of any property and proceeds acquired by criminal conduct, including the means of duress, to their rightful owners' <www.icty.org/sid/135>. For the corresponding provision at the ICTR see Art 23(3) of the ICTR Statute <http://www.unictr.org/Portals/0/English%5CLegal%5CStatute%5C2010.pdf>.

[7] C McCarthy, *Reparation and Victim Support in the International Criminal Court* (Cambridge University Press 2012) 47.

[8] Art 75 of the Rome Statute states:

> 1. The Court shall establish principles relating to reparations to, or in respect of, victims, including restitution, compensation and rehabilitation. On this basis, in its decision the Court may, either upon request or on its own motion in exceptional circumstances, determine the scope and extent of any damage, loss and injury to, or in respect of, victims and will state the principles on which it is acting.
> 2. The Court may make an order directly against a convicted person specifying appropriate reparations to, or in respect of, victims, including restitution, compensation and rehabilitation. Where appropriate, the Court may order that the award for reparations be made through the Trust Fund provided for in article 79.
> 3. Before making an order under this article, the Court may invite and shall take account of representations from or on behalf of the convicted person, victims, other interested persons or interested States.
> 4. In exercising its power under this article, the Court may, after a person is convicted of a

68(3) of the Rome Statute allows victims to participate in proceedings;[9] participation before the Court may occur at various stages of the proceedings and may take different forms. The judges have the discretion to give directions as to the timing and manner of this participation.[10]

The second way in which the Rome Statute caters for victims is the possibility of payment of reparations. The Court can make an order against a convicted person specifying the appropriate reparation for the victims or their beneficiaries.[11] This reparation may take the form of restitution, indemnification or rehabilitation. The Court may order reparations to be paid through the TFV, which was established by the Assembly of States Parties.[12]

The reparations mandate of the TFV is the result of the bifurcated mandate of the ICC. Rule 98 of the ICC Rules of Procedure and Evidence stipulates that the TFV can award reparations to victims under Article 75(2), which mandates the ICC to make an order directly against a convicted person specifying appropriate reparations in respect of victims. The TFV is also mandated to provide general assistance to victims and their families, which can take the form of physical rehabilitation, material support and psychological rehabilitation.[13]

> crime within the jurisdiction of the Court, determine whether, in order to give effect to an order which it may make under this article, it is necessary to seek measures under article 93, paragraph 1.
>
> 5. A State Party shall give effect to a decision under this article as if the provisions of article 109 were applicable to this article.

(Rome Statute of the International Criminal Court, (2002) 2187 UNTS 90.)

[9] Art 68(3) of the Rome Statute states:

> As an exception to the principle of public hearings provided for in article 67, the Chambers of the Court may, to protect victims and witnesses or an accused, conduct any part of the proceedings in camera or allow the presentation of evidence by electronic or other special means. In particular, such measures shall be implemented in the case of a victim of sexual violence or a child who is a victim or a witness, unless otherwise ordered by the Court, having regard to all the circumstances, particularly the views of the victim or witness.

[10] Rule 89(1) of the ICC Rules of Procedure and Evidence (adopted by the Assembly of States Parties (3-10 September 2002) OR ICC-ASP/1/3). Victims may file submissions before the Pre-Trial Chamber when the Prosecutor requests its authorisation to investigate. They may also file submissions on all matters relating to the competence of the Court or the admissibility of cases. More generally, victims are entitled to file submissions before the Chambers of the Court at the pre-trial stage, at trial, and during the appeals process.

Participation in the Court's proceedings will in most cases take place through a legal representative and will be conducted 'in a manner which is not prejudicial or inconsistent with the rights of the accused and a fair and impartial trial.'

[11] Art 75(2) Rome Statute.

[12] 'Establishment of a fund for the benefit of victims of crimes within the jurisdiction of the Court, and of the families of such victims' (9 September 2002) Res ICC-ASP/1/Res.6.

[13] 'Learning from the TFV's Second Mandate: From Implementing Rehabilitation Assistance to Reparations' <http://www.trustfundforvictims.org/sites/default/files/imce/TFV%20Programme%20Report%20Fall%202010.pdf>.

To trigger the ICC's ability to award reparations it is necessary that a person be convicted of a crime within the jurisdiction of the Court. Accordingly, had Lubanga been found innocent, the Court could not have made a reparations order.[14] The fact that the Rome Statute ties the payment of reparations to the guilt of the accused raises a greater concern. It can be asked whether this puts pressure on the Court to make a conviction.[15] If it is clear that a large number of victims have suffered and need reparation, the Court might be too hasty in making a finding of guilt for the purposes of securing a means by which to alleviate victims' suffering.

But the TFV's hands are not entirely tied until a conviction is made. The TFV has a more flexible mandate; it may provide general assistance to victims whose injury cannot be causally linked to the conduct of the convicted persons (assuming one can always make such a clear distinction) and can do so at any time – before or after the verdict. Under this part of its two-fold mandate, for which it is not reliant on an order of the Court, the TFV has already assisted thousands of victims in concrete and meaningful ways.[16]

According to one commentator, the TFV may play a crucial role 'in closing the gap between expectations of victims who typically have both an urgent psychological need for justice and an urgent need for material support, and what the ICC itself can offer them'.[17]

In terms of the implementation of the TFV's reparations mandate, the ICC may order that money and other property collected through fines or forfeiture from a convicted person be transferred to the TFV for use in the implementation of the reparations reward.[18] As was clear from the *Lubanga* case, the accused will often claim to be indigent and the Court will have to find other sources of funding. The TFV has the mandate to complement such resources through voluntary contributions.[19]

One of the most important characteristics of the ICC framework is the distinction it makes between victim participation and reparation. In domestic legal jurisdictions (such as Germany) victim participation is linked to a claim for civil damages in a criminal action. The Rome Statute deviates from

---

14 The Court found Thomas Lubanga Dyilo guilty of the crime of conscripting, enlisting and using child soldiers. See *Prosecutor v Thomas Lubanga Dyilo* (Judgment pursuant to Article 74 of the Statute) ICC-01/04-01/06-2842 (14 March 2012) para 1358.

15 M Swart, 'Was the ICC's Lubanga Judgment a Fair One?' (*Business Day* 19 March 2012).

16 For more information on the various projects of the Trust Fund for Victims in Africa see <http://www.trustfundforvictims.org/>.

17 See M Glasius, 'What is Global Justice and Who Decided? Civil Society and Victim Responses to the International Criminal Court's First Investigations' (2009) 31 Human Rights Quarterly 517.

18 Cf ibid 516.

19 For more on the politics surrounding donors see S Kendal, 'Donor's Justice' (2011) 24 Leiden Journal of International Law 3.

this conception. Participation in pre-trial and trial proceedings and claims for reparations are independent procedures.[20] Even victims who do not participate in the Court proceedings can potentially be recipients of reparations.

It must be recognized, however, that the ICC, in its *Lubanga* decision, gave victims an important role that exceeded the statutory regime.[21] The interests of victims formed an integral part of the *Lubanga* trial. This was particularly evident from the degree of victim participation in the case, in which as many as 129 victims took part.[22] The interests of victims were also injected directly into the trial in the form of the participation of Paolina Massada, Principal Counsel of the Office of Public Counsel for Victims (OPCV),[23] who represented victims during the closing arguments in the *Lubanga* trial. The heightened importance the ICC attributed to victims in the trial proceedings has, however, been subject to scholarly criticism. According to Damaška, the greatest stress with regard to the rights of the accused at international criminal tribunals stems from the 'ennobling ambition' to place victims at the heart of their mission.[24] In the view of Damaška, the conflicting demands generated by the tension between protecting victims and the accused can be difficult to resolve.[25]

III. THREE TENSIONS

1. *The tension between the reparations mandate of the Court and the general assistance mandate of the Trust Fund for Victims*

The tension between the reparations mandate of the Court, as implemented by the TFV, and the general assistance mandate of the TFV has been described as the main tension running through the ICC system[26] and has led

---

[20] S SáCouto and K Cleary, 'Victims Participation in the Investigations of the ICC' (2008) 17 Transnational Law and Contemporary Problems 87.

[21] See *Prosecutor v Thomas Lubanga Dyilo* (Judgment) (n 14).

[22] Ibid para 16.

[23] The OPCV was established in order to effectively assist victims in exercising their rights, or to represent them before the Chambers, as provided for in the Regulations of the Court. See <http://www.icc-cpi.int/NetApp/App/MCMSTemplates/Content.aspx?NRMODE=Published&NRNODEGUID={007C8D7C-8B11-4E11-8D92-57E1326E40C1}&NRORIGINALURL=/Menus/ICC/Structure+of+the+Court/Victims/Office+of+Public+Counsel+for+Victims/Frequently+Asked+Questions.htm&NRCACHEHINT=Guest#Q_4>.

[24] M Damaška 'The Competing Visions of Fairness: The Basic Choice for International Criminal Tribunals' (2011) 36 North Carolina Journal of International Law and Commercial Regulation 372–373.

[25] Ibid 373 *et seq*.

[26] F Mégret, 'Of Shrines, Memorials and Museums: Using the International Criminal Court's Victims Reparation and Assistance Regime to Promote Transitional Justice' (2010) 16 Buffalo Human Rights Law Review 4, 12–13.

Mégret to describe the system as 'profoundly dual, hybrid, even schizophrenic'.[27] The fact that the Court's reparations mandate is of a more conventionally 'legal' nature (in the sense that the reparations order is a product of the legal process) could place it in conflict with the more humanitarian ambitions of the TFV. Although the Court and the TFV represent two different paradigms, it is important that there be coherence between the Court's reparations mandate and the general assistance role of the TFV.

An intellectual tension exists between court-ordered reparations and the assistance role of the TFV. The logic of reparations is conceptually different from that of TFV assistance. The TFV is not a judicial body and follows a pattern that resembles domestic reparations schemes – its work has been described as falling between humanitarian and welfare logics and is not tied to the finding of guilt.[28] It is analogous to welfare in that it is funded by voluntary contributions from third parties including States, NGOs and individuals. TFV assistance creates the following conundrum: if the ICC is perceived both as the primary institution from which victims are to seek reparation and as an institution of international criminal justice, then what is done for victims will be dependent upon the outcome of proceedings. If, on the other hand, one considers that the TFV takes the leading role when it comes to victims, then rehabilitation and assistance are what victims can primarily expect from the Rome Statute institutions.[29]

This creates the concern that those victims who have not been 'lucky' enough to have been harmed by a particular accused will have no legal claim to reparations.[30] It can be argued that this leads to a privileging of some victims over others, which is a concern that directly relates to the selection of victims.

The problem of selectivity is an overarching concern that runs through international criminal justice generally and which affects the Rome Statute's reparations regime. This could potentially cause tension and conflict between victim groups. The fact that the investigation and prosecution of crimes at the ICC is necessarily selective has important implications for reparations. In light of the fact that reparations cannot be effected in the absence of a conviction, one can speak of a 'double selectivity' – at a prosecutorial level as well as with regard to reparations.

The *Lubanga* case gave rise to the first ICC reparations decision which offers some guidance as to the relationship between the Court and the TFV. In the *Lubanga* reparations decision the Court drafted principles of reparations in

---

27 Ibid 4.

28 Idem.

29 Idem.

30 Ibid 12.

accordance with its Article 75 duty.[31] It can be argued that the Court failed to live up to expectations in its formulation of reparations principles. The lack of clarity with regard to reparations is illustrated by the fact that the Court has still not provided a clear definition of the harm requirement and the element of causation. However, the inadequacies of the process of drafting principles are not the focus of this chapter.[32] The Trial Chamber allocated a specific role to the TFV. It was decided that the Chamber would rely on the TFV for the implementation of the reparations award.[33] A newly constituted Trial Chamber will assist in the implementation.[34] Both States Parties to the Rome Statute and non-States Parties will be required to cooperate to give effect to the reparations awards. The Court stated that it declined to issue specific orders to the TFV on the implementation of reparations.[35] This of course means that the Court did not state any specific amount to be paid to victims. This accordingly vests the TFV with a great deal of responsibility, and it can be questioned whether it is good for the Court to defer the specificities of a matter as important as financial reparations to a non-judicial body. It is also not clear that the Court will always defer the implementation of reparations awards to the TFV. The Court is not bound by its decision in the *Lubanga* case and is free to alter the way in which it structures reparations awards in future decisions. While the *Lubanga* decision defers the actual implementation of reparations to the TFV and this can be considered as an attempt to bridge the two frameworks, the decision does not resolve the tensions inherent in the bifurcated mandate of the ICC, nor does it clarify the relationship between the Court and the TFV.

As in the case of the Court, the TFV is confronted by the problem of selectivity. In terms of victim support, the TFV is limited to supporting victims in situation countries. This means that many thousands of victims of international crimes will be left to dysfunctional or non-existent domestic mechanisms to obtain reparation.[36] At the same time it is not realistic to expect the TFV to assist all victims of international crimes worldwide.

---

[31] Art 75 of the Rome Statute states:

> 1. The Court shall establish principles relating to reparations to, or in respect of, victims, including restitution, compensation and rehabilitation. On this basis, in its decision the Court may, either upon request or on its own motion in exceptional circumstances, determine the scope and extent of any damage, loss and injury to, or in respect of, victims and will state the principles on which it is acting.

[32] For criticism of the decision see M Swart, 'The Lubanga Reparations Decision: A Missed Opportunity?' (2013) 32 Polish Yearbook of International Law 294–316.

[33] *Prosecutor v Thomas Lubanga Dyilo* (Decision establishing the principles and procedures to be applied to reparations) ICC-01/04-01/06-2904 (7 August 2012) paras 106, 261.

[34] Ibid para 286.

[35] Ibid para 287.

[36] McCarthy (n 7) 71.

As a division of the ICC, the TFV should carve out a distinct identity and not duplicate the work of development agencies and NGOs distributing aid. The assistance provided by the TFV should be awarded on the basis of recognition of an entitlement resulting from harm suffered in the context of the commission of international crimes.[37] It is vital that there should be coherence between the TFV and the Court; in light of scarcity of resources it might for example make sense to give aid or assistance as a matter of priority to those unlikely to obtain reparations.[38] There should further be coherence between the ICC reparations mandate and transitional justice mechanisms such as truth-seeking.[39]

2. *The distinguishing factors of the common law and civil law, and the consequences for reparations*

It has often been said that the ICC inherited the legacy of the Nuremberg Tribunal and the ad hoc tribunals. The Nuremberg Tribunal has been described as a truly American creation and as being heavily dominated by common law procedure and tradition.[40] The ICTY and ICTR were also heavily influenced by common law.[41] The Statute of the ICTY reflects the fundamental features of the adversarial system.[42]

The major differences between civil law and common law are widely known. In common law systems, proceedings take the form of a contest between two parties, which is geared towards the establishment of procedural truth. The judge acts mainly as a referee between the parties. In the words of Chayes 'the case is organized and the issues defined by exchanges between the parties.'[43] The victim has no particular status in this two-party model.[44]

---

37 Mégret (n 26) 24.

38 Idem.

39 According to Margarrell, it is by now accepted that reparations form an essential part of transitional justice initiatives and post conflict processes. See L Margarrell, 'Reparations in Theory and Practice' International Center for Transitional Justice (2007) <http://ictj.org/publication/reparations-theory-and-practice>.

40 It is widely acknowledged that US was the driving force behind the International Military Tribunal. See F Smith (ed), *The American Road to Nuremberg: the Documentary Record, 1944–1945* (Hoover Press 1982); A Orie, 'Accusatorial v Inquisitorial Approach in International Criminal Proceedings,' in A Cassese, P Gaeta and JRWD Jones (eds), *The Rome Statute of the International Criminal Court – A Commentary* vol II (Oxford University Press 2002) 1456–1463, 1492.

41 See A Cassese, *International Criminal Law* (1st edn, Oxford University Press 2003) 384.

42 Idem.

43 A Chayes, 'The Role of the Judge in Public Law Litigation' (1976) 89 Harvard Law Review 1283.

44 Cassese (n 41) 628. Whereas some jurisdictions allow for compensation claims flowing from criminal conviction, compensation is usually paid in cases involving civil wrongs such as

Traditionally victims act as witnesses and may give victim impact statements but their role does not extend much beyond this. The effect of the judgment will usually also be confined to the parties to the litigation.[45]

In civil law systems the search for truth is said to play a more pronounced role. The judge is the master of the proceedings and has the duty to seek the truth.[46] The judge may question the accused and witnesses and order evidence to be produced. In some systems the judge may even be involved in the gathering of evidence during the pre-trial investigation.[47]

The above summary describes the general features of the two systems but does not capture the nuances and varieties of domestic models. Increasingly domestic models consist of a mixture of common law and civil law. For example, the French, Belgian and Dutch systems have been described as 'moderately inquisitorial'.[48]

The Rome Statute can be regarded as a mixture of procedural features of the two traditions.[49] The merger is a compromise solution, resulting from the articulation of different positions during the negotiations preceding the adoption of the Rome Statute.[50] It does not represent a victory of one legal

---

tort or delict. Under Cambodian law, civil parties may claim compensation in criminal cases for damages they suffered from the crimes being tried. Before the Extraordinary Chambers in the Courts of Cambodia (ECCC), which is of a hybrid international-domestic nature, victims of a crime within the jurisdiction of the ECCC may participate in proceedings and claim reparation, pursuant to the ECCC Internal Rules, which are based on the Cambodian Criminal Code, which in turn reflects French criminal procedure. See Zegveld (n 4) 89. In French law, a civil action can be brought jointly with a penal action before a criminal court. According to Article 2 of the Code of Criminal Procedure, civil action for damages caused by a crime, misdemeanour or offence is open to all who have personally suffered damage as a direct result of the offence. See C Howard, 'Compensation in French Criminal Procedure' (1958) 21 Modern Law Review 387.

[45] Chayes (n 43) 1283.

[46] Cassese (n 41) 373. See also M Damaška 'Evidentiary Barriers to Conviction and Two Models of Criminal Procedure: A Comparative Study' (1973) 121 University of Pennsylvania Law Review 513 *et seq*.

[47] Judge Wald described the difference between the two systems as follows: common law systems rely on parties to make their case with the judge or jury as umpire and is characterised by detailed rules governing the admissibility of evidence by the court. The civil law system, on the other hand, uses an investigating judge to supervise the compilation of a dossier that can include a more wide-ranging evidence than that permitted at common law to which the defendant responds at trial. MA Glendon et al, *Comparative Legal Traditions* (2nd edn, West Group 1994) 179–183.

[48] P de Hert, 'Legal Procedures at the International Criminal Court' in R Haveman, O Kavran and J Nicholls (eds), *Supranational Criminal law: A System Sui Generis* (Intersentia 2003) 94.

[49] According to Orie the result of this compromise was that the basic elements of procedure have lost their anchorage in a coherent system. See A Orie (n 40) 1494.

[50] K Ambos, 'International Criminal Procedure: Inquisitorial, Adversarial or Mixed?,' in M Bohlander (ed) *International Criminal Justice: A Critical Analysis of Institutions and Procedures* (Cameron May 2007) 429.

system over another but creates a new system. The ICC model has been described as based to an extent 'on the civil law notion of *partie civile*, where civil parties can be enjoined into criminal proceedings with a view to claiming damages'.[51]

The Rome Statute and the Rules of Procedure and Evidence are infused with elements of both the adversarial and the inquisitorial systems, where elements of one system are introduced into the framework of another. The procedure during the trial itself tends towards the adversarial model, even if the Rome Statute authorises the judge to play an active role during the trial proceedings.[52] Judges do not have the obligation to extend the taking of evidence to include all the facts and evidence that are relevant for the establishment of the truth, which is the decisive characteristic of an adversarial procedure. Instead, the Prosecution and Defence have the role of investigating and presenting the evidence for their respective cases during the trial.[53]

What is the relevance of this hybrid nature of the Court for reparations? It is typically the common lawyer who feels uncomfortable with the Court's reparations mandate. In civil law jurisdictions it is not at all unusual to integrate victims into criminal proceedings. But even in systems that involve victims in the criminal justice process to a greater extent, the role of victims remains secondary. In countries where civil or adhesion proceedings are possible, such as France, Austria and Germany,[54] the dichotomy between the two bodies of law – criminal and civil – is less pronounced. For instance, the French *Code de procedure pénal*[55] establishes the right to civil action for victims who suffer harm caused directly by a crime.[56]

The *partie civile* procedures in the French and German legal systems illustrate possible alternative models of integrating victims and reparations claims into criminal law.[57] The civil law models illustrate that it is not unusual for a criminal court to award reparations and consider the views and needs of

---

[51] REDRESS, 'Justice for Victims: The ICC's Reparations Mandate' (20 May 2011).

[52] GGJ Knoops, *Theory and Practice of International and Internationalised Criminal Proceedings* (Kluwer Law International 2005) 6.

[53] S Kirsch, 'The Trial Proceedings Before the ICC' (2006) 6 International Criminal Law Review 58 *et seq*.

[54] The Nebenklage procedure in the German Criminal system allows the victims to take part in the trial on nearly equal footing with lawyers for the defense and the state, therefore the so-called Nebenklagerin (second accuser) serves as subsidiary prosecutor. See S Walther, 'Reparation in the German Criminal Justice System: What Is, and What Remains to Be Done' (2000) 7 International Review of Victimology 265–280.

[55] Art 2 of the Criminal Procedure Code provides for the *partie civile* procedure.

[56] G Mueller, 'Lessons of Comparative Criminal Procedure' (1966) 15 American University Law Review 358.

[57] See CO Lapie, 'The Partie Civile in the Criminal Law of France' (1928) 10 Journal of Comparative Legislation & International Law 41–42.

victims. On the other hand, in common law systems,[58] historically, remedies were awarded in private law litigation rather than in criminal proceedings.[59] However, common law systems such as the US and UK are increasingly providing 'space' for victims in criminal law proceedings.[60]

Whereas civil law countries generally tend to downplay the dichotomy between criminal law and civil law and are more comfortable with collapsing the distinction between the interests of the State and the individual, the distinction is more pronounced in common law countries. By including the adjudication of reparations in a criminal court the Rome Statute seems to resemble the French and other civil law jurisdictions to a certain extent. The reparations scheme envisaged in the Rome Statute is not a mere imitation of the French system, but creates a unique and alternative model of reparations.

The joinder of civil claims and penal proceedings offers advantages in a domestic setting. In theory, permitting victims to be parties to prosecution proceedings not only empowers them but offers a measure of retribution while allowing them to obtain damages faster than would be possible before a civil court. Whereas this might be the case in domestic settings it is however not clear that this would also be an advantage in the context of international criminal law. The joinder of civil claims and penal proceedings also allows for maximisation of judicial and administrative resources. A 'merged' process might be cheaper for the victim than going through a separate civil process.[61]

Commentators have expressed the concern that the accusatorial process at the Court may be negatively affected by the expanded role given to victims as it may influence the right of the accused to a fair, unbiased and speedy

---

[58] G Shalev and Y Adar 'The Law of Remedies in a Mixed Jurisdiction: The Israeli Experience' (2008) 12 Electronic Journal of Comparative Law <http://www.ejcl.org/121/art121-1.pdf>. See also Chayes (n 43) 1282 on the interdependence of rights and remedies in a common law system.

[59] In common law systems a remedy would be commonly defined as 'the legal system's response to the commission of a civil wrong'. (Shalev and Adar (n 58) 9.)

[60] See, for example, P Rock, *Constructing Victims' Rights, the Home Office, New Labour and Victims* (Oxford University Press 2004) and J Doak, 'Victims' Rights in Criminal Trials: Prospects for Participation' (2005) 32 Journal of Law and Society 294.

[61] Art 25 of the Statute of the Special Tribunal for Lebanon (STL) does not merge civil and criminal proceedings as such but makes provision for reparations by means of a two-step mechanism that hurdles the division of (international) criminal and (domestic) civil proceedings. In essence the STL recognises that victims may have claims to reparations but refers them to the national courts. When the Tribunal has found the accused guilty, a victim may bring an action for compensation in a Lebanese or other national court, or any other competent body on the basis of that judgment. The STL judgment shall be final and binding on the criminal responsibility of the convicted person. National legal action will however not be *dependent* on the STL's recognition of the victims. Nevertheless, the STL's recognition of the harm suffered by the victims will be of great assistance to those bringing claims before domestic courts. See Zegveld (n 4) 90 and STL Statute <http://www.stl-tsl.org/en/documents/statute-of-the-tribunal/statute-of-the-special-tribunal-for-lebanon>.

trial.[62] This concern should not be overstated since the ICC process is in any event not *purely* accusatorial, and concerns regarding speedy trials at the international criminal tribunals have arisen for many reasons other than delays that might be caused by victim participation. Since the Rome Statute system is an inherently mixed system (containing elements of both the inquisitorial and adversarial systems as well as novel features), the Court will have to engage in a continuous process of resolving the tension between the demands of the accusatorial model and those of the inquisitorial model. What is unusual about the ICC system is that it brings victims and accords them a special status. In this regard neither the traditional common law nor civil law systems can assist. The Court will have to find its own path.

3. The contrast between civil and criminal law proceedings

The act of awarding reparations is often seen to resemble the payment of 'damages' in civil (tortious) proceedings. The ICC's reparations mandate therefore upsets traditional understandings and expectations of the difference between the role of civil courts and criminal courts. Critics such as Liesbeth Zegveld have pointed to the absence of a substantive body of law applicable to reparations claims at the ICC. She has suggested a full emancipation of the criminal trial from the civil reparations hearing as well as the establishment of an international civil court.[63]

According to ICC Regulation 56 '[t]he Trial Chamber may hear the witnesses and examine the evidence for the purposes of a decision on reparations in accordance with article 75, paragraph 2, at the same time as for the purposes of a trial.'[64]

Zegveld argues that the testimony of victims – often emotional and accusatory – can affect the objectivity of judges.[65] She writes that by separating the compensation proceedings from the criminal trial, the presumption of innocence can be fully upheld during the latter. For example, in Belgian law victim reparations claims may be dealt with exclusively in a separate hearing.[66] Zegveld also argues that one advantage of splitting the trial stage from the compensation stage is that it would allow judges to deal with the question of reparations after the accused has already been convicted.[67]

---

[62] C Jorda and J de Hemptinne, 'The Status and Role of the Victim,' in Cassese et al (n 40) 1387–1383.

[63] Zegveld (n 4) 109.

[64] Regulations of the Court, adopted by the judges of the Court (26 May 2004) ICC-BD/01-01-4 Reg 53.

[65] Zegveld (n 4) 110.

[66] MEI Brienen & EH Hoegen, 'Victims of Crime' (2000) 22 European Criminal Justice Systems 151.

[67] Zegveld (n 4) 110.

The priority of the judges should be to ensure an expeditious trial for the accused. The time and logistical demands presented by the reparations mandate of the ICC could affect the judges' ability to facilitate a fair and expeditious trial. This is another reason why it would be better to deal with the question of reparations after the accused has already been convicted. Zegveld further argues that judges in international criminal tribunals are not specialised in the complex matters relating to victims' reparations claims.[68]

In response to Zegveld it can be argued that however ambitious and logistically challenging it might be for the ICC to carry out its reparations mandate, it is fitting given the aims of the Court and of international criminal justice for the Court to have the dual role of prosecution and reparations. However, it might be necessary to collapse the separation of criminal and civil law in order to achieve this.

In terms of ensuring the objectivity of ICC judges, I submit that the solution is not to eliminate the reparations role but to appoint judges who are equipped to order reparations and who are able to separate the question of criminal guilt of the accused from the reparations claims of the victims. From this point of view it was fitting for the Trial Chamber in the *Lubanga* case to defer certain aspects of decision making (with regard to implementation) to the TFV, staffed by experts in the field of reparations.

IV. CONCLUSION

The tensions highlighted in this chapter represent only some of the difficulties brought to the fore by the ICC reparations regime. To avoid potential conflict between victims groups *inter se* and between victims and other interested groups, the relationship between the ICC's reparative function, the TFV assistance orientation and the greater needs of societies in transition should be carefully managed. It is especially important that the relationship of the Court and the TFV be of a complementary (and not competitive) nature. At present it seems as if the relationship is partly one of dependence – the Court will often be dependent on the TFV for the implementation and funding of its reparations orders.[69]

Unless the Court prepares itself for the challenges and potentially disruptive nature of the involvement of victims, a dark shadow of unmet expectations will be cast over proceedings. To help manage the expectations of victims and to create a coherent system, the Court can draw inspiration from domestic contexts. The Court should examine domestic mass claims proce-

---

[68] Ibid 108.

[69] This was clear from the ICC's first decision on reparations. See *Prosecutor v Lubanga* (Reparations) (n 33).

dures, contemporary international law and developments at the domestic level. For reasons of consistency, predictability and fairness it is important that the ICC provides a framework for deciding on reparations. The *Lubanga* reparations decision of August 2012 is an early indication that the Court will not hesitate to draw liberally from domestic systems.[70]

It is vital for the credibility and legitimacy of the Court that it manage and resolve the tensions created by the reparations mandate and that it formulate reparations principles that will instil trust and confidence in the mandate of the Court as soon as possible.

---

[70] Ibid.

PART 5

The International Criminal Court Ten Years Later and Prospects for the Future

The International Criminal Court at Ten

*William A. Schabas** **

I. INTRODUCTION

When assessing the 10th anniversary of the International Criminal Court (ICC) one is necessarily confronted with a question as to when the actual birthday of the Court is. The institution itself now celebrates 17 July, and it is apparently a much appreciated paid holiday for employees at the Court, who take advantage of the day off to soak up the sun at Scheveningen beach. But the Court wasn't really 'born' on 17 July, which is the day the Rome Conference concluded in 1998 with the famous vote by which the Statute was adopted. The Rome Statute requires 60 ratifications for entry into force,[1] and this was only achieved on 17 April 2002. Article 126 says that entry into force takes place about 2 months after the requisite ratifications, so the magic date might be 1 July 2002. It is an important date in any event, because it marks the starting point of the Court's temporal jurisdiction,[2] but the Court wasn't functional on 1 July 2002. Judges and a Prosecutor had not yet been elected, and the subsidiary instruments required by the Statute, the Rules of Procedure and Evidence and the Elements of Crimes had not yet been adopted. The ICC was only in a position to actually begin its judicial activi-

* OC MRIA, Professor of International Law, Middlesex University; Professor of International Criminal Law and Human Rights, Leiden University; Emeritus Professor of Human Rights Law, National University of Ireland Galway; Editor-in-Chief, Criminal Law Forum.

** This contribution, which served as the basis for the key-note speech by Professor Schabas at the conference on 10th anniversary of the International Criminal Court (21 June 2012, London), is an update of an article first published in (2011) 22 Criminal Law Forum and adjusted for the publication in this book. Reprinted with permission of the author and publisher (Springer).

1 Rome Statute of the International Criminal Court, (2002) 2187 UNTS 90, Art 129. See RS Clark, 'Article 126', in O Triffterer (ed), *Commentary on the Rome Statute of the International Criminal Court* (2nd edn, CH Beck et al 2008) 1775–1776.

2 Art 11 Rome Statute. See SA Williams, 'Article 11', in Triffterer (n 1) 539–545.

ties in June 2003, when the Prosecutor was sworn into office. Thus, the Court actually has several possible birthdays. Its employees would no doubt be delighted if every one of these were to be celebrated with a paid day off. For the purposes of this article, let us say that the ICC is 'about' 10 years old. The aim of this short article is to consider some features of the institution's work in this first decade of its activity.

II. TOO MANY JUDGES, TOO LITTLE WORK

It is often overlooked that when the Rome Statute was adopted, the ad hoc tribunals for the former Yugoslavia and Rwanda had been operational and engaged in trial work for only a few years. Most of the rich lessons from their activity in the procedure (and substance) of international criminal law had yet to be learned. Thus, when the first trial began at the ICC in 2009 it was using a procedural model that had been designed more than a decade earlier. The invaluable lessons learned from the experience of the ad hoc tribunals were not taken into account at all.

The procedural system of the United Nations international tribunals had been largely left to the judges, whereas that of the ICC was more rigorously codified by the states that negotiated the Statute and the Rules of Procedure and Evidence. Many felt the Rome system was better, and certainly it more closely resembled models in domestic legal systems. But while this may have been an advantage, there were also disadvantages with the inflexibility of the scheme. At the United Nations tribunals, the Rules of Procedure and Evidence have been subjected to a constant process of fine tuning and amendment. The judges have adjusted the procedure in light of experience but also to accommodate changes in the nature of the case load. Although the same should be possible at the ICC, in practice there is nothing of the sort. The Rules of Procedure and Evidence have never been amended. While complex when compared with the ad hoc tribunals, the amending process at the ICC should not be so terribly difficult. On closer examination, it seems that the failure to amend the procedural regime is not so much a function of the difficulty of the process as a genuine resistance to the idea.

Outside the ICC's own institutions, much thought is given to amendment among academics.[3] But within the Court, and the Assembly of States Parties, the idea took hold that it was premature to contemplate amendments with respect to the procedure, structures and other operational aspects. The theory

---

[3] RS Clark, 'Possible Amendments for the First ICC Review Conference in 2009' (2007) 4 New Zealand Yearbook of International Law 103 and C Burchard, O Triffterer and J Vogel (eds), *The Review Conference and the Future of the International Criminal Court* (Kluwer Law International 2010).

was that a 'full cycle' (arrest, confirmation hearing, trial, appeal) should be completed before any changes would be considered. The approach contrasts rather sharply with the attitude taken at the ad hoc tribunals. Perhaps there is some merit in this more conservative and cautious position. It may be the reflection of the involvement of diplomats both in the Assembly of States Parties and within the ICC itself (where they are, strictly speaking, former diplomats). Diplomats might be nervous about reopening compromises that were negotiated with difficulty, fearful that one change would lead to a cascade. Thus, although given the opportunity to make minor (and perhaps major) repairs to the system at the Kampala Review Conference, there was a refusal to consider the matter. Instead, much time was consumed at Kampala with a series of 'stocktaking sessions', which were a mix of academic conference and NGO campaign meeting. While interesting and worthwhile in a sense, they hardly merited the expense and energy of bringing more than a thousand people to central Africa. The term 'stocktaking' implied introspection, but there was very little of that in reality. Most of the sessions involved hectoring States Parties about their obligations to the Court, rather than reflection on the problems within the Court. There was also a sense that these and similar activities had been conceived rather late in the preparations for Kampala once it was understood that the agenda of amendments – which was, after all, the purpose of the Review Conference – would be rather more slender than many observers would have expected.

Actually, it takes little imagination to see how the procedure can be improved, the pre-trial and trial activity simplified, and the ICC made more efficient. In that sense, the Kampala Conference was a missed opportunity. An unfortunate message was delivered of an institution that is rather reluctant to acknowledge its shortcomings and that seems content with its performance.

One of the innovations in the Rome Statute is the confirmation hearing, the preliminary proceeding at which the Pre-Trial Chamber is to determine whether there are 'substantial grounds' to go to trial.[4] The confirmation hearing can add up to a year to the length of the proceedings as a whole. Its enthusiasts explain that it adds a layer of protection against abusive trials, which may well be true. In four cases, the confirmation hearing resulted in dismissal of the charges, which is reassuring to defence lawyers (and troubling, to the extent that it reflects misjudgment by the Prosecutor).[5]

---

[4] Art 61 Rome Statute. See K Shibahara and WA Schabas, 'Article 61', in Triffterer (n 1) 1171–1181.

[5] *Prosecutor v Abu Garda* (Decision on the Confirmation of Charges) ICC-02/05-02/09 (8 February 2010); *Prosecutor v Callixte Mbarushimana* (Decision on the confirmation of charges) ICC-01/04-01/10-465-Red Pre-Trial Chamber I (16 December 2011); *Prosecutor v Callixte Mbarushimana* (Judgment on the appeal of the Prosecutor against the decision of Pre-Trial Chamber I of 16 December 2011 entitled 'Decision on the confirmation of charges') ICC-

However, in all such arguments, a cost-benefit analysis is central. Is the added length to the proceedings, especially if the accused is in custody, worth the investment in time and resources that is involved?

The closest that the ad hoc tribunals come to a confirmation hearing is the so-called Rule 61 Procedure. Under the Rules of Procedure and Evidence of the ad hoc tribunals, when an arrest warrant cannot be executed there is a special procedure at which evidence may be produced and witnesses called. The accused is, of course, not present at the hearing, and may not even be represented by counsel.[6] At the conclusion of the hearing, the Trial Chamber may determine 'there are reasonable grounds for believing that the accused has committed all or any of the crimes charged in the indictment'. Rule 61 was adopted as a compromise intended to assuage critics from continental European justice systems who thought that the lack of an *in absentia* procedure would seriously hamper the work of the Tribunal.[7] The main distinction is that a Rule 61 proceeding does not pronounce a sentence. In the early years of the International Criminal Tribunal for the former Yugoslavia, several hearings were held pursuant to Rule 61, but the practice was discontinued once the Tribunal had defendants in custody and the suggestion that it could only function if it could conduct *in absentia* hearings no longer made any sense.[8] Reflecting on the procedure, Louise Arbour said it was 'detrimental'

01/04-01/10-514 Appeals Chamber (30 May 2012); *Prosecutor v Francis Kirimi Muthaura, Uhuru Muigai Kenyatta and Mohammed Hussein Ali* (Decision on the Confirmation of Charges Pursuant to Article 61(7)(a) and (b) of the Rome Statute) ICC-01/09-02/11-382-Red Pre-Trial Chamber II (23 January 2012); *Prosecutor v William Samoei Ruto, Henry Kiprono Kosgey and Joshua Arap Sang* (Decision on the Confirmation of Charges Pursuant to Article 61(7)(a) and (b) of the Rome Statute) ICC-01/09-01/11-373-Red Pre-Trial Chamber II (23 January 2012).

[6] *Prosecutor v Karadžić* et al (Review of the Indictment Pursuant to Rule 61 of the Rules of Procedure and Evidence) IT-95-5-R61 & IT-95-18-R61 (11 July 1996) para 4. But see *Prosecutor v Rajić* (Review of the Indictment Pursuant to Rule 61 of the Rules of Procedure and Evidence) IT-95-12-R61 (13 September 1996); *Prosecutor v Rajić* (Separate Opinion of Judge Sidhwa) IT-95-12-R61(13 September 1996) paras 10-16.

[7] *Prosecutor v Rajić* (n 6): 'A Rule 61 proceeding is not a trial in absentia. There is no finding of guilt in this proceeding'. *Prosecutor v Dragan Nikolić* (Review of Indictment Pursuant to Rule 61) IT-94-2-R61 (20 October 1995): 'The Rule 61 procedure [...] cannot be considered a trial in absentia: it does not culminate in a verdict nor does it deprive the accused of the right to contest in person the charges brought against him before the Tribunal.'

[8] See F Patel King, 'Public Disclosure in Rule 61 Proceedings Before the International Criminal Tribunal for the Former Yugoslavia' (1997) 29 New York University Journal of International Law and Policy 523; M Thieroff and EA Amley, Jr, 'Proceeding to Justice and Accountability in the Balkans: The International Criminal Tribunal for the Former Yugoslavia and Rule 61' (1998) 23 Yale Journal of International Law 231; BT Hildreth, 'Hunting the Hunters: The United Nations Unleashes its Latest Weapon in the Fight against Fugitive War Crimes Suspects – Rule 61' (1998) 6 Tulane Journal of International and Comparative Law 499; AL Quintal, 'Rule 61: The "Voice of the Victims" Screams Out for Justice' (1998) 36 Columbia Journal of Transnational Law 723.

to the work of the Prosecutor.[9] Neither the International Criminal Tribunal for Rwanda nor the Special Court for Sierra Leone ever showed any interest in Rule 61 proceedings. They are now little more than a footnote, and with hindsight look like efforts to create work for judges and prosecutors at an institution without defendants. In that sense, there are obvious similarities with the confirmation hearing of the ICC. As the institution gets busier, it seems likely that the confirmation hearing will be reduced in scale until at some point there is a willingness to eliminate it altogether.

The Regulations of the ICC require that the decision on the confirmation hearing be issued within sixty days of its conclusion.[10] Working within this requirement, the Pre-Trial Chambers have issued lengthy rulings in which the facts and law are reviewed.[11] The time limit is useful, because where one is not imposed, the judges generally take much, much longer to issue written rulings. On the arguably simpler issue of whether or not to issue an arrest warrant, they have sometimes taken several months.[12] By comparison, issuance of an arrest warrant at the ad hoc tribunals is a matter of a few days.

Questions about the utility of the confirmation hearing inexorably lead to thoughts about the value of the Pre-Trial Chamber itself. Again, this is a feature introduced in the Rome Statute that has no equivalent at the ad hoc tribunals, where the same issues are very adequately dealt with by a single pre-trial judge. A minimum of one-third of the entire cohort of judges at the ICC is tied up with this pre-trial work. If the Chamber were abolished, there would be more judges for trials which are, after all, the bread and butter of the institution.

At the other end of the system sits the Appeals Chamber. There was no appeal at Nuremberg or Tokyo. When the Yugoslavia Tribunal was established in the early 1990s, the text of the International Covenant on Civil and Political Rights made an effective right of appeal a *sine qua non*. Proposing inclusion of a right of appeal for the Yugoslavia Tribunal, the Secretary-General's Report said 'such a right is a fundamental element of individual civil and political rights and has, *inter alia*, been incorporated in the International Covenant on Civil and Political Rights. For this reason, the Secretary-General has proposed that there should be an Appeals Chamber.'[13]

---

9 L Arbour, 'The Crucial Years' (2004) 2 Journal of International Criminal Justice 397.

10 Regulations of the Court, Adopted by the judges of the Court (26 May 2004) ICC-BD/01-01-4 Reg 53.

11 For example, *Prosecutor v Lubanga* (Decision on the Confirmation of the Charges) ICC-01/04-01/06 (29 January 2007); *Prosecutor v Katanga* et al (Decision on the Confirmation of the Charges) ICC-01/04-01/07 (30 September 2008); *Prosecutor v Bemba* (Decision Pursuant to Article 61(7)(a) and (b) of the Rome Statute on the Charges of the Prosecutor Against Jean-Pierre Bemba Gombo) ICC-01/05-01/08 (15 June 2009).

12 For example, *Prosecutor v Bashir* (Decision on the Prosecution's Application for a Warrant of Arrest against Omar Hassan Ahmad Al Bashir) ICC-02/05-01/09 (4 March 2009).

13 Report of the Secretary-General Pursuant to Paragraph (2) of Security Council Resolution 808 (1993), UN Doc S/25704 (1993) para 116.

The implication, confirmed by the reference to Article 14(5) of the International Covenant, was that this was to be an appeal of the final verdict. The corresponding provision, Article 25 of the Statute of Yugoslavia Tribunal said: 'The Appeals Chamber shall hear appeals from persons convicted by the Trial Chambers or from the Prosecutor on the following grounds.'[14] But the judges themselves soon determined that in addition to an appeal of conviction – the only requirement imposed by human rights law – interlocutory matters could also be dealt with.[15] The idea stuck, and was incorporated in the Rome Statute.[16]

By the time the ICC completed its first full cycle of judicial elections, in early 2012, a full-time five-judge Appeals Chamber (together with professional assistants and secretarial help) had occupied a floor of the Court's premises for nearly the entire period without ever engaging in the fundamental reason for its existence: appeal by an accused of a conviction. The Appeals Chamber has barely managed to keep itself occupied with interlocutory appeals. The occasional decisions are generally sparsely reasoned and there are few separate or dissenting opinions. The job could very well have been accomplished with a panel of part-time or standby judges, called to The Hague as required and remunerated according to the work that they actually accomplish.

Would the sky fall in if there were no interlocutory appeal at all? There might be variations in procedure from one chamber to another, but that is something that many justice systems accept as a fact of life. Some argue the virtue of 'clarifying' the law so as to ensure 'legal certainty'. But it might be more constructive for a Court in its early years to 'let a hundred flowers bloom', and to encourage experimentation and innovation. The Rome Statute contemplates a division of labour whereby the Pre-Trial and Trial Chambers are enriched by a large proportion of judges with criminal trial experience. That makes sense, but the consequence may be that there is less criminal trial experience at the Appeals Chamber, and a tendency for it to be top-heavy with judges from the international law stream. This means that tricky determinations about trial procedure made by experienced judges working at the coal face are being second-guessed by those who are probably less familiar with daily life in the courtroom.

A much-heralded innovation in the Rome Statute is the recognition of a role for victims of crime. The Statute's provisions concerning victim participation might well have been interpreted relatively narrowly. Instead, an elaborate and costly regime of victim representation and participation has

---

[14] Statute of the International Criminal Tribunal for the former Yugoslavia, UN Doc S/RES/827 (1993), annex, Art 25(1).

[15] Rules 72(B), 73(B), 108*bis*(A) Rules of Procedure and Evidence.

[16] Art 82 Rome Statute. See C Staker, 'Article 82', in Triffterer (n 1) 1475–1480.

developed. Much of the institutional energy of the ICC in its first decade has been devoted to addressing this. But it is not apparent that the right scheme for victim participation has been found. One suspects that if the victims understood that many millions had been invested – mainly in professional salaries and international travel – in order to ensure the respect of their rights, they might ask if they could simply be given the money instead. The continental procedural model of the *partie civile* on which victim participation was premised seems very remote from what we actually see in the Chambers of the ICC.

One example of this indulgence is the Trust Fund for Victims, whose establishment is called for by Article 79 of the Rome Statute.[17] As it was understood, this was to provide a mechanism for seizing the assets of the wealthy warlords and tyrants upon successful prosecution by the Court. Of course, to date it has collected nothing of the sort, because no trials have been completed.[18] It was probably unrealistic to view the defendants as a reliable source of resources that might be used to address issues of compensation and restitution for victims. At the ad hoc tribunals, most of the defendants have been declared indigent for the purposes of legal aid. Even the notorious Charles Taylor, widely alleged to have billions tucked away in foreign bank accounts, was not declared to be capable of paying his own lawyers' fees because the money could not be found. And proof of assets for the purposes of legal aid should not be nearly as demanding as for the seizure of bank accounts and other property.

The Fund itself gets a limited income in the form of voluntary contributions from the wealthier States Parties. The money is being spent on a range of projects in regions where the Court is active. For the year 2010, the Fund expected an income of something under 2 million euro in such gifts. It had budgeted an operating cost of 1.2 million euro. This is an expensive way to do what amounts to overseas development assistance. Maybe States should give their money to the UNDP or Oxfam, and let the Trust Fund become inoperative until such time as the Prosecutor is astute enough to catch a wealthy defendant.

III. THE CHALLENGE OF SELECTING SITUATIONS AND CASES

Although the procedural issues pose interesting challenges, it may be that the crux of the difficulty facing the ICC is substantive. After all, this is where the real differences lie between the Court and the ad hoc institutions. James

---

[17] Art 79 Rome Statute. See M Jennings, 'Article 79', in Triffterer (n 1) 1439–1442.

[18] Although the Lubanga trial has been completed, it is currently pending before the Appeals Chamber.

Crawford, who chaired the International Law Commission drafting committee in the early 1990s, has said that the statute it prepared was what the Commission thought would meet general acceptance. Professor Crawford has suggested that the world may not have been ready for the more radical concepts that emerged from the Rome Conference. If he is right, this may help us to understand the difficulties that the Court faces in becoming operational and effective.

The Rome Statute makes an important distinction between 'situations' and 'cases'. The process of prosecution begins with identification of a 'situation' rather than a 'case'. Thus, we have the 'Situation in the Democratic Republic of the Congo' and the 'case' of Thomas Lubanga, leader of a combatant faction in a civil war accused of recruiting child soldiers. There is the 'Situation in northern Uganda' and the 'case' of Joseph Kony, head of the Lord's Resistance Army.

The great originality of the ICC compared with all of its predecessors is that the Prosecutor selects both the 'situation' and the 'case'. At the other institutions, starting with Nuremberg, the 'situation' has invariably been selected by the political body that created the tribunal. The Prosecutor at these institutions only selects the 'case'. In 1945, the four-power London Conference charged the International Military Tribunal with delivering justice to 'the major war criminals of the European axis'. The four prosecutors concurred about the individuals they would prosecute. Even there, it seems they were instructed by their various governments in making this choice. In the course of the trial, the judges heard evidence of war crimes perpetrated by the Allied forces – the Katyn massacre, unrestricted naval warfare – but were without jurisdiction to address these issues. Had one or more of the prosecutors suggested that these matters be dealt with in the interests of 'balance' and fairness, he would have been quickly replaced by someone prepared to live within the Tribunal's mandate.

When the International Criminal Tribunal for the former Yugoslavia was established in 1993, it was said that the shortcomings at Nuremberg had been corrected. A specific provision in the Statute enshrines the independence of the Prosecutor. The Prosecutor is appointed by the Security Council, and 'shall not seek or receive instructions from any Government or from any other source'.[19] But he or she must still live within the confines of the narrow jurisdictional scheme established by the Security Council. At the ad hoc tribunals, the Prosecutor's discretion is limited to the choice of 'cases'. The 'situation', on the other hand, is part of his job description and he cannot change it. This was also the International Law Commission's vision of the prosecutor of an international criminal court, but one that the Rome

19 Art 16(2) ICTY Statute.

Conference did not endorse. Indeed, the *proprio motu* authority of the Prosecutor enshrined in Article 15 of the Rome Statute has been hailed out as one of the great achievements of the negotiations.[20]

Political factors are not entirely absent in the selection of 'situations' at the ICC. Alongside the *proprio motu* authority of the Prosecutor is the power given to the Security Council[21] and to States Parties[22] to refer 'situations', thereby 'triggering' the exercise of jurisdiction, to use the jargon of the Court. But it is a trigger with a safety catch, because the Prosecutor is not obliged to proceed at the behest of the Security Council or a State Party. He or she may even decline to pursue the agenda set by the Security Council or a State Party, subject to a vague and untested degree of judicial supervision.[23] To date, the Prosecutor has never resisted the initiatives of the Security Council or States Parties. The four self-referrals, from Uganda, the Democratic Republic of the Congo, the Central African Republic and Mali were in practice instigated by the Prosecutor rather than the State Party concerned. It seems likely that the referral letters were drafted in The Hague and simply sent to the national capitals for signature. The Security Council referrals of the situations in Darfur and Libya were welcomed because they brought the Court to the centre of some of the great international crises of the day. Indeed, it was for situations like Darfur and Libya that the ICC was created.

The enthusiasm for the *proprio motu* authority of the Prosecutor was the result of two different and perhaps somewhat disparate objectives: to free the Court from the hegemony of the Security Council, and to create an institution where the decisions about targets for prosecution are based upon judicial rather than political criteria. One nourished the other. Adversaries of the Security Council invoked the goal of an apolitical prosecutor without giving much thought to how this would work in practice. Fans of the independent and impartial prosecutor transposed models from domestic justice systems, where all serious crimes against the person receive attention, without adequate reflection about the different imperatives of an international system.

When Luis Moreno-Ocampo took office in June 2003, he could build on much experience from his predecessors at Nuremberg, Tokyo, The Hague and Arusha. But in the selection of 'situations', he was in virgin territory. A team of lawyers hired to set up the Office had prepared draft Regulations that attempted to parse the matter of selecting situations. The initial draft Regulations contemplated a highly transparent process of the selection of

---

20 Art 15 Rome Statute. See M Bergsmo & J Pejić, 'Article 15', in Triffterer (n 1) 581–593.

21 Art 13(b) Rome Statute. See SA Williams and WA Schabas, 'Article 13', in Triffterer (n 1) 563–574.

22 Art 14 Rome Statute. See A Marchesi, 'Article 14', in Triffterer (n 1) 575–579.

23 Art 53 Rome Statute. See M Bergsmo and P Kruger, 'Article 53', in Triffterer (n 1) 1065–1076.

situations based upon objective judicial standards. The Prosecutor himself quickly understood that the Rome Statute did not provide much guidance on what those standards really were. Moreover, he was astute enough to recognize that mechanistic application of regulations such as those drafted by the advance team might have unexpected consequences that would be politically unwise. In the result, the draft Regulations were not adopted. Much later, the Prosecutor proposed Regulations where the issue of selection of situations was addressed in a vague manner, and in such a way as to provide him with essentially unlimited discretion.

Some students of the Rome Statute have read Article 15 as suggesting that the Prosecutor is required to act relying upon information received, from whatever source, as long as there is a 'reasonable basis' to proceed. This is an absurdly unrealistic interpretation in light of the resources of a Court that has been barely able to deal with a handful of cases in a decade and that now appears overwhelmed by the new situations that have arisen quite unpredictably in Libya and Côte d'Ivoire. The drafters at Rome gave little thought as to the basis on which the Prosecutor would exercise his phenomenal discretion. Had they done so, it is likely that they would have been unable to agree. When they attempted to codify the exercise of the authority to decline to proceed in the case of referral by the Security Council or a State Party, the best they could come up with was 'interests of justice' as a criterion. It was a way of avoiding clarification and it amounted to a lack of regulation, although there have been naïve attempts to interpret the 'interests of justice' formulation so as to make it say more than it really does.

The Rome Statute itself advances three concepts that may assist in the application of prosecutorial discretion: complementarity, gravity and the 'interests of justice'. The first of these creates a presumption in favour of national jurisdictions, directing the Court not to proceed when national jurisdictions are willing or able to prosecute. Article 17 of the Statute offers some instruction about the scope of 'unwillingness' and 'inability'.[24] The issues lend themselves to a reasonably objective assessment. The same cannot be said of such stunningly nebulous concepts as 'gravity' and the 'interests of justice'. These notions are so malleable as to provide any imaginative prosecutor with a rationale for what may be, in reality, rather arbitrary choices.

In order to avoid the challenge of selecting situations, early in his term the Prosecutor essentially abdicated the responsibility. He rather quietly encouraged some States to refer situations to the Court and then proceeded on this basis without challenging the validity of such choices. He used a novel interpretation of Article 14, by which States could 'self-refer' situations within their own territory. The Prosecutor explained that States Parties had decided

---

[24] Art 17 Rome Statute. See SA Williams and WA Schabas, 'Article 17', in Triffterer (n 1) 605–625.

to refer the situations in Uganda, the Democratic Republic of the Congo and the Central African Republic, and acted as if he was virtually bound to proceed in the absence of evidence that the situations were inadmissible. The Prosecutor did the same when the Security Council referred the 'situation in Darfur', in March 2005.

This was an expedient by which the Prosecutor avoided selecting a situation on his own. But even then, it soon became apparent that situations were a Matrioshka doll, and that there were situations within situations. When he obtained the first arrest warrants, in 2005, in the 'situation in Uganda', the targets were the Lord's Resistance Army rebels. The big human rights NGOs took the Prosecutor to task for failing to proceed against the pro-government forces as well. It was at this point that he discovered 'gravity', a term buried in the Statute and essentially forgotten or overlooked, until that point, by academic writers in the major commentaries.[25] Justifying his focus on the rebels, the Prosecutor said they were killing many more people than the government forces, and this meant they should be prioritized by the Court. He suggested he would get to the pro-government forces later, but never did. There was the lingering suspicion of an agreement, or perhaps only a tacit understanding, by which Museveni's helpful 'self-referral' of the situation in Northern Uganda meant the focus would be on Museveni's enemies rather than on himself.

In practice, it seemed that the fabled de-politicized Prosecutor was in fact not immune to political factors. Soon, gravity was invoked once again to explain why the Prosecutor had decided to reject the many complaints about violations of the Rome Statute perpetrated by British troops in Iraq. He explained that many more people were being killed in Uganda and in the Congo, so these areas deserved the attention of the Court as a priority. The explanation was unconvincing, because the evidence of the massive death toll in Iraq was notorious. The Prosecutor seemed to be confusing 'situations' and 'cases', comparing the 'cases' of alleged deaths in British custody in Iraq with the 'situations' of mass killings in Uganda and the Congo. Days later, he announced that he was proceeding against Thomas Lubanga, a Congolese warlord, on charges of recruitment of child soldiers. But if the Democratic Republic of the Congo was inherently more serious than Iraq, because of the number of deaths, why wasn't the Prosecutor dealing with murder rather than that arguably less important crime of recruitment?

---

[25] SA Williams, 'Article 17', in O Triffterer (ed), *Commentary on the Rome Statute of the International Criminal Court* (Nomos 1999) 393. See also M Bergsmo and P Kruger, 'Article 53', in ibid 708–709; JT Holmes, 'Complementarity: National Courts *versus* the ICC', in A Cassese, P Gaeta and JRWD Jones (eds), *The Rome Statute of the International Criminal Court: A Commentary* vol I (Oxford University Press 2002) 667–686; G Turone, 'Powers and Duties of the Prosecutor', in ibid 1153–1154; É David, 'La Cour pénale internationale' (2005) 313 *Recueil des cours* 248–251.

James Crawford may well have been right to suggest that the world is not ready for a Court with an independent and impartial prosecutor, analogous to what we expect in the national justice system of a functional, democratic society that is based upon the rule of law. International human rights courts, like the European Court of Human Rights, have held that there is a procedural obligation upon States to investigate and prosecute all serious crimes against the person. But the theory does not lend itself to a simplistic application in the international criminal law environment. The ICC cannot prosecute all atrocities that go unpunished at the national level. Choices are inevitable. The Prosecutor claims he makes them on the basis of judicial standards. But the whiff of politics is inescapable.

Possibly this is what really ails the Court. Seductive as the vision of an independent Prosecutor may be, the idea that the choices of situations are left to one unaccountable individual, who employs vague concepts of 'gravity' and 'interests of justice' to explain these, is perhaps not the ICC's greatest strength but rather its greatest flaw. At the Rome Conference, the drive to eliminate a role for the Security Council in the determination of 'situations' was understandable. But it may have caused another problem in the neglect of the ineluctable role of politics. The challenge, as the ICC enters its second decade, may be to find ways to remedy the situation by governing and regulating the role of political factors in the choice of 'situations' rather than pretending that they are simply absent.

IV. TOWARDS THE SECOND DECADE

There is a strong impression that after the euphoric success of the Rome Conference and the precocious entry into force of the Statute, the actual operations of the ICC have been a disappointment. Afflicted with a cumbersome and inflexible procedural regime, there is nevertheless resistance to contemplation of any reforms. The Court lacks vision and leadership. Its employees exude frustration and even demoralization. The ardour of the African states that ratified the Statute in large numbers, proving its appeal to countries of the South confronted with internal conflict, has cooled.

Compare this with the accomplishments of the United Nations tribunals at a similar stage in their development. Nine years after the adoption of the Security Council resolution establishing the International Criminal Tribunal for the former Yugoslavia, it had completed the trials of 25 accused persons. In 18 cases, even the appeals were finished. Forty-six people were in detention in The Hague, compared with five for the ICC. The International Criminal Tribunal for Rwanda cannot claim to have been quite as productive, but its performance is still rather stellar when set beside that of the ICC. Nine years after its establishment, it had completed the trials of 13 accused. Several appeals had also been adjudicated. And at the same age, the Special Court for Sierra Leone had completed three trials of nine defendants through to the appeals stage.

The Prosecutor has been rather dismissive of criticism about the ICC poor performance. Yet he has himself been responsible for forecasts that have failed to materialize. A year after taking office, the Prosecutor proposed a budget based upon the proposition that '[i]n 2005, the Office plans to conduct one full trial, begin a second and carry out two new investigations'.[26] A flow chart derived from the Prosecutor's plans indicated that the first trial before the Court would be completed by August 2005.[27] He became somewhat less ambitious in 2006, when a three-year strategic plan proclaimed the expectation that the Court would *complete* two 'expeditious trials by 2009, and … conduct four to six new investigations'.[28] In fact, only one trial started in 2009. No reasonable observer would use the adjective 'expeditious' to describe its glacial pace. In February 2010, a new three-year strategic plan from the Office of the Prosecutor said the Court would finish the three trials then underway or about to begin, and start 'at least one new trial'. In addition, the Prosecutor said he intended to continue ongoing investigations in seven cases, and conduct 'up to four new investigations of cases'.[29] In fact, by early 2011 not even one trial was even close to completion. The first judgment only came in early 2012, seven years behind schedule, and was followed by a second at the end of the year.[30] These mistaken projections reflect an unrealistic assessment of the difficulties facing the institution.

But there are many encouraging signs that it continues to enjoy the confidence of a large number of States, including many who have yet to join the Court. In early 2011, the Court presented itself as one of the useful options to deal with evolving crises in Libya and Côte d'Ivoire. When the Security Council referred Libya to the Court, both the Prosecutor and the Pre-Trial Chamber reacted with a sense of urgency that neither had shown years earlier when it had been asked to do the same thing in Darfur. Another sign of health is the successful adoption of amendments at the Kampala Conference that will eventually permit the ICC to exercise jurisdiction over the crime of aggression. While the pace of ratification has slowed, political changes such as the jasmine revolution in the Arab countries open up new opportunities.

---

26 Draft Programme Budget for 2005, ICC-ASP/3/2 para 159.

27 Ibid 49.

28 OTP, 'Report on Prosecutorial Strategy' (14 September 2006) 3.

29 OTP, 'Prosecutorial Strategy, 2009-2012' (1 February 2010) 2.

30 By the end of 2012, the Court had delivered two trial judgments in cases against Thomas Lubanga Dylo and Mathieu Ngudjolo Chui. (See *Prosecutor v Thomas Lubanga Dylo* (Judgment) ICC-01/04-01/06-2842 (14 March 2012) and *Prosecutor v Mathieu Ngudjolo* (Judgment) ICC-01/04-02/12 (18 December 2012).)

Tunisia's accession to the Rome Statute in June 2011 is a positive indication in this respect.

The Court remains confronted by the need to address shortcomings that have manifested themselves in its first years of operation. Other international courts and tribunals – the International Court of Justice and the European Court of Human Rights, for example – also face challenges to adjust as the world changes around them. But there is confidence in their continued existence as a more or less permanent fixture of the global order. This cannot yet be said as safely about the ICC. It must address its problems with a greater sense of urgency, and one of concern that if there is a failure to do so adequately, States may begin to lose the enthusiasm for the institution with which it has been blessed since the 1990s.

The ICC and its First Judgment in the Lubanga Case: One Giant Leap for Mankind, One Small Step for the Court?

*Andraž Zidar**

On 14 March 2012, in the year that marked 10th anniversary of the functioning of the International Criminal Court (ICC), the Court delivered its first judgment in a case against Thomas Lubanga Dyilo, a former militia leader in the province of Ituri in the Democratic Republic of Congo (DRC).[1] When the Prosecutor decided to launch proceedings against Lubanga in 2006 the case against him seemed to be a relatively easy case that would lead to prompt rendition of justice under the Rome Statute.[2] Proceedings against Lubanga went hand in hand with the expectations of the public to see the first criminal court of universal aspiration handing down justice against perpetrators of the most atrocious crimes.

At first, the ICC case against Lubanga seemed a win-win situation for all concerned.[3] Before Lubanga was transferred to The Hague the Congolese authorities accused him of genocide, crimes against humanity, murder, illegal detention and torture.[4] Prosecution of all these offences requires significant resources and expertise and it was not clear whether the Congolese judicial

* Dorset Senior Research Fellow in Public International Law at the British Institute of International and Comparative Law. Author wishes to express sincere thanks to Aletta van der Merwe, Olympia Bekou, Ruth Kennedy, Sotirios Lekkas, Shehara de Soysa and Nicole Urban for useful comments in the course of the preparation of this contribution.

1 For a good overview of the case see S Kammer, 'Deconstructing Lubanga, the ICC's First Case: the Trial and Conviction of Thomas Lubanga Dyilo' (2012) AMICC, Institute for the Study of Human Rights, Columbia University.

2 Rome Statute of the International Criminal Court, (2002) 2187 UNTS 90.

3 WA Schabas, 'Prosecutorial Discretion *v.* Judicial Activism at the International Criminal Court' (2008) 6 Journal of International Criminal Justice 757.

4 M Happold, '*Prosecutor* v *Thomas Lubanga*, Decision of Pre-Trial Chamber I of the International Criminal Court, 29 January 2007' (2007) 56 International and Comparative Law Quarterly 713.

authorities would pursue the case further.[5] The Prosecutor of the ICC, on the other hand, chose to charge Lubanga only with the offence of enlisting, conscripting and using child soldiers, despite the record of large-scale allegations of sexual violence and other crimes in Ituri.[6] Thus, after Lubanga's transfer to the ICC it seemed that all protagonists would be satisfied.[7] Lubanga avoided criminal charges for genocide and crimes against humanity as well as harsh detention conditions in DRC, the Congolese authorities handed over prosecution of a complex case to the ICC, and the Prosecutor was looking forward to a trial that promised an expeditious outcome.[8]

However, proceedings against Lubanga lasted for six years, and as they unfolded a number of serious questions arose as to the relationship between major actors before the Court, the application of general principles of criminal law, and procedure to the Rome Statute legal framework. In hindsight one could say that the *Lubanga* proceedings showed an ambivalent oscillation, often present in international criminal justice, 'between the wish to punish those individually responsible for large humanitarian disasters and the danger of becoming a show trial.'[9] On the other hand, several commentators welcomed the first trial judgment as a historic moment, a success, a cause for celebration and a major step in the history of the ICC.[10] The first judgment of the ICC is a natural cause for celebration for any proponent of international criminal justice. Nevertheless, the aim of this contribution is to provide a more critical analysis of the most pertinent legal issues arising from the *Lubanga* case and offer recommendations on how to resolve dilemmas to the benefit of the future work of the ICC.

The contribution will focus on the trial stage of the *Lubanga* case, with references to other phases (pre-trial and sentencing stages). The first question under consideration will be the use of intermediaries by the Prosecution. At present, the Rome Statute framework does not provide a definition of an intermediary. This led to difficulties in the *Lubanga* case with regard to the mandate, responsibility and reliability of intermediaries. The next question is

---

[5] Cf Schabas (n 3) 744.

[6] See J Locke, 'Chapter 11: Indictments', in L Reydams, J Wouters and C Ryngaert (eds), *International Prosecutors* (Oxford University Press 2012) 618 and Kammer (n 1) 3.

[7] Lubanga's transfer, however, took place on the basis of the Court's decision on jurisdiction of the ICC and admissibility of the case. (See *Prosecutor v Thomas Lubanga Dyilo* (Decision on the Prosecutor's Application for a warrant of arrest) ICC-01/04-01/06 Pre-Trial Chamber I (10 February 2006).)

[8] See Schabas (n 3) 743–744, 757–758 and Happold (n 4) 717–718.

[9] M Koskenniemi, 'Between Impunity and Show Trials' (2002) 6 Max Planck Yearbook of United Nations Law 1.

[10] G Acquaviva, 'Foreword' (2012) 10 Journal of International Criminal Justice 881, Kammer (n 1) 1, 21 and TR Liefländer, 'The *Lubanga* Judgment of the ICC: More than just the First Step?' (2012) 1 Cambridge Journal of International and Comparative Law 191.

the observance of the principle of legality. Although the *Lubanga* judgment is consistent with the principle of legality in Article 22 of the Rome Statute, the issue of sexual violence led to arguments and interpretations, notably in a sentencing decision and in two individual opinions by Judge Odio Benito, which could raise doubts in light of this pivotal principle in criminal justice. Finally, the contribution will touch upon some questions related to criminal liability. It will first explore the meaning of co-perpetration under the Rome Statute. This also opens discussion as to whether indirect intention (*dolus eventualis*) is envisaged under the Rome Statute. There are sound arguments which support this form of criminal liability in the ICC legal framework.

I. THE USE OF INTERMEDIARIES BY THE PROSECUTION

An intermediary usually denotes a private individual or an organisation that assumes some official functions and acts as a bridge between the official agency and addressees. This mechanism is, for example, known in the law of the United States where official institutions transfer certain prerogatives to individuals or groups and authorise them to act as their agents.[11] In essence this means that some working activities of an official agency are outsourced to private individuals or associations.[12] This may be for a variety of reasons: the official institution is not adequately organised to perform a certain function, the exercise of activities is geographically too distant to be performed by that agency, the official agency is not disposed of adequate capacity to fulfil the task and because there is a need to achieve cost reductions.[13]

The major problem that ensues from such a delegation of official powers is that it severs the link between the mandate of a public authority and the performance of working tasks in practice. This can pose serious questions about accountability and transparency of intermediaries.[14] Therefore, the use

---

[11] See, for example, A Stein, 'Healthcare Intermediaries' (2006-2007) 29 Regulation 20–25, D Isaak, 'FCPA Compliance – Navigating the Minefield of Intermediaries' (2008) 17 Currents International Trade Law Journal 22–27, S Issacharoff and DR Ortiz, 'Governing through Intermediaries' (1999) 85 Virginia Law Review 1627–1670 and BD Bayer, 'Membership Associations as Attorney-Client Intermediaries' (1968) University of Illinois Law Forum 65–74.

[12] In recent years the most known case of governmental outsourcing pertains to military functions. See, for example, PW Singer, 'Outsourcing War' (2005) 84 Foreign Affairs 119–132 and LA Dickinson, 'Outsourcing Covert Activities' (2012) 5 Journal of National Security Law and Policy 521–537.

[13] See, in general, M Weidenbaum, 'Outsourcing: Pros and Cons' (2005) 48 Business Horizons 311–315.

[14] This applies particularly to intermediaries taking part in political life or to contractors exercising military roles. (See Issacharoff and Ortiz, 'Governing through Intermediaries' (n 11) 1664 *et seq*, Singer, 'Outsourcing War' (n 12) 131–132 and S Chesterman, *One Nation under Surveillance* (Oxford University Press 2011) 112–130)

of intermediaries should rely on a precisely defined arrangement (mandate) of provided services and regular control to ensure intermediaries' compliance with legal standards.[15] Experience from domestic criminal proceedings, in particular, demonstrates that the use of intermediaries for prosecutorial activities is highly dubious. Analysis has shown that 'prosecution outsourcing diminishes the sort of accountability and transparency demanded of, and theoretically provided by, public prosecutors.'[16] This can lead further to the perception of increased danger of corruption and conflicts of interest.[17]

A. The problem of the definition of an intermediary in the Rome Statute legal framework

The legal framework of the Rome Statute does not provide a definition of the intermediary. Neither the Rome Statute nor the Rules of Procedure and Evidence make reference to this mechanism.[18] In the context of the ICC, intermediaries were local humanitarian and aid relief workers who, for reasons of security and knowledge of local circumstances, were recruited to assist ICC prosecutions. Thus, their humanitarian engagement and expertise were supplemented with the exercise of prosecutorial functions.[19]

In the *Lubanga* case, the Prosecution chose to rely substantially on the assistance of individuals, that later came to be known as intermediaries, during the investigation stage in Ituri in 2004 and 2005.[20] After arriving in Ituri, the representatives of the Office of the Prosecutor (OTP) encountered a difficult and unforeseen situation on the ground, since militias were still active.[21] Investigators came to the conclusion that in such a precarious situation witnesses would be put at risk if investigators contacted them directly.[22]

---

[15] Such is experience with intermediaries who perform financial services overseas. (See Isaak, 'FCPA Compliance – Navigating the Minefield of Intermediaries' (n 11) 22–23, 25–26.)

[16] RA Fairfaix, 'Outsourcing Criminal Prosecution?: The Limits of Criminal Justice Privatization' (2010) University of Chicago Legal Forum 284.

[17] Ibid 286.

[18] Cf CM de Vos, 'Someone who Comes between One Person and Another' (2011) 12 Melbourne Journal of International Law 218–219.

[19] MS Jacques, 'The OTP v Thomas Lubanga Dyilo: The Challenges of Using "Intermediaries" in the International Criminal Court', (2011) Humanitarian Law Perspectives, Australian Red Cross 3.

[20] See *Prosecutor v Lubanga* (Judgment) (n 49) para 125 *et seq*. Although the Lubanga case was the first example of the use of intermediaries, it was equally relevant in proceedings against Katanga and Ngudjolo. (See International Bar Association, 'Witnesses before the International Criminal Court (2013) 43 and C Buisman, 'Delegating Investigations: Lessons to be Learned from the Lubanga Judgment (2013) 11 Northwestern Journal of International Human Rights 32, 40 *et seq*.)

[21] Kammer (n 1) 9.

[22] See *Prosecutor v Lubanga* (Judgment) (n 49) paras 159–161.

Investigators likewise faced security threats during performance of their activities.[23] Thus, although security risks to potential witnesses were at the forefront, it seems that security concerns of investigators were equally important.[24] Faced with such a situation, the investigative team chose to build relationships with local NGOs and human rights activists to reach out to potential witnesses.[25] Eventually, these individuals began to act as 'intermediaries' in that they assisted the investigative team in identifying witnesses and victims to participate at trial.[26] In the course of time intermediaries became the main driving force behind the production of evidence for the *Lubanga* trial.

However, during the trial of Lubanga it emerged that some intermediaries may have attempted to persuade individuals to give false evidence and that some of the intermediaries were in contact with each other.[27] This cast a shadow of doubt over activities of intermediaries in general and on the fairness of the trial as a whole. During the *Lubanga* proceedings there were also no formal mechanisms at the ICC to supervise intermediaries. Thus, the content of this mechanism was ambiguous and the rules of the game were not known.

As mentioned previously, the Trial Chamber realised that there had been ample opportunities for intermediaries to influence witnesses in regards to statements they provided to the Prosecution.[28] Therefore the Court devised a procedural mechanism to decide on the release of identities of dubious intermediaries to the Defence. Disclosure of identities to the Defence was to be decided on an individual basis. The threshold for disclosure was *prima facie* evidence that the intermediary had been in contact with witnesses whose incriminating evidence had been materially questionable. In such a case the Court proceeded to consider disclosing the identity to the Defence. When deciding on disclosure the Court also took into account the assessment of the Victims and Witnesses Unit for protective measures for an intermediary.[29]

---

23 Ibid paras 151–152, 155, 162.

24 Women's Initiatives for Gender Justice, 'DRC: Lubanga Judgement — the Prosecution's investigation and use of intermediaries' (2012) Legal Eye on the ICC, see 'Security risks and impacts' <http://www.iccwomen.org/news/docs/WI-LegalEye8-12-FULL/LegalEye8-12.html#2>.

25 See *Prosecutor v Lubanga* (Judgment) (n 49) para 167.

26 Kammer (n 1) 9–10.

27 *Prosecutor v Thomas Lubanga Dyilo* (Redacted Decision on Intermediaries) ICC-01/04-01/06-2434-Red2 Trial Chamber I (31 May 2010) paras 135, 139.b.

28 Ibid para 138.

29 See ibid para 139.d. For an overall treatment of this issue see M Eikel, 'Witness Protection Measures at the International Criminal Court: Legal Framework and Emerging Practice' (2012) 23 Criminal Law Forum 97–133.

However, when the Trial Chamber ordered the disclosure of the identity of a particular intermediary the Prosecution refused to comply arguing that this would compromise the security of that person.[30] The Trial Chamber concluded that in such circumstances a fair trial of the accused was no longer possible, nor was it possible to do justice, because the judges had lost control of a significant aspect of trial proceedings.[31] The Trial Chamber ordered a stay of proceedings and the release of the defendant.[32] It was particularly striking that the OTP appeared to argue that it had autonomy to comply with, or disregard, the orders of the Chamber, depending entirely on its own interpretation of responsibilities under the Rome Statute framework.[33]

On appeal, however, the Appeals Chamber rejected the arguments of the Prosecution and upheld the principle of judicial autonomy. It went on to emphasize that under the Rome Statute, the Trial Chamber is the ultimate guardian of a fair and expeditious trial and its authority is subject only to the powers of the Appeals Chamber.[34] It held that orders of the Chambers are binding and should be treated as such by all parties before the Court.[35] Even if there was a conflict between the orders of a Trial Chamber and the Prosecution's perception of its duties as the prosecution, the OTP was obliged to comply with the orders of the Trial Chamber.[36] At the same time the Appeals Chamber also held that the continuation of fair proceedings was possible and annulled the stay of proceedings and the release of the defendant.[37] On the basis of previously mentioned procedural mechanism the Trial Chamber managed to bring the trial against Lubanga to a comprehensive close. However, in the trial judgment the Chamber criticized the way that the Prosecution resorted to the use of intermediaries. It held that the Prosecution should not have delegated its responsibilities to the intermediaries, especially since their activities were essentially unsupervised.[38]

---

[30] *Prosecutor v Thomas Lubanga Dyilo* (Judgment on the appeal against the decision of Trial Chamber I of 8 July 2010) ICC-01/04-01/06-2582 OA 18 Appeals Chamber (8 October 2010) para 12.

[31] *Prosecutor v Thomas Lubanga Dyilo* (Redacted Decision on Prosecution's Urgent Request for Variation of the Time-Limit to Disclose the Identity of Intermediary 143) ICC-01/04-01/06-2517-Red Trial Chamber I (8 July 2010) para 31.

[32] See *Prosecutor v Lubanga* (Judgment on the appeal against the decision of 8 July 2010) (n 30) paras 16-17.

[33] *Prosecutor v Lubanga* (Redacted Decision on the Identity of Intermediary 143) (n 31) para 21.

[34] *Prosecutor v Lubanga* (Judgment on the appeal against the decision of 8 July 2010) (n 30) para 47.

[35] Ibid para 1.

[36] Ibid paras 2, 54.

[37] See ibid paras 55-62 and *Prosecutor v Thomas Lubanga Dyilo* (Judgment on the appeal against the oral decision of Trial Chamber I of 15 July 2010) ICC-01/04-01/06-2583 OA 17 Appeals Chamber (8 October 2010) paras 22–27.

[38] *Prosecutor v Lubanga* (Judgment) (n 49) para 482.

B. Proposed (draft) documents on intermediaries

Proceedings against Lubanga thus brought to light the problem of the trustworthiness of intermediaries, non-reliability of evidence gathered by them and the necessity of submitting this mechanism to the formal supervision of the Court. In response to these issues, the Registry of the ICC in 2009 initiated consultations to establish guidelines on intermediaries.[39] This section will provide a short analysis of the draft 'Guidelines Governing the Relations between the Court and Intermediaries' that emerged during consultations and offer views on how to improve proposals contained therein. [40] At present, guidelines are yet to be finalised and adopted at a session of the Assembly of State Parties to the Rome Statute.[41]

The draft guidelines define an intermediary as follows:

> An intermediary is someone who comes between one person and another; who facilitates contact or provides a link between one of the organs or units of the Court or Counsel on the one hand, and victims, witnesses, beneficiaries of reparations and/or affected communities more broadly on the other.[42]

Although this description is very general, it contains one essential element of the notion of intermediaries: this is an individual who acts as a channel of communication or facilitator of transactions (inter-mediate) between two sides, in this case between the Court and people in conflict affected communities. Intermediaries should not function as agents of any side because that would compromise their equidistant position. However, in the framework of the ICC a problem was that intermediaries often acted as informal agents of the Court, in particular of the OTP.[43]

A look at the range of functions, as described in the draft guidelines on intermediaries, shows that this concept comprises some activities that potentially

---

[39] Witnesses before the ICC (n 20) 44 and International Criminal Court, 'Project to Define Policies Governing Relations between the ICC and Intermediaries' (Draft) (May 2010) 3 (unofficial document, on file with author).

[40] See International Criminal Court, 'Draft Guidelines Governing the Relations between the Court and Intermediaries' (Draft) (April 2012) (unofficial document, on file with author). The draft guidelines are a working document and not available in the public domain. However, they represent a summary of policies and practices of the ICC with regard to intermediaries.

[41] See ICC ASP, 'Report of the Bureau on the Strategic planning process of the International Criminal Court' (6 November 2012) ICC-ASP/11/30 paras 11–18, ICC ASP, 'Strengthening the International Criminal Court and the Assembly of States Parties (21 November 2012) ICC-ASP/11/Res 8 para 50 and Witnesses before the ICC (n 20) 45.

[42] Draft Guidelines (n 40) 5. The definition didn't undergo any significant changes from the beginning of the consultative process on intermediaries (see Project to Define Policies (n 39) 9).

[43] See de Vos (n 18) 218, 233-234 and Jacques (n 19) 3, 14.

conflict with the idea of an impartial intermediary.[44] The majority of functions envisage intermediaries as a channel of informative communication between the Court and victims or witnesses.[45] However, one specific function in the draft guidelines is also to assist 'a party or participant to *conduct investigations by identifying evidentiary leads and/or witnesses* and *facilitating contact with (potential) witnesses*'.[46] The annexe to the draft guidelines elaborates on the activities within the ambit of the investigative function of intermediaries. They are as follows:

- To monitor the situations and document international crimes;
- To assist in the preservation of evidence;
- To assist the OTP to locate and contact witnesses and other investigative leads and/or to maintain contacts between the OTP and witnesses (for investigation and protection);
- To assist the Defence Counsel to contact potential witnesses and collect evidence for a particular submission; and
- To assist legal representatives of victims to contact potential witnesses and collect evidence for a particular submission.[47]

These activities can be mandated by various organs of the Court: the Defence Counsel, the Office of the Public Counsel for Victims (OPCV) and the OTP. The first three activities fall within the domain of the OTP, the fourth is to assist the Defence and the fifth relates to the work of the OPCV. According to the above list an 'intermediary' is supposed to act as an extended arm of one of the parties to the trial to conduct investigative activities on the ground. This points to an inherent contradiction in the design of the intermediary under the ICC framework. We have seen that the rationale for the intermediary is to facilitate communication between the Court and witnesses, victims and other individuals in the field. However, investigative activities would make the intermediary work for one of the Court's organs. As practice demonstrates, that organ would be mainly the Prosecution.[48]

This is problematic for two reasons: first, the intermediary becomes an agent of one of the Court's organs and exercises his or her function on the

---

[44] The draft guidelines first enumerate main functions of intermediaries, which are further narrowed down to more specific activities within those functions.

[45] For an overview of all roles see Draft Guidelines (n 40) 6 and Project to Define Policies (n 39) 4–6.

[46] Draft Guidelines (n 40) 6 (emphasis added).

[47] 'Annex I: Summary of the main tasks conducted by intermediaries (by function and by unit/organ)' to Draft Guidelines (n 40) 1.

[48] Cf Jacques (n 19) 14–15.

basis of an investigative hypothesis or even bias.[49] This runs contrary to the very concept of the intermediary. Secondly, the framework of an investigative function presupposes investigations for various parties in different directions of investigation (the OTP and the OPCV on one side and the Defence on the other side). This blurs the distribution of activities and puts the intermediary into a position of a potential, if not real, conflict of interests.

The concept of intermediaries also suffers from serious defects in terms of imprecise content, the scope of the mandate and the mechanism for accountability. More specifically, the most pertinent drawbacks of using intermediaries for the Court's proceedings are as follows:

- the Court lacks sufficient mechanisms to control or monitor the activities of intermediaries;
- intermediaries are usually affiliated with particular interest groups, which might not be consistent with the best interest of the victims; and
- some intermediaries may work with various organs and sections of the Court at the same time, which can have adverse consequences.[50]

One can understand why the Court introduced intermediaries in its work. Often the Court does not have easy access to victims and witnesses who live in remote geographical areas. Likewise, in liaising with people from the conflict-affected communities it may lack sufficient cultural and societal expertise. In addition, security concerns may make it impossible for the ICC staff to visit and openly work in high risk areas.[51] In such circumstances it is useful and necessary to have contacts with local non-governmental or community-based organizations or individuals.

However, as underlined previously, the major deficiency of the proposed design of the intermediary in the ICC framework is that it embodies various conflicting roles, incompatible with adverse interests of parties before the Court. REDRESS aptly pointed to this problem:

> As has been demonstrated in the Lubanga case, an intermediary might work with separate organs of the Court or Counsel and this may be used as a line of defence to challenge their credibility or the credibility of the witnesses. In this light, the Draft Guidelines should specifically address

---

49 See *Prosecutor v Thomas Lubanga Dyilo* (Judgment) ICC-01/04-01/06-2842 (14 March 2012) paras 205, 482. For an in depth discussion on investigative bias and its epistemological implications on judicial proceedings see BM Zupančič, *The Owl of Minerva* (Eleven International Publishing 2008) 65–82.

50 Project to Define Policies (n 39) 13. See also Witnesses before the ICC (n 20) 44, 47 and Buisman (n 20) 58, 61.

51 Project to Define Policies (n 39) 12–13.

areas of conflict or multiple engagements that could affect their work or that of another organ/counsel. This is particularly important as new situations and permutations of conflicts of interest may arise.[52]

The function to assist the OTP is especially precarious since, as the *Lubanga* case revealed, the Prosecutor engaged intermediaries to perform investigative activities, thus turning them into an extended arm of the OTP.[53] But intermediaries should not act as substitutes for core functions within the Court's mandate and, in particular, perform activities in place of investigators.[54] Therefore, the prosecutorial (and possibly also the defensive) dimension should be removed altogether from the concept of the intermediary. Individuals who work with the Prosecution should not be included in the framework of intermediaries. Instead, the Prosecutor should find alternative means by which to engage local experts to perform investigative and evidentiary activities for the OTP. One possible solution for the OTP would be to improve its field presence and establish a permanent presence of its official representatives in the region under investigation.[55] Overall, however, the formal arrangement for intermediaries should put more emphasis on the consistency of procedural justice with the requirement of fairness and impartiality in proceedings before the ICC.

II. THE PRINCIPLE OF LEGALITY AND INTERPRETATION OF 'ACTIVE PARTICIPATION IN HOSTILITIES' AND 'HARM CAUSED TO THE VICTIMS'

Another important issue in the *Lubanga* case was the interpretation of certain expressions in the legal regime under the Rome Statute,[56] specifically pertaining to using children to participate actively in hostilities (Article 8(2)(e)(vii)

---

[52] REDRESS, 'Comments on the Draft Guidelines Governing Relations between the Court and Intermediaries' (15 October 2010) 4.

[53] That this is a realistic perception of the current work of intermediaries is clear also from the following description: 'Intermediaries perform a range of functions which are necessary for the ICC to do its work effectively. This may include, for example, assisting prosecution or defense investigators in identifying evidentiary leads and helping to contact potential witnesses. [...]' (Open Society Justice Initiative, 'Intermediaries and the International Criminal Court: A Role for the Assembly of States Parties' (December 2011) 2.)

[54] Victims' Rights Working Group, 'Intermediaries' Guidelines: Outstanding Issues' (April 2011) 2 and Buisman (n 20) 57.

[55] Buisman (n 20) 80–81 and Human Rights Watch, 'Unfinished Business: Closing Gaps in the Selection of ICC Cases' (2011) 46.

[56] For the purpose of this section I understand interpretation as 'the process of assigning meaning to texts and other statements for the purposes of establishing rights, obligations, and other consequences relevant in a legal context.' (M Herdegen, 'Interpretation in International Law', in R Wolfrum (ed), *The Max Planck Encylopedia of Public International Law* vol VI (Oxford University Press 2012) 260.)

of the Rome Statute) and to causing harm to victims (Rule 145(1)(c) of Rules of Procedure and Evidence)[57]. Interpretation of these provisions is particularly interesting in the context of sexual violence against children in two individual judicial opinions of Judge Odio Benito and in the reasoning of the Trial Chamber at the sentencing stage. These interpretations and reasoning raise concerns from the point of view of the principle of legality.

The Trial Chamber convicted Thomas Lubanga Dyilo for the crime of conscripting and enlisting children under 15 of age years and using them to participate actively in hostilities ((Article 8(2)(e)(vii)).[58] He was sentenced to 14 years' imprisonment.[59] Public opinion welcomed this conviction.[60] However, several public voices – notably some NGOs – harboured expectations that Lubanga would answer for accusations of sexual violence.[61] During the armed conflict in Ituri members of the *Union des Patriots Congolais/Force Patriotique pour la Libération du Congo* (UPC/FPLC) under Lubanga's control committed acts of sexual violence against girls and young women on a large scale. Victims of such violence suffer severe consequences such as post-traumatic stress disorder over a prolonged period of time and endure an immense physical and emotional ordeal.[62]

However, the Prosecutor decided not to pursue allegations of sexual violence against Lubanga.[63] The decision on the confirmation of charges by the Pre-Trial Chamber included only criminal offences focused on the enlisting, conscripting and the use of child soldiers.[64] This has led many observers to criticise the limited scope of the charges and to express doubts as to the credibility and relevance of the ICC.[65] Nevertheless, the OTP repeatedly

---

57 Rules of Procedure and Evidence, Adopted by the Assembly of States Parties (3-10 September 2002) OR ICC-ASP/1/3.

58 *Prosecutor v Lubanga* (Judgment) (n 49) para 1358.

59 *Prosecutor v Thomas Lubanga Dyilo* (Decision on sentence) ICC-01/04-01/06 (10 July 2012) para 107.

60 See eg The Independent, 'Congo Warlord Thomas Lubanga Convicted of Using Child Soldiers (14 March 2012) <http://www.independent.co.uk/news/world/europe/congo-warlord-thomas-lubanga-convicted-of-using-child-soliders-7566058.html> and Amnesty International, 'DRC: ICC Conviction of Thomas Lubanga Welcomed' (14 March 2012) <http://www.amnesty.org.uk/news_details.asp?NewsID=19998>.

61 See eg FIDH, 'Crimes of Sexual Violence and the Lubanga Case: Interview with Patricia Viseur Sellers' (16 March 2012) <http://www.fidh.org/Crimes-of-sexual-violence-and-the> and Women's Initiatives Gender Justice, 'First Sentencing Judgement by the ICC: The Prosecutor v. Thomas Lubanga Dyilo' (11 July 2012) <http://www.iccnow.org/documents/ Press-Statement-on-Lubanga-Sentencing.pdf>.

62 See *The War Within the War: Sexual Violence against Women and Girls in Eastern Congo* (Human Rights Watch 2002).

63 The OTP presumably avoided charges for sexual violence because of a lack of evidence. (See Kammer (n 1) 3.)

64 See *Prosecutor v Lubanga* (Decision on the Confirmation of Charges) (n 71) 175–176.

65 Locke (n 6) 618–619.

referred to sexual violence during the trial stage, which fuelled pre-existing frustrations of victims about the narrow scope of the charges.[66] At the sentencing stage the Trial Chamber voiced its strong disappointment with work of the former Prosecutor:

> The Chamber strongly deprecates the attitude of the former Prosecutor in relation to the issue of sexual violence. He advanced extensive submissions as regards sexual violence in his opening and closing submissions at trial, and in his arguments on sentence he contended that sexual violence is an aggravating factor that should be reflected by the Chamber. However, … the former Prosecutor fail[ed] to apply to include sexual violence or sexual slavery at any stage during these proceedings.[67]

The question as to whether Lubanga should be convicted for acts of sexual violence led to disagreements among judges on a number occasions and, in particular, to two individual opinions of Judge Elizabeth Odio Benito. At the trial stage Judge Odio Benito pleaded for an extension of the crime of using child soldiers to encompass elements of sexual violence. Furthermore, at the sentencing stage she suggested the interpretation of the suffering of victims as a direct consequence of acts of sexual nature. Although these views did not influence the judicial outcome of the case, the line of argument contained therein is intriguing because it runs counter to the principle of legality. Thus, two individual opinions of Judge Odio Benito, as well as the sentencing decision of the Trial Chamber, require thorough examination. We shall first give an overview of the principle of legality under the Rome Statute and then proceed to examination of the meaning of 'active participation' at the trial stage and of the content of 'causing harm to victims' at the sentencing stage.

A. The principle of legality in the Rome Statute

The principle of legality is a general principle of law and one of the most important achievements of the Western legal tradition. It is encapsulated in the Latin maxim *nullum crimen, nulla poena sine lege*.[68] This means that law alone determines and defines an offence and decrees the penalty. Such a prescription acts as a safeguard of individual liberty from any arbitrary encroachment on the part of the public authorities (ie the State).[69] In its

---

[66] S Vasiliev, 'Chapter 13: Trial' in Reydams, Wouters and Ryngaert (n 6) 748–749.

[67] *Prosecutor v Lubanga* (Decision on sentence) (n 59) para 60 (footnotes omitted).

[68] See J Hall, *General Principles of Criminal Law* (2nd edn, Bobbs-Merrill 1968) 28–30, 34–35, 58 and MC Bassiouni, *Introduction to International Criminal Law* (Transnational Publishers 2003) 178–179.

[69] *Consistency of Certain Danzig Legislative Decrees with the Constitution of the Free City* (Advisory Opinion) PCIJ Rep Series A/B No. 65, 51, 56.

Article 22, the Rome Statute enshrines the principle of legality reflecting *nullum crimen sine lege* in the following terms:

> 1. A person shall not be criminally responsible under this Statute unless the conduct in question constitutes, at the time it takes place, a crime within the jurisdiction of the Court.
> 2. The definition of a crime shall be strictly construed and shall not be extended by analogy. In case of ambiguity, the definition shall be interpreted in favour of the person being investigated, prosecuted and convicted.[70]

In the Rome Statute framework, this principle manifests the following constituent elements: an accused individual ought to be convicted on the basis of written criminal norms (*lex scripta*), pre-existing and approved by the States Parties to the Rome Statute (*lex praevia*), defining prohibited conduct and setting out the related sentence (*lex certa*), which cannot be interpreted by analogy (*lex stricta*).[71]

The purpose of the requirement of *lex stricta* is that the defendant must be aware in advance of all elements of the crime, which at the trial stage form the so-called 'major premise'. The 'major premise' of the criminal offence should be clear and not subject to further extension by the judge.[72] In this context it is apt to refer to one of the founding fathers of modern criminal law, Cesare Beccaria. He eloquently expressed this requirement in his classical treatise *On Crimes and Punishments*:

> The judge should construct a perfect syllogism about every criminal case: the major premise should be the general law; the minor, the conformity or otherwise of the action with the law; and the conclusion, freedom or punishment. Whenever the judge is forced, or takes it upon himself, to construct even as few as two syllogisms, then the door is opened to uncertainty.[73]

70 The third paragraph of Art 22 is omitted.

71 *Prosecutor v Thomas Lubanga Dyilo* (Decision on the Confirmation of Charges) ICC-01/04-01/06 Pre-Trial Chamber I (29 January 2007) para 303 and K Ambos, '*Nulla poena sine lege* in International Criminal Law' in R Haveman and O Olusanya (eds), *Sentencing and Sanctioning in Supranational Criminal Law* (Intersentia 2006) 21.

72 On the major premise see Zupančič (49) 36-38, 62-63, 247-248 and 315 *et seq*.

73 C Beccaria, *On Crimes and Punishments and Other Writings* (ed R Bellamy, trans R Davies, V Cox and R Bellamy, Cambridge University Press, 1995 [1764]) 14.

The Rome Statute follows the postulate of strict construction and interpretation of statutes in criminal law.[74] The purpose of this maxim is to instruct 'the judge to remain anchored to the authoritatively established and the ordinary meaning of the words and to resolve his doubts in favour of the accused.'[75] Article 22(2) of the Rome Statute prescribes a ban on broad or extensive interpretation of international criminal rules. This principle entails that one is not allowed to broaden, by way of interpretation, the scope of rules criminalizing conduct for the purpose of making them applicable to instances not specifically envisaged by those rules.[76]

B. The trial stage: the meaning of the 'active participation' of children in hostilities

The requirement of *lex stricta* is relevant in relation to the interpretation of 'active participation' of child soldiers in hostilities at the trial stage. Although the Prosecution, as we have seen, did not include offences related to sexual violence in charges against Lubanga, the OTP and victims' representatives advocated that using children to participate actively in an armed conflict implies that they were subjugated to acts of sexual violence.[77]

The Chamber majority, comprising Judges Fulford and Blattmann, declined such an approach. They refused to accept the charge of sexual violence because the facts relating to the sexual violence were not presented at a previous stage and thus not included in the Court's decision on the confirmation of charges.[78] This is in line with Article 74(2) of the Rome Statute requiring that the decision of the Trial Chamber 'shall not exceed the facts and circumstances described in the charges and any amendments to the charges.' Consequently, Lubanga was found guilty of the use of child soldiers, with no reference to elements of sexual violence.

In a separate and dissenting opinion to the judgment at the trial stage Judge Odio Benito disagreed with the Chamber majority. In her view the judgment should have taken into account not only the criminal act itself but also the suffering of the victims.[79] She argued that the Chamber has the

---

[74] B Broomhall, 'Article 22, *Nullum crimen sine lege*' in O Triffterer (ed), *Commentary on the Rome Statute of the International Criminal Court: Observers' Notes, Article by Article* (CH Beck, Hart, Nomos 2008) 714.

[75] Hall (n 68) 47. Jerome Hall here refers to the principle of legality, however, this assertion comes in the context of consideration of strict construction and interpretation. (Ibid 39–47.)

[76] A Cassese, *International Criminal Law* (2nd edn, Oxford University Press 2008) 48. See also WA Schabas, *An Introduction to the International Criminal Court* (3rd edn, Cambridge University Press 2007) 201-202 and Werle (n 86) 34.

[77] See *Prosecutor v Lubanga* (Judgment) (n 49) paras 574, 577–578, 589, 598 and 629.

[78] Ibid para 630.

[79] Separate and Dissenting Opinion of Judge Odio Benito, *Prosecutor v Lubanga* (Judgment) (n 49) para 8.

responsibility to define the crime based on applicable law, which she understood very broadly and beyond the scope of the Rome Statute.[80] According to Judge Odio Benito it is 'necessary and a duty of the Chamber to include sexual violence within the legal concept of "use to participate actively in the hostilities"'.[81] She went on to assert that the fact that the charges brought by the Prosecution against the accused did not include sexual violence should not have served as an impediment to this duty.[82] Thus, according to Judge Odio Benito, the meaning of 'active participation' should be extended to elements of sexual violence.[83]

In international humanitarian law there is a discrepancy in the degree of protection of children in armed conflicts. Additional Protocol I (1977) prohibits 'direct' participation of children in international conflicts.[84] On the other hand, Additional Protocol II (1977), which covers non-international conflicts, excludes any participation of children in hostilities.[85] In adopting the term 'active participation' of children in hostilities, the Rome Conference to some degree remedied this discrepancy and extended protection of children in armed conflicts to prohibit a broader range of participation than 'direct participation'.[86] The underlying reasoning behind this provision – 'to participate actively' – is therefore to keep children out of armed hostilities and to take into account the risks to their physical and psychological wellbeing resulting from such involvement.[87]

Amongst the elements of the crime of using, conscripting or enlisting child soldiers there is nothing to suggest this crime would encompass

---

[80] See ibid paras 6–7, 15.

[81] Ibid para 17.

[82] Ibid paras 15 and 17. However, contrast this opinion to the following views of Beccaria: 'The first consequence ... is that laws alone can decree punishments for crimes, and that this authority resides only with the legislator ... No magistrate ... can justly establish of his own record any punishment for any member of the same society. ... Therefore, a magistrate may not, *on any pretext of zeal or concern for the public good whatsoever*, increase the punishment laid down by law for a miscreant citizen.' (Beccaria (n 73) 12 (emphasis added).) Beccaria refers to punishment in terms of punishability.

[83] See Separate and Dissenting Opinion of Judge Odio Benito (n 79) para 20.

[84] See Art 77(2) of the Protocol Additional to the Geneva Conventions of 12 August 1949, and relating to the Protection of Victims of International Armed Conflicts (Protocol I) (adopted 8 June 1977, entered into force 7 December 1979) 1125 UNTS 3.

[85] See Art 4(3)(c) of the Protocol Additional to the Geneva Conventions of 12 August 1949, and relating to the Protection of Victims of Non-International Armed Conflicts (Protocol II) (adopted 8 June 1977, entered into force 7 December 1978) 1125 UNTS 609.

[86] M Cottier, 'Participation of Children in Hostilities' in Triffterer (n 74) 470-471. For more on the meaning on 'active participation' see G Werle, *Principles of International Criminal Law* (TMC Asser Press 2005) 332-333 and R Graf, 'The International Criminal Court and Child Soldiers: An Appraisal of the *Lubanga* Judgment' (2012) 10 Journal of International Criminal Justice 960-966.

[87] Cottier (n 86) 471.

elements of sexual violence as part of the *actus reus*.[88] Similarly, no such traces are detectable in the preparatory works.[89] Rather, active participation of children in hostilities implies their assistance in the conduct of hostilities.[90] The Preparatory Committee for the Rome Diplomatic Conference specified in more detail what 'active participation' stands for:

> The words 'using' and 'participate [actively]' have been adopted in order to cover both direct participation in combat and also active participation in military activities linked to combat such as scouting, spying, sabotage and the use of children as decoys, couriers or at military checkpoints. It would not cover activities clearly unrelated to the hostilities such as food deliveries to an airbase or the use of domestic staff in an officer's married accommodation. However, use of children in a direct support function such as acting as bearers to take supplies to the front line, or activities at the front line itself, would be included within the terminology.[91]

In the *Lubanga* case, in addition to the Trial Chamber,[92] the Pre-Trial Chamber likewise confirmed this interpretation.[93] The Special Court for

---

[88] See *Elements of Crimes*, Official Records of the Assembly of States Parties to the Rome Statute of the International Criminal Court, First session, New York, 3-10 September 2002 (United Nations publication, Sales No. E.03.V.2 and corrigendum), part II.B, reprinted as publication of the International Criminal Court, The Hague, 2011, 31, 39. See also C Garraway, 'Article 8(2)(b)(xxvi) – Using, Conscripting or Enlisting Children' in RS Lee (ed), *The International Criminal Court: Elements of Crimes and Rules of Procedure and Evidence* (Transnational Publishers 2001) 205–206.

[89] However, in the Rome Statute there is a number of war crimes related to sexual violence. Inclusion of these crimes represents a significant step in the progressive law-making in international criminal law. (See M Cottier, 'Rape and other Forms of Sexual Violence' in Triffterer (n 74) 431–454 and R Cryer *et al*, *An Introduction to International Criminal Law and Procedure* (Cambridge University Press 2010) 253–258.)

[90] Cf Cryer et al (n 89) 310.

[91] *Report of the Preparatory Committee on the Establishment of the International Criminal Court* (14 April 1998) UN Doc A/CONF.183/2 in United Nations Diplomatic Conference of the Plenipotentiaries on the Establishment of an International Criminal Court – Rome, 15 June – 17 July 1998 - *Official Records* vol III 18. See also Cottier (n 86) 471 (footnotes omitted) and WA Schabas, *The International Criminal Court: A Commentary on the Rome Statute* (Oxford University Press 2010) 253–254.

[92] See *Prosecutor v Lubanga* (Judgment) (n 49) para 621 *et seq*. The Trial Chamber added that a determination what constitutes 'active participation' can only be made on a case-by-case basis (ibid para 628).

[93] See *Prosecutor v Lubanga* (Decision on the Confirmation of Charges) (n 71) paras 261–267. See also *The Prosecutor v Germain Katanga and Mathieu Ngudjolo Chui* (Decision on the Confirmation of Charges) ICC-01/04-01/07 Pre-Trial Chamber I (30 September 2008) para 250.

Sierra Leone in the *Brima* case reached a similar conclusion.[94] Therefore, in terms of international criminal law there is a common understanding as to the notion of 'active participation'.[95] It is not logically possible to interpret this expression in the direction of Judge Odio Benito's expansive reasoning that '[s]exual violence is an intrinsic element of "use to participate actively in hostilities"' and that '[g]irls who are used as sex slaves or "wives" of commanders or other members of the armed group provide essential support to the armed groups.'[96] [97] Such a reading of 'sexual violence' into the conduct of using children in hostilities would violate the strict construction requirement and amount to a prohibited analogy under the Rome Statute (Article 22(2)).[98]

C. *The sentencing stage: the content of the 'harm caused to victims'*

The next issue related to *lex stricta* refers to the sentencing stage. Two factors are problematic here. The first is that the Trial Chamber allowed new evidence (eg on sexual violence) to be admitted at the sentencing stage irrespective of whether it extended the scope of the confirmation of the charges. The second was the line of reasoning in the dissenting opinion of Judge Odio Benito trying to establish a nexus between Lubanga's conduct and acts of sexual violence, although logical reasoning does not support such a conclusion.

---

[94] See *Prosecutor v Alex Tamba Brima et al* (Judgment) SCSL-2004-16-T Trial Chamber II (20 June 2007) paras 736-737.

[95] It seems that a perspective from international humanitarian law (IHL) is a different one. Although recommendations of the International Committee of the Red Cross emphasize that there is no difference in terms of quality and degree between 'direct' and 'active' participation of individuals in hostilities, in the IHL context such 'direct' participation applies only to conduct of hostilities. (See 'Interpretative Guidance on the Notion of Direct Participation in Hostilities under International Humanitarian Law' (2008) 90 International Review of the Red Cross 991–1047, especially 1012 *et seq*.) This further rules acts of sexual violence out of the scope of 'active participation' in hostilities.

[96] Separate and Dissenting Opinion of Judge Odio Benito (n 79) para 20.

[97] Even one author who is sympathetic to a gender-inclusive definition of child soldiers does not extend her argument as far as Judge Odio Benito. Cf: 'Also unique to the Paris Principles is the special recognition given to the situation of female child soldiers. Among the many gender provisions included, the Paris Principles address the recruitment of girl soldiers, the sexual-based violence they experience, and the particular problems and stigmas that female child soldiers face when they are released from armed groups. [...] The Rome Statute of the ICC does not define a child soldier in the same manner as aspirational documents such as the Paris Principles but rather adheres more closely to earlier documents such as the CRC.' (K Gallagher, 'Towards a Gender-inclusive Definition of Child Soldiers: The Prosecutor v. Thomas Lubanga' (2010–2011) 7 Eyes on the ICC 121 (footnotes omitted).)

[98] K Ambos, 'The First Judgment of the International Criminal Court (*Prosecutor* v. *Lubanga*): A Comprehensive Analysis of the Legal Issues' (2012) 12 International Criminal Law Review 137, n 156.

The Trial Chamber stated that the Prosecutor's omission to charge Lubanga with sexual crimes is not determinative of the relevance of these acts for the purposes of sentencing.[99] It reasoned that evidence admitted at the sentencing stage can exceed the facts and circumstances in the confirmation of charges, provided that the defence has had a reasonable opportunity to address them.[100] The Trial Chamber's argument was that it can consider sexual violence under Rule 145(1) of the Rules of Procedure and Evidence in the context of elements such as: the harm caused to the victims; the nature of unlawful behaviour; the circumstances of the manner of the commission of the crime and if the crime was committed with particular cruelty.[101] To this the Trial Chamber added requirements – which were to be satisfied beyond reasonable doubt – that: (i) child soldiers had been subjected to sexual violence; and (ii) this consequence could have been attributed to Lubanga in terms of his culpability. If these procedural standards were taken into account, there would be, according to the Trial Chamber, no consequential unfairness in including sexual violence as a relevant factor in the determination of the sentence.[102]

After examining the evidence, the Chamber majority, again comprising Judge Fulford and Judge Blattmann, concluded that

> the link between Mr Lubanga and sexual violence, in the context of the charges, has not been established beyond reasonable doubt. Therefore, this factor cannot properly form part of the assessment of his culpability for the purposes of sentence.[103]

The conclusion of the majority on this point is reasonable. However, it is problematic that the Trial Chamber referred to the issue of sexual violence in the course of the determination of sentence in the first place. The problem is that the causal link between allegations of sexual violence (in this context as harm), criminal responsibility and consequent sentence of the defendant is doubtful if these allegations did not form part of the confirmation of charges at the pre-trial stage. From the established doctrinal point of view the 'principle of causation designates and requires a causal relationship between legally proscribed harms and conduct.'[104] An essential aspect of the causal principle is that the defendant's conduct was a *necessary* condition of the

[99] *Prosecutor v Lubanga* (Decision on sentence) (n 59) paras 67.
[100] Ibid para 29.
[101] Ibid paras 67–68. See also Art 145(1)(c) Rules of Procedure and Evidence.
[102] *Prosecutor v Lubanga* (Decision on sentence) (n 59) para 69.
[103] Ibid para 75.
[104] Hall (n 68) 247.

caused harm.[105] In other words, the harm caused must be attributable to the defendant on the basis of his criminal conduct. This leads to the establishment of criminal responsibility, which serves as a basis for the determination of the punitive sanction (sentence).[106] A causal nexus must therefore exist, through the establishment of criminal responsibility, between the harm caused and the prescribed sanction.

However, in the *Lubanga* case the Court determined the criminal responsibility of Lubanga on the basis of a charge not related to sexual violence. This rules out the nexus between sexual violence and the harm suffered by victims for this particular type of allegations. If the Trial Chamber were to establish a link between sexual violence and suffering of victims (ie harm), it would amend the previous determination of criminal liability with elements of sexual violence. This would amount to the *ex post facto* application of laws (extension of the major premise of the offence) and go against the requirement of strict interpretation under the Rome Statute.

In her dissenting opinion to the Court's decision on sentence Judge Odio Benito contended that during the trial the Chamber received ample evidence of the use of sexual violence against recruited boys and girls during their involvement with the UPC/FPLC. The evidence pointed to 'harsh conditions of children in the recruitment camps and the sexual violence they suffered (mainly but not exclusively the girls)'.[107] In an attempt to attribute sexual violence to Lubanga she referred to Lubanga's speech at Rwampara army camp where he told recruits and other soldiers that training can involve 'suffering'. However, upon closer inspection this reference turns out to be misplaced. Nowhere in his speech did Lubanga refer to imposing punishment on soldiers or to sexual violence. The context of the 'suffering' in his speech was that of 'suffering' during ordinary military training.[108] From this no causal nexus ensues between the conduct of Lubanga for which he was found guilty and acts of sexual violence against children recruited by the

---

105 Ibid 282. For a detailed study see A Eser, 'The Principle of "Harm" in the Concept of Crime: A Comparative Analysis of the Criminally Protected Legal Interests' (1966) 4 Duquesne University Law Review 345–417.

106 Hall (n 68) 213, 225, n 47.

107 Dissenting Opinion of Judge Odio Benito, *Prosecutor v Lubanga* (Decision on sentence) (n 59) para 6. She enumerated evidence with regard to sexual violence explicitly in paras 14, 16–18.

108 The relevant paragraph reads: '[…] in view of the responsibility we have towards you, because I know we are united, aren't we? Well, we took an initiative and as soon as you finish your training and you're given your weapons, you have to go and ensure that safety and security of the population, and this is a very important task to carry out before God and humanity. You shouldn't take this work lightly. This type of work is of great importance. *It can involve suffering whilst you are being trained.* However, it's all to train your endurance and to ensure that you have the capacity. And if a member of the population sees you wearing a uniform, that they feel they can sleep tightly because somebody is guarding their safety.' (Ibid para 15, emphasis added in the original.)

UPC/FPLC. While Judge Odio Benito admitted that acts of sexual violence 'may not have been the deliberate intention of the convicted person', she nevertheless stated that sexual crimes 'may be attributed to Mr Lubanga since he was found guilty beyond reasonable doubt of the crimes that caused such harms to the child victims and their families.'[109] But this line of reasoning is founded on a fallacy. The correlation between the 'harm caused to victims' in the sense of sexual violence and Lubanga's criminal liability is not established. Firstly, Lubanga's reference to 'suffering' in training camps did not refer to suffering as a consequence of sexual violence. Secondly, since Lubanga was not charged with acts of sexual violence at the pre-trial stage, such charges cannot be brought in at the sentencing stage. In short, these arguments espoused in the dissenting opinion of Judge Odio Benito are below the standard of guilt 'beyond reasonable doubt' as prescribed by Article 66(3) of the Rome Statute.

The line of argument in two individual opinions of Judge Odio Benito and to a lesser degree also the reasoning of the Trial Chamber at the sentencing stage, is problematic from the perspective of the *lex stricta* component of the principle of legality. A classic violation of this principle would be when the general premise of a crime were framed on the basis of concerns of public morality or public policy.[110] This would make the normative premise collapse into the factual reality, which can result in the *ex post facto* application of the law.[111] The consequence of such an operation would be legal uncertainty.[112] These arguments display a logic that would run contrary to the principle of legality under the Rome Statute and therefore have to be disputed.

From a broader perspective there are a number of reasons that explain Judge Odio Benito's arguments (and also of the Trial Chamber at the sentencing stage) with regard to accounts of sexual violence in DRC. First, it is true that the OTP failed to articulate legal qualifications of sexual violence in the *Lubanga* case without giving an explicit explanation for their approach. However, adjudicators cannot replace the prosecution and extend criminal

---

[109] Ibid paras 20, 21.

[110] In one of the first international cases in the area of criminal law the Permanent Court of International Justice stated that 'sound popular feeling may mean different rules of conduct in the minds of those who are to act in accordance therewith. It is for this reason that that legislation is necessary in order to lay down the precise limits between *morale* and law.' (*Consistency of Certain Danzig Legislative Decrees* (n 69) 53.) From a domestic perspective see *Shaw v DPP* [1961] UKHL 1, [1962] AC 220 and its analysis in A Ashworth, *Principles of Criminal Law* (Oxford University Press 2009) 58–59 and MJ Allen, *Textbook on Criminal Law* (Oxford University Press 2009) 10–11.

[111] For a detailed analysis see Zupančič (n 49) 296–299.

[112] See *Knuller v DPP* [1973] AC 435 and R Card, *Card, Cross and Jones, Criminal Law* (Oxford University Press 2006) 16–17.

charges against a defendant on their own motion.[113] Secondly, judges should not use criminal law arguments to sanction the accused in ways contrary to the principle of legality under the Rome Statute.[114] We must harbour all compassion for victims of sexual violence in DRC and seek to provide adequate remedies for the suffering and consequences that were caused to them. Fortunately, the regime under the Rome Statute can provide remedies for their grievances through the reparations scheme. [115] However, if criminal charges are not brought against the accused on that account then the fundamental postulates of criminal justice do not allow the law to be extended contrary to the principle of legality. Such an extension, based on analogy, would reduce strict norms of international criminal law to vague considerations of morality or public policy, which would be contrary to the contemporary understanding of international criminal law.[116]

III. CRIMINAL LIABILITY ISSUES: CO-PERPETRATION AND INDIRECT INTENT (*DOLUS EVENTUALIS*)

The *Lubanga* cases also addressed a set of issues related to criminal liability. The Trial Chamber found Lubanga guilty of co-perpetratorship as envisaged in Article 25(3)(a) of the Rome Statute (to commit a crime 'jointly with another'). Under this mode of liability the Court relied on the concept of 'essential contribution' to the common plan that results in the commission of a crime.[117] The Court held that the decisive issue is 'whether the co-perpetrator

113 This would amount to 'khadi justice'. See Zupančič (n 49) 44.

114 One explanation for this may be an alleged intellectual rift in international criminal law between international humanitarian lawyers and criminal lawyers. As emphasised by Roelof Haveman: 'Compared to criminal jurists, humanitarian law jurists seem to be less interested in human rights when it comes to the trials of individuals, at least as far as the human rights of the person accused of having violated humanitarian law are concerned. … To give an example with respect to definitions of crimes: for an international humanitarian jurist who is not trained in criminal law, strict crime definitions only pose problems. … This means in fact that international humanitarian jurists must learn to reason as criminal jurists and, though seemingly to a lesser extent, vice versa.' (R Haveman, 'The Context of the Law' in R Haveman, O Kavran and J Nicholls (eds), *Supranational Criminal Law* (Intersentia 2003) 32–33).

115 The regime of the Rome Statute endowed the Court with broad remedial powers destined for reparation of victims and post-conflict rehabilitation of the society. For reparations of victims in the *Lubanga* case see *Prosecutor v Thomas Lubanga Dyilo* (Decision establishing the principles and procedures to be applied to reparations) ICC-01/04-01/06-2904 Trial Chamber I (7 August 2012). For reparation of victims of sexual offences see ibid paras 189, 207–209.

116 Ambos likewise understands the dissent of Judge Odio Benito at the trial stage rather 'as a policy speech for certain constituencies in the NGO community than a strict judicial analysis'. (Ambos (n 98) 138, n 156.)

117 *Prosecutor v Lubanga*, Judgment (n 58) paras 999, 1006, 1018.

performs an essential role in accordance with the common plan, and it is in this sense that his contribution, as it relates to the exercise of the role and functions assigned to him, must be essential.'[118] In addition, the Trial Chamber went on to establish the mental element (*mens rea*) of the accused on the basis of 'risk' that the consequence (result) of the criminal act will occur in the future.[119]

However, neither of the two concepts is an original invention of the Trial Chamber and instead derives from the reasoning of the Pre-Trial Chamber in its decision on the confirmation of charges. Furthermore, both concepts form part of two complex doctrines dwelled upon by the Pre-Trial Chamber – the control of the crime theory and the mental element of indirect intent or *dolus eventualis*.[120] Employed in isolation from these doctrinal backgrounds, 'essential contribution' and 'risk' with regard to the consequence bring more confusion than clarity into the judgment of the Court.[121] Therefore, both issues deserve a comprehensive consideration. The first issue under scrutiny will be the concept of co-perpetration as developed by the Chamber's majority. This notion will be juxtaposed with the separate opinion of Judge Fulford. His disagreement with the element of 'essential contribution' will also serve as a starting point for the examination of the mental element under the Rome Statute, in particular with regard to the existence of indirect intention (*dolus eventualis*) in the liability scheme under the Rome Statute.

A. Co-perpetration under Article 25(3)(a) and the element of 'essential contribution'

Article 25(3)(a) of the Rome Statute states that a person shall be criminally responsible and liable for punishment for a crime if that person:

> Commits such a crime, whether as an individual, jointly with another or through another person, regardless of whether that other person is criminally responsible;

This provision describes a category of perpetration which covers the following modes of criminal liability: direct perpetration, co-perpetration and perpetration by means.[122] Through different stages of proceedings the Court

---

[118] Ibid para 1000.

[119] Ibid paras 983, 986, 1011.

[120] See *Prosecutor v Lubanga* (Decision on the Confirmation of Charges) (n 71) paras 317–367.

[121] For a recent analysis of these issues see Liefländer (n 10) 203–208.

[122] See K Ambos, 'Article 25, Individual Responsibility', Special Print, in Triffterer (n 74) 748–755, Schabas (n 91) 427–430 and A Eser, 'Individual Criminal Responsibility' in A Cassese, P Gaeta and JRWD Jones (eds), *The Rome Statute of the International Criminal Court: A Commentary* vol I (Oxford University Press 2002) 789–795. From the comparative perspective see also GP Fletcher, *Rethinking Criminal Law* (Little Brown 1978) 637 *et seq*.

considered the criminal responsibility of Lubanga to be that of co-perpetration.[123] At the stage of the confirmation of charges the Pre-Trial Chamber read this provision in the context of the German doctrine known as 'control of the crime theory'.[124] The purpose of this doctrine is to delineate the zone of liability that exists between principals and accessories. It covers both direct and indirect perpetration. Thus, if a perpetrator is absent from the scene of the crime but nevertheless exercises 'control' or 'hegemony' over the execution of the crime, he or she falls under the concept of co-perpetration.[125] According to the Pre-Trial Chamber, co-perpetration based on joint control relies on the division of essential tasks for the purpose of committing a crime between two or more persons acting in a concerted manner. In that concept, the joint control of the crime corresponds to the essential contribution of co-perpetrators.[126] The control of the crime theory thus entails the following five elements:

> *Objective elements*
> i. the existence of an agreement or common plan between two or more persons;
> ii. the co-ordinated essential contribution made by each co-perpetrator resulting in the realisation of the objective elements of crime;
>
> *Subjective elements*
> iii. the suspect must fulfil the subjective elements of the crime in question;
> iv. the suspect and the other co-perpetrators must all be mutually aware and mutually accept that implementing their common plan may result in the realisation of the objective elements of the crime; and
> v. the suspect must be aware of the factual circumstances enabling him or her to jointly control the crime.[127]

Although the Trial Chamber majority (on this issue consisting of Judges Blattmann and Odio Benito) did not rely expressly on the above scheme of

---

[123] *Prosecutor v Lubanga* (Decision on the Prosecutor's Application for a warrant of arrest) (n 7) para 96, *Prosecutor v Lubanga* (Decision on the Confirmation of Charges) (n 71) para 321 *et seq* and *Prosecutor v Lubanga*, Judgment (n 49) para 978 *et seq*.

[124] T Weigend, 'Intent, Mistake of Law and Co-perpetration in the *Lubanga* Decision on Confirmation of Charges' (2008) 6 Journal of International Criminal Justice 478–480 and Separate opinion of Judge Fulford (*Prosecutor v Lubanga* (Judgment) (n 49)) para 10.

[125] The control of the crime theory was developed by a German scholar Claus Roxin. For a description of the doctrine in the English language see Fletcher (n 122) 655–656, 666–667, 672–673 and Werle (n 86) 123–124. For a critical assessment see JD Ohlin, 'Joint Intentions to Commit International Crimes' (2011) 11 Chicago Journal of International Law 721 *et seq*.

[126] *Prosecutor v Lubanga* (Decision on the Confirmation of Charges) (n 71) paras 346–347.

[127] Ibid paras 342–367.

the Pre-Trial Chamber, it nevertheless confirmed the reading of Article 25(3)(a) through the lens of this doctrine. The Chamber majority put its main emphasis regarding criminal liability for co-perpetration on the element of 'essential contribution' and reasoned as follows: 'None of the participants exercises, individually, control over crime as a whole but, instead, the control over the crime falls in the hands of a collective as such.'[128] This presupposes that 'the accused does not need to be present at the scene of the crime, as long as he exercised, jointly with others, control over the crime.'[129] The majority concluded that liability for co-perpetration requires two objective elements: (i) the existence of an agreement or common plan between two or more persons that will result in the commission of the crime; and (ii) that the accused provided an essential contribution to the common plan that resulted in the commission of the crime.[130] These are distinguishing criteria for delimiting principal liability, which requires a greater contribution, from a lesser accessory liability.[131] In other words, perpetrators or principals (this applies to co-perpetrators as well) are directly liable for the violation of the norm, while accessories are derivatively liable.[132]

Judge Fulford objected to the introduction of the control of the crime theory by the Pre-Trial Chamber into the legal regime of the Rome Statute. However, for the sake of fairness and to allow the accused to be informed in detail of the nature, cause and content of the charges against him,[133] he accepted the general test employed by the Trial Chamber on co-perpetration, which included the element of 'essential contribution'.[134] He criticised the position of the Pre-Trial Chamber from the perspective that such an interpretation of co-perpetration is too far-fetched and has no origin in the text of the Rome Statute.[135] The control of the crime theory originates in the German legal system and is closely related to the situation after WWII. In addition, the German legal system determines the sentencing range on the basis of the mode of liability under which an individual is convicted. In that context it is necessary to draw clear distinctions between principals and accessories.[136] On

[128] *Prosecutor v Lubanga* (Judgment) (n 49) para 994 (footnote omitted).

[129] Ibid para 1005.

[130] Ibid para 1006.

[131] See ibid paras 998–999.

[132] Fletcher (n 122) 636, 638.

[133] Charges were formally determined in the decision of the Pre-Trial Chamber on the confirmation of charges.

[134] Separate opinion of Judge Fulford (n 124) paras 2, 20–21.

[135] Ibid paras 3, 12.

[136] Judge Fulford disagreed with a reading of Article 25(3) that establishes a clear dividing line between various forms of liability. It is, however, important to establish distinctions between different forms of liability for the sake of clearly differentiating between principals and accessories. (See KJ Heller, 'The Rome Statute in Comparative Perspective', in KJ Heller and MD Dubber (eds), *The Handbook of Comparative Criminal Law* (Stanford University Press 2010) 605–606.)

the other hand, sentencing under the Rome Statute is not restricted in this way and such strict considerations do not apply. Thus, before adopting a particular domestic doctrine, the Court should investigate its compatibility with the Rome Statute framework.[137]

Judge Fulford emphasized that according to the plain, textual reading of Article 25(3)(a) the verb 'commits' requires a contribution to the commission of the crime.[138] This does not mean that the contribution must involve direct, physical participation at the execution stage of the crime, which would exclude an absent perpetrator. The word 'commits' simply requires an operative link between the individual's contribution and the commission of the crime.[139] On the basis of a plain reading of the words 'jointly with another' from Article 25(3)(a) the following elements of co-perpetration can be established:

a) the involvement of at least two individuals;
b) coordination between those who commit the criminal act, which may take the form of an agreement, common plan or joint understanding, expressed or implied, to commit a crime or to undertake action that, in the ordinary course of events, will lead to the commission of the crime;
c) contribution to the crime, which may be direct or indirect, provided that there is a causal link between the individual's contribution and crime;
d) intent and knowledge, as defined in Article 30 of the Statute, or as 'otherwise provided' elsewhere in the Court's legal framework.[140]

This approach provides a realistic basis for the Court to conduct its work.[141] Its advantage is that it grounds co-perpetration in the original meaning of Article 25(3)(a) and provides an original understanding of this concept under the Rome Statute.[142] The two main elements of this understanding are: (i) that a co-perpetrator makes a contribution – direct or indirect – to the commission of the crime (objective element) and (ii) that he or she has the mental element – intent or knowledge (according to Article 30 of the Rome

---

[137] See Separate opinion of Judge Fulford (n 124) paras 10-11.

[138] This interpretation is in line with canons of the Vienna Convention on the Law of Treaties. Cf: 'A treaty shall be interpreted in good faith in accordance with the ordinary meaning to be given to the terms of the treaty of their context and in the light of its object and purpose.' (Art 31(1) of the Vienna Convention on the Law of the Treaties (signed on 23 May 1969 and entered into force 27 January 1980) 1155 UNTS 331.)

[139] Separate opinion of Judge Fulford (n 124) paras 13, 15.

[140] Ibid para 16.

[141] Ibid para 17.

[142] This approach moves the notion of co-perpetration further away from the concept of joint criminal enterprise developed by the International Criminal Tribunal for the former Yugoslavia. (Cf Schabas, *The International Criminal Court* (n 91) 422, 436.)

Statute) – to commit the crime as a co-perpetrator (subjective element). The contribution of a co-perpetrator must be of such intensity that it falls in the criminality zone required for perpetration and needs not be 'essential'. Therefore, because a plain, ordinary reading of Article 25(3) yields results that also cover the criminal contribution of perpetrators absent from the scene of the crime, there is no need to transplant the 'control of the crime theory' and infuse ambiguity into the Rome Statute. The Court should, in the first place, base itself on the text of the Rome Statute and interpret it on the basis of its ordinary meaning and in light of its object and purpose. A reference to a specific doctrine from a particular domestic context should only be read as a supplementary source after the means of interpretation under the Rome Statute have not yielded a useful result.

B. Mental element under Article 30 of the Rome Statute and dolus eventualis

Judge Fulford also disagreed on the interpretation of the mental element, which opens a more in-depth debate on the existence of indirect intent (*dolus eventualis*) in the Rome Statute.[143] The Chamber majority interpreted the phrase from Article 30 'awareness that a consequence will occur in the ordinary course of events' as a matter of probability. According to the majority this phrase means that participants in the crime anticipate, based on their knowledge and how events ordinarily develop, that the consequence will occur in the future.[144] This prognosis involves consideration of the concepts of 'possibility' and 'probability', which are inherent to the notions of 'risk' and 'danger'. Since co-perpetrators only 'know' consequences of their conduct once they have occurred, the relevant standard should be that co-perpetrators – at the time they agree on a common plan and through its implementation – must know the existence of a risk that the consequence will occur.[145]

However, this investigation on different forms of probability is inconsistent and does not make much sense from a doctrinal standpoint.[146] Upon

---

143 Separate opinion of Judge Fulford (n 124) para 15. Judge Fulford, however, did not embark on the discussion concerning *dolus eventualis*.

144 See *Prosecutor v Lubanga* (Judgment) (n 49) para 1012.

145 Idem.

146 The assessment of the Chamber majority is confusing and inconsistent from a logical point of view. The majority interprets the phrase 'will occur in the ordinary course of events' as one of mere 'possibility', 'probability', 'risk' or 'danger'. The majority thus situates 'will occur' in the sphere of probability. However, when the Chamber majority confronts the phrase 'will occur' with 'may occur' – the latter implying probability – it declines the use of 'may occur' (which would imply *dolus eventualis*) with an argument that it would contradict the plain language of the Rome Statute. Since the Chamber majority interprets both, 'will occur' and 'may occur', as expressions of probability one fails to see a difference between them. (See ibid paras 983, 986, 1011–1012.)

closer examination it seems that the interpretation of the Chamber majority is a remnant of the Pre-Trial Chamber's reasoning on the mental element of individual liability that supported the concept of *dolus eventualis*. The Pre-Trial Chamber devised a number of arguments in favour of incorporating *dolus eventualis* in the framework of Article 30 of the Rome Statute.[147] However, the Trial Chamber majority disagreed with the Pre-Trial Chamber on this point and excluded *dolus eventualis* from the liability scheme under the Rome Statute.[148]

Although Lubanga was condemned on the basis of direct intent, the disagreement between the two chambers poses the important question of the inclusion of *dolus eventualis* in criminal responsibility under the Rome Statute, which is meaningful for future case law of the Court.

1. *Insights from comparative criminal law*

During the negotiations at the Rome Conference it was questionable whether the mental element in what is the current Article 30 would encompass *dolus eventualis*. It seems that divisions on this issue between Common Law and Civil Law lawyers left *dolus eventualis* out of further discussions on Article 30.[149] This, however, does not mean that the final text of Article 30 automatically excludes the concept of *dolus eventualis*.[150]

In that context it is useful to look at relevant provisions of the Model Penal Code (MPC). Several scholars point to the fact that in many instances the Rome Statute closely follows provisions of the MPC.[151] This applies likewise to the mental element of the Rome Statute 'that is similar to, and almost

---

147 See *Prosecutor v Lubanga* (Decision on the Confirmation of Charges) (n 71) paras 349–355.

148 *Prosecutor v Lubanga* (Judgment) (n 49) para 1011. The Trial Chamber majority followed argumentation of the Pre-Trial Chamber II in the Bemba case, which argued against the use of *dolus eventualis* under the Rome Statute (see *Prosecutor v Jean-Pierre Bemba Gombo* (Decision on the Charges) ICC-01/05-01/08-424 (15 June 2009) paras 357, 360–369).

149 See DK Piragoff and D Robinson, 'Article 30, Mental element' in Triftterer (n 74) 850, 860 n 67 and P Saland, 'International Criminal Law Principles', in RS Lee (ed), *The International Criminal Court: The Making of the Rome Statute* (Kluwer Law International 1999) 205. For an in-depth examination of legislative history see ME Badar 'Dolus Eventualis and the Rome Statute without It?' (2009) 12 New Criminal Law Review 444–452.

150 This is a suggestion by the Pre-Trial Chamber II in the Bemba case (see supra n 148). However, the Pre-Trial Chamber II erroneously equates *dolus eventualis* with recklessness (cf infra n 159).

151 See ME Badar, 'The Mental Element in the Rome Statute of the International Criminal Court: A Commentary From a Criminal Law Perspective' (2008) 19 Criminal Law Forum 475–476, Heller (n 136) 602–603, 609, Fletcher (infra n 155) 316–318 and A Eser, 'Mental Element – Mistake of Fact and Mistake of Law' in Cassese, Gaeta and Jones (n 122) 909–910.

certainly based on, the approach taken by the Model Penal Code.'[152] This is hardly surprising since the MPC represents the most authoritative codification of criminal law principles in the English language.[153] In Section 2.02.(2) the MPC enlists the following provisions on culpability for acting purposely or knowingly:

> (a) Purposely.
> A person acts purposely with respect to a material element of an offense when:
> (i) if the element involves the nature of his conduct or a result thereof, it is his conscious object to engage in conduct of that nature or to cause such a result; and
> (ii) if the element involves the attendant circumstances, he is aware of the existence of such circumstances or he believes or hopes that they exist.
> (b) Knowingly.
> A person acts knowingly with respect to a material element of an offense when:
> (i) if the element involves the nature of his conduct or the attendant circumstances, he is aware that his conduct is of that nature or that such circumstances exist; and
> (ii) if the element involves a result of his conduct, he is aware that it is practically certain that his conduct will cause such a result.[154]

This provision of the MPC covers two forms of intent; direct intent (*dolus directus*) described as 'purposely'; and indirect intent (*dolus eventualis*) formulated as 'knowingly'. There is a clear division drawn between them.[155] According to the MPC the main components (material elements) in these definitions are conduct, result/consequence and circumstances.[156] If the two levels of intent are classified according to these components, the following is apparent:

---

[152] Heller (n 136) 603.

[153] On the importance of the MPC in the American context see PH Robinson, 'United States' in Heller and Dubber (n 136) 565 and ME Badar, *The Concept of* Mens Rea *in International Criminal Law: The Case for a Unified Approach* (Hart Publishing 2013) 100.

[154] *Model Penal Code and Commentaries (Official Draft and Revised Comments)*, Part I, General Provisions §§ 1.01 to 2.13 (The American Law Institute 1985) 225–226.

[155] See GP Fletcher, *The Grammar of Criminal Law: American, Comparative and International* vol 1 (Oxford University Press 2007) 317–318. Fletcher points out that the origins for a distinction between 'purposely' and 'knowingly' derives from the German doctrine and its differentiation between *dolus directus* and *dolus eventualis*.

[156] Model Penal Code and Commentaries (n 154) 229 (including n 1) and Badar (n 153) 101.

	Purposely	**Knowingly**
Conduct	It is his conscious object to engage	Awareness that his conduct is an element of the offense
Consequence/result	It is his conscious object to cause a result	Awareness that it is practically certain that his conduct will cause a result
Circumstances	Awareness that they exist/ Belief or hope that they exist	Awareness that they exist

The first significant difference between 'purposely' and 'knowingly' is in relation to the prohibited conduct. Acting purposely requires an intense volitional requirement that the conduct is in the author's conscious object to engage. On the other hand, acting 'knowingly' presupposes a cognitive element in that the author must be aware that his conduct is an element of an offense.

However, the key differentiation between the two modes of responsibility is the attitude towards the result of the author's conduct. Action is purposive with respect to the result if it was actor's *conscious object* to cause such a result.[157] In other words, a perpetrator *wills* a result. The situation is different, however, in case of acting knowingly when the actor is simply *aware* that the prohibited result is practically certain to follow from his conduct.[158] The gist of the distinction between the two culpability levels – purposely (*dolus directus*) and knowingly (*dolus eventualis*) – is thus the presence or absence of a positive desire to cause the result.[159]

According to comparative criminal law theory, the approach towards the result in *dolus eventualis* goes in two directions. One approach follows the Common Law system and emphasizes the degree of risk that the result will occur. In this objective approach (with an emphasis on cognition) the actor

---

[157] Fletcher (n 155) 317–318 and Robinson (n 153) 574.

[158] Model Penal Code and Commentaries (n 154) 233.

[159] Robinson (n 153) 574. Section 2.02.(2)(c) MPC covers also the third degree of culpability, that is, if a perpetrator acts 'recklessly' (known also as advertent negligence). The distinguishing factor between 'knowingly' and 'recklessly' again resides in the sphere of the result. In the case of acting knowingly the result must satisfy the threshold of practical certainty whereas in case of acting recklessly the perpetrator must be aware of a substantial risk. (See Model Penal Code and Commentaries (n 154) 236–237 and Robinson (n 153) 574.) This is worth emphasizing because international lawyers frequently confuse *dolus eventualis* with recklessness. (Fletcher (n 155) 317 and Badar (153) 112.)

takes a very high risk and is 'practically certain' that the consequence will occur. What is controlling, therefore, is actual risk and knowledge of risk.[160] This is also the standard of the MPC (as noted above).[161] The second approach, predominant in the Continental legal tradition, emphasises the actor's attitude toward the risk. This approach implies that the perpetrator 'reconciles himself' or 'makes peace' with the consequence of the crime,[162] which essentially means that he 'assents' to the consequences of the crime. Here the emphasis is on the subjective posture towards the result (volitional element), even if the risk that the consequence will occur is lower.[163] At this point it must be added that the subjective approach towards the result moves the emphasis of *dolus eventualis* from the focus on the consequence to the attitude towards the conduct.[164]

On the basis of these insights we can come to the following conclusions. Differences between direct intent and *dolus eventualis* are in the attitude towards the conduct and the result. If the actor wills a conduct or a result, such an action is purposive and implies direct intent. However, if the actor is 'solely' aware that his conduct is of the required nature or that the result is practically certain to occur, it is a case of *dolus eventualis*. From the comparative perspective, the attitude towards the result presupposes two approaches. The subjective (volitional) approach puts an emphasis on the intensity of the actor's attitude towards the result (acquiescence). Under the objective (cognitive) approach, on the other hand, the focus is on the result, which must be 'practically certain' to follow after the prohibited conduct. Both approaches can be part of the notion of *dolus eventualis*.

2. *A fresh look at the mental element under Article 30 of the Rome Statute*

We can apply insights from comparative criminal law also to the wording of the mental element in the Rome Statute. Article 30 reads as follows:

---

[160] Fletcher (n 122) 446–447. This approach derives from the (utilitarian) work of Jeremy Bentham. Cf: 'It is also to be observed, that into the account of the consequences of the act, are to be taken not such only as might have ensued, were intention out of the question, but such also as depend upon the connexion there may be between these first-mentioned consequences and the intention. The connexion there is between the intention and certain consequences is, as we shall see hereafter, a means of producing other consequences. In this lies the difference between rational agency and irrational.' (J Bentham, *An Introduction to the Principles of Morals and Legislation* (Batoche Books 2000 [1781]) 61–62.)

[161] The MPC draws a divisive line between *dolus eventualis* and recklessness on the basis of the degree of risk. *Dolus eventualis*, as stated above, necessitates 'practical certainty'. Recklessness, on the other hand, requires 'probability less than substantial certainty'. (See Model Penal Code and Commentaries (n 154) 236 (including n 13) and 248 (n 42).)

[162] Fletcher (n 122) 325-326 and Werle (n 86) 113.

[163] See Fletcher (n 122) 325-326, 445–447.

[164] Cf ibid 448.

1. Unless otherwise provided, a person shall be criminally responsible and liable for punishment for a crime within the jurisdiction of the Court only if the material elements are committed with intent and knowledge.
2. For the purposes of this article, a person has intent where:
   (a) In relation to conduct, that person means to engage in the conduct;
   (b) In relation to a consequence, that person means to cause that consequence or is aware that it will occur in the ordinary course of events.
3. For the purposes of this article, 'knowledge' means awareness that a circumstance exists or a consequence will occur in the ordinary course of events. 'Know' and 'knowingly' shall be construed accordingly.

The stipulation in Article 30(1) that the material elements of a crime under the Rome Statute require 'intent and knowledge' is different from the terminology employed in the MPC in that it does not relate to various degrees of liability but to elements of that liability.[165] Therefore, we cannot compare 'intent and knowledge' to 'purposely' and 'knowingly'.[166] Rather, the 'intent and knowledge' requirement marks a distinction between volitional and cognitive conditions of criminality. For the establishment of criminal liability the Rome Statute requires their cumulative presence at the time of the criminal conduct.[167]

However, from this point on the wording of Article 30 largely follows the tradition of the Common Law. As we have seen before, the two levels of liability in the MPC consist of the following components: conduct, circumstances and result/consequence. The same goes for liability under the Rome Statute.[168] On the basis of the elements that comprise Article 30 the following two options arise:

165 It is worth noting that in terms of structure and wording the Art 30 of the Rome Statute resembles sections 5.2 and 5.3 of the Australian Commonwealth Criminal Code adopted in 1995. (See <http://www.austlii.edu.au/au/legis/cth/consol_act/cca1995115/sch1.html>.)

166 Cf Fletcher (n 155) 316–317. See also K Ambos, 'General Principles of Criminal Law in the Rome Statute' (1999) 10 Criminal Law Forum 22. Ambos, however, doubts as to whether *dolus eventualis* is included in Art 30 of the Rome Statute. (See ibid 21–22.)

167 Werle (n 86) 102, 103. See also Eser (n 122) 905 and Schabas (n 91) 475.

168 See *Prosecutor v Thomas Lubanga Dyilo* (Judgment) (n 49) para 1007, M Kelt and H von Hebel, 'General Principles of Criminal Law and the Elements of Crimes', in Lee (n 88) 21 and Piragoff and Robinson (n 149) 852.

	Rome Statute Option A	**Rome Statute Option B**
Conduct	Means to engage	Means to engage
Consequence	Means to cause it	Awareness that it will occur in the ordinary course of events
Circumstance	Awareness that it exists	Awareness that it exists

If we juxtapose these two combinations to definitions in the MPC we realise that the Rome Statute Option A closely corresponds to the category of 'purposely' or direct intent. The same applies to the Rome Statute Option B in relation to the category 'knowingly' or *dolus eventualis*. There are, however, three distinctions that need to be mentioned.

The first distinction relates to conduct. In the MPC 'purposely' requires that it is in the actor's 'conscious object to engage in conduct', whereas Option A requires a slightly lesser threshold that the perpetrator 'means to engage in the conduct'. On the other hand, the definition of 'knowingly' in the MPC presupposes that the actor is aware of the nature of his or her conduct, while Option B again requires that the actor 'means to engage in the conduct'. In comparative terms this is a subjective understanding of intent, which encompasses indirect intent.[169] It seems that this general expression in the Rome Statute was formed to accommodate conduct under both forms of intent – active engagement and 'acquiescent engagement'. It is important to keep in mind that intention, which is the highest degree of criminal liability, logically implies 'some element, although minimal, of desire or willingness to do the action'.[170] At the same time this anticipates a high degree of volition with regard to the conduct that we could describe as the 'clear state of mind'. This standard is higher than that of the MPC for 'knowingly' but still lower than that required for the direct intent or 'purposely' (eg 'conscious object to engage').

The second difference relates to the consequence. For acting 'knowingly' the MPC requires that the actor is 'aware that it is practically certain that his conduct will cause such a result'. Option B sets a seemingly higher threshold

[169] The subjective approach is common in Australian criminal law. Under section 5.2 of the Commonwealth Criminal Code and under part 2.2.7 of the Model Criminal Code the intention with regard to conduct is formulated with an expression 'means to engage' which includes indirect intent. (S Bronitt, 'Australia' in Heller and Dubber (n 136) 58.) See also M Findlay, S Odgers and S Yeo, *Australian Criminal Justice* (Oxford University Press 1999) 15–17.

[170] Piragoff and Robinson (n 149) 859. See also Badar (n 149) 467.

in that the perpetrator is aware that the consequence 'will occur in the ordinary course of events'. The formulation in the Rome Statute prompted some to claim that it encapsulates absolute certainty and thus allows only for direct intent under the Rome Statute.[171] However, the difference between the two formulations is much narrower than it seems at first sight. Firstly, assessment of a future event (that is, the result or consequence of a criminal act) is always an exercise in probability.[172] It would be unrealistic to impose a requirement that the actor must be aware with absolute certainty that the consequence will occur in the future.[173] On the other hand, this threshold must be still high enough not to blur the distinction between intention and lower levels of culpability, such as recklessness and negligence. It is reasonable to interpret, therefore, the expression of the Rome Statute ('will occur in the ordinary course of events') as awareness of practical certainty that the consequence will occur in the future.

The third variance pertains to the combination of material elements. The text of the MPC under both forms of liability ('purposely' and 'knowingly') allows for the alternative presence of the two material elements: either the conduct or the result. Article 30(1), on the other hand, requires that the material elements 'are committed with intent and knowledge', which brings a strong conjunctive requirement in the scheme of the mental element under Article 30.[174] This would require cumulative presence of all material elements, but most importantly of the conduct and of the consequence.[175] In terms of Option B, which is central to our discussion on *dolus eventualis* under the Rome Statute, this would mean that all of its components have to be fulfilled. In terms of the conduct there would have to be an intense subjective element ('clear state of mind') of the perpetrator. In terms of consequence there would have to be practical certainty that the result will occur in the ordinary course of events. This arrangement for *dolus eventualis* under the Rome Statute is a high threshold, setting the bar higher than is required for 'knowingly' in the MPC (but still lower than for 'purposely'). Because of the qualified nature of material elements in Article 30 we could say that the Rome Statute endorses a notion of indirect intent that could be labelled as *dolus eventualis* of the first degree.

---

171 See Cryer et al (n 89) 386–387.

172 Otherwise we would be living in the world of Phillip Dick's *Minority Report*. See PK Dick, 'The Minority Report', in *The Collected Short Stories of Phillip K. Dick: Minority Report* (Gollanz 2001) 71–102.

173 Cf Model Penal Code and Commentaries (n 154) 236, n 13.

174 Eser (n 181) 904-908 and Piragoff and Robinson (n 149) 854–855.

175 See *Prosecutor v Lubanga* (Judgment) (n 49) paras 1007–1010, in particular 1010 and *Prosecutor v Lubanga* (Decision on the Confirmation of Charges) (n 71) paras 351–355, in particular 352.ii. This argument comes from the reasoning of the Pre-Trial Chamber, which introduced a cumulative approach to *dolus eventualis* albeit with lower thresholds than suggested in this contribution.

In conclusion it can be said that *dolus eventualis* exists under the Rome Statute in terms of the concept described above in Option B. This concept, however, presupposes high standards with regard to material components. Attitude towards the conduct, expressed as a standard 'means to engage' implies a clear state of mind of the author with regard to actions or omissions and ensuing harm (comparable to the standards 'reconciles himself' 'or makes peace' with the result). In addition, attitude concerning the result itself has to follow the standard that the perpetrator is practically certain that his conduct will lead to such a result.[176] Thus, a clear state of mind and practical certainty with regard to result are both necessary for *dolus eventualis* under the Rome Statute. Finally, there must be an awareness regarding the circumstance of the offence. This element is less important for our discussion but it likewise has to satisfy a high threshold.[177]

At the end of this section it has to be emphasised, however, that in the *Lubanga* case the condemnation of the defendant by the Court did not rely on indirect intent. Thomas Lubanga was found guilty on the basis of direct intent.[178] Nevertheless, confrontation of the arguments between the Pre-Trial and the Trial Chamber served as the inspiration to examine this important issue in more detail, also in the context of the MPC as being a possible source of interpretation of the Rome Statute on the mental element. From this discussion it follows that there are good arguments to support *dolus eventualis* as part of the responsibility scheme under the Rome Statute.[179] However, to date the case law of the ICC remains diverse and inconsistent on this issue[180] and doctrinal opinions vary as to whether the Rome Statute encompasses it.[181] In the last instance it will fall to the Appeals Chamber of the ICC to determine whether *dolus eventualis* forms part of the mental element under the Rome Statute.

---

[176] On these two elements see *Prosecutor v Lubanga* (Decision on the Confirmation of Charges) (n 71) para 352.ii.

[177] According to Heller 'awareness that a circumstance exists' goes beyond the standard of a 'high probability' of a circumstance's existence in the MPC. (Heller (n 136) 604.)

[178] See *Prosecutor v Lubanga* (Judgment) (n 49) paras 1356–1357.

[179] See Badar (n 149) 435, 467 and Badar (153) 382–400.

[180] As mentioned previously, Pre-Trial Chamber II and Trial Chamber I excluded this concept, whereas Pre-Trial Chamber I endorsed it.

[181] See Eser (n 122) 792, A Eser, 'Mental Element – Mistake of Fact and Mistake of Law' in Cassese, Gaeta and Jones (n 122) 901, 915–916, 932–933, Schabas (n 91) 475–476, Piragoff and Robinson (n 149) 850–851, 860–861, JD van der Vyver, 'The International Criminal Court and the Concept of *Mens Rea* in International Criminal Law' (2004) 12 University of Miami International and Comparative Law Review 63–67 and E van Sliedregt, *Individual Criminal Responsibility in International Law* (Oxford University Press 2012) 45–48.

IV. CONCLUSION

An appraisal of the Court's first trial judgment in the *Lubanga* case is not an easy task. Throughout the process we witnessed the rocky path of judicial proceedings. To a certain degree a slow pace of proceedings in the *Lubanga* case is understandable; the Rome Statute embodies elements of various systems, traditions and levels of criminal justice. This makes it a very complex legal regime.[182] The Court is continuously faced with the task of reconciling these elements through decisions on concrete issues. In the *Lubanga* case the Trial Chamber managed to deliver a logically consistent and persuasive judgment that led to the first conviction under the Rome Statute. This judgment is in line with aspirations of the public that 'the ICC is the nail in the coffin of the long-standing culture of impunity that leaders and planners of international crimes have for too long enjoyed.'[183] From this perspective, the conviction of Lubanga for the crime of enlisting, conscripting and using child soldiers does represent 'one giant leap for mankind'.

At the same time, contradictions embedded in the Rome Statute necessitate a quest for further coherence of the legal regime under the Rome Statute. The following are some specific challenges that arise out of the *Lubanga* case. As we have seen already, the use of intermediaries by the Prosecution posed a major problem for the Court. Intermediaries should serve as a channel of communication between the Court and witnesses and victims on the ground. If the general idea of intermediaries is to be consistent with the Rome Statute, the role, mandate and accountability of intermediaries must be defined in precise terms. Since the work of intermediaries is based on equidistance and impartiality, agents who perform investigative activities for the Prosecution must be taken out of the scheme of intermediaries, integrated into the institutional capacity of the OTP and possibly be located in the region where there is an ICC investigation.

The Prosecution must also undertake a more profound and comprehensive assessment of charges against potential perpetrators. In the *Lubanga* case the omission of charges for sexual violence raised doubts among international and local commentators about the legitimacy of the trial. It also prompted some judges on the bench to look for a 'remedy' for this prosecutorial omission in an extended interpretation of the crime of using child soldiers that was infused with elements of sexual violence. However, this is highly problematic. If adopted, such a solution would merge the roles of prosecutor and judge and would be incompatible with fundamental principles of the contemporary concept of criminal justice. In particular, it would be contrary to the princi-

[182] On the complexity in international criminal law in general see Bassiouni (n 68) 1–8.

[183] The Board of Editors, 'The Rome Statute: A Tentative Assessment' in Cassese, Gaeta and Jones, vol II (n 122) 1901.

ple of legality under the Rome Statute, which the ICC – as a criminal court *par excellence* – must resolutely uphold.

Finally, consideration of the topic of criminal liability also opened a number of issues. The Pre-Trial Chamber judges had justified Lubanga's co-perpetration liability on the basis of the 'control of the crime theory'. This is a specific doctrine in the German criminal law system, which is foreign to the legal framework of the Rome Statute. Although the majority of the Trial Chamber did not expressly rely on the control of the crime theory, it implicitly confirmed it through acceptance of its 'essential contribution' component. Instead, the judges should have applied a realistic approach and developed an autonomous interpretation of co-perpetration under the Rome Statute. On the other hand, the Trial Chamber did not follow the *obiter dictum* of the Pre-Trial Chamber that the mental element under the Rome Statute encompasses indirect intention (*dolus eventualis*). Insights from comparative criminal law – in particular from the MPC – provide sound arguments in favour of *dolus eventualis* as part of the liability scheme under the Rome Statute.

Overall, one can agree with an assessment that the judgment in the *Lubanga* case was legally solid and factually well-founded, which makes it a remarkable achievement.[184] However, all challenges and dilemmas that arose in the course of the judicial proceedings in the *Lubanga* case described above demonstrate that the Court will have to proceed through a number of smaller steps to bring solid coherence into the legal regime under the Rome Statute. The *Lubanga* case is only the first step in the right direction.

[184] Acquaviva (n 10) 885.

The International Criminal Court: Where Do We Stand after 10 Years? A Perspective from Civil Society

*Marek Marczynski**

I. INTRODUCTION

The establishment of the International Criminal Court (ICC) brought a lot of hope to the victims of genocide, crimes against humanity and war crimes around the world. It was also a tremendous achievement for civil society, which in the mid-1990s was becoming increasingly global.

As a result of the fall of communism and the end of the bipolar distribution, many foresaw the world moving towards a global system based on democratic values and universal respect for human rights. While those hopes materialised in some parts of the world, what happened in other parts was quite contradictory. The new, post-Cold War era of international relations started at the beginning of the 1990s with deadly conflicts in Rwanda, Sierra Leone, Chechnya and other parts of the Soviet Union and in the former Yugoslavia. Hundreds of thousands of people lost their lives, millions were displaced and the true number of victims of other gross human rights violations will probably never be established.[1]

* Director of Campaigns and Policy at Index on Censorship, Editor-in-Chief of the Birkbeck Law Review and previously Deputy Director in Europe and Central Asia Programme at the International Secretariat of Amnesty International, London.

[1] While it is beyond the scope of this article to provide full and comprehensive statistics of the number of victims of crimes under international law committed during the 1990s worldwide, the extent of atrocities committed during that decade was massive. According to estimates between 500,000 and 1 million people were killed during the genocide in Rwanda. (See A Des Forges 'Leave None to Tell the Story: Genocide in Rwanda' (Human Rights Watch 1999) <http://www.hrw.org/legacy/reports/1999/rwanda/Geno1-3-04.htm#P95_39230>). At least 50,000 people lost their lives during the 1991–2002 civil war in Sierra Leone; 20,000 were left mutilated and it is estimated that 2.5 million people were internally and externally displaced. (See M Meredith, *The State of Africa. A History of the Continent since Independence* (Simon & Schuster 2011) 572). According to estimates between 50,000 and 64,000 women might have been victims of sexual violence during the conflict. (See: '"We will kill you if you cry": Sexual Violence in the Sierra Leone Conflict' (Human Rights Watch 2003) 25 <http://www.hrw.org/sites/default/

But what happened at the beginning of the 1990s was also the birth of a global civil society, which, in response to those atrocities, united victims across continents in their struggle for human rights and in the fight against impunity. What initially started as a relatively small initiative grew over the years into the Coalition for the International Criminal Court which today includes 2,500 organisations from 150 countries across the world.[2]

From July 1994, when the International Law Commission presented to the UN General Assembly its final draft of what later became the Rome Statute, it took eight years to establish the functioning International Criminal Court in 2002.[3] Since the very beginning, Amnesty International has supported this initiative, contributing its expertise to the development of the Rome Statute as well as lobbying governments to ratify it and support international justice.

On 1 July 2002, together with the 60th ratification of the Rome Statute, the ICC became a central part of an emerging system of international justice. This new system is composed of domestic investigations and prosecutions of

---

files/reports/sierleon0103.pdf>). According to various estimates during the wars in the former Yugoslavia (1991-1999) between 100,000 and 200,000 people lost their lives. However, the numbers are highly contested by all parties to the conflicts. The most reliable statistics of the victims of the war in Bosnia and Herzegovina were collected by the Research Documentation Centre from Sarajevo in their publication entitled *The Bosnian Book of the Dead*, which recorded almost 96,000 dead. (See 'After years of toil, book names Bosnian war dead' (*Reuters* 15 February 2013) <http://www.reuters.com/article/2013/02/15/us-bosnia-dead-idUSBRE91E0J220130215>). Similar statistics of the casualties in other republic of the former Yugoslavia are not publicly available. Only during the war in Bosnia and Herzegovina between 20,000 and 50,000 women were raped. (See: 'The Women of Bosnia and Herzegovina are Still Waiting' (Amnesty International September 2009), 5).

[2] An informal steering committee of the Coalition for an International Criminal Court was established in New York in February 1995 by the following NGOs: Amnesty International, Arab League for Human Rights, Associación por los Derechos Humanos, Canadian International Centre for Human Rights and Democratic Development, European Law Students Association, Fédération Internationale des Ligues des Droits de l'Homme, Human Rights Watch, Inter-African Union for Human Rights, International Commission of Jurists, Lawyers Committee for Human Rights, No Peace Without Justice, Parliamentarians for Global Action, Women's Caucus for Gender Justice in the ICC, World Federalist Movement which also was asked to act as the Secretariat of the Coalition. The Coalition quickly expanded in numbers of NGOs contributing to its work. In 1998 the number of NGOs participating in the work of the Coalition increased to 800 members and 235 of them were accredited to participate in the Rome Conference. On the role of non-governmental organizations in the establishment of the ICC see WR Pace and M Thieroff, 'Participation of Non-Governmental Organizations' in RS Lee (ed), *The International Criminal Court – The Making of the Rome Statute: Issues, Negotiations, Results* (Kluwer 1999). For the most updated information about the membership in the Coalition for the International Criminal Court (CICC) see the website of the Coalition <http://iccnow.org/?mod=coalition>.

[3] 'Draft Statute for an International Criminal Court', in Report of the International Law Commission on its forty-sixth session, UN Doc A/49/10 (1994) Yearbook of the International Law Commission vol II, 20.

core crimes under international law. It includes States exercising universal jurisdiction over those crimes on behalf of the international community and international and internationalized criminal courts.

II. SUCCESSES OF INTERNATIONAL JUSTICE

The idea of international justice was born long before the creation of the ICC. However, it was only in the 1990s that it achieved a new dimension and significant momentum, due to the specific political and historic situation, but also thanks to the strong support of civil society.[4] Now, 20 years later, international criminal justice is an essential component of the global system of international relations, with the ICC at its centre.[5]

Recent developments serve as proof that international justice has been a largely successful endeavour. Charles Taylor was convicted by the Special Court for Sierra Leone in April 2012.[6] The International Criminal Tribunal for the former Yugoslavia continued moving towards completion of its mandate, continuing to hear several trials, including that of Ratko Mladić and Radovan Karadžić. While there has been some fair criticism of the work of both ad hoc tribunals which preceded the ICC, overall they have largely delivered what they were created for by bringing many of those responsible to justice; by developing international criminal law; and by playing a positive role in making sure that justice is delivered at the national level.[7]

---

4 The first known idea for the establishment of an international criminal court was presented by Gustave Moynier in 1872. See CK Hall, 'The First Proposal for a Permanent International Criminal Court' (1998) 38 International Review of the Red Cross 57.

5 Since the 1990s the importance of international justice and the use of different international justice mechanisms to respond to crimes under international law has been increasing. The UN Security Council established ad hoc criminal tribunals (ICTY and ICTR) to respond to crimes committed in the 1990s. Also several hybrid criminal courts (composed of both international and domestic staff) were established with the support of the international community. They include the Special Panels for Serious Crimes in Dili, Timor-Leste; the international panels in Kosovo; the Special Court for Sierra Leone; the War Crimes Chamber of the State Court of Bosnia and Herzegovina and the Extraordinary Chambers in the Courts of Cambodia. The importance of international justice in international relations is also recognised directly in the Rome Statute. Article 13(b) equips the UN Security Council (UNSC) with power to refer situations outside immediate jurisdiction of the ICC and by doing so it provides for a new tool that the UNSC has for situations which pose a threat to international peace and security in accordance with Chapter VII of the UN Charter.

6 *Prosecutor v Taylor* (Judgement) Case SCSL-03-01-T (18 May 2012).

7 The ICTY has indicted 161 persons, proceedings against 126 accused have been completed as of 1 September 2012, see <http://icty.org/sections/TheCases/KeyFigures>. The ICTR has completed 45 cases as of 1 September 2012; 17 cases were pending appeal. In 10 cases the accused were acquitted, see the website of the Tribunal <http://www.unictr.org/Cases/StatusofCases/tabid/204/Default.aspx>.

The ICC, which was established in response to the atrocities of the 1990s is now a fully functioning institution. On 14 March 2012, the ICC delivered its first judgment, convicting Thomas Lubanga Dyilo of the war crime of enlisting, conscripting and using children under the age of 15 in hostilities in the Democratic Republic of the Congo.[8] The Trial Chamber subsequently sentenced him to fourteen years' imprisonment.[9] On 7 August 2012 Trial Chamber I issued its landmark decision establishing the principles and procedures to be applied to reparations.[10]

The ICC has begun investigating and is seeking to prosecute crimes in the Central African Republic, Cote d'Ivoire, the Democratic Republic of the Congo, Kenya, Libya, Darfur, Mali and Uganda. The Prosecutor is also determining whether to exercise her *proprio motu* powers to open new investigations into alleged crimes in other places including Afghanistan and Colombia. Several serving or former heads of state including Omar Al-Bashir, Muammar Gaddafi, Laurent Gbagbo and Uhuru Kenyatta have been the subject of ICC arrest warrants, something which even 20 years ago was completely unthinkable.[11]

Although Omar Al-Bashir has yet to be surrendered to the ICC an increasing number of States are refusing to host him in their territory. The change of venue in June 2012 of the African Union Summit to Addis Ababa following Malawi's refusal to offer President Bashir safe haven is an indication that some African countries are becoming more and more willing to comply with their legal obligations under the Rome Statute. This is true notwithstanding the risk of breaking ranks with respect to the African Union, which has called on its members not to cooperate with the ICC and specifically not to execute the arrest warrant against President Bashir.[12]

With 122 States already parties to the Rome Statute and with several more States that have announced their intention to ratify shortly, the ICC is becoming a truly global court.[13] Under the influence of the Rome Statute,

---

[8] *Prosecutor v Thomas Lubanga Dyilo* (Judgment pursuant to Article 74 of the Statute) ICC-01/04-01/06 (14 March 2012).

[9] *Prosecutor v Thomas Lubanga Dyilo* (Decision on Sentence pursuant to Article 76 of the Statute) ICC-01/04-01/06 (10 July 2012).

[10] *Prosecutor v Thomas Lubanga Dyilo* (Decision Establishing the Principles and Procedures to be Applied to Reparations) Case ICC-01/04-01/06 (7 August 2012).

[11] For an overview see UN General Assembly, 'Report of the International Criminal Court to the United Nations for 2011/2012' (14 August 2012) A/67/308.

[12] Assembly of the African Union, 'Decision on the Progress Report of the Commission on the Implementation of Decision Assembly/AU/Dec.270(XIV) on the Second Ministerial Meeting on the Rome Statute of the International Criminal Court (ICC) Doc. Assembly/AU/10(XV)', Fifteenth Ordinary Session, 25–27 July 2010, Kampala, Uganda' (27 July 2010) Assembly/AU/Dec.295(XV).

[13] In April 2012 the authorities of El-Salvador announced their willingness to ratify the Rome

some States are adopting implementing legislation which criminalises conduct which constitutes a crime under international law in their national legal frameworks and which also allows for better cooperation with the ICC in judicial matters. The positive impact of the Rome Statute on the domestic legislations globally goes far beyond its States Parties. According to the recent global survey by Amnesty International 166 States (approximately 86% of all States) have defined one or more crimes under international law (war crimes, crimes against humanity, genocide and torture) in their domestic legislation and 147 States (approximately 76% of all States) provided for universal jurisdiction for at least one of those crimes.[14] Although the impact of the Rome Statute on domestic legislation of States which are not parties to the treaty may only be characterised as indirect it seems obvious that the developments of international criminal law embodied in the Rome Statute have also influenced the behaviour of States which have not yet ratified the treaty. This impressive achievement gives a legal framework for the creation of the global system of international justice.

III. CHALLENGES AHEAD OF THE ICC

Despite its successes the ICC, as many other international justice mechanisms before it, also faces several challenges which need to be addressed so it can effectively deliver what it was created for – justice, truth and reparation for the victims of the most serious crimes.

To be able to respond to new situations, as well as to conduct its current work, the ICC requires strong budgetary and political support from States Parties. For the Court to be effective it also has to receive unequivocal support from the Security Council which should exercise its responsibility for the maintenance of international peace and security. In order to be fully relevant the ICC should also prioritise rebuilding its relationship with African

---

Statute. According to media reports the government was drafting the relevant legislation at the time, see 'El Salvador espera reconocer a la CPI este mismo año' (*La Prensa Grafica* 11 April 2012) <http://www.laprensagrafica.com/el-salvador/politica/257505-el-salvador-espera-reconocer-a-la-cpi-este-mismo-ano>. In March 2011 the authorities of Malaysia expressed their readiness to ratify. Reportedly the final decision on the deposition of the ratification instrument was pending the approval of the government, see 'Malaysian Bar commends Malaysian Government's intention to ratify the Rome Statute' (Malaysian Bar 15 March 2011) <http://www.malaysianbar.org.my/press_statements/press_release_malaysian_bar_commends_malaysian_governments_intention_to_ratify_the_rome_statute.html>; 'Asia-Pacific Update' (Coalition for the International Criminal Court July 2011) <http://iccnow.org/documents/Asia_Update_Issue7.pdf>.

14 See *Universal Jurisdiction: A Preliminary Survey of Legislation around the World – 2012 Update* (Amnesty International 2012) <http://www.amnesty.org/en/library/info/IOR53/019/2012/en>.

States. The Prosecutor has a leading role to play in this regard. In the paragraphs that follow I will address those issues briefly.

1. Budget

The first challenge to the effective functioning of the ICC is the need to secure a sufficient budget.[15] It has proven to be a complicated task. Calls for a so called 'zero-growth' budget were made on several occasions by the ICC's largest financial contributors and during the Assembly of States Parties (ASP) in November 2012. Prior to the 2012 ASP, the Budget and Finance Team of the Coalition for the International Criminal Court had observed that if the ICC was turned into a 'resource driven' not 'crime driven' Court it could 'curtail the independence of the Prosecutor, prevent the rest of the Court from fulfilling its mandate and render the Court irrelevant and ineffective in many situations'.[16]

The battle over the 2013 budget was an important one as it came at a time when crimes within the jurisdiction of the Court were being committed at an alarming rate around the world. The need for the ICC to be able to respond to those challenges and bring justice to the victims is now as pressing as ever. There is no doubt that in order for the ICC to remain effective and to be one of the significant features of post-Cold War international relations it needs a sufficient budget to operate.

Although the ICC is active already in eight African locations, there are legitimate expectations that it will step into other situations where there are serious doubts about the authorities' ability and willingness to act, including Afghanistan, Colombia and Georgia, which will obviously cost money. While the concerns about the most efficient use of the money available are fair, they should not serve as an excuse to, *de facto*, deprive victims of crimes under international law of access to justice.

For now the attempts to impose a 'zero-growth' budget seem to have largely stopped following opposition to the idea by the majority of States Parties at the November 2012 ASP and after a sustained campaign by global civil society as part of the Coalition for the International Criminal Court which once again stood firmly behind the Court.[17] However, as the impact

---

[15] For a more comprehensive analysis of the key discussions surrounding the ICC budget see J O'Donohue, 'Financing the International Criminal Court' (2013) 13 International Criminal Law Review 269–296.

[16] Coalition for the International Criminal Court – Budget and Finance Team, 'Comments on the Proposed Programme Budget for 2013 of the International Criminal Court and other matters' (20 September 2012) <http://www.iccnow.org/documents/BF_Commentary_on_2013_Budget_FINAL.pdf>.

[17] See Coalition for the International Criminal Court, 'Report on the 11th Session of the Assembly of States Parties to the Rome Statute 14-21 November 2012, The Hague, The

of the current economic crisis is still felt strongly in several States Parties it will also be pertinent in the upcoming years to make sure that the need to provide justice does not fall victim to the calls for austerity measures to be imposed on the Court.

2. The role of the Security Council

Pending universal ratification of the Rome Statute, the Security Council has a crucial role to play in referring further crimes outside the ICC's immediate jurisdiction and by so doing allowing victims to see justice.

While international justice is now a crucial element of international relations in the 21st century and the Security Council plays a central role in this regard, some observe that it is difficult to escape the feeling that the way the Security Council acts with regards to international justice is, at least at times, politicised. [18]

As crimes against humanity and war crimes are being committed in Syria initiatives by some members of the Security Council to refer the situation to the ICC Prosecutor have consistently been blocked by Russia and China.[19] The inaction of the Security Council, apart from denying justice to the victims of the most heinous crimes, also negatively impacts on the perception of the ICC and on international justice in general which is often seen as politicised and one-sided. As the death toll in Syria increases some have asked whether the Council is still fit for its role of ensuring international peace and security. The Prime Minister of Turkey, Recep Tayyip Erdoğan, called for a reform of the Security Council after the body again failed to take any meaningful action to address the humanitarian crisis is Syria.[20]

The Security Council needs to stand firmly behind the ICC and make sure that States cooperate with it fully. The issue is especially crucial when it comes to situations like Libya and Darfur, which were referred to the ICC Prosecutor by the Council itself.

The main problem which arises in relation to both referrals is the vague, imprecise and weak language that was used by the Security Council in its resolutions in relation to the obligation of States to cooperate with the ICC. In both referral resolutions the Security Council merely stated that the countries

---

Netherlands' (2012) <http://www.iccnow.org/documents/CICC_Report_on_the_11th_ASP_session.pdf>.

[18] DP Forsythe, 'The UN Security Council and Response to Atrocities: International Criminal Law at the P-5' (2012) 34 Human Rights Quarterly 840–863.

[19] See C Baldwin and L Leicht, 'Syria, a Path to Justice' (Human Rights Watch 6 August 2012) <http://www.hrw.org/news/2012/08/06/syria-path-justice>.

[20] J Adetunji, 'Turkey Calls for UN Security Council Reform Over Failure to Pressure Syria' (*The Guardian* 13 October 2012) <http://www.guardian.co.uk/world/2012/oct/13/turkey-un-security-council-reform-syria>.

in question were to 'cooperate fully with and provide any necessary assistance to the Court and the Prosecutor' without explicitly stating that such cooperation should be guided by the respective provisions of the Rome Statute.[21] To make the situation even more confusing both resolutions provided that 'States not party to the Rome Statute have no obligation under the Statute'.[22] This very general and seemingly contradictory wording left a lot of space for interpretation of the scope of the obligation of the referred States, which are not States Parties to the Rome Statute, to cooperate with the ICC.[23]

As it was to be discovered soon after the referral resolutions were adopted, imprecise legal drafting can have detrimental effects on the prospects of bringing those allegedly responsible for crimes under international law to justice. From on the start both Sudan and Libya have refused to cooperate with the Court and have failed to surrender the individuals against whom the ICC has issued arrest warrants.[24]

The question pertinent for referrals of situations involving States which are not parties to the Rome Statute is: does the Rome Statute, including Part 9, apply to those States by virtue of a Security Council resolution? If it does, what are the implications? Further, can a State, which is not a State Party to the Rome Statute, insist on its rights under the Statute and at the same time reject its obligations under Part 9 thereof?

The Libya situation is a good example of the problem. It was referred to the Prosecutor of the ICC by Security Council Resolution 1970 adopted on 26 February 2011.[25] The language used in operative paragraph 5 of the Resolution imposed the obligation on the Libyan authorities to 'cooperate fully with and [to] provide any necessary assistance to the Court and the Prosecutor'. In the same paragraph the resolution also recognised that Libya did not have a pre-existing obligation to cooperate with the ICC as it is not a State Party to the Rome Statute.

Deciding on Libya's submission regarding the arrest of Saif Al-Islam Gaddafi the judges clarified that the language contained in Resolution 1970

---

21 UNSC Res 1593 (2005), (31 March 2005) UN Doc S/RES/1593, para 2 <http://www.icc-cpi.int/NR/rdonlyres/85FEBD1A-29F8-4EC4-9566-48EDF55CC587/283244/N0529273.pdf>; UNSC Res 1970 (2011) (26 February 2011) UN Doc S/RES/1970, para 5 <http://icc-cpi.int/NR/rdonlyres/081A9013-B03D-4859-9D61-5D0B0F2F5EFA/0/1970Eng.pdf>.

22 Idem.

23 See D Akande, 'The Effect of Security Council Resolutions and Domestic Proceedings on State Obligations to Cooperate with the ICC' (2012) 10 Journal of International Criminal Justice 299–324.

24 See Report of the International Criminal Court to the United Nations for 2011/2012 (n 11) 9, 11.

25 UNSC Res 1970 (2011) (26 February 2011) UN Doc S/RES/1970 <http://icc-cpi.int/NR/rdonlyres/081A9013-B03D-4859-9D61-5D0B0F2F 5EFA/0/1970Eng.pdf>.

'means that the Statute, and especially its Part 9, is the legal framework within which Libya must comply with the Surrender Request.'[26] It was also further decided that the 'Libyan authorities ... are required to work within the cooperation framework provided by the Statute.'[27]

Despite the decision by Pre-Trial Chamber I, which clarified the scope of the country's obligation to cooperate with the Court, the Libyan authorities have failed to respect this obligation, while the Security Council has remained completely silent on the issue.

In the meantime in violation of Article 55 of the Rome Statute as well as other human rights treaties binding upon Libya such as the International Covenant on Civil and Political Rights, Saif al-Islam Gaddafi has been reportedly held *incommunicado* in a secret location and the extent of his access to a lawyer in respect to proceedings brought by central authorities is unclear.[28] Since his capture by rebels, Saif Al-Islam Gaddafi has not appeared in the courts of the Libyan State. He has, however, appeared in court in rebel-held Zintan. While those fair trial concerns were not taken fully into consideration by Pre-Trial Chamber I in its decision on the admissibility of the case, some authors have argued that they signify an important indication of a 'substantial collapse' or 'unavailability' of the justice system as per Article 17(3) of the Rome Statute, which in turn merits admissibility of the case before the ICC.[29]

Another regrettable episode of this case came in June 2012 when four staff of the ICC, including Saif Al-Islam Gaddafi's legal counsel, were arrested by the Zintan militia and detained for a month, accused of spying while visiting their client.[30] The detention of the four ICC staff was a stark violation of the Rome Statute and the obligation to cooperate with the Court imposed on Libya by the Security Council.

Interestingly, while the Libyan authorities have rejected their obligation to cooperate with the Court as required by the Rome Statute they have been rigorously exercising their rights under the same Statute to challenge the admissibility of both the cases against Saif Al-Islam Gaddafi and Abdullah

---

26 *Prosecutor v Saif Al-Islam Gaddafi* (Decision on Libya's Submissions Regarding the Arrest of Saif Al-Islam Gaddafi) ICC-01/11-01/11-72 (7 March 2012) para 12.

27 Idem.

28 'Is Libya Too Scared to Put Saif Gaddafi on Trial?' (*The Independent* 16 August 2013) <http://www.independent.co.uk/news/world/africa/is-libya-too-scared-to-put-saif-gaddafi-on-trial-8771495.html>.

29 J O'Donohue and S Rigney, 'The ICC Must Consider Fair Trial Concerns in Determining Libya's Application to Prosecute Saif al-Islam Gaddafi Nationally' (*EJIL Talk!* 8 June 2012) <http://www.ejiltalk.org/the-icc-must-consider-fair-trial-concerns-in-determining-libyas-application-to-prosecute-saif-al-islam-gaddafi-nationally/> .

30 Amnesty International, 'International Criminal Court staff detained in Libya must be released immediately' (15 June 2012) <http://www.amnesty.org.au/news/comments/28929/>.

Al-Senussi and to request suspension of its obligation to surrender Saif Al-Islam Gaddafi.

It is worth pointing out that the Libya legal impasse could have easily been avoided if more careful and clear language was used in the Security Council resolution referring Libya to the ICC Prosecutor.

Challenges to an effective cooperation of States with international criminal tribunals are not new or surprising. Indeed ad hoc tribunals faced similar obstacles. However, it seems they were better equipped to address them, as any legal ambiguity as to the scope of the obligation of States to cooperate with them was largely resolved in advance by the Security Council itself. For example, in its Resolution 827, which established the International Criminal Tribunal for the former Yugoslavia (ICTY), in contrast with the subsequent Resolutions 1593 and 1970, the Security Council clearly defined the scope of state cooperation with the ad hoc tribunal.[31] In its Resolution the Security Council decided that:

> all States shall cooperate fully with the International Tribunal and its organs in accordance with the present resolution and the Statute of the International Tribunal and that consequently all States shall take any measures necessary under their domestic law to implement the provisions of the present resolution and the Statute, including the obligation of States to comply with requests for assistance or orders issued by a Trial Chamber under Article 29 of the Statute.[32]

Unlike the resolutions referring Darfur and Libya to the Prosecutor of the ICC, Resolution 827 makes it clear that state cooperation with the ICTY should be guided by its Statute. Clear reference is made to a specific provision of the Statute (Article 29) which defines the scope of such cooperation. Further, Article 29 of the ICTY Statute (which was adopted as an annexe to Resolution 827) explicitly sets the scope of this obligation by stating that:

> 1. States shall co-operate with the International Tribunal in the investigation and prosecution of persons accused of committing serious violations of international humanitarian law.
> 2. States shall comply without undue delay with any request for assistance or an order issued by a Trial Chamber, including, but not limited to:
> (a) the identification and location of persons;
> (b) the taking of testimony and the production of evidence;
> (c) the service of documents;

[31] UNSC Res 827 (1993) (25 May 1993) UN Doc S/RES/827. <http://icty.org/x/file/Legal%20Library/Statute/statute_827_1993_en.pdf>.

[32] Ibid para 4.

(d) the arrest or detention of persons;
(e) the surrender or the transfer of the accused to the International Tribunal.[33]

If similar language had been used when the Security Council referred Darfur and Libya to the Prosecutor of the ICC much of the legal ambiguity would have been avoided. More importantly, the Security Council should have taken more forceful action to ensure Libya's compliance with its own resolution. Sadly, its commitment to international justice seems to be undermined as no meaningful action followed even when the ICC staff were unlawfully detained by the Zintan militia in June 2012.

Similarly, the surrender of Omar Al-Bashir to the ICC has not been on the top of the Security Council agenda. The Council has hitherto not taken any action with respect to the two non-cooperation decisions issued in December 2011 by the Pre-Trial Chamber against Chad and Malawi – both of which are States Parties to the Rome Statute and which have failed to arrest and surrender Omar Al-Bashir to the ICC upon his visits to both countries.[34]

The silence of the UN Security Council with regards to both situations it referred to the Prosecutor of the ICC could have a long-term, detrimental effect on the ICC. This inaction also sends a very negative political message and undermines the role of the Security Council itself, which seems to be unable to vigorously enforce its own resolutions pursuant to Chapter VII of the UN Charter.

3. Relationship with African States

African countries played a very important role in establishing the ICC and now 34 countries from the continent are States Parties to the Rome Statute. Côte d'Ivoire which until 15 February 2013 was not a State Party had prior to that accepted the exercise of jurisdiction by the ICC under Article 12(3) of the Rome Statute. The first three situations addressed by the ICC were self-referrals from African countries, namely Uganda, the Democratic

---

33 Updated Statute of the International Criminal Tribunal for the former Yugoslavia (United Nations September 2009) <http://icty.org/x/file/Legal%20Library/Statute/statute_sept09_en.pdf>.

34 *Prosecutor v Omar Hassan Ahmad Al-Bashir* (Decision Pursuant to Article 87(7) of the Rome Statute on the Failure by the Republic of Malawi to Comply with the Cooperation Requests Issued by the Court with Respect to the Arrest and Surrender of Omar Hassan Ahmad Al Bashir) ICC-02/05-01/09-139 (12 December 2012); *Prosecutor v Omar Hassan Ahmad Al-Bashir* (Decision Pursuant to Article 87(7) of the Rome Statute on the refusal by the Republic of Chad to Comply with the Cooperation Requests Issued by the Court with Respect to the Arrest and Surrender of Omar Hassan Ahmad Al Bashir) ICC-02/05-01/09-140 (13 December 2012).

Republic of the Congo and the Central African Republic. Recently also the government of Mali made a request of the ICC that it step in to provide justice to the victims of the conflict in the country.[35]

Against this background, the relationship between the African Union and the ICC in recent years has been far from satisfactory. One of the areas of tension has been the lack of cooperation of African States with the ICC in the arrest and surrender of Omar Al-Bashir.[36] Several African countries – some of which are States Parties to the Rome Statute – have hosted President Al-Bashir and have failed to fulfil their legal obligations under the Rome Statute. In its decisions the African Union has called on its members not to cooperate in arresting and surrendering him to the ICC.[37]

Similarly the current proposals advanced to create jurisdiction over crimes under international law of the African Court of Human and People's Rights are driven by efforts to establish an alternative jurisdiction to the ICC.[38] Although on the surface the idea seems positive, the complex challenge of partially transforming the African Court into a regional criminal court, the cost impact for an already underfunded human rights system and the lack of any clarity about its relationship with the ICC – including the potential for duplication and conflict – all raise serious questions about the initiative.[39]

While vigorous discussions are taking place in Africa about the new approach to international justice, the ICC is fully functioning and able to investigate and prosecute crimes under international law to the highest standard. The relationship of any regional criminal court with the ICC must be defined in such a way that does not undermine the jurisdiction of the ICC or States' obligations to cooperate with it. African States Parties to the Rome Statute have a crucial role to play in this regard.

On the other hand the ICC should engage with and respond better to the concerns which underlie the African Union proposals. They are based on the assertion that the ICC seems to be prosecuting accused in connection with situations only in Africa and by doing so targeting only African leaders. While those arguments are neither fair nor accurate, the ICC needs to play a

---

35 Referral Letter by the Government of Mali (13 July 2012) <http://icc-cpi.int/NR/rdonlyres/A245A47F-BFD1-45B6-891C-3BCB5B173F57/0/ReferralLetterMali130712.pdf>.

36 For more information about the discussion please see SM Weldehaimanot, 'Arresting Al-Bashir: the African Union's Opposition and the Legalities' (2011) 19 African Journal of International and Comparative Law 208.

37 See Decision on the Progress Report of the Commission on the Implementation of Decision Assembly/AU/Dec.270(XIV) (n 12).

38 See Weldehaimanot (n 36) 218–220.

39 See Joint Letter to the Justice Ministers and Attorneys General of the African States Parties to the International Criminal Court Regarding the Proposed Expansion of the Jurisdiction of the African Court of Justice and Human Rights (3 May 2012) <http://www.hrw.org/sites/default/files/related_material/Letter_on_African_Court_May_2012.pdf>.

more proactive role in challenging some of those assumptions and championing justice for African victims.

The new ICC Prosecutor Fatou Bensouda, who is from Africa, is already playing a very positive role in challenging some of the negative perceptions of the Court in the continent. It is encouraging that when taking office, the Prosecutor set out a number of priorities which, if implemented, may lead to increased support for the ICC, including in Africa. They include reviewing the quality and efficiency of investigations and prosecutions, clarifying the process through which the Office of the Prosecutor (OTP) conducts preliminary examinations and developing a strong gender policy.[40]

The first set of priorities in particular, which deal with the questions of preliminary examinations and investigations, are of the highest importance and will be closely followed by African States. The accusations of the alleged bias of international justice (and the ICC in particular) against Africa aired by some States of the African Union is well known and go beyond the issue of the surrender of Omar Al-Bashir.[41] There is no doubt that there are indeed plenty of situations in countries outside Africa which have ratified the Rome Statute and in which crimes under international law have been committed. Situations like Afghanistan and Georgia seem not to receive a great deal of public attention from the OTP[42] and the preliminary examination of Palestine was eventually closed, exposing the OTP to criticism.[43] This creates a perception of imbalance as to where the ICC is conducting its investigations.[44] Addressing the situations in other continents in a transparent way may send a positive message that the Prosecutor is looking beyond Africa and championing justice for victims around the world.

An objective look into the ICC's current investigations also suggests that there is some room for improvement. As observed in September 2011 by Human Rights Watch, which has been supportive of the Court since its creation, '[d]ecisions made to date in the DRC, Uganda, CAR, and Darfur situations have already damaged the ICC's credibility and legitimacy, especially

---

40 'International Criminal Court – Office of the Prosecutor Briefing' (Issue 134; 10 November–19 December 2012) <http://www.icc-cpi.int/iccdocs/otp/wb/OTP-Briefing-134-Eng.pdf>.

41 See HJ Richardson, 'African Grievances and the International Criminal Court: Issues of African Equity under International Criminal Law', in VO Nmehielle (ed), *Africa and the Future of International Criminal Justice* (Eleven Publishing 2012) 81–123 and P Clark and N Waddell (eds), *Courting Conflict* (Royal African Society 2008). See also a recent decision by the African Union adopted at its extraordinary session in October 2013: Assembly of the African Union, 'Decision on Africa's Relationship with the International Criminal Court (ICC)', 13 October 2013, Addis Ababa, Ethiopia, Ext/Assembly/AU/Dec.1(Oct.2013).

42 Richardson (n 41) 111–112.

43 J Dugard, 'Palestine and the International Criminal Court Institutional Failure or Bias?' (2013) 11 Journal of International Criminal Justice 563–570.

44 Weldehaimanot (n 36) 235 and Richardson (n 41) 112.

in Africa, and could undermine its long-term mission to fight against impunity. Some decisions have led to a sense that the OTP is not responding adequately to the justice needs identified by affected communities—that is to say, that the OTP simply "doesn't get" what is needed to redress the serious crimes committed.'[45] The report recommended that the OTP review all current investigations and that it develop more coherent and effective strategies in each situation.[46] It also made specific suggestions related to each situation which included for example expanding the scope of investigations; identifying the criminal responsibility of individuals higher up the chain of command and extending investigations to all parties to the conflict in question conflict.[47]

The disconnection of the ICC from the victims has also been prominently voiced since *Lubanga* judgment. It was felt that the engagement of the OTP with intermediaries was inappropriate. In addition to the concerns related to the fair trial guarantees for the accused which were raised by Lubanga's counsel and which were addressed at various stages of the proceedings, it was also observed that the way the OTP used intermediaries exposed them, as well as some of the witnesses, to future threats and intimidation.[48] The trial has also shown that much more needs to be done to ensure meaningful and effective participation of witnesses.[49]

In this context the issue of the budget arises once again. The importance of outreach programmes and engagement with victims (also by maintaining field presence) has been one of the lessons learnt from the ad hoc tribunals.[50] Yet, exactly those services were prioritised for cuts in previous budget discussions. It is absolutely imperative that outreach and engagement activities with victims remain among the core functions of the Court and are, as such, included in the future ICC budgets. Ultimately the Court was created to bring justice *to the victims* and therefore engaging with them in a meaningful way is absolutely crucial.

---

[45] *Unfinished Business: Closing Gaps in the Selection of ICC Cases* (Human Rights Watch 2011) <http://www.hrw.org/sites/default/files/reports/icc0911webwcover.pdf>.

[46] Ibid 46.

[47] Ibid 48–49.

[48] See O Bueno, 'Lubanga Found Guilty: Opinion Divided in Congo' (*The Lubanga Trial* 20 March 2012) <http://www.lubangatrial.org/2012/03/20/lubanga-found-guilty-opinion-divided-in-congo/>; P Wegner, 'What Went Wrong During the Lubanga Trial (*Justice in Conflict* 14 March 2012) <http://justiceinconflict.org/2012/03/14/what-went-wrong-during-the-lubanga-trial/>.

[49] L Catani, 'Victims at the International Criminal Court: Some Lessons Learned from the Lubanga Case' (2012) 10 Journal of International Criminal Justice 905–922.

[50] JN Clark, 'International War Crimes Tribunals and the Challenge of Outreach' (2009) 9 International Criminal Law Review 99–116.

Other priority areas highlighted by the new Prosecutor Fatou Bensouda are also important from an African perspective. Among them is the need to ensure that gender-based crimes receive more prominence in the investigation and prosecution of cases.[51] In the past Amnesty International has expressed its concerns that for example in the *Lubanga* case gender-based crimes against girls were not included among the charges.[52] As a result it left victims of those terrible crimes without access to justice and possibly also without full reparations. Although during the trial the ICC judges were presented with witness testimonies and other evidence of rape and other gender-based violence, no related charges were brought by the Prosecutor.[53] In the absence of such charges Lubanga, although convicted, was not found guilty of gender-based violence.

In its subsequent decision Trial Chamber I ruled in August 2012 on the principles and procedures to be applied to reparations and, upon the finding of Lubanga's indigence, entrusted the task of providing reparations to the Trust Fund for Victims. While Trial Chamber I in its decision elaborated on the need for a gender-sensitive approach to reparations, it also concluded that '"damage, loss and injury," which form the basis of a reparations claim, must have resulted from the crimes of enlisting and conscripting children under the age of 15 and using them to participate actively in the hostilities.'[54] However, it also clarified that '[r]eparations should not be limited to "direct" harm or the "immediate effects" of the crimes of enlisting and conscripting children under the age of 15 and using them to participate actively in the hostilities, but instead the Court should apply the standard of "proximate cause".'[55]

The actual availability of reparations for the victims of gender-based violence in the DRC boils down to the understanding of the meaning of 'proximate cause', which is also open to interpretation. In the worst case scenario what it may mean, when those principles are applied to the actual reparations proceedings, is that victims of gender-based violence might not be able to benefit directly and fully from them as the 'damage, loss and injury' they suffered was not – according to the judgement – caused by the crimes of enlisting and conscripting children under the age of 15 and using them to participate actively in the hostilities. If this happens it will leave those victims yet again disillusioned with the international justice process and the ICC itself will lose yet another group of its supporters in Africa, which it desperately needs.

---

51 International Criminal Court – Office of the Prosecutor Briefing (n 40) 1.

52 Amnesty International, 'Landmark ICC Verdict over Use of Child Soldiers' (14 March 2012) <http://www.amnesty.org/en/news/landmark-icc-verdict-over-use-child-soldiers-2012-03-14>.

53 W Brown, 'Lubanga: Why the ICC must do better' (*Thomson Reuters Foundation* 14 March 2012) <http://www.trust.org/item/?map=lubanga-why-the-icc-must-do-better/>.

54 *Prosecutor v Thomas Lubanga Dyilo* (Decision Establishing the Principles and Procedures to be Applied to Reparations) ICC-01/04-01/06 (7 August 2012) 247.

55 Ibid 249.

In order to ensure confidence in the international justice process the new Prosecutor has a crucial role to play in addressing the concerns identified in this section. As she embarks on this daunting task she needs to benefit from the vigorous support of the States Parties.

V. CONCLUSION

On the 10th anniversary of the ICC there are many reasons to celebrate. What was once a distant dream is now a reality that brings hope to victims of genocide, crimes against humanity and war crimes. The first truly global, permanent international criminal court exists and is ready to bring justice, truth and reparation to victims.

The Court now enjoys the support of 122 States which is the considerable majority of all States. Since its establishment it has grown into a fully functioning judicial institution with decisions contributing to the development of international criminal law. In its first 10 years, four serving or former Heads of State have been subject to its arrest warrants, which sends a clear message that no one is above the law. Through its impact on the domestic legislations of States around the world, the majority of which define at least some crimes under international law and allow for universal jurisdiction in respect thereof, the Rome Statute extends its reach beyond its States Parties.

However, in order to be fully relevant in the second decade of its existence the ICC has to tackle several challenges.

As was argued in this article, the first challenge is securing a sufficient budget for this still growing judicial institution. In times of the economic crisis and global calls for austerity measures the main financial contributors to the ICC's budget have been advocating a 'zero-growth' budget. Although those calls have been challenged by the majority of States Parties, which eventually led to the rejection of those ideas during the 2012 ASP, they may still be revived in near future. If the ICC is to maintain its pivotal position on the international justice landscape of the 21st century it is imperative that the Court has the resources it needs to conduct its work effectively.

Another challenge is the role of the Security Council which has often not taken its leadership role in matters of international peace and security. While the failure of the Security Council to refer Syria to the Prosecutor of the ICC has revitalised the calls for its reform, it also raised doubts about the idea of international justice which again was seen by some as politicised.

In the situations where the Security Council did take action – as in respect of Darfur and Libya – the support was only half-hearted and resulted in weak and ambiguous language in the referrals. This unclear language has contributed to the obstruction of the international justice process by Libya as explained above. The lack of serious commitment of the Security Council to the ICC has further been evident by the lack of any meaningful enforcement of its own referral resolutions.

The last key challenge ahead of the ICC, as the Court enters the second decade of its existence, is the need to dramatically improve its relations with Africa. The new Prosecutor has a leading role to play in this regard. While some past mistakes of the ICC in Africa could be attributed to her predecessor, Fatou Bensouda has a crucial role to play to rebuild Africa's future with the ICC. The fact that the Prosecutor herself comes from Africa gives her additional legitimacy and leverage in African countries.

In addition, under the leadership of Fatou Bensouda the OTP needs to look outside Africa to bring justice to victims of crimes under international law in other parts of the world. It can do so by conducting transparent preliminary examinations into crimes purportedly committed in countries which have ratified the Rome Statute from other continents. Sadly, as crimes under international law are being committed across the world, she has plenty of situations to choose from.

The OTP must also be able to respond better to the needs on the ground in the situations currently under investigation. It must come up with more coherent and effective strategies for each of the situations under investigation. As one of the key lessons from the *Lubanga* case the OTP also must not cut corners by making inappropriate use of intermediaries. The OTP's efforts to understand the local dynamics better must be combined with robust outreach efforts and engagement with victims by other parts of the Court. Last but not least in order to remain relevant the OTP must put gender issues at the top of its agenda. This should include not only the bringing of gender-based charges wherever relevant but also an overall gender sensitive approach to the way the OTP, and indeed the rest of the Court, conducts its work.

As the Court enters its second decade of existence the drafters of the Rome Statute can indeed be proud of it. Its achievements at its young age are already impressive. However, like all growing international institutions the ICC needs strategic, political and financial support from the international community. Without it the Court will never be able to live up to its expectations and the world regress to its previous state, at the beginning of the 1990s, where the perpetrators of atrocities acted with impunity while the rest of the world simply looked on.

PART 6

Conclusion

A Look at the International Criminal Court from the Bench

*Sir Adrian Fulford**

When I first joined the Court back in those heady days in New York in 2003, it seemed to me then that my nine-year term would simply never end and my role had been fixed for eternity. And yet – it feels like only moments later - bar the sentence in Lubanga and some guidance as to reparations, for me it is all over. I cannot overstate what a privilege and – despite many exotic and unexpected frustrations – a pleasure it has been. Challenging, most certainly, in so many – but nearly always the best possible – ways.

I suspect the Court for all ex-judges (to borrow from the novelist Dodie Smith) will become like a dear Octopus from whose tentacles one never quite escapes; but nor, in our innermost hearts, would we ever wish to do so.

Although we had the Rome Statute framework to guide us, so much needed to be resolved for the first time by the first judges in the first case. In many areas we simply had a blank sheet of paper, with the ad hoc tribunals very often providing the only relevant guidance, if any was to be found at all. Judges are usually hidebound by precedent and risk appellate censure if they depart from established practice. Not so, certainly during our early days at the ICC. It was a once in a lifetime opportunity to sit back and work out what we believed was best for the Court, rather than simply applying, with a tiny margin of residual discretion, the received wisdom of generations of earlier judges. Whether we got it right will be revealed by the Appeals Division and some of our decisions have provided interesting academic debate. Indeed, I have rediscovered something I had forgotten from my university days – the strange and chilling draught of some academic commentary. No doubt gentle at home and kindly to dumb beasts, a few learned writers become merciless when they sit in front of their computers and begin their analysis of the work of the Court, even to the extent of eviscerating the judges for the style of our footnotes and the language in which we have

* Lord Justice of Appeal at the Court of Appeal of England and Wales and former Judge at the ICC. The address was delivered on 21 June 2012 at the International Conference on 10th Anniversary of the International Criminal Court, which took place at the Foreign and Commonwealth Office.

quoted academic sources. One eminent professor has complained that the bench (which contains two Spanish-speaking judges) cited his work in Spanish rather than in German. It is necessary to have a very thick hide as a judge. The ICC has contributed to my rhinoceros skin.

But I get ahead of myself and instead I should follow the narrative advice of the King of Hearts in Alice in Wonderland – begin at the beginning, go on to the end and then stop.

It can be useful when significant landmarks are reached (in this instance, the Court a decade after its work started and at the end of the first trials) to stand back in order to look at the institution in the round, to assess it from a macro rather than a micro point of view. Forget the detail for a moment, and instead, see how it all looks from what might be called the commanding heights. Well, I gaze round this audience and notice many seasoned campaigners – perhaps including just a few hardened cynics – but notwithstanding your baleful gaze, my assessment is that the landscape picture, with some exceptions, is not a bad one in mid 2012, notwithstanding that our lives are dominated by our rather austere and inconvenient converted courthouse (of Dutch post-modernist style, built originally for the giant telephone company KPN and located in a somewhat unprepossessing light industrial suburb of Den Haag). But, then, without the generosity of the Kingdom of the Netherlands we would have no home at all, and we owe our host country a considerable debt of gratitude.

There has been far too much exaggerated talk over the last 10 years, but cutting away the nonsense, my view is that our global impact has been widespread, in that the Court is well known and, I am pleased to detect, not a little feared. Although it is not empirically verifiable, the anecdotal, diffusely available evidence is too strong to be wrong or ignored. Troops from the world's properly-organised armed forces not infrequently require written instructions on the precise scope of the rules of engagement when going into combat – what is within and what is without their military remit. The real and expressed concern is they need protection from an unscheduled visit to our war crimes court, should they be accused of having exceeded proportionate battlefield tactics.

The default position of politicians, journalists and commentators when confronted with a possible dire humanitarian atrocity is to invoke the likelihood of the Court's scrutiny, and – although 10 years ago this would have seemed unimaginable – the current administration in the US is clearly more than happy to adopt this line. Although he was executed without a trial, Colonel Gaddafi at the time of his detention was expected to face justice at our Court, along with certain other prominent members of his family and wider entourage. The fact that events have more recently turned sour is the product of the current lawlessness in Libya rather than a change in mood or expectation on the part of the international community.

Elections are said to have gone wrong in Kenya and Côte d'Ivoire and the Court swings into action (I was on the bench for the first appearance of Laurent Gbagbo, the former President of Côte d'Ivoire last year), and those allegedly involved in violence associated with this democratic process are being investigated and may go on trial; whenever government troops fire on protestors, they know (and the press is keen to remind them) our prosecutor is quietly watching and waiting. Indeed, modern technology is one of the main enemies of the ruthless and the violent, in that any expression of public repression is liable to end up first on YouTube and a little later as part of the prosecution case at the ICC. Video evidence, even from a handheld mobile phone, can be extremely powerful. Furthermore, the Court has a long memory and we have started to demonstrate that justice has a habit of catching up with alleged perpetrators in the fullness of time (as the arrest warrant against the current Sudanese Defence Minister, Abdel Raheem Muhammad Hussein, for crimes against humanity and war crimes committed in 2003 and 2004, has shown).

I believe the stage has now been reached when the continued refusal by some of the major, as well as the lesser, powers to join the Court increasingly resembles an admission on the part of at least some of them that they have domestic problems that have not been (or are not being) handled sufficiently well and which they fear are potentially criminally justiciable. If that is the case, it is not something to be proud of. Put another way, if you have nothing to fear, why refuse to sign up to international criminal justice as 120 other countries have done, seemingly with no identifiable ill effect? And the argument that the Court cannot be trusted looks increasingly self-serving and unfounded. No sustainable contention has yet been advanced that any of our proceedings to date have been vitiated by political or other bias on the part of the judiciary or the other organs of the Court, and it could be said (although this will seem like self praise, which it is assuredly not meant to be) that the experience of the first trial over which I have presided has at least been an object lesson in judicial independence given we stayed the proceedings twice and ordered the release of the accused because of material unfairness on the part of the last prosecutor when he failed to discharge his disclosure obligations to the defence. The evidence in the first two cases will have taken over two years in each instance, and bearing in mind the painstaking investigation by both of these first trial Chambers, I suspect it is unlikely that the Court will be accused of refusing to hear testimony, or to consider documents, that either party believed to be relevant.

It is well known that the President of Sudan can only travel to those few countries that will not extradite him to the ICC, and – possibly most important of all – the Americans have not vetoed the Court's involvement in the Sudan and Libya (countries over which we do not have jurisdiction absent a UN Security Council Resolution). Let us not forget how grim it looked at the outset, in that after the Rome Statute reached the critical 60 ratifications in 2002 that automatically brought the institution into being, President Bush's first administration sent a note to the UN Secretary General on 6 May 2002 suspending his country's signature (which had been appended by President Clinton in the dying days of his administration) and indicating the US had no obligations towards the Court. However, during Bush's second term (perhaps most particularly once the frank and colourful John Bolton had disappeared from the administration), this strident tone disappeared, and following President Obama's election, America began full engagement and cooperation with the Court. Whether in due course a president will submit the treaty for Senate ratification is perhaps, in reality, a notable but secondary issue at this early stage in our existence. The more important indicator as regards our success is that the US provides, certainly in circumstances that are acceptable to them, a significant level of help and cooperation.

Therefore, the eagle-eyed view is, alarums and difficulties notwithstanding, essentially promising. I believe we have made a somewhat unexpected and not unimportant impact on world consciousness – most people who have ready access to international news are aware, certainly in a general sense, of our presence on the world stage. But not only are we known: I believe we have additionally achieved a certain and real deterrent effect, that has included demonstrating to the international community that the safe havens of old have become rather insecure. You can run, but the holes for hiding, in the global village, are not as well concealed or as readily available as once they were, and, as Charles Taylor (the former President of Liberia) found to his cost, these days – when substantial international leverage can be and sometimes is applied – your hosts may suddenly find it expedient to hand you over for trial.

I don't want to overstate this. There was excessive talk when the Court was set up that our arrival marked the end of impunity. That was too grandiose; too self-important; too vainglorious. But I do believe we have contributed to a critical shift in consciousness that best finds its expression with the BBC news reporter who casually reports that his sources are of the view that our Court will be the next resting place for whichever alleged despot or murderous general is under the spotlight for suspected war crimes. Rather like at school when the automatic result of bad behaviour in class certainly used to be some form of detention, so the unconscious reflex position now is that human rights abuses of a sufficiently egregious kind are likely to lead the alleged perpetrator to the Netherlands.

The importance of that change in approach should not be underestimated – in my view it is no mean result for this fledgling institution.

So much of the view from the peaks.

The devil, as always, lurks in the detail, and the microbial view is the one that has given me some real sleepless nights. And there are some strange campaign tales which lack of time and my continued connection with the institution mean must remain untold.

Instead, in the limited time I want to say just a few words on what I believe needs to be and can be fixed, in order to avoid cases that run into eternity, as *Lubanga* surely did. The proceedings overall simply should not have taken anything like the time we spent on them.

Although I am reliably informed that the Assembly of States Parties has no inclination to amend the Statute, some practical steps can be taken that would substantially improve our proceedings.

In the course of other speeches, I have developed ideas for change that I strongly believe in which I will not rehearse this evening, such as the desirability of delegating much of the work of the trial chambers, at least before the opening of the trials themselves, and possibly even during parts of the trial process, to a single judge; far greater use of video link technology to avoid bringing witnesses half way round the world for 2–4 hours of evidence; introducing a broader range of evidence by way of deposition that enables the parties and participants to question some of the less important witnesses, without it all being played out at snails pace in Court before the judges, with only a very small portion of the material then featuring in counsel's closing submissions; and a more rigorous insistence that the parties reach agreement on the areas of undisputed evidence, in order to avoid those significant tracts of testimony which turn out not to be the subject of any questioning or dispute. And there are many more.

Instead, I want to focus on one issue and one issue only. When I was first selected as the British candidate I caused two or three very senior officials in this building to turn a lighter shade of pale when I asked whether the Court was going to have access to armed forces – perhaps a small rapid reaction force – to enable it to arrest perpetrators on both sides and to secure evidence in hostile environments. After much polite coughing, it became clear that this was perhaps not the best item to include in my campaign strategy for election when sitting in the Indonesian lounge at the UN meeting the ambassadors who would be casting their votes for or against my candidature. So, I let the notion lapse and I hasten to say, I do not resurrect it now. But the underlying reason for proposing it remains for me as vibrant and urgent as ever.

Ignoring for these purposes the nonetheless urgent question of whether the Court remains at risk of being perceived as only, or mainly, prosecuting those who turned out to be the losers of internal civil wars or other disputes, I want instead to focus on the need for the Court to secure evidence at the outset that will be available to be used at all stages of the proceedings. Put on the most basic level, I ask rhetorically what is *really* the point of launching a case based on the contents of one or more unverified NGO reports which in turn will be inadmissible at trial, and when the authors of the report or reports will not be called, not least because they cannot give anything other than potentially unreliable hearsay evidence? Apart from the advantage of commencing the proceedings sooner rather than later, is it truly in the interests of the Court and the wider interests of justice to arrest an alleged perpetrator, taking him or her through the confirmation stages of the case when the prosecution are not in possession of the core elements of its case for trial (when the evidential requirements and the standard of proof are far more rigorous and taxing) and when it does not even necessarily know which, if any, witnesses will be available to support its case before the trial chamber? Approached in this way, the pre-trial stage does not help the later trial to any great extent at all, save it merely serves to establish that the case is not frivolous or improperly motivated. What it will not have shown is whether there will ever be a case that stands a reasonable prospect of resulting in a conviction based on evidence that meets trial standards. Instead of handing a trial-ready case over to the trial chamber, an essentially new case will be put together.

Accordingly, the prosecution needs in my view either to wait until realistic investigations can take place or it ought to have the support and assistance from the international community to go into the country concerned in order to secure the evidence for its case, essentially for all stages of the proceedings.

Mary Tudor is reputed to have said that after she died it would be found that the word 'Calais' had become engraved on her heart. For me, it might be the word 'intermediary', because of the problems that occurred in the *Lubanga* Trial that we have described in the Article 74 Decision. I fully recognise the problems that can exist as regards security, but if elements of the prosecution's investigative function are passed to others outside the Office of the Prosecutor (OTP) there is a risk that you lose control of the integrity and reliability of the evidence and the process. In my judgment, the OTP must always take responsibility for identifying, interviewing and investigating the reliability of the witnesses it intends to call. For witnesses whose evidence may be challenged, all reasonable checks should be made as to their reliability and honesty. That is one of the core elements of prosecutorial responsibility, which should not, save in exceptional and justified circumstances, be delegated, sub-contracted or otherwise passed to others. I need not rehearse the problems we have had, but it is better that trials are delayed rather than the Court receiving testimony that has unknown or potentially dubious origins that may have fatally undermined it.

Therefore, one of my principal parting pleas from the Court is that the prosecution is given the assistance by the international community it needs in order to carry out its investigative function properly, and that as a result there is a real element of consistency and reliability in the evidence at all stages in the proceedings, in the sense that a case is launched when the prosecution is able to rely on *prima facie* reliable material that it is anticipated will be available at trial. I am not suggesting that all of the evidence needs to have been obtained, but the core elements should have been secured or there should be a reasonable expectation that this will occur.

Returning for one final moment to the Olympian heights, the ICC is a really exciting and still youthful institution, both in terms of its mere 10 years of existence and the average age of the people working in it. The amount of maternity and paternity leave is quite astonishing (I have never seen so many photographs of newborn babies) and the levels of commitment, enthusiasm and hard work on the part of many members of the staff is exemplary. It does feel like a visit to a brave and courageous new world, but voyages of exploration are invariably attended by vicissitudes and challenges. There will be – there have been – mistakes at the beginning, but as I said at the outset I believe the Court has had surprising and impressive triumphs. And we have now finally reached a new and critical stage, when the first trials are ending. The ground mercifully closes over ex judges with incredible speed, and I will soon join the forest of footnotes that litter counsel's submissions and the Court's decisions. It has been a real pleasure and privilege to have played a part and I thank you for giving me this short period to unburden myself of a few personal views on the strengths and weaknesses of an institution with which I am proud to have been associated.

*Annexes**

* These annexes were compiled by Shehara de Soysa, Research Assistant, British Institute of International and Comparative Law. A bibliography follows Annexe 3.

Annexe 1 – Activities of the Court

States Parties to the Rome Statute

	2010	2011	2012	2013
States Parties	113	114	120	122
Africa	31	33	33	34
Asia-Pacific	15	18	18	18
Eastern Europe	18	18	18	18
Latin America and Caribbean	25	26	27	27
Western Europe and Other	25	25	25	25

Activities of the Court

	2008/9	2009/10	2010/11	2011/12	2012/13
Judicial Proceedings	• *Lubanga* • *Katanga and Ngudjolo Chui* • *Bemba Gombo* • *Al-Bashir* • *Abu Garda* • *Kony, Otti, Odhiambo and Ongwen*	• *Kony, Otti, Odhiambo and Ongwen* • *Lubanga* • *Katanga and Ngudjolo Chui* • *Bemba Gombo* • *Ahmad Harun and Ali Kushayb* • *Al-Bashir* • *Abu Garda* • *Banda and Jerbo*	• *Lubanga* • *Katanga and Ngudjolo Chui* • *Mbarushi-mana* • *Bemba Gombo* • *Al-Bashir* • *Banda and Jerbo* • *Ruto, Kosgey and Sang* • *Muthaura, Kenyatta and Hussein Ali* • *Muammar Gaddafi, Saif Al-Islam Gaddafi, Al-Senussi*	• *Lubanga* • *Katanga and Ngudjolo Chui* • *Mbarushi-mana* • *Ntaganda* • *Mudacu-mura* • *Bemba Gombo* • *Al-Bashir* • *Banda and Jerbo* • *Abdel Raheem Muhammad Hussein* • *Ruto, Kosgey and Sang* • *Muthaura, Kenyatta and Hussein Ali*	• *Lubanga* • *Katanga and Ngudjolo Chui* • *Mbarushi-mana* • *Ntaganda* • *Bemba Gombo* • *Al-Bashir* • *Banda and Jerbo* • *Abdel Raheem Muhammad Hussein* • *Ruto and Sang* • *Muthaura and Kenyatta* • *Saif Al-Islam Gaddafi and Al-Senussi*

(*continued overleaf*)

Activities of the Court (*continued*)

	2008/9	2009/10	2010/11	2011/12	2012/13
Judicial Proceedings (*continued*)				• *Muammar Gaddafi, Saif Al-Islam Gaddafi and Al-Senussi* • *Laurent Gbagbo*	• *Laurent Gbagbo* • *Simone Gbagbo*
Situations under investigation	• Democratic Republic of the Congo (DRC) • Uganda • Central African Republic (CAR) • Darfur, Sudan	• DRC • Uganda • CAR • Darfur, Sudan • Kenya	• DRC • Uganda • CAR • Darfur, Sudan • Kenya • Libya	• DRC • Uganda • CAR • Darfur, Sudan • Kenya • Libya • Côte d'Ivoire	• DRC • Uganda • CAR • Darfur, Sudan • Kenya • Libya • Côte d'Ivoire • Mali
Preliminary examination	• Afghanistan • Colombia • Côte d'Ivoire • Georgia • Kenya • Palestine	• Afghanistan • Colombia • Côte d'Ivoire • Georgia • Guinea • Palestine	• Afghanistan • Colombia • Côte d'Ivoire • Georgia • Guinea • Honduras • Rep. of Korea • Nigeria • Palestine	• Afghanistan • Colombia • Georgia • Guinea • Honduras • Rep. of Korea • Mali • Nigeria • Palestine	• Afghanistan • Colombia • Georgia • Guinea • Honduras • Registered vessels of the Union of the Comoros, the Hellenic Republic and the Kingdom of Cambodia • Nigeria • Republic of Korea • Mali • Palestine

Mechanisms Triggering the Jurisdiction of the Court

Type of referral	Instances	Situations
Referral by a State party pursuant to Article 13(a), Rome Statute	4	• Uganda • Democratic Republic of Congo • Central African Republic • Mali
Referral by the UN Security Council pursuant to Article 13(b), Rome Statute	2	• Libya • Darfur, Sudan
Authorisation by Pre-Trial Chamber of request by the Prosecutor to initiate investigation *proprio motu*, pursuant to Article 13(c), Rome Statute	2	• Kenya • Côte d'Ivoire[1]

Situations before the Court

Situation	Date of Referral	Decision to Open Investigation
Uganda	29 January 2004	29 July 2004
Democratic Republic of Congo	19 April 2004	23 June 2004
Central African Republic	7 January 2005	22 May 2007
Darfur, Sudan	31 March 2005	6 June 2005
Kenya	n/a	31 March 2010[2]
Libya	26 February 2011	–
Côte d'Ivoire	n/a	3 October 2011[3]
Mali	13 July 2012	–

[1] Côte d'Ivoire, then a non-State party, declared its acceptance of the jurisdiction of the Court, pursuant to Art 12(3), Rome Statute on 18 April 2003.

[2] Pre-Trial Chamber II authorisation to open investigation.

[3] Pre-Trial Chamber III authorisation to open investigation.

Judicial Proceedings

Situation	Accused	Stage of Proceedings	Prosecution request for issue of Arrest Warrant/ Summons to Appear
Uganda	Joseph Kony, Vincent Otti, Okot Odhiambo and Dominic Ongwen	Pre-trial	6 May 2005
	Raska Lukwiya	Case terminated	6 May 2005
Democratic Republic of the Congo	Thomas Lubanga Dyilo	Appeals	13 January 2006
	Germain Katanga	Trial	25 June 2007
	Mathieu Ngudjolo Chui	Appeals	25 June 2007
	Bosco Ntaganda	Pre-trial	12 January 2006
	Callixte Mbarushimana	Charges declined	20 August 2010
	Sylvestre Mudacumura	Pre-trial	13 June 2012
Central African Republic	Jean-Pierre Bemba Gombo	Trial	9 May 2008
Darfur, Sudan	Ahmad Harun and Ali Kushayb	Pre-trial	27 February 2007
	Omar Hassan Ahmad Al Bashir	Pre-trial	14 July 2008
	Bahar Idriss Abu Garda	Charges declined	20 November 2008
	Abdallah Banda Abakaer Nourain	Trial	20 November 2008
	Saleh Mohammed Jerbo Jamus	Case terminated	20 November 2008
	Abdel Raheem Muhammad Hussein	Pre-trial	2 December 2011

Judicial Proceedings (*continued*)

Situation	Accused	Stage of Proceedings	Prosecution request for issue of Arrest Warrant/ Summons to Appear
Kenya	William Samoei Ruto and Joshua Arap Sang	Trial	15 December 2010
	Henry Kiprono Kosgey	Charges declined	15 December 2010
	Uhuru Muigai Kenyatta	Trial	15 December 2010
	Francis Kirimi Muthaura	Charges withdrawn	15 December 2010
	Muhammad Hussein Ali	Charges declined	15 December 2010
	Walter Osapiri Barasa	Pre-trial	30 July 2013
Libya	Saif Al-Islam Gaddafi and Abdullah Al-Senussi	Pre-trial	16 May 2011
	Muammar Gaddafi	Case terminated	16 May 2011
Côte d'Ivoire	Laurent Gbagbo	Pre-trial	25 October 2011
	Charles Blé Goudé	Pre-trial	12 December 2011
	Simone Gbagbo	Pre-trial	7 February 2012
Mali	–	–	–

Annexe 2 – Financial Overview

Budget

Year	Proposed Budget (Euros)	Approved Budget (Euros)
2010	102,980,000	103,623,300
2011	107,020,000	103,607,900
2012	117,730,000	108,800,000
2013	118,750,000	115,120,300[4]
2014	126,070,000	121,656,200[5]

Division of Funds

Programme	2010 (Euros)	2011 (Euros)	2012 (Euros)	2013 (Euros)
Judiciary	10,743,700	10,669,800	10,284,000	10,697,900
Office of the Prosecutor	26,828,300	26,598,000	27,723,700	28,265,700
Registry	59,631,100	61,611,400	65,041,700	64,520,900
Secretariat of the Assembly of States Parties	4,272,800	2,728,200	2,777,300	2,951,700
Interim Premises	–	–	–	5,901,500
Secretariat of the Trust Fund for Victims	1,221,600	1,205,200	1,450,600	1,580,000
Project Director's Office (permanent premises)	584,200	492,200	1,337,200	996,700
Independent Oversight Mechanism	341,600	303,100	185,500	205,900
TOTAL	**103,623,300**	**103,607,900**	**108,800,000**	**115,120,300**[6]

[4] The Netherlands and Mexico undertook to contribute €2,950,700 and €130,000 respectively, to the expense of interim premises. These contributions had the effect of reducing the level of the 2013 budget appropriations to be assessed for contributions by States Parties from €115,120,300 to €112,039,600 (Programme Budget for 2013, etc., 21 November 2012 – Resolution ICC-ASP/11/Res.1, paras 2 and 3).

[5] The budget appropriations that need to be assessed for contributions by States Parties will be reduced from 121,656,200 to 118,595,000, as the host State will continue to contribute to the costs in relation the Interim Premises and those States Parties that have opted for the one-time payment and have paid in full such payments for the permanent premises will not be assessed for the contributions to support the cost of interest on the loan of the host State in

Assessed Contributions[7]

State party	2010 (Euros)	2011 (Euros)	2012 (Euros)	2013 (Euros)
Afghanistan	6,155	6,153	6,449	8,851
Albania	15,388	15,382	16,123	17,814
Andorra	10,771	10,767	11,286	14,229
Antigua and Barbuda	3,078	3,076	3,225	3,585
Argentina	441,625	441,461	462,732	769,376
Australia	2,974,427	2,973,322	3,116,592	3,693,497
Austria	1,309,486	1,309,000	1,372,074	1,421,110
Bangladesh	n/a	15,382	16,123	11,204
Barbados	12,310	12,306	12,898	14,229
Belgium	1,654,169	1,653,555	1,733,231	1,777,284
Belize	1,539	1,538	1,612	1,793
Benin	4,616	4,615	4,837	5,378
Bolivia	10,771	10,767	11,286	16,022
Bosnia & Herzegovina	21,543	21,535	22,572	30,251
Botswana	27,698	27,687	29,022	30,251
Brazil	2,478,945	2,478,025	2,597,428	5,225,079
Bulgaria	58,473	58,451	61,268	83,694
Burkina Faso	4,616	4,615	4,837	5,378
Burundi	1,539	1,538	1,612	1,793
Cambodia	4,616	4,615	4,837	7,171
Canada	4,934,808	4,932,977	5,170,672	5,314,150
Cape Verde	n/a	n/a	1,611	1,793
Central African Republic	1,539	1,538	1,612	1,793

(continued overleaf)

respect of the Permanent Premises Project (Programme Budget for 2014, etc. 27 November 2013 - Resolution ICC-ASP/12/Res.1, paras 2–4).

[6] Idem.

[7] Pursuant to Art 117, Rome Statute, the calculation of the Court's scale of assessment = assessment rate of the State Party in the UN scale / sum of assessment rates of all States Parties to the Court in the UN scale * 100%. The UN scale of assessment fixes the maximum assessment rate at 22% of the Court's budget (Report of the Court on the methodology for its scale of assessment, 1 November 2012 – ICC-ASP/11/44, paras 3 and 6).

Assessed Contributions (*continued*)

State party	2010 (Euros)	2011 (Euros)	2012 (Euros)	2013 (Euros)
Chad	3,078	3,076	3,225	3,585
Chile	363,147	363,013	380,505	594,818
Colombia	221,582	221,499	232,172	461,267
Comoros	1,539	1,538	1,612	1,793
Congo	4,616	4,615	4,837	8,851
Cook Islands	1,539	1,538	1,612	1,793
Costa Rica	52,318	52,298	54,818	67,672
Côte d'Ivoire	n/a	n/a	n/a	n/a
Croatia	149,260	149,204	156,394	224,415
Cyprus	70,783	70,757	74,166	83,694
Czech Republic	537,028	536,828	562,695	687,363
Democratic Republic of the Congo	4,616	4,615	4,837	5,378
Denmark	1,132,529	1,132,108	1,186,658	1,202,073
Djibouti	1,539	1,538	1,612	1,793
Dominica	1,539	1,538	1,612	1,793
Dominican Republic	64,628	64,604	67,717	80,108
Ecuador	61,550	61,528	64,492	78,316
Estonia	61,550	61,528	64,492	71,257
Fiji	6,155	6,153	6,449	5,378
Finland	870,939	870,616	912,566	924,327
France	9,421,839	9,481,342	9,872,161	9,960,432
Gabon	21,543	21,535	22,572	35,629
Gambia	1,539	1,538	1,612	1,793
Georgia	9,233	9,229	9,674	12,436
Germany	12,337,792	12,333,213	12,927,484	12,717,167
Ghana	9,233	9,229	9,674	24,985
Greece	1,063,284	1,062,890	1,114,105	1,136,194
Grenada	n/a	641	1,612	1,793
Guatemala	n/a	n/a	22,565	48,065

Assessed Contributions (*continued*)

State party	2010 (Euros)	2011 (Euros)	2012 (Euros)	2013 (Euros)
Guinea	3,078	3,076	3,225	1,793
Guyana	1,539	1,538	1,612	1,793
Honduras	12,310	12,306	12,898	14,229
Hungary	447,780	447,613	469,182	473,703
Iceland	64,628	64,604	67,717	48,065
Ireland	766,303	766,019	802,929	744,391
Italy	7,692,270	7,689,415	8,059,927	7,921,312
Japan	19,280,686	19,273,528	20,202,216	19,292,211
Jordan	21,543	21,535	22,572	39,214
Kenya	18,465	18,458	19,348	23,192
Latvia	58,473	58,451	61,268	83,694
Lesotho	1,539	1,538	1,612	1,793
Liberia	1,539	1,538	1,612	1,793
Liechtenstein	13,849	13,844	14,511	16,022
Lithuania	100,020	99,982	104,800	129,966
Luxembourg	138,489	138,437	145,108	144,195
Madagascar	4,616	4,615	4,837	5,378
Malawi	1,539	1,538	1,612	3,585
Maldives	n/a	n/a	1,612	1,793
Mali	4,616	4,615	4,837	7,171
Malta	26,159	26,149	27,409	28,458
Marshall Islands	1,539	1,538	1,612	1,793
Mauritius	16,926	16,920	17,735	23,192
Mexico	3,625,323	3,623,977	3,798,597	3,280,407
Moldova	n/a	3,076	n/a	n/a
Mongolia	3,078	3,076	3,225	5,378
Montenegro	6,155	6,153	6,449	8,851
Namibia	12,310	12,306	12,898	17,814
Nauru	1,539	1,538	1,612	1,793
Netherlands	2,854,403	2,853,343	2,990,831	2,945,521
New Zealand	420,082	419,926	440,160	450,511

(*continued overleaf*)

Assessed Contributions (*continued*)

State party	2010 (Euros)	2011 (Euros)	2012 (Euros)	2013 (Euros)
Niger	3,078	3,076	3,225	3,585
Nigeria	120,023	119,979	125,760	160,329
Norway	1,340,262	1,339,764	1,404,320	1,515,560
Panama	33,853	33,840	35,471	46,272
Paraguay	10,771	10,767	11,286	17,814
Peru	138,489	138,437	145,108	208,394
Philippines	n/a	n/a	145,108	274,273
Poland	1,274,094	1,273,622	1,334,991	1,640,148
Portugal	786,307	786,015	823,889	844,106
Rep. of Korea	3,477,602	3,476,311	3,643,815	3,551,095
Rep. of Moldova	n/a	n/a	3,225	5,378
Romania	272,361	272,260	285,378	402,446
Saint Kitts and Nevis	1,539	1,538	1,612	1,793
Saint Lucia	n/a	1,538	1,612	1,793
Saint Vincent and the Grenadines	1,539	1,538	1,612	1,793
Samoa	1,539	1,538	1,612	1,793
San Marino	4,616	4,615	4,837	5,378
Senegal	9,233	9,229	9,674	10,644
Serbia	56,934	56,913	59,655	71,257
Seychelles	n/a	3,076	3,225	1,793
Sierra Leone	1,539	1,538	1,612	1,793
Slovakia	218,504	218,423	228,948	304,524
Slovenia	158,492	158,434	166,068	178,143
South Africa	592,423	592,203	620,738	662,490
Spain	4,888,645	4,886,831	5,122,301	5,294,543
Suriname	4,616	4,615	4,837	7,171
Sweden	1,637,243	1,636,635	1,715,495	1,709,612
Switzerland	1,738,801	1,738,155	1,821,908	1,864,563
Tajikistan	3,078	3,076	3,225	5,378

Assessed Contributions (*continued*)

State party	2010 (Euros)	2011 (Euros)	2012 (Euros)	2013 (Euros)
The Former Yugoslav Rep. of Macedonia	10,771	10,767	11,286	14,229
Timor-Leste	1,539	1,538	1,612	3,585
Trinidad and Tobago	67,706	67,680	70,942	78,316
Tunisia	n/a	n/a	48,369	64,087
Uganda	9,233	9,229	9,674	10,644
United Kingdom	10,161,982	10,158,211	10,647,681	9,223,100
Tanzania	12,310	12,306	12,898	11,204
Uruguay	41,547	41,531	43,532	92,657
Vanuatu	n/a	n/a	1,478	1,793
Venezuela	483,170	482,992	506,265	1,116,587
Zambia	6,155	6,153	6,449	10,644
TOTAL	**103,623,300**	**103,607,900**	**108,800,000**	**112,039,600**[9]

Voluntary Contributions

Project	Contributor	2010 (Euros)	2011 (Euros)	2012 (Euros)
Internship and Visiting Professionals Programme[9]	European Commission Finland Norway Australia Netherlands Rep. of Korea Switzerland	846,581 27,300 20,000 12,500 18,805 5,670 17,063	–	–

(*continued overleaf*)

[8] See supra (n 4).

[9] The Internship and Visiting Professionals Programme supports interns and visiting professionals in Judiciary, Office of the Prosecutor and Registry at the Court (Financial Statements for the Period 1 January to 31 December 2010, 26 July 2011 – ICC-ASP/10/12 – para 5.1, 51).

Voluntary Contributions (*continued*)

Project	Contributor	2010 (Euros)	2011 (Euros)	2012 (Euros)
European Commission Contracts[10]	European Commission	–	1,031,155	1,049,694
	Finland	–	30,000	40,000
	Australia	–	–	10,000
	Denmark	–	–	22,709
	Rep. of Korea	–	7,805	30,000
	Mac Arthur Foundation	–	68,199	–
	MFA Netherlands	–	19,068	50,000
	Municipality of The Hague	–	4,000	–
	Switzerland	–	31,250	35,000
Least Developed Countries[11]	Australia	50,000	50,000	50,000
	Finland	46,638	15,023	–
	Ireland	25,000	10,000	5,000
	Luxembourg	20,000	30,000	–
	Poland	10,000	10,000	5,000
Joint Regional Seminar with African Union (Ethiopia)[12]	Australia	–	5,000	5,000
	Ireland	–	5,000	–
	Organisation Internationale de la Francophonie	–	15,933	17,949
	MFA Netherlands	–	–	10,000

[10] As of 1 April 2010, the European Commission Contracts comprise the Internship and Visiting Professionals Programme and the Defence Counsel Seminar (Financial Statements for the Period 1 January to 31 December 2011, 28 August 2012 – ICC-ASP/11/12 – p 39, Schedule 7).

[11] On 12 September 2003, the Assembly of States Parties (ASP) decided upon the establishment of a trust fund for the participation of the least developed countries in the work of the Assembly and its subsidiary bodies, and called upon States, international organizations, individuals, corporations and other entities to contribute voluntarily to the fund (Establishment of a trust fund for the participation of the least developed countries in the activities of the Assembly of States Parties, 12 September 2003 – ICC-ASP/2/Res.6, para 1). The fund is administered by the Secretariat of the ASP and covers travel costs related to the participation of representatives of the least developed countries and other developing states at the ASP meeting (Financial Statements for the Period 1 January to 31 December 2010, 26 July 2011 – ICC-ASP/10/12 – para 5.1, 5.2).

[12] The Joint Seminar with African Union in Ethiopia was for the purposes of improving the participants' knowledge of the technical aspects of the Rome Statute and the Court's work (Financial Statements for the Period 1 January to 31 December 2011, 28 August 2012 – ICC-ASP/11/12 – para 5.1, 5.2).

Voluntary Contributions (*continued*)

Project	Contributor	2010 (Euros)	2011 (Euros)	2012 (Euros)
Regional Seminar in Yaoundé[13]	France Organisation Internationale de la Francophonie	15,000 59,403	– –	– –
Regional Seminar in Tunis[14]	France Organisation Internationale de la Francophonie	– –	20,000 52,250	– –
Dakar Seminar[15]	Organisation Internationale de la Francophonie	3,580	–	–
Legal Tools Project[16]	European Commission Finland Germany Netherlands	49,987 35,000 44,500 10,000	69,982 35,000 – 30,000	150,031 – – –
Defence Counsel Seminar[17]	European Commission Rep. of Korea Finland Switzerland Netherlands	64,930 17,744 2,700 1,688 1,398	–	–

(*continued overleaf*)

[13] The Regional Seminar in Yaoundé was run by the Registry to support the organisation of local seminars for local experts including judges, lawyers, politicians, NGOs to raise awareness and knowledge of the Court around the world. The first seminar took place in Dakar at the end of 2009 (Financial Statements for the Period 1 January to 31 December 2010, 26 July 2011 – ICC-ASP/10/12 – para 5.1, 5.2).

[14] The Regional Seminar in Tunis was organised by the Court to provide interactive training on the Rome Statute to leading law professionals of the Maghreb countries and some countries of Middle East (Egypt, Jordan Lebanon and Syria) with a view to enhancing States' cooperation with the Court (Financial Statements for the Period 1 January to 31 December 2011, 28 August 2012 – ICC-ASP/11/12 – para 5.1, 5.2).

[15] See supra (n 11).

[16] The Legal Tools Project is run by the Office of the Prosecutor to facilitate and coordinate the introduction, implementation and use of the Legal tools project, in particular the Case matrix, by users outside the Court (Financial Statements for the Period 1 January to 31 December 2010, 26 July 2011 – ICC-ASP/10/12 – para 5.1, 5.2).

[17] Defence Counsel Seminar is run by the Registry to finance the consultations between the Court and the legal professional represented by the counsels on the Court's list of counsel (Financial Statements for the Period 1 January to 31 December 2010, 26 July 2011 – ICC-ASP/10/12 – para 5.1, 5.2).

Voluntary Contributions (*continued*)

Project	Contributor	2010 (Euros)	2011 (Euros)	2012 (Euros)
General Trust Fund[18]	Austria	10,000	–	–
	Rep. of Korea	10,549		
	Uganda	48,370		
	Finland	8,850		
	Belgium	35,475		
	Municipality of The Hague	–		4,500
Special Fund for Relocations of Witnesses[19]	Denmark		131,881	
	Finland		300,000	
	Germany	–	200,000	–
	Ireland		50,000	
	United Kingdom		234,196	
	Luxembourg		–	20,000
Family visit for indigent detainees[20]	Germany	–	170,000	
TOTAL		**1,518,728**	**2,625,742**	**1,504,883**

[18] The General Trust Fund is used for the Victims and Witnesses Unit to organise an annual one-day seminar on protection (Financial Statements for the Period 1 January to 31 December 2010, 26 July 2011 – ICC-ASP/10/12 – para 5.1, 5.2).

[19] The Special Fund for Relocations was established to assist States which are willing but do not have the capacity to enter into relocation agreements with the Court with cost neutral solutions, aimed at increasing the number of effective relocations and building local capacity to protect witnesses (Financial Statements for the Period 1 January to 31 December 2011, 28 August 2012 – ICC-ASP/11/12 – para 5.1, 5.2).

[20] The Family visit for indigent detainees was established to fund family visits for indigent detainees (Financial Statements for the Period 1 January to 31 December 2011, 28 August 2012 – ICC-ASP/11/12 – para 5.1, 5.3).

Annexe 3 – Human Resources

Staff Count

	2010	2011	2012	2013
Established posts	686	702	702	690
Approved General Temporary Assistance (GTA)	165	192	188	152
Interns	90	86	82	70
Visiting professionals	1	7	5	12
Consultants	62	49	44	47
Elected officials / judges	23	23	23	21
TOTAL	1,027	1,060	1,044	992

Geographic Representation of Professional Staff

Region	Nationality	2010	2011	2012	2013
Africa	Algeria	0	0	1	1
	Benin	1	1	1	1
	Burkina Faso	1	1	1	1
	Cameroon	1	1	1	1
	Chad	1	0	0	0
	Democratic Republic of the Congo	2	2	2	2
	Côte d'Ivoire	0	1	2	2
	Egypt	3	4	4	4
	Gambia	3	2	2	2
	Ghana	2	2	2	2
	Guinea	1	1	1	1
	Kenya	3	3	3	3
	Lesotho	1	1	1	1
	Malawi	0	1	1	1
	Mali	2	2	2	2
	Mauritius	0	0	1	1
	Niger	2	3	3	3
	Nigeria	7	5	4	3
	Rwanda	1	1	1	1
	Senegal	3	3	3	3
	Sierra Leone	4	3	3	3
	South Africa	7	8	10	10
	Togo	1	1	1	1
	Tunisia	1	1	0	0
	Uganda	1	2	2	2
	Tanzania	2	2	2	2
	Zimbabwe	0	1	1	1
Africa Total		**50**	**52**	**55**	**54**

Geographic Representation of Professional Staff (*continued*)

Region	Nationality	2010	2011	2012	2013
Asia	China	0	0	1	1
	Cyprus	1	1	1	1
	Iran	4	4	4	4
	Japan	5	4	4	3
	Jordan	1	1	1	1
	Lebanon	2	2	2	2
	Mongolia	1	1	1	1
	Palestine	1	1	1	1
	Philippines	1	1	2	2
	Rep. of Korea	2	2	1	1
	Singapore	2	3	2	2
	Sri Lanka	1	1	1	1
Asia Total		**21**	**21**	**21**	**20**
Eastern Europe	Albania	1	1	1	1
	Belarus	1	0	0	0
	Bosnia and Herzegovina	1	1	1	1
	Bulgaria	2	1	1	1
	Croatia	5	5	4	4
	Georgia	1	1	1	1
	Poland	1	1	1	1
	Romania	6	6	5	7
	Russian Federation	1	1	2	2
	Serbia	3	4	5	4
	Former Yugoslav Rep. of Macedonia	1	1	1	0
	Ukraine	1	1	1	1
Eastern Europe Total		**24**	**23**	**23**	**23**

(*continued overleaf*)

Geographic Representation of Professional Staff (*continued*)

Region	Nationality	2010	2011	2012	2013
GRULAC[21]	Argentina	3	4	5	4
	Brazil	3	2	1	1
	Chile	1	1	2	2
	Colombia	5	5	6	6
	Costa Rica	3	1	1	1
	Ecuador	2	2	2	3
	Mexico	2	2	2	2
	Peru	3	3	4	3
	Trinidad and Tobago	4	4	4	2
	Venezuela	2	2	2	2
GRULAC Total		**28**	**26**	**29**	**26**
WEOG[22]	Australia	18	16	12	12
	Austria	3	3	3	2
	Belgium	10	11	11	10
	Canada	14	14	15	13
	Denmark	1	1	1	1
	Finland	3	3	3	3
	France	45	45	44	46
	Germany	16	16	14	12
	Greece	2	2	3	3
	Ireland	4	4	7	6
	Italy	9	10	10	11
	Netherlands	17	17	18	19
	New Zealand	3	4	4	4
	Portugal	2	3	3	4
	Spain	9	8	10	11
	Sweden	2	1	1	1
	Switzerland	2	1	1	1

21 Latin American and Caribbean Group.
22 Western European and Others Group.

Geographic Representation of Professional Staff (*continued*)

Region	Nationality	2010	2011	2012	2013
	United Kingdom	24	26	27	28
	United States of America	11	11	9	9
WEOG Total		**195**	**196**	**196**	**196**
Total number of nationalities		74	75	77	76
TOTAL		**318**	**318**	**324**	**319**

Sources for Annexes

ANNEXE 1

States Parties to the Rome Statute – <http://www.icc-cpi.int/en_menus/asp/states%20parties/Pages/the%20states%20parties%20to%20the%20 rome%20statute.aspx> – retrieved 30 September 2013

Report of the Committee on Budget and Finance on the work of its fourteenth session, 6 July 2010 – ICC-ASP/9/5

Report of the Committee on Budget and Finance on the work of its sixteenth session, 17 June 2011 – ICC-ASP/10/5/

Report of the Committee on Budget and Finance on the work of its eighteenth session, 9 August 2012 – ICC-ASP11/5

Report of the Committee on Budget and Finance on the work of its twentieth session, 7 June 2013 – ICC-ASP/12/5/Rev.1

Fifth Report of the International Criminal Court to the United Nations for 2008/2009, 17 September 2009 – A/64/356

Sixth Report of the International Criminal Court to the United Nations for 2009/2010, 19 August 2010 – A/65/313

Seventh Report of the International Criminal Court to the United Nations for 2010/2011, 19 August 2011 – A/66/309

Eighth Report of the International Criminal Court to the United Nations for 2011/2012, 14 August 2012 – A/67/308

Ninth Report of the International Criminal Court to the United Nations for 2012/13, 13 August 2013 – A/68/314

Report on Preliminary Activities 2013, November 2013 – <http://icc-cpi.int/en_menus/icc/press%20and%20media/press%20releases/Documents/OTP%20Preliminary%20Examinations/OTP%20-%20Report%20%20Preliminary%20Examination%20Activities%202013.PDF > – retrieved 10 December 2013

The Court Today – http://www.icc-cpi.int/iccdocs/PIDS/publications/TheCourtTodayEng.pdf – retrieved 30 September 2013

ANNEXE 2

Proposed Programme Budget for 2010 of the International Criminal Court, 30 July 2009 – ICC/ASP/8/10

Proposed Programme Budget for 2011 of the International Criminal Court, 2 August 2010 – ICC/ASP/9/10

Proposed Programme Budget for 2012 of the International Criminal Court, 21 July 2011 – ICC/ASP/10/10

Proposed Programme Budget for 2013 of the International Criminal Court. 16 August 2012 – ICC/ASP/11/10
Proposed Programme Budget for 2014 of the International Criminal Court, 29 July 2013 – ICC/ASP/12/10
Programme Budget for 2010, etc., 26 November 2009 – Resolution ICC-ASP/8/Res.7
Programme Budget for 2011, etc., 10 December 2010 – Resolution ICC-ASP/9/Res.4
Programme Budget for 2012, etc., 21 December 2011 – Resolution ICC-ASP/10/Res.4
Programme Budget for 2013, etc., 21 November 2012 – Resolution ICC-ASP/11/Res.1
Programme Budget for 2014, etc., 27 November 2013 – Resolution ICC-ASP/12/Res.1
Report of the Committee on Budget and Finance on the work of its fourteenth session, 6 July 2010 – ICC-ASP/9/5
Report of the Committee on Budget and Finance on the work of its sixteenth session, 17 June 2011 – ICC-ASP/10/5/
Report of the Committee on Budget and Finance on the work of its eighteenth session, 9 August 2012 – ICC-ASP11/5
Report of the Committee on Budget and Finance on the work of its twentieth session, 7 June 2013 – ICC-ASP/12/5/Rev.1
Report of the Court on the methodology for its scale of assessment, 1 November 2012 – ICC-ASP/11/44
Rome Statute of the International Criminal Court (1998) 2187 UNTS 3
Financial Statements for the Period 1 January to 31 December 2010, 26 July 2011 – ICC-ASP/10/12
Establishment of a trust fund for the participation of the least developed countries in the activities of the Assembly of States Parties, 12 September 2003 – ICC-ASP/2/Res.6
Financial Statements for the Period 1 January to 31 December 2011, 28 August 2012 – ICC-ASP/11/12
Financial Statements for the Period 1 January to 31 December 2012, 7 August 2013 – ICC-ASP/12/12

ANNEXE 3

Report of the Committee on Budget and Finance on the work of its fourteenth session, 6 July 2010 – ICC-ASP/9/5
Report of the Committee on Budget and Finance on the work of its sixteenth session, 17 June 2011 – ICC-ASP/10/5/
Report of the Committee on Budget and Finance on the work of its eighteenth session, 9 August 2012 – ICC-ASP11/5
Report of the Committee on Budget and Finance on the work of its twentieth session, 7 June 2013 – ICC-ASP/12/5/Rev.1

Contributors

Amal Alamuddin is a barrister at Doughty Street Chambers who specialises in international law and human rights. She appears in English and international courts – including the International Criminal Court and the International Court of Justice – and advises individuals and governments. She has been appointed as an adviser to UN Special Envoy Kofi Annan on Syria, and as Counsel to the Inquiry by the UN Special Rapporteur on Counter-Terrorism and Human Rights on the use of drones in armed conflict. She has also previously practised at the international courts and tribunals in The Hague. She holds a BA/LLB from the University of Oxford and an LLM from New York University School of Law.

Professor M Cherif Bassiouni is Emeritus Distinguished Research Professor of Law at DePaul University and President Emeritus of the International Human Rights Law Institute. He is a prolific writer and editor, and frequently lectures at universities around the world. He holds an LLB from the University of Cairo, a JD from Indiana University, an LLM from John Marshall Law School and an SJD from George Washington University in addition to several honorary degrees. He has acted as Chairman of the Drafting Committee of the United Nations Diplomatic Conference on the Establishment of an International Criminal Court.

Professor Olympia Bekou is Professor of Public International Law and Head of the International Criminal Justice Unit of the University of Nottingham Human Rights Law Centre. She studied law at the Democritus University of Thrace in Greece, undertook an LLM at the University of Cambridge and obtained a PhD from the University of Nottingham. Previously she was a fellow of the Max Planck Institute for Foreign and International Criminal Law. She leads capacity building projects and is responsible for the National Implementing Legislation Database of the ICC's Legal Tools Project.

Henry Bellingham MP has been the Member of Parliament for North West Norfolk for 26 years. After studying law at Magdalene College, Cambridge, he was called to the Bar. He has served on three different Select Committees, from 2006 to 2010 was Shadow Minister for Legal Services, the Court Service, the Judiciary and Family Law, and from 2010 to 2012 was Minister for Africa, the Caribbean, the Overseas Territories, the UN and conflict issues at the Foreign and Commonwealth Office.

Gaelle Carayon is a Legal Officer on the ICC programme at the REDRESS Trust where she has worked with victims in ICC situation countries including the DRC, Côte d'Ivoire, Kenya and Uganda. She holds a Bachelor's degree in Political Science and Government from the Institut d'Etudes Politiques de Lyon and an LLM in International Human Rights Law from the University of Essex. Previously she worked for the UN High Commissioner for Refugees in Tanzania as Resource Mobilisation and Donor Reporting Officer.

Pieter de Baan is the Executive Director of the Secretariat for the ICC Trust Fund for Victims. He holds a degree in Modern History from Leiden University, where he also undertook post-graduate study in International Law. Prior to joining the Trust Fund for Victims, he held management and advisory positions at SNV Netherlands Development Organization and at ARCADIS Euroconsult/BMB Management Consultants. On behalf of the International Secretariat of Amnesty International, he established in 1995 a trial observation routine regarding the ICTY.

Dr Mark Ellis is Executive Director of the International Bar Association, London, and an Adjunct Professor at the Florida State University College of Law. He holds a JD and BS (Economics) from the same institution, a PhD from King's College London, and was twice a Fulbright Scholar at the Economic Institute in Zagreb, Croatia. Previously he was the first Executive Director of the Central European and Eurasian Law Initiative and is a member of the Disciplinary Advisory Panel to the Defence Counsel for the ICTY and ICTR. He has published extensively on international humanitarian law, war crimes tribunals and the development of the rule of law.

Shehara de Soysa is a research assistant in the Public International Law programme at the British Institute of International and Comparative Law. She obtained her LLB from King's College London and LLM in Public International Law from Leiden University. Her research interests include international humanitarian law, international criminal law and the law on the use of force.

Sir Adrian Fulford was appointed to the Court of Appeal in March 2013. He recently served a nine-year term as a judge of the ICC, during which he presided over the *Lubanga* case, the Court's first trial, and was president of the Trial Division for three years. He studied at the University of Southampton, was called to the Bar and appointed Queen's Counsel in 1994 and High Court judge in 2002. He has vast experience in publishing as both editor and contributor.

Dr Federica Gioia is a Legal Officer at the ICC and Associate Professor at the Università Cattolica, Piacenza. She holds a law degree from the Università

Cattolica del Sacro Cuore, and obtained her PhD at the Università degli Studi di Ferrara. Previously she held the post of Legal Officer at the United Nations Commission on International Trade Law and was a Visiting Professor at Leiden University for five years.

Dr Fabricio Guariglia is Prosecutions Coordinator in the Office of the Prosecutor at the ICC, after nine years as Senior Appeals Counsel in the Office of the Prosecutor. He holds a law degree from the University of Buenos Aires and a PhD from the University of Münster. Previously, he was a Legal Officer and latterly Appeals Counsel in the Office of the Prosecutor at the ICTY and was a member of the Argentine delegation to the ICC Preparatory Committee and the Rome Conference. He has published widely on international criminal law, comparative criminal law and human rights law. Academic appointments have included the position of visiting fellow at the London School of Economics.

Dr Annika Jones is a Lecturer in Law at the University of Exeter. She completed her undergraduate degree in law, her LLM in International Criminal Justice and Armed Conflict and her PhD at the University of Nottingham. She is a fellow of the Forum for International Criminal and Humanitarian Law (FICHL) and has worked for a number of years on the development of the National Implementing Legislation Database as part of the ICC's Legal Tools Project.

Marek Marczynski is Director of Campaigns and Policy at Index on Censorship and Editor-in-Chief of the Birkbeck Law Review. He undertook studies at the Nicolas Copernicus University, the University of Sarajevo and the University of Bologna in international relations, public international law and human rights. Previous posts include Deputy Director of the Europe and Central Asia Programme at the International Secretariat of Amnesty International in London. Prior to that, he led Amnesty International's work on international justice. He is a co-founder of the Institute of Global Responsibility.

H E Judge Howard Morrison CBE QC is the elected UK judge at the International Criminal Court currently sitting as a trial judge at the ICTY. He studied law at the University of London and Inns of Court School of Law before being called to the Bar by Grays Inn in 1977. He has held judicial positions in Fiji and served as an ad hoc Attorney General in the Caribbean before defending in cases at both the ICTY and ICTR. He was appointed to the UK judiciary in 2004 and served as a Senior Judge of the Sovereign Base areas of Cyprus and as a judge of the STL. He lectures on international criminal and humanitarian law worldwide and is a Bencher of Grays Inn and an Honorary

Professor of Law at Leicester University and Senior Fellow of the Lauterpacht Centre for International Law at Cambridge University.

Professor William A Schabas OC MRIA is Professor of International Criminal Law and Human Rights at Leiden University, Professor of International Law at Middlesex University, Emeritus Professor of Human Rights Law at National University of Ireland Galway, Honorary Professor at the Chinese Academy of Social Sciences, visiting fellow at the University of Oxford, and Associate Professor at the Université du Québec à Montréal. He is also Chairman of the Irish Centre for Human Rights, an associate member at 9 Bedford Row International, London, Editor-in-Chief of *Criminal Law Forum*, president of the Irish Branch of the International Law Association and chair of the International Institute for Criminal Investigation. He holds BA and MA degrees in history from the University of Toronto and LLB, LLM and LLD degrees from the University of Montreal, as well as honorary doctorates in law. He has published widely, chiefly on international criminal law and international human rights law.

Professor Mia Swart is Professor of International Law at the University of Johannesburg and a research associate of the South African Institute of Advanced Constitutional, Public and International Law. She undertook a BA at the University of South Africa, an LLB at the University of Cape Town, an LLM at Humboldt University and obtained her PhD from Leiden University. Previously she was a Research Fellow at the Bingham Centre for the Rule of Law and Assistant Professor at Leiden University. She holds the title of Honorary Associate Professor at the University of the Witwatersrand in Johannesburg, where she was previously an Associate Professor. She has published on transitional justice, international criminal law, and comparative constitutional law.

Dr Andraž Zidar is the Dorset Senior Research Fellow in Public International Law at the British Institute of International and Comparative Law. He studied at the Universities of Ljubljana (univ dipl iur) and Padua (EMA), and obtained a PhD in international law from the Graduate Institute of International and Development Studies, Geneva. Previously he held the post of Director General for International Law and Protection of Citizens at the Ministry of Foreign Affairs of Slovenia, lectured on international and constitutional criminal law and was a human rights diplomat at the Mission of Slovenia to the UN Office in Geneva. He has published on international law, human rights, diplomacy and international relations and is Editor-in-Chief of a Slovenian book collection on international law.